ELDER ABUSE:

CONFLICT IN THE FAMILY

ELDER ABUSE

Conflict in the Family

Edited by

KARL A. PILLEMER
University of New Hampshire

ROSALIE S. WOLF
University of Massachusetts Medical Center

Auburn House Publishing Company
Dover, Massachusetts

Library of Congress Cataloging in Publication Data

Elder abuse.

   Includes index.
   1. Aged—Abuse of. 2. Aged—Abuse of—Prevention.
3. Aged—Family relationships. I. Pillemer, Karl A.
II. Wolf, Rosalie S.
HV6626.3.E43 1986   362.6′042   86-14014
ISBN 0-86569-133-9

Printed in the United States of America

FOREWORD

There is a kernel of truth in the stereotype of the university as an "ivory tower." To a certain extent, the book-laden walls shield scholars and scientists from the "real" world. Like other stereotypes, however, this image is mostly false. Rather than taking place in isolation, what goes on in the ivory tower typically reflects the cultural and ideological concerns of the historical period and the society. This is especially true of the social sciences, and perhaps even more true of sociology than the other social sciences. The issues which have preoccupied sociologists have usually been aspects of society that were the object of concern by society at large. One need only look at the work of the founders of modern sociology, such as Emile Durkheim, whose study of suicide and alienation reflected the concern with "moral decline" that so preoccupied late Victorian society.

This book illustrates the connection between contemporary social concerns and the concerns of academics. The aged are the fastest growing segment of the population. The elderly are becoming more powerful, not only because of increasing numbers, but also because they are increasingly represented by organizations with growing sophistication and power such as the American Association of Retired Persons. At the same time, old solutions to their needs are becoming nonsolutions. For example, with smaller size families, there are fewer children to assume responsibility for aged parents. Moreover, the old system of the adult sons providing economic support, and adult daughters or daughters-in law providing care, is less and less a viable arrangement; the percentage of women who devote full time to homemaking has drastically declined and that trend is likely to continue.

No one knows whether there is more conflict and abuse between the generations than some years back, but there is certainly more awareness and concern. Society is recognizing "elder abuse" as a problem. *Newsweek*, *Parade*, and many other magazines and newspapers have published feature stories. Congressional hearings have been held. Many states enacted "adult protective" legislation similar to the child abuse legislation which all the states had passed by the early 1970s. Thus, the appearance of this volume is one more testimony to the responsiveness of the scholarly world to the real world, and one more blow to the idea of the academy as an ivory tower.

There is, however, a way in which the ivory tower metaphor is correct. An implicit social contract underlies society's support of the academy. The terms of the contract free the scholar from having to deal with the real world *and also* place on him or her the obligation to produce insights and knowledge that are unlikely to be produced by those caught up in the day-to-day demands of the real world. Society shields and supports the academy in the hope of finding new approaches to old issues or innovative approaches to new problems. This book illustrates the value of that contract. It shows how we can attain new insights into tragic and sensational events by approaching them from a scholarly perspective, thereby allowing the power of history and theory to be brought to bear on the solution of an ancient problem.

MURRAY A. STRAUS
Family Research Laboratory and Department of Sociology,
University of New Hampshire

CONTENTS

INTRODUCTION

by Karl A. Pillemer and Rosalie S. Wolf

Conflict in the family lives of older people has recently emerged as an important area of study. As the fifteen chapters in this book demonstrate, such conflict can take a wide variety of forms. Some families have difficulty meeting the needs of impaired older relatives, and in others elderly parents and adult children come into conflict over scarce economic resources. Spouses who have had difficulties throughout their married lives can find these problems intensifying in later life. The stressful life events and social isolation that at times accompany old age exacerbate family conflicts. In some cases, tensions result in abusive behavior toward the elderly.

Gerontologists are now turning their attention to the difficulties aged persons and their families experience. These investigators are now asking: Why does conflict and abuse occur in families of the elderly? What can be done to prevent and treat these problems? It is the goal of this book to improve our understanding of conflict in late-life families and of elder abuse by presenting new theory and research on these topics.

The theme of this volume is by no means entirely new; over the years, social scientists have described and analyzed conflict in older persons' family lives. One notable interest has been in intergenerational conflict. Fifty years ago, social theorist Karl Mannheim argued that different generations occupy divergent social and existential worlds. He held that individuals born into a given generation experience a particular configuration of sociopolitical events as they grow up; this sets them off as a special group. Young people come into contact with preexisting institutional arrangements and, because their viewpoint is fresh, question the established structures. Thus the generations differ in the basic way in which they see the world.[1]

---

[1]Karl Mannheim, "The Problem of Generations," in *Essays on the Sociology of Knowledge*, ed. Paul Kecskemeti (London: Routledge and Kegan Paul, 1952), pp. 276-332; Vern L. Bengston and Neil E. Cutler, "Generations and Intergenerational Relations," in *Handbook of Aging and the Social Sciences*, eds. Robert H. Binstock and Ethel Shanas (New York: Van Nostrand Reinhold, 1976), pp. 130-159.

While it would not be appropriate to apply Mannheim's macro-level analysis directly to the microlevel phenomena of family conflict and abuse, his point that the generations differ in their perceptions of social world is relevant. Parent and child may have different expectations for the amount of care older people deserve and disagree as to proper conduct toward parents in other areas. Mannheim's work is thus useful because it alerts us to the possibility of conflictual relationships between the elderly and their off-spring. Support for this potential conflict between the aged and younger generations comes as well from anthropological studies of a variety of cultures and from historical evidence; these studies have shown conflict to be in part the result of structural inequalities in society.[2]

Another body of literature has also examined conflict and the aged, but with a more specific focus on individual families. This work has been conducted by psychologists, often in an attempt to bring a clinical understanding to family problems. One notable example is the work of John Herr and John Weakland.[3] Families, in these authors' terms, may "fight for blood"—that is, engage in serious verbal conflict and even physical violence. Herr and Weakland identify power struggles between family members as the major source of such conflict. For example, as the physical and economic powers of an aged person diminish, children and spouses may become more assertive than previously. As family members jockey for new positions, conflict can erupt.

Thus, although there is considerable evidence that kin frequently play a positive role in the lives of the elderly, a conflict perspective is not unknown. Some observers have acknowledged that conflict, an important dynamic in all families, may be heightened by stressors associated with advanced age, including increased frailty, lack of economic resources, retirement, and the death of close friends and family members. The chapters in this book reflect such an interest and attempt to shed light on the question: What are the causes and consequences of conflict between the aged and their relatives?

In addition to examining strain and conflict in late-life families, this volume has another goal: to present new research and theory regarding the problem of elder abuse. Although elder abuse is certainly not a new phenomenon (see Chapters 1 and 2), it has come to the public's attention only recently as a social problem. Since the "discovery" of elder abuse in the past decade, interest

---

[2]Nancy Foner, *Ages in Conflict* (New York: Columbia University Press, 1984).
[3]John J. Herr and John H. Weakland, *Counseling Elders and their Families* (New York: Springer, 1979).

has grown rapidly. Many states have passed mandatory reporting laws and begun elder protective services programs. Exploratory studies have documented the existence of elder abuse and attempted to shed light on its causes.

However, as critics have amply pointed out, these early studies suffered from serious methodological weaknesses. The problems include reliance on interviews with professionals rather than with victims and their families, failure to use comparison groups, and imprecise definitions of "elder abuse," which make results from various studies difficult to compare. Further, random sample surveys on this issue are lacking, so we have no reliable estimates of the extent of elder abuse.

We are thus in a curious situation, in which major intervention programs are being designed for a problem that we do not yet know how to define, the extent of which is unknown, and the causes of which remain obscure. This book attempts to add to our knowledge in these areas by presenting new data and by taking a fresh look at existing information. By viewing elder abuse not as a separate problem, but as one aspect—albeit extreme—of family conflict in later life, the book ties the study of elder maltreatment to more general research on the aging family.

Part I presents an overview of old-age family conflict from historical, literary, psychological, and sociological perspectives. Peter Stearns in Chapter 1 traces the historical pattern of old-age family conflict, beginning with pre-industrial Western society and continuing through the present day. He notes that there is little direct evidence that abuse existed in the 19th and early 20th centuries. In contemporary society, according to Stearns, the growing attention to the problem of elder abuse may be an artifact of new definitions, more rigorous standards, and the increased numbers and visibility of old people. On the other hand, economic pressure for younger family members and the loss of tight community structures, which in the past protected members from abuse, may have heightened family conflict.

Shulamit Reinharz uses examples from history, legend, and literature to show in Chapter 2 that elder abuse is not a new problem but rather an "unbroken saga in the relations between adults and their elders." Two motifs emerge from her study: the first is that the relations among the generations are conflictual, a result of younger people struggling with their elders for power; the second theme emphasizes respect, honor, and love. Recognition of the interplay of these two contrasting themes enables us to put elder abuse and other relations between adults and their parents in proper perspective.

In Chapter 3, Victor Cicirelli constructs a model based on attachment theory to explain children's neglect of their aged parents. According to the model, attachment behaviors to parents are a function of the child's prior feelings of attachment, the parent's dependency, and the child's sense of filial obligation. Children with weak attachment bonds may ignore or neglect increasingly dependent parents. Neglect also may result if the children perceive their parent's traits as undesirable or if they sense that the parents played a part in fostering a rivalrous relationship between them and their siblings.

Linda George in Chapter 4 analyzes the role of the social norms of reciprocity and solidarity in creating the stress associated with family caregiving. Under ordinary circumstances, these competing norms can be balanced, but providing care to a chronically ill older adult can lead to long-term inequality and personal distress. From a longitudinal study of victims of Alzheimer's disease and related disorders, she shows that caregiving spouses experience little normative conflict and that when tensions exist, it is usually with other members of the support network. Issues of equity arise most frequently with adult child caregivers. However, for both groups, the norm of solidarity and affection are powerful.

In Chapter 5, Andrew Boxer and his colleagues discuss intergenerational conflict among three generations of male family members. The authors report that even though patterns of attachment and emotional relatedness may change over the course of life, and sometimes result in conflict, men across the generations also report significant ties to one another.

Part II focuses more specifically on elder abuse and neglect. In Chapter 6, Margaret Hudson reports on the status of research on elder mistreatment. She notes that no substantiated profile of the abuser and abused can be drawn from existing studies because of methodological problems in their designs. The lack of uniformity of definition has been a barrier in developing detection and reporting systems. Although various treatment models have been described, very little has been written about their effectiveness. Hudson closes with an appeal for definitional consensus and the expansion of the research base.

Tanya Johnson in Chapter 7 identifies the problems that have plagued previous efforts to define elder abuse and outlines a new definition. According to Johnson, elder mistreatment is a state of self-inflicted or other-inflicted suffering unnecessary to the maintenance of the quality of life of an older person. Elder mistreatment, in her view, can take the form of one or more behavioral manifestations: physical, psychological, sociological, or legal. It can be measured by determining the frequency of abusive acts (in

Johnson's terms, "intensity") and the number of types of abuse to which the victim is exposed ("density"). As the author demonstrates, this definition has implications for future research and for treatment of elder abuse.

In Chapter 8, Linda Phillips draws on various theoretical models to explain elder abuse and proposes an explanation based on symbolic interactionism. Viewed within this framework, elder abuse can be conceptualized as inadequate or inappropriate role performance arising from misperceptions by both the elder and the caretaker. Although it has certain limitations, the symbolic interactionist approach is able to capture the complex and dynamic nature of elder abuse situations.

Using data from an evaluative study of three model projects on elderly abuse, Rosalie Wolf reports in Chapter 9 on a series of analyses that examined the nature of five types of maltreatment—physical, psychological, and material abuse, and active and passive neglect—and their relationship to four causal factors. No single theory or set of variables alone could explain the occurrence of abuse and neglect; instead, the results underscored the different characteristics of each type of mistreatment. The three model projects were also evaluated in terms of their success in resolving cases, the degree to which they established a referral network in their communities, and the replicability of each intervention model. Based on this evaluation, Wolf offers suggestions for future research and policy.

In Chapter 10, Karl Pillemer reports on a study of five risk factors for physical elder abuse. He explores the relationship of these factors to abuse using data from interviews with victims and matched control cases. He outlines a "path diagram," showing how the abuser's psychological state may be directly related to violence or can result in dependency on the victim, which may also lead to abuse. The social isolation of abusive families appears to exacerbate the situation. Based on his findings, Pillemer cautions researchers against concentrating exclusively on the caregiver-burden model of elder abuse and suggests that a domestic violence paradigm that focuses on the characteristics of the abuser may be more useful.

Part III shifts the focus from discussions of definitions, theories, and risk factors to intervention models and elder abuse policy. It is important to note that the recommendations of some of the authors in this section are not just limited to elder abuse, but also address the problems of aging families in a more general way. Mark Edinburg in Chapter 11 points out that the application of family therapy principles and practice to the care of the elderly has great potential for helping families handle the stresses of later life. Family-oriented approaches can aid in understanding and improving family problem-solving ability and are particularly useful in dealing with stressful situations brought on by life events such as chronic illness and disability, death, divorce, or institutionalization. Edinburg recommends, however, that better criteria for evaluating the effectiveness of family-oriented approaches be identified, instruments for assessment refined, and comparisons made between family-oriented intervention and other treatment modalities.

Francis Caro discusses the problem of caregiver burden in Chapter 12 and relates it to present policy on in-home care. He reports on a research study of the circumstances in which caregiving becomes burdensome. Caro warns that a balance must be struck between family responsibility and formal support in developing a home care system. Publicly funded services should not only encourage the participation of the informal system but also be concerned with the welfare of both the elder care recipient and the informal caregiver.

In Chapter 13, Alan Sager proposes an alternative to publicly funded home care. He suggests that voluntary, mutual-aid approaches to providing and financing long-term care should be developed. Sager discusses several projects based on this self-help model that are in operation in the United States and elsewhere. He contends that growing needs for care and declining traditional long-term care resources require the further development of voluntary aid efforts.

Still another approach to intervention is described in Chapter 14 by Edward Ansello and his colleagues, based on the "environmental press model," which they have found useful for understanding the complex interaction of factors that create situations in which elder abuse occurs. According to the model, if an individual's level of competence and the environment's demand (or "press") are not in synchrony, maladaption occurs. They propose a variety of intervention strategies based on this model.

In the final chapter, Stephen Crystal raises the issue of whether elder abuse should be addressed by categorical programs—the current policy direction in this country—or be viewed as a problem to be handled within the generic social service system. He builds a case for considering abuse as only one aspect of the larger issue of meeting the needs of the frail elderly. Further, he questions the utility of mandatory reporting laws, which seriously compromise the traditional privileged relationship between client and practitioner. Crystal holds that the major need is to develop a comprehensive set of services which can respond to the entire range of problems old persons experience.

Acknowledgments

In preparing this volume, we have been helped by a number of individuals. These include J. Jill Suitor, Murray Straus, and David Finklehor of the Family Research Laboratory at the University of New Hampshire; Susan McMurray-Anderson of the University Center on Aging at the University of Massachusetts Medical Center; Mary Ann LaFleur of the University of New Hampshire History Department; and Robert Jolley of the University of New Hampshire Department of Social Services. We are also grateful for the editorial advice of Clare McMillan, and the assistance of Patty Fanning in preparing the manuscript. Finally, we would like to acknowledge the invaluable help of the editorial staff at Auburn House, especially that of Eugene Bailey and Margaret Kearney.

KARL A. PILLEMER
ROSALIE S. WOLF

THE CONTRIBUTORS

EDWARD F. ANSELLO is Acting Director of the University of Maryland Center on Aging and the author of over four dozen papers, articles, and books on adulthood and aging, including a text on criminal victimization of the elderly. He is a Fellow of the Gerontological Society of America.

ANDREW M. BOXER is the Coordinator of the Clinical Research Training Program in Adolescence in the Department of Psychiatry at the Michael Reese Hospital and Medical Center. He has also served on the Committee on Human Development at the University of Chicago. His research interests include adolescence and adult family relations.

FRANCIS G. CARO is Director of the Institute for Social Welfare Research of the Community Service Society of New York. A sociologist, he has been active in the field of applied research, with special interest in community-based long-term care for a variety of functionally disabled populations. His most recent publication examines home care in New York City.

VICTOR G. CICIRELLI is Professor of Developmental and Aging Psychology in the Department of Psychological Sciences at Purdue University. He holds Ph.D.'s from the University of Michigan and Michigan State University. He is the author of *Helping Elderly Parents: Role of Adult Children* and has published numerous articles presenting research on family relationships in later life.

JUDITH COOK has published research in the areas of familial reactions to death from childhood cancer, teaching styles of university professors, lawyer-social work conflict in juvenile courts, parental burden in coping with offspring with chronic mental illness, and feminist epistemology. Her current research includes studies of vocational transitioning among mentally ill adolescents and the effects of opening sealed adoption records on adoptees, birth parents, and adoptive families.

BERTRAM J. COHLER is William Rainey Harper Professor of Social Sciences in the college and Professor in the departments of Behavioral Sciences (Human Development), Psychiatry, Education, and Divinity at the University of Chicago. His research interests include interpretive life course, social science and mental health, and well-being in the latter half of life.

STEPHEN CRYSTAL is Chief of the Division of Health Care Sciences, School of Medicine, University of California at San Diego. He previously directed the Center for Human Services Research and Development at New York City's Human Resources Administration. He has been principal investigator of a four-year national study of adult protective services.

MARK A. EDINBURG is Director of the Center for the Study of Aging, University of Bridgeport, and a Licensed Clinical Psychologist with a practice in Fairfield, Connecticut. He spent the 1985–1986 academic year at the Brookdale Center on Aging of Hunter College (N.Y.). He is author or co-author of *Communication in the Nursing Context, Mental Health Practice with the Elderly*, and the forthcoming *Talking with Your Parents: A Guide for Children of the Elderly*.

LINDA K. GEORGE is Professor of Psychiatry and Associate Director of the Center for the Study of Aging and Human Development at Duke University. Her major research interests include stress and coping in later life, the epidemiology of psychiatric disorders, and health services research. She is the author or co-author of five books, twenty-seven chapters, and fifty-one journal articles on these topics.

MARGARET F. HUDSON is Associate Professor of Primary Care Nursing at the University of North Carolina at Chapel Hill. A gerontological nurse practitioner, she has conducted two major studies of elder mistreatment. She is co-editor of *Elder Neglect and Abuse: An Annotated Bibliography*, and co-author of a chapter on the same topic in the forthcoming *Annual Review of Gerontology and Geriatrics*.

TANYA JOHNSON is a family sociologist who teaches at North Carolina State University in Raleigh, N.C. Most recently, she has been a postdoctoral fellow at the Center for the Study of Aging and Human Development at Duke University, where she has been conducting a research project on Social Indicators of Families at Risk for Elder Abuse. Her publications in family violence focus on child abuse and elder abuse. Included in the latter area are *Elder Neglect and Abuse: An Annotated Bibliography* (with Margaret Hudson and James O'Brien) and "Elder Neglect and Abuse: A Review of the Literature" (with Margaret Hudson), in the forthcoming *Annual Review of Gerontology and Geriatrics*.

NANCY R. KING is Deputy Director of the Center for Women Policy Studies in Washington, D.C. She has a background in gerontology, with a focus on public policy and long-term care. She is editor of the CWPS journal, *RESPONSE to the Victimization of Women and Children*.

LINDA R. PHILLIPS is Assistant Professor in the College of Nursing at the University of Arizona, Tucson. Her writings on elder abuse, which appear in gerontological and nursing journals, draw on both practical experience and theoretical considerations. She is the co-author of *Confusion: Prevention and Care*.

KARL A. PILLEMER is Assistant Professor of Sociology at the University of New Hampshire, where he is also a Research Associate in the Family Research Laboratory. His current research interests include the family relations of the elderly, long-term care, and domestic violence.

SHULAMIT REINHARZ teaches social gerontology, qualitative methods, and social psychology in the Sociology Department at Brandeis University. Among her recent publications are *On Becoming a Social Scientist* and *Psychology and Community Change*. Two additional books on aging are in preparation: *Aging on the Kibbutz,* and an edited volume entitled *Qualitative Gerontology*.

ALAN SAGER is Associate Professor at the Boston University School of Public Health. He has studied the reliability of professional decision making in long-term care and the shape of affordable urban hospital services. He recently published "The Opiate of the Managers," a study of competition in health care. He is author of *Planning Home Care with the Elderly*.

PETER N. STEARNS is Heinz Professor of History at Carnegie-Mellon University and editor-in-chief of the *Journal of Social History*. He has written widely in the field of old-age history and on related policy issues, authoring or editing *Old Age in European Society, Old Age in Pre-Industrial Society,* and *Old Age in a Bureaucratic Society*. His next book, on the history of emotions, deals with anger in the American past.

GEORGE TALER is assistant professor of Family Medicine and Director of the Division of Geriatric Medicine at the University of Maryland School of Medicine. He completed his residency in Family Medicine at the University of Maryland Hospital and a fellowship in Geriatric Medicine at the Jewish Institute for Geriatric Care, New Hyde Park, New York.

ROSALIE S. WOLF is Associate Director of the University Center on Aging at the University of Massachusetts Medical Center and Assistant Professor in the Departments of Medicine and Family and Community Medicine. She holds a Ph.D. from the Florence Heller School at Brandeis University. She has directed two federally funded projects on elder abuse and neglect. Her other major research interests lie in the organization and delivery of long-term care services.

Part One

FAMILY CONFLICT IN LATER LIFE

Chapter 1

OLD AGE FAMILY CONFLICT: THE PERSPECTIVE OF THE PAST

by Peter N. Stearns

Efforts to substantiate the existence of familial abuse of the elderly are, without question, elusive in the present, and unfathomable in the past. The extent of previous levels of conflict, even if researchers could agree on a single definition of the phenomenon, is unknown. Therefore, the most obvious question concerning the historical record—Is abuse today higher or lower than in the past?—cannot be answered. To be sure, historians have not explicitly inquired into elder abuse as a discrete subject, and while it may be possible, and perhaps even desirable, to try to improve our empirical knowledge of trends, we cannot expect real precision, even with the additional effort.

Nevertheless, the considerable attention of late that historians have given to past conditions of old age has a bearing on present interest in the problem of familial conflict. The changing context and probable patterns of abuse do emerge, raising interesting questions about current trajectories. What is clear is that conflict is not a purely modern issue. Gerontological interest in history has too often been confined to a "tradition is good, modern is worse" contrast, which appears to apply to the subject of abuse. Thus we

Note: My thanks to my colleague, W. Andrew Achenbaum, for a critical reading and constructive suggestions.

see respected and useful elders in pre-modern society standing above serious family squabbles in a rural world in which Biblical injunctions to honor one's parents had real meaning. But then modernity, serpentlike, disrupted this Eden, robbed the elderly of their protective veneration, and increased their dependence on often-resentful younger kin.

The use of this type of modernization theory to explain changes in old age could present such a picture. The first point to establish, however, is that this use of history would result in serious distortions. Abuse certainly predates modernization in Western culture and may, in fact, have been more serious in the pre-modern past than in more recent times. With the rise of an urban, industrial society, the familial context of old age shifted, altering the leading causes of familial conflict and possibly reducing the amount of conflict itself. The new pattern of family life, established with industrialization, is thus the second main vantage point to explore.

Many historians, however, are questioning a modernization approach to old age history, not only because of its oversimplification of pre-modern tradition—and therefore of the impact of urbanization and industrialization—but also because it posits too straightforward a modern trajectory. Vital changes have occurred in the lives of the elderly through the initial onset of modernization as well as through developments within the past 60 years. Thus it is important to explore a distinction between modern and more strictly contemporary trends and to deal with the possibility that familial conflict has taken some new directions in recent decades.

One pattern in the historical mosaic is clear: Aside from general laments about the heedlessness and ingratitude of the young, a recurrent theme is discernible in Western history. That theme is a specific focus on the problem of intergenerational conflict involving the elderly. During the past several centuries, this theme has gone through three cycles. The first was concern about conflict, which ran high in the 17th and 18th centuries, as witness the sometimes tense injunctions to respect one's elders. The second cycle saw a lessening of concern during the 19th and early 20th centuries, despite vigorous interest in family problems of other sorts. Recently, in the third cycle, the theme has been renewed, in appropriately modern, social scientific language—as the present volume abundantly suggests. Does abuse itself follow the same tripartite periodization? Or do other factors account for the relative silence of the middle period, or for the new articulation of the past two decades? Here, we begin to provide a framework for understanding this historical progression.

The Pre-Industrial Setting

A number of cultures have generated value systems that seem to inhibit familial tensions surrounding the elderly. In some cases—in India and China, for example—a religious component of ancestor worship enhances the more familiar injunctions to honor fathers and mothers.[1] The Western tradition, at least as it can be captured from the late-Middle Ages onward, unquestionably contained strong appeals for veneration of the elderly. Into the 18th century, religious-sponsored family manuals urged respect for and obedience to parents, to the exclusion of reciprocal obligation toward the young. For those who were not only old but male and reasonably prosperous, a number of public signs seem to have carried these injunctions out in practice. In colonial New England, the elderly received disproportionate shares in public officeholding; they also received pride of place in church seating. There is no reason to doubt that such appeals for respect carried over into family settings to some extent. Yet, ironically, familiar tensions surrounding the elderly may have been greater than those that surfaced in public life.[2]

Property Relationships

In the early modern Western tradition, the elderly stood at the hub of a set of property relationships that had wide and often unfavorable effects on younger family members. Generally speaking, until older family members relaxed their hold on property control, the young could not form families of their own and could not aspire to full economic or even sexual adulthood. In Western Europe, marriages were characteristically late for the common people—age 27 or 28 was the norm among peasants and artisans—and a surprisingly high rate remained single permanently.[3] Many younger kin were inclined, in this situation, to view their elders as unadulterated nuisances whose passing could only be welcome—like the French peasant who, on his father's death, noted starkly in his diary, "My father died today; now I can do as I please," before going on to more pressing issues such as the state of the livestock.[4]

Although property tensions stood at the core of family conflicts surrounding old age in the Western tradition, other issues may have added fuel to the fire. Western styles of child rearing, for example, involved considerable use of force and frequent isolation of children from parental attention, in a pattern designed to break children's will. This system was not uniform, nor necessarily unloving, and it did usually serve to evoke obedience from children themselves. But the same system could build up tensions that gained expression when parents themselves became somewhat enfeebled. Repressed, even unknown, during the parental prime, these hostilities could burst forth when the same parents reached more vulnerable years.[5]

Thus generational tensions over property, unusually great in Western society because of the peculiar pattern of late marriage, produced a potential for disputes between the elderly and their younger kin that appeals for veneration could not necessarily dampen. These tensions were also fed at times by sexual tensions in a society that did not readily countenance heterosexual expression before marriage and were exacerbated by other familial hostilities. Indeed, the appeals for veneration themselves may well have been a sign of tension, for authorities often seemed to be protesting too much, urging respect precisely because it was so uncertain in fact. Even the imagery of old age was ambivalent, with considerable emphasis on unfortunate passions, such as avarice, that emphasized the elderly's seemingly greedy defense of property. The simple fact was that Western society did not form the kind of unified extended family in which economic operations were seen as a function of the entire family unit. Extended families existed, especially in those instances in which older parents co-resided with late-born children who had yet to reach maturity. But the value system argued for a demarcation between generations, more than for a merging of their interests.[6]

Familial Tensions

Signs of familial tension abounded in pre-modern Western society. In some European countries, the elderly were carefully housed separately from younger kin, once the latter had acquired property control. Small cottages built to the rear of the main dwelling may have reduced daily disputes, but they also symbolized the lack of mutual interests that could produce tension. Many older people were forced into almshouses and hospitals, both of which were, well into the 19th century, dominated by the elderly, even though they were not expressly designed for them.[7] To be sure, many of these impoverished old people had no families available at all; some had never married; some had families that were simply too poor to offer relief. But some families tried to cast dependent elderly out, even against community norms that tried to maintain responsibility in such cases.

Tensions displayed against older women, within families as well as in larger communities, played a significant role in the witchcraft craze that swept through many parts of Western society from the 16th to the later 17th centuries. Conflicts with older women were not alone responsible for witchcraft fears, to be sure, but a disproportionate number of older women were victims. Two key reasons seem to have been the threat that their existence posed to access to property by younger kin and the burdens they placed on family resources. Add to this a pervasive belief in Western culture of the non-usefulness and danger of postmenopausal women, and a portion of the witchcraft brew was concocted.[8] The witchcraft craze did end, perhaps because older women learned greater caution and docility. But more specific hostilities persisted, as in the frequent cases in which older widows who managed to remarry were attacked or shamed by gangs of youths.[9]

Outright physical violence was directed against older men as well. During the 18th century, for example, men over 50 were the most frequent murder victims in France. While available data do not allow exact reconstruction of the patterns of these crimes in detail, there is enough nonscientific evidence to suggest that most of the murders were familial, generated by the tensions of pro-longed control over property and blockage of the aspirations of younger kin.

Most revealing of all, because they were widespread and dura-ble, were the legal arrangements older people had to resort to in order to try to assure their livelihood against neglect by younger relatives. When older men sought to retire because of failing health or other reasons, or sought to protect their wives in case of their death, they frequently had elaborate contracts drawn up to assure a food supply and housing from those children who would take over the property. The fearful wording of these documents suggests not a casual statement of intent but an anxious awareness of the potential for later neglect. Specificity down to monthly pecks of potatoes followed from prior conflict within the family, or awareness that such conflict was likely as soon as the elderly surrendered their basic weapon in a familiar power struggle—the weapon of ownership.[10]

The factors that generated familial tensions and outright abuse, and the evidence of such conflicts, do not add up to any uniform patterns. Not all old men and women were deprived of respect and even affection. Aside from vagaries of personality, both on the part of younger kin and on that of the elderly themselves, certain situations were conducive to less-than-average dispute. In colonial America, for example, a country blessed with relatively abundant resources in land, many families were able to provide for younger

kin in advance of outright retirement by older farmers and without
great tension on either side.[11] Even in Western Europe, recent
evidence suggests that partial property transfers took place more
frequently than had been realized, before parental death and
sometimes before marriage of the youngest child. While such
transfers may have reflected prior conflict, sometimes they flowed
from mutual economic advantage and positive affection, as in
colonial America. Among other things, the American situation
permitted an earlier average marriage age. On the other hand, the
concentration of poorer families and the general increase in crowding along the Eastern seaboard during the 18th century produced
some familial conflicts quite similar to the standard European
model of the period. Indeed, the availability of land in America,
and the particular value placed on independence, could sometimes
generate new sources of dispute. When teenaged apprentices,
because of the open spaces and fewer village and guild restrictions,
saw greater prospects for independent livelihood, they might, like
the young Ben Franklin, quarrel bitterly with their fathers over
the disposition of their own training.[12] The colonial American
pattern, in sum, displays certain modifications of characteristic
Western family tensions, but not a really different framework.

Historians have agreed, despite some nuances of difference, that
old age in preindustrial Western society was a rocky state, despite
certain ascriptive advantages over more recent conditions. Although rates of family conflict can rarely be suggested with any
precision, the frequency of such conflict, and the institutions such
as retirement contracts to which it gave rise, forms one key reason
for this generally gloomy assessment. Family life was not easy for
many old people, and they were abundantly aware of the fact.[13]

The Modern Setting: Industrialization's Impact

Pre-industrial family tensions, though admittedly diverse, must be
noted for their own sake, lest we be tempted to posit some false
golden age against which modern horrors of abuse must be contrasted. There is no conflict-free utopia in our recallable past, and
there may indeed be some deep-seated tensions in Western culture concerning old age that underlie current as well as past abuse.

But the pre-industrial pattern must also be recognized in order
to bring out the surprisingly complex generational relationships in
more recent history. Some of the key tensions that informed old
age in the pre-modern Western family were gradually modified by
the forces of industrialization that took shape in the late 18th and

early 19th centuries. Unquestionably, industrialization was hostile to old age in several respects: It tended to vaunt youthful energy over the traditionalism associated with the elderly, and to enhance the economic insecurities of old age, as a growing percentage of the population found itself permanently propertyless. We will return to these points later. Tensions of this sort showed most clearly in the public forum—in the workplace and in the generally youth-oriented culture. Within families, on the other hand, industrialization ironically reduced some traditional irritants in the relations between old people and younger kin.

Reduction in Tensions Between Elderly and Younger Kin

The most important shift entailed the reductions of the power of older parents to determine the economic fate and marital choices of their children. This change was gradual and incomplete, but its direction was steady. With the separation of work from home, which industrialization brought about, and the reduction in property ownership as the basis for survival, young people had more options through which they could establish independence at a relatively early age. Through factory work, a male could support himself by age 17 or 18. Rising rates of marriage and declining marriage ages, along with a general decrease in parental power to select mates or supervise sexual activity before marriage, reflected the new generational relationship. While the new patterns were most pronounced among urban workers, they spread to some extent to middle-class families.[14]

The growing opportunities for freedom in work and courtship did not produce a new warfare between children and older parents. Particularly in the working class, abundant signs of close ties remained, as most children continued to live at home at least until marriage, and many older people, particularly widows, later co-resided with their children. What occurred was not in fact a disruption in relations but a change in their base, with the overwhelming power of the elderly reduced, and traditional kinds of conflicts reduced as well. Supplementing this shift, especially again in the working class, was the development of new functions for the elderly, such as taking care of grandchildren so that younger women could work or at least shop.[15]

With property-generated conflict declining, other changes in the family environment contributed to a lessening of tension, or at least to its less overt and recognized expression. From the late 18th century onward, a new middle-class ideology of a loving family became increasingly widespread. Child-rearing methods changed, with a reduction of physical discipline and an effort to win closer emotional ties between parent (particularly mother) and child. Conceivably, this shift also reduced hostilities in later life between adults and their elderly parents. Certainly, the general notion that the family was supposed to provide a loving refuge from the tensions of the outside world encouraged a belief that conflict and the family were incompatible.[16] This demanding ideal was applied particularly to parent-child and husband-wife contacts, but was readily extended to older relatives as well. Thus the imagery of the elderly began to shift, notably in the case of women. Instead of the witch picture of the 17th century, the 19th century generated the image of a rosey-cheeked and benign, if somewhat passive, grandmother.

Historian David Hackett Fischer has put the case this way: Changing family relations from the 18th to the 19th centuries notably reduced the power of the elderly but generated a more loving emotional environment.[17] This shift admittedly remains to be established empirically, through data from actual families as opposed to images. But signs of increasing grief over the death of older parents—the forerunner of a phenomenon even more abundantly clear in the 20th century—provide at least one interesting indication.[18]

Finally, contacts between the elderly and younger kin were increasingly mediated by women. In the property-dominated framework of family life in the 18th century, the elderly were most likely to be oriented toward the families of sons; daughters, unless unmarried, were expected to gravitate to their husbands' orbit. Extended households thus most commonly entailed relationships with married sons. In the 19th century this arrangement began to shift. Elderly people who co-resided with adult children came almost invariably to choose daughters. Further, co-residence most typically involved widowed mothers rather than elderly couples or widowed fathers. An increasing difference in marriage age between men and women, plus a growing gap in life expectancy in the latter's favor, made it more and more probable that the older person seeking shelter in the household of younger kin would be female. Hence the most common extended family tie, residentially, was a mother-daughter tie. This shift was occurring at the same time as a particular emphasis developed on an ideal of feminine love and companionship—and avoidance of familial anger—as the bedrock of family life. Bonds among women were encouraged to be particularly close, and some large and durable patterns, most notably the close bonds formed among working-class wives and their mothers, do seem to have formed on this basis.[19]

In sum, structural changes in family life reduced some key traditional tensions, while other changes in family culture—unquestionably, realized only imperfectly in fact—also worked toward a reduction of conflict.

New Perceptions of the Elderly by Younger Kin: The Image of Inability

To be sure, this is hardly the whole story. Modern conditions also created or enhanced other sources of tension in the familial environment for the elderly. Two changes were particularly significant. First, the elderly were increasingly perceived and in some ways treated as useless. The industrial culture of the 19th and early 20th centuries placed a premium on the real or imagined virtues of youth. New societal commitments, in such forms as mass education, went far more to the young than to other groups. Revealingly, after about 1820, when Americans lied about their age they pretended to be younger than they actually were. In earlier times, Americans were more likely to pretend they were older—and therefore worthier—than they were. The young were seen as possessing the energy and ability to assimilate new ways, a vital trait in a changing society where what was novel was deemed desirable.

This general spirit translated into family life. Initially in the middle classes, and later more generally, child-rearing manuals began to gain ground as sources of authority, instead of the experiences of the elderly. Further, these manuals shifted gears every 20 years or so, altering previous advice about feeding, discipline, and the like. These frequent changes promoted a belief that the elderly were positively irrelevant in family counsels.

In a special version of this pattern, second-generation immigrant families often confronted a huge gap between the language and values of older relatives and what they themselves and their children were learning about American ways. Here was a fruitful source not only of a growing feeling of isolation on the part of many older people, but of active dispute about how the family was run.[20]

The second change in the familial environment was that the urban elderly became increasingly likely to be economically dependent on younger kin. A similar development occurred among the growing number of propertyless agricultural workers. Property became less widely distributed, and hence lost value in procuring support or bargaining power in old age. The elderly also found it increasingly difficult to retain factory jobs, encountering reductions of income and skill level and growing periods of unemployment in the face of competition from machines and younger workers.[21] Well before the establishment of pension plans, the pattern of forced retirement or partial retirement took shape in urban areas. It is far from clear whether the services that the elderly could provide younger kin in the form of babysitting and occasional chores, or the new emotional bonds that might be forming, were sufficient to compensate for the tensions that growing economic need could place on younger family members.

Lack of Evidence of Elderly Abuse in 19th and 20th Centuries

When the elderly came to be regarded as relatively useless and also vulnerable because they were dependent, the potential for abuse might actually have been greater, in terms of frequency if not severity, than when the elderly had been seen as frustrating power-wielders. However, there is almost no evidence of direct abuse of the elderly in the 19th and early 20th centuries. Perhaps such evidence will emerge in further inquiry. It may be that abuse was concealed because of pervasive beliefs that the conflict that did take place should not be occurring in a properly loving family. Perhaps the elderly were simply not seen as sufficiently important to warrant reformist attention.

This last point, especially, is hard to refute. Yet it was precisely because of new beliefs about the ideal family that 19th-century reformers were willing to probe abuses of other family members. Child abuse and wife-beating, although not entirely new subjects of concern, received growing attention during the first decades of industrialization, not so much because they were increasing as because new standards were being applied. Attacks on familial abuse provided an excellent opportunity for middle-class observers to tout their values over the presumed vices of working-class, black, or immigrant families. Perhaps, again, the elderly were simply left out of this pattern. They were seen as less innocent and improvable than children, and less pure than ideal women; therefore, it may be that no one bothered to inquire into what was happening to them in the family environment. Interestingly, then, the first century plus of industrialization produced no signs of a widespread elder abuse problem. This fact is in contrast with the pre-industrial centuries, when laments about disobedient and disrespectful children abounded, and in contrast to the past few decades, when the subject of elderly abuse has surfaced even more explicitly.

A few novels, to be sure, raised the issue. In the 1880s, for example, Sarah Orne Jewett, in *The Country of the Pointed Firs*, wrote of pervasive physical abuse of elderly people in working-class families; the only solution she saw was to board the elderly out in other families, where tensions would be less great. Josephine Laurell's 1934 novel, *The Years Are So Long*, dealt with problems of frequent arguments between old people and younger kin, although mainly in the context of the damage imposed on all family members by the Depression. However, even such literary references are scarce. Old people themselves, admittedly mainly from the middle class, managed to convey in their writings concern about issues such as health problems and the sense of being bypassed by changing modern values. However, they produced no direct comment on abuse or conflict within the family, on whose symbolic cohesion and, often, economic support they of course depended.

This is not to say that abuse and conflict were nonexistent. There are even some oblique signs of disputes that could perhaps not be articulated directly. Older workers frequently lamented their uncertainty about their economic future, claiming that they did not know where they could turn: "I'll go where the wind blows me, or to the poorhouse, or I'll die."[22] Partly, of course, this was a comment on the new burdens of poverty and joblessness in the industrial economy, but it indirectly commented as well on the unreliability of one's children as sources of support. Later in the 19th century, the elderly began disproportionately to fill the ranks of the expanding insane asylums, with the initiative for institutionalization typically coming from younger kin.[23] Here, quite possibly, was a statement that disputes with the elderly could be rationalized, and ended, by means of assumptions that the old had lost their mental balance—a sign, therefore, of a host of conflicts that could not be directly admitted in principle.

These examples notwithstanding, it appears that conflict and abuse were becoming less common than they had been before. Alternatively, families may simply have become more reticent about conflict. When a problem is not discussed, it may be because there are overriding reasons not to perceive it, which is surely a viable hypothesis for developments during the first century of industrialization. But it is also likely that the problem of conflict became less severe.

Shifts in the familial context of the elderly during the second quarter of the 20th century may further have reduced the conflicts that did exist, however unacknowledged. The decades between the 1920s and the 1950s are widely seen as a historic watershed in the history of the elderly in recent centuries, for two related reasons that both bear on the potential for familial conflict. First, retirement support became more available than ever before, greatly reducing the economic dependency of many elderly on younger kin. Second, the elderly began to separate themselves residentially from younger kin, in one of the great modern changes in family structure.

Retirement Support for the Elderly

The establishment of mass retirement as a normal phenomenon, undergirded by pension support, may of course have generated tensions, particularly during the first transitional decades. Many older workers initially feared retirement; only from the late 1950s onward do polls indicate that most older workers have switched from expectations that retirement would bring new health, psychic, and economic problems to a belief that retirement is on the whole a pleasurable state.[24] Until this shift was made, the newly generalized patterns of retirement may have increased anxieties among not only the elderly but also other family members. Given the low levels of support and limited coverage of the initial Social Security program and other pension schemes, retirement may often have increased dependency, as employers' zeal to rid themselves of expensive older workers outstripped the support provided. Again, this is a problem still not fully resolved, but ameliorated only with Social Security extensions in the 1960s and early 1970s. Retirement support may have also generated disputes within the family about kin obligations. Evidence suggests that workers who reached retirement age in the 1950s and before continued to believe that support should come from family, not from state programs tainted somewhat by welfare labels. Yet younger family members, more comfortable with Social Security provisions with which they had grown up, readily disclaimed their traditional responsibility in light of new sources of aid. Here, too, tensions subsided with time; by the 1960s most retirees agreed with younger kin that familial economic support should not play a primary role in maintaining old age.[25]

On balance, then, the development of retirement as a normal experience palliated some of the tensions undoubtedly produced by the growing economic dependency of older people under the impact of industrialization. As the experience became increasingly standard and anticipated by all family members and as the number of retirees below the poverty line declined, these effects became increasingly clear. To be sure, retirement provided new sources of tension, with older workers now around the house increasingly, disrupting earlier family routines. Changes in the power balance between husband and wife, with the latter gaining increasing ascendancy in later years, followed from retirement and may have produced a new set of conflicts, though mainly within the elderly household itself.[26]

The Residential Revolution

The second great 20th-century change, the residential revolution, significantly reduced the daily contact between older people and younger kin, and therefore the potential for nagging conflicts. During the 19th century, as in pre-industrial times, a substantial minority of older people had lived in the households of younger kin. Another large group maintained one or more children in their own households. In all, in 1900 approximately 60 percent of all older people lived in one or the other of these arrangements. Both arrangements declined precipitously from the 1920s onward. Co-residence with younger children waned as the birth rate dropped and, during the baby boom, the age of childbearing declined. More interestingly still, because it involved a more explicit decision within the family, the number of elderly living in the households of younger children dropped rapidly as well. By the 1960s, 89 percent of all older people lived alone, with a spouse, or with nonrelatives.[27]

This dramatic change could, of course, have produced bitter conflict. It would be easy to hypothesize a pattern in which younger kin, selfishly tired of dealing with older parents, kicked the elders out, amid bitter dispute on both sides. In fact, it is the smoothness of the residential revolution that is remarkable. All parties seem to have agreed that the new arrangements made sense, to the extent that change was virtually unremarked. Other structural shifts, such as the pattern of younger couples living together before marriage, provoked much clearer outrage and tension. There is some evidence that younger kin sometimes regretted the decision of older parents to live separately, worrying about their ability to care for themselves, but there is no sign that this concern was pushed to the point of major conflict or abuse.

The only clear conflict involved in the residential revolution was in fact apparently resolved by the revolution itself. Many older people cited their concern about powerlessness and irrelevance in a younger household, and particularly the tension they felt when confronted with the noisy lifestyles of teenaged grandchildren,[28] as a reason for wanting their own space. They used the new resources available through growing prosperity and pension funds to provide this space, with a resultant lessening of family conflict.

Thus the two great changes of the 20th century seem directly to have attacked the two sources of conflict that seemed most ominous during the earlier industrial decades, in which respect for the elderly had declined. Retirement income lessened economic dependency, and the change in residential patterns helped alleviate the problem of generational dispute. Both these developments highlight the probability that some tensions in the 19th century have thus far escaped our notice, in terms of direct and detailed evidence; but both suggest also a trajectory of conflict reduction.

The Contemporary Setting

In addition to the firm historical finding of a distressingly solid tradition of familial conflict surrounding the elderly in Western society, the historical perspective also reveals an important change in the nature of the sources of conflict in the mid-20th century and the possibility also of a decline in the frequency and severity of conflict itself. But now we confront the most immediate problem requiring historical perspective: the rapid increase during the past 15 years of concern about the problem of elder abuse.

A New Periodization

The idea of a recent shift in historical patterns is not startling. To be sure, most gerontologists who have dabbled in historical context at all have tended to favor a fairly simple traditional-modern dichotomy, in which modern trends, once launched, proceed fairly directly to and through the present. We already know that this approach is not fully satisfactory for old age history, even aside from the vital point that the traditional cannot be equated with unqualified good, and the modern with unadulterated bad. In many ways, modern trends for a full century did less to change the basic conditions of old age than did the pension support and residential revolutions of the past half-century. A "modern" history of old age since the 1920s and 1930s differs considerably from a history of old age in modernizing society during the preceding century.

On other topics, also, a division must frequently be made between initial industrial patterns and more contemporary trends. Thus, during much of the 19th and early 20th centuries, the per capita rates of crimes of violence stabilized or even decreased, reflecting better policing and more firmly ingrained methods of self-control, as well as a growing tendency to turn to crimes of property over crimes against persons.[29] Yet crime patterns from the mid-20th century have established a different set of trends, in which violent crime rises once again, on a per capita basis and also, at least until very recently, in relation to the rates of property crime. Here, in ways that may be highly relevant to the more specific issue of abuse of the elderly, is a clear distinction between modern and contemporary developments—in historians' parlance, a need to establish and explain a new periodization that separates the century roughly 1850 to 1950, from the decades thereafter.

Is Abuse Increasing or Is the Problem Being Redefined?

In dealing with a contemporary versus modern periodization for familial conflict, however, two lines of analysis must be pursued. They are not inherently contradictory, but may in theory be separate. The growing concern about elder abuse, which clearly separates the contemporary period from the preceding century, may itself be an artifact—the product of factors other than the phenomenon to which it is addressed. It is also possible that the problem of abuse is itself increasing, and so explains or partly explains the first development.

New attention to familial abuse sometimes results not from new abuse, but from new attention and newly rigorous standards. Current concern about the sexual abuse of children, for example, involves the construction of new definitions of what is abusive—which is not to say that the concern is wrong, but rather that it may create a misleading impression of a rising incidence of a problem when in fact what has happened is that the problem has been in part restated. There are several reasons to suspect that the current concern about abuses within the family, including those affecting the elderly, has been generated in part by factors separate from the problems to which it is addressed. At several points in American history—most recently, the 1920s—a reform interest discouraged from a sweeping legislative approach has turned to moral and family reform with unusual intensity, usually with strong implications that the family problems had taken a turn for the worse. The waning of Progressive sentiment and the realization that many Progressive reforms had not had desired results turned many reformers, in the politically conservative climate of the 1920s, to family issues. If only people would run their families better, then problems such as illegitimacy, delinquency, and poor school behavior would go away. Something of a similar mood seems to have hit American society in the aftermath of the Great Society, as reformers again sought unassailable moral issues through which they could hope to effect change, largely outside a now-conservative legislative arena.

And this time, concern focuses on the elderly as well. The growth in numbers of the elderly enhances their visibility and brings a growing legion of professionals with something of a personal stake in finding problems to which they can address remedies. Now that new legislative reforms for the elderly seem largely unrealistic, and as the game changes to defense of gains previously won, attention to family conduct almost naturally rises. Again, this is not to argue that the new concerns are factually incorrect or wrongly directed, though at times, it can be argued, earlier concern about family abuse involved efforts to impose middle-class values on family situations with some unforeseen and undesirable results.[30] But even when the campaign against abuse is fiercely waged, it is important to retain the possibility that some portion of the war emanates not from changes in the enemy, but in larger forces that shape the fighters for justice.

It is, of course, possible that abuse is actually becoming an increasing problem, rather than simply being redefined and more zealously hunted without its basic pattern greatly changing. The most elementary verification of this hypothesis again eludes us, for the simple reason that prior rates of familial conflict cannot be established with even rough precision, particularly for the preceding modern period. Yet, just as we argued that the absence of complaint about abuse during the first industrial decades may suggest a low incidence level, at least compared with other familial abuses and to the pre-industrial pattern, so we must now entertain the possibility that the new outcry against elder abuse reflects changes in the contours of the problem. There are reasons to believe that the outcry results in part from other factors; for example, the growing size and political clout of the old-age population may increase the visibility of certain issues without necessarily changing their shape. However, we must consider whether a new period has opened up in the history of familial environment of the elderly that has led to increased rates of elder abuse.

Changes in the Contemporary Setting and
in the Elderly Population

Regarding the possibility of a significant contemporary shift in patterns of abuse and conflict, two factors merit examination: (1) changes in the larger environment and (2) the working out of prior changes in the position of the elderly themselves. Particularly interesting, although not conclusive, is the way these two general factors interweave.

Growing economic insecurity and the lack during the 1970s of significant improvements in per capita real income placed substantial burdens on American families. It has been demonstrated that the economic downturn of the late 1970s and early 1980s had a direct impact on rates of child abuse, especially in families of the unemployed.[31] One response to economic pressure, among other causes, has been the increased involvement of women in the labor force outside the home. This may aid the economic fortunes of the family, but only by placing increased strain on women and reducing the extent that women can or choose to serve their earlier modern function as a primary contact between the nuclear family and its older relatives.[32] Other tensions within the family, including declining parental authority, might also rebound in worsening relations with the elderly, as the latter become targets for conflicts generated at first in other relationships. Not only economic insecurity but also the growing emotional constraint placed on workers with the proliferation of tightly regimented white-collar jobs may increasingly be turning the family into an outlet for emotional frustration—an odd but recognizable perversion from its earlier idealization as a haven from the outside world. Here, too, the elderly, as vulnerable family members along with young children, may bear the brunt of new attack.[33] Tensions within specific groups feed into this altered environment. The alienation of white-collar workers who discover toward mid-life that the fabled mobility ladder is not theirs to climb; the steady increase in the number of unskilled, poor and transiently employed; and, of course, the rise of often-strained, single-headed households are particularly noteworthy developments in recent decades, with potential for producing heightened family conflict.

Changes in the elderly population have some interesting consequences as well. The increase in the elderly population means more than growing visibility for problems in this sector. It also means that individual families have more elderly relatives to deal with, in some fashion, than ever before. Changes in the young-old ratio, so often invoked in dealing with retirement support, have emotional implications as well, in potentially stretching the reserves of young and old alike. The particularly rapid growth in the old-old population, with its medical and economic needs, represents another unfamiliar and possibly demanding experience for many families. Improved medical ability to prolong life amid considerable debility may also increase the burden, annoyance, and vulnerability of many older people in family care, although the earlier history of the elderly bears some similarities, as death often came somewhat slowly, but typically at earlier stages of old age.

At the same time, the long-run implications of the earlier changes in the 20th century context for old age may now have unforeseen consequences. It is widely recognized that in the 1970s the elderly fared better economically than did other segments of the population. This development fueled many speculations about potential generational antagonism spilling over into American politics, as the young would resist the demands of the old on their tax dollars.[34] Few of these speculations have to date borne close empirical scrutiny, as young and old alike generally agree on Social Security issues and as politically hostile generational camps have not clearly emerged. But the possibility of generational antagonism over differing fortunes within the family does merit inquiry. As the old loudly insist on retirement rights, seem largely to enjoy retirement, and yet can be perceived as functionless by already-strained wage earners, they may provoke unexpected resentments.

The residential separation of the elderly, although at first a source of conflict reduction, may have adverse consequences as well. The separation does not eliminate tight intergenerational bonds, but it may lessen their power. It leaves the elderly more literally isolated, and so more vulnerable, than before. It produces inevitable dislocation when, after a long period of separate residence, medical or economic dependency forces reintegration of an older relative into the household.

Finally, the residential separation of the elderly serves to reduce the informal community supervision that may previously have protected them against frequent abuse. In pre-industrial society, family members of all ages operated in a community environment which, most historians agree, limited family abuse to some extent. This village or neighborhood environment was weakened by 19th-century urbanization, which is one reason that reformers and the police intervened increasingly in family disputes.[35] For the elderly, however, the perpetuation of co-residence with younger kin, in a majority of cases, may have maintained some collective inhibitions, as the family itself served as some check against individual abuse. Obviously, neither family nor community prevented all abuse; but these structures did constrain individual behavior while keeping most cases of mild abuse out of wider public purview. For the elderly, the most substantial alteration of this kind of small-group protection may have occurred, not with industrialization itself, but more recently with the move toward residential isolation. The result would be both a growing problem of conflict degenerating into abuse and a growing perception of the need for outside, non-family restraints.

Conclusion

Historical perspective on the issue of old age and family conflict produces a complex mixture of firm findings about past problems and shifts in conflict-generating issues, and open questions. Vexing questions about previous rates of abuse, the impact of a changing environment during the decades of industrialization, and the relationship of the contemporary decades to past patterns merit further inquiry, though they may never be fully resolved. Historians of old age have produced considerable information about some of the sweeping changes that accompanied the experience of old age in the past two centuries, but they have not provided detailed micro-analyses that would unearth the richest lodes of data on such current issues as elder abuse. Yet the leading problems of interpretation, though distressingly unresolved, are themselves useful in guiding inquiry about current behaviors, quite apart from the fact that a number of firm findings inhibit errors about the larger historical context.

Anyone concerned about elder abuse in any systematic way must confront the following, essentially historical questions: Is abuse increasing, or are we merely perceiving rates of abuse that previously passed unnoticed? If the former, what major factors are involved in this recent historical change? And if the latter, what is provoking us to take this new look at old problems, and what unintended consequences might flow from the impulse to redefine family problems? Understanding the intricacy of old age family history and of the recency of some of the most important shifts in the lives of older people helps refine the questions and provide some guiding hypotheses as we seek to grasp the relationship of present to past in order better to grasp the present itself.

Endnotes

1. Sylvia Vatuk, "Old Age in India," in *Old Age in Preindustrial Society,* ed. Peter N. Stearns (New York: Holmes & Meier, 1982), pp. 70–103; Erdman Palmore, *The Honorable Elders: A Cross-Cultural Analysis of Aging in Japan* (Durham, N.C.: Duke University Press, 1975).
2. Jean-Louis Flandrin, *Families in Former Times: Kinship, Household and Sexuality,* trans. R. Southern (Cambridge: Cambridge University Press, 1979); David Hackett Fischer, *Growing Old in America* (New York: Oxford University Press, 1977).
3. J. Hajnal, "European Marriage Patterns in Perspective," in *Population in History,* eds. D. V. Glass and D.E.C. Eversly (Chicago: Aldine Press, 1964), pp. 101–43.
4. Peter N. Stearns, *Old Age in European Society: The Case of France* (New York: Holmes & Meier, 1978), p. 43.
5. Flandrin, *Families in Former Times;* David Hunt, *Parents and Children in History* (New York: Basic Books, 1970).
6. Simone de Beauvoir, *The Coming of Age,* trans. P. O'Brien (New York: G. P. Putnam's, 1972); Peter Laslett, "A History of Aging and the Aged," in *Family Life and Illicit Love in Earlier Generations,* ed. Peter Laslett (Cambridge: Cambridge University Press, 1977), pp. 174–213.
7. Glenn C. Altschuler and J. M. Saltzgaber, "Clearinghouse for Paupers: The Poorfarm of Seneca County, New York, 1830–1860," *Journal of Social History* 17, no. 4 (1984), pp. 573–600; Olwen Hufton, *The Poor of Eighteenth Century France* (New York: Oxford University Press, 1975); H. C. Johanson, "The Position of the Old in the Rural Household in a Traditional Society," in *Chance and Change: Social and Economic Studies in Historical Demography in the Baltic Areas,* eds. S. Akerman et al. (Odense, Denmark: Christianson, 1978), pp. 122–30.
8. Edward Bever, "Old Age and Witchcraft in Early Modern Europe," in *Old Age in Preindustrial Society,* ed. Peter N. Stearns (New York: Holmes & Meier, 1982), pp. 150–90.
9. Natalie Z. Davis, *Society and Culture in Early Modern France* (Stanford: Stanford University Press, 1975), pp. 116–17.
10. Lutz Berkner, "The Stem Family and the Developmental Cycle: An 18th-Century Austrian Example," *American Historical Review* 77 (1972), pp. 398–414; Keith Thomas, "Age and Authority in Early Modern England," *Proceedings of the British Academy* 62 (1976), pp. 233–48; Stearns, *Old Age in European Society,* pp. 72ff.
11. Philip J. Greven, Jr., *Four Generations: Population, Land and Family in Colonial Andover, Massachusetts* (Ithaca, N.Y.: Cornell University Press, 1970); Richard M. Smith, ed., *Land, Kinship and Life Cycle* (Cambridge: Cambridge University Press, 1985). For a view of growing tensions in America toward the end of the 18th century, based on new ideas of personal independence but probably also growing crowding along the eastern seaboard, see Fischer, *Growing Old in America,* pp. 75–78, describing how one father believed he had to arm himself against a violently abusive son. Fischer implies that this kind of tension mounted at this time, due to ideological

changes prompting greater youth freedom; but it seems more probable that this was a well-recorded instance of a common type of conflict in what was still a pre-industrial setting.

12. Benjamin Franklin, *Autobiography* (New York: Crowell, 1962), pp. 23ff.

13. Lawrence Stone, "Walking Over Grandma," *New York Review of Books* 24 (1977), pp. 10–16.

14. Edward Shorter, *The Making of the Modern Family* (New York: Basic Books, 1975).

15. Michael Anderson, *Family Structure in Nineteenth-Century Lancashire* (Cambridge: Cambridge University Press, 1971).

16. Carol Z. Stearns and Peter N. Stearns, *Anger: The Struggle for Emotional Control in America's History* (Chicago: University of Chicago Press, 1986), chapter 3.

17. Fischer, *Growing Old in America,* pp. 75ff.

18. Paul C. Rosenblatt, *Bitter, Bitter Tears: Nineteenth-Century Diarists and Twentieth-Century Grief Theories* (Minneapolis: University of Minnesota Press, 1983).

19. Mirra Komarovsky, *Blue Collar Marriage* (New York: Norton, 1967); Colin Rosser and Christopher Harris, *The Family and Social Change* (New York: Oxford University Press, 1965); Peter N. Stearns, "Old Women: Some Historical Observations," *Journal of Family History* 5(1980), pp. 44–57; Daniel Scott Smith, "Historical Change in the Household Structure of the Elderly in Economically Developed Societies," in *Old Age in Preindustrial Society,* ed. Peter N. Stearns (New York: Holmes & Meier, 1982), pp. 248–74.

20. W. Andrew Achenbaum, *Old Age in a New Land: The American Experience Since 1790* (Baltimore: Johns Hopkins University Press, 1978); Fischer, *Growing Old in America;* Carole Haber, "Mandatory Retirement in 19th Century America: The Conceptual Basis for a Work Cycle," *Journal of Social History* 12, no. 1 (1979), pp. 77–97.

21. Brian Gratton, *The Elderly in Boston* (Philadelphia: Temple University Press, 1986); Janese Reiff, Michel Dahlin, and Daniel Scott Smith, "Rural Push and Urban Pull: Work and Family Experiences of Older Black Women in Southern Cities, 1880–1900," *Journal of Social History* 16, no. 4 (1983), pp. 37–48.

22. J.P.A. Villeneuve-Bargemont, *Economie politique chretienne* (Paris, 1835), II, p. 275.

23. Gerald N. Grob, "Directions in Old Age History Research," in *Old Age in a Bureaucratic Society,* eds. David Van Tassel and Peter N. Stearns (Westport, Conn.: Greenwood, 1986).

24. Gail Buchwalter King and Peter N. Stearns, "The Retirement Experience as a Policy Factor: An Applied History Approach," *Journal of Social History* 14, no. 4 (1981), pp. 589–626; Herbert S. Parnes and Gilbert Nesbet, *Work and Retirement: The Longitudinal Experience of Men* (Cambridge, Mass.: MIT Press, 1981).

25. Tamara K. Hareven, *Family Time and Industrial Time* (Cambridge: Cambridge University Press, 1982), pp. 116–19; William Graebner, *A History of Retirement* (New Haven: Yale University Press, 1980).

26. David Guttman, "The Premature Gerontocracy," in *Death in the American Experience,* ed. Adrien Mack (New York: Wiley, 1973).

27. Daniel Scott Smith, "Life Course, Norms and the Family System of Older Americans in 1900," *Journal of Family History* 4 (1979), pp. 285–98; Smith, "Historical Change"; Frances Kobrin, "The Fall in Household Size and the Rise of the Primary Individuals in the United States," *Demography* 13 (1976), pp. 127–38; Frances Kobrin, "The Primary Individual and the Family: Changes in Living Arrangements in the United States since 1940," *Journal of Marriage and the Family* 38 (1976), pp. 233–39.

28. Suzanne Pacaud and M. D. Lahalle, *Attitudes, comportements, opinions des personnes agees dans le cadre de la famille moderne* (Paris: Presses Universitaires, 1969).

29. Roger Lane, *Violent Death: The Social Significance of Suicide, Accident and Murder in Nineteenth-Century Philadelphia* (Cambridge, Mass.: Harvard University Press, 1980); Eric M. Monkkonen, "A Disorderly People? Urban Order in the Nineteenth and Twentieth Centuries" (Paper delivered at the Bi-annual Meeting of the American Studies Association, September 28–30, 1979).

30. Christopher Lasch, *Haven in a Heartless World: The Family Beseiged* (New York: Basic Books, 1977).

31. Paula M. Rayman and Barry Bluestone, *Out of Work: The Consequences of Unemployment in the Hartford Aircraft Industry* (Washington, D.C.: U.S. Government Printing Office, 1982); Phyllis Moen, E. L. Kain, and Glen Elder, Jr., "Economic Conditions and Family Life: Contemporary and Historical Perspective," in *American Families and the Economy,* eds. R. Nelson and F. Skidmore (Washington, D.C.: National Academy Press, 1983), pp. 335–37.

32. Ethel Shanas, "The Family as a Support System in Old Age," *Gerontologist* 19 (1979), pp. 169–74; Elaine Brody, *Long-Term Care for Older People* (New York: Human Sciences Press, 1977).

33. Lasch, *Haven in a Heartless World;* Stearns and Stearns, *Anger,* ch. 6.

34. Robert S. Kaplan, *Financial Crisis in the Social Security System* (Washington, D.C.: American Enterprise Institute, 1978); William C. Mitchell, *The Popularity of Social Security* (Washington, D.C.: American Enterprise Institute, 1977).

35. For a fuller discussion of the complex impact of community decline on familial abuse over time, and efforts to compensate through more formal agencies, see Peter N. Stearns, "Child Abuse in Historical Perspective," *New Designs for Youth Development* (forthcoming); Linda A. Pollock, *Forgotten Children: Parent-Child Relations from 1500 to 1800* (Cambridge: Cambridge University Press, 1984).

Chapter 2

LOVING AND HATING ONE'S ELDERS: TWIN THEMES IN LEGEND AND LITERATURE

by Shulamit Reinharz

This chapter provides a framework from which to view one aspect of kinship relations, the social-psychological bond between adults and their parents. On the basis of Greek myths, Biblical passages, legends, fairy tales, anthropological material, ceremonies, novels, plays, psychoanalytic theory, and famous crimes, two contradictory themes can be seen: In certain circumstances adults are expected to abuse their elders and in others, to respect them. These literary and historical sources also demonstrate that, contrary to public opinion, "elder abuse" is not a new problem that has emerged because of the increased proportion of elderly people in the population, or because of "the breakdown of the nuclear family," economic uncertainty, or the loss of a sense of neighborliness and community. Rather, elder abuse represents an unbroken saga in the relations between adults and their elders. These cultural products give testimony to persistent intergenerational cruelty. This tradition of abuse, however, is challenged by the equally forceful norm of respect for elders. Thus respect and disdain together define intergenerational relations. They form the twin cultural themes of honor and contempt and are experienced as hating and loving.

The first theme asserts that the relation among generations is

Note: I acknowledge gratefully the assistance of Professors Gordon Fellman and Scott McNall, who commented on an earlier draft of this chapter.

25

conflictual and that the passage of power from generation to generation comes about through younger people overpowering their elders. The aggression of adult children toward their parents takes many forms, the most extreme case of which is murder. (*Matricide* is mother-murder, *patricide* is father-murder, and *parricide* refers to murder of either parent.) The extent to which this theme is embedded in cultural products suggests that it is "natural" to want to overcome one's elders and that social norms must be established to ward off this desire. It is "natural" to compete with them, to be jealous of their power and rights, to ignore their opinions, to want to separate from them, and even to do away with them.

The second theme emphasizes respect, loyalty, commitment, honor, and love and is equated with civilization, morality, and religion. Just as the first theme is frequently portrayed as "natural," so, too, the loving, protective attitude toward parents has become defined as "natural." Within the "respect paradigm," the notion of harming one's parents is considered repugnant, immature, inhuman, a sign of madness, and an impossibility.

The "data" used to support the existence of these two themes are historical and literary texts, examples of which are included in this chapter. These materials suggest the broad contours of the relation between adults and their parents—the need to destroy and the requirement to protect. Recognition of the uninterrupted saga of these two contrasting attitudes may enable us to put elder abuse and other relations between contemporary adults and their parents in perspective. As our population ages, and as families come to be made up of multiple generations, it becomes increasingly important for policy makers and professionals to understand intergenerational relationships.

Greek Mythology

Stories about offspring, particularly sons, who kill their parents or wish for their death abound in world literature. Myths are codes for prescribed and proscribed behavior;[1] they justify prevalent practices, while also being vehicles to project wishes, desires, and hatreds.[2] In Greek mythology, parricide is an essential component of the explanation of the world's creation. In Greek creation myths, generativity and continuity occur when a rebellious son (sometimes aided by the mother) banishes his father. The rebellious son takes revenge against his father, sometimes castrating him, takes his power, and then kills him. These elements are all present in the following passage:[3]

> *Uranus fathered the Titans upon Mother Earth, after he had thrown his rebellious sons, the Cyclopes, into Tartarus, a gloomy place in the Underworld, which lies as far distant from the earth as the earth does from the sky. . . . In revenge, Mother Earth persuaded the Titans to attack their father; and they did so, led by Cronus, the youngest of the seven, whom she armed with a flint sickle. They surprised Uranus as he slept, and it was with the flint sickle that the merciless Cronus castrated him, grasping his genitals with the left hand (which has ever since been the hand of ill-omen) and afterwards throwing them, and the sickle too, into the sea by Cape Drepanum.*
>
> *The Titans then released the Cyclopes from Tartarus, and awarded the sovereignty of the earth to Cronus. However, no sooner did Cronus find himself in supreme command than he confined the Cyclopes to Tartarus again together with the Hundred-handed Ones and, taking his sister Rhea to wife, rules in Ellis.*
>
> *Cronus married his sister Rhea, to whom the oak is sacred. But it was prophesied by Mother Earth, and by his dying father Uranus, that one of his own sons would dethrone him. Every year, therefore, he swallowed the children whom Rhea bore him: first Hestia, then Demester and Hera, then Hades, then Poseidon. Rhea was enraged. She bore Zeus, her third son, at dead of night on Mount Lycaeum in Arcadia. . . .*
>
> *Zeus grew to manhood among the shepherds of Ida, occupying another cave; then sought out Metis the Titaness, who lived beside the Ocean stream. On her advice he visited his mother Rhea, and asked to be made Cronus's cup-bearer. Rhea readily assisted him in his task of vengeance; she provided the mustard and salt, which Metis had told him to mix with Cronus's honeyed drink. Cronus, having drunk deep, vomited up . . . Zeus's elder brothers and sisters. They sprang out unhurt and, in gratitude, asked him to lead them in a war against the Titans, who chose the gigantic Atlas as their leader; for Cronus was now past his prime.*
>
> *The war lasted ten years but, at last Mother Earth prophesied victory to her grandson Zeus, if he took as allies those whom Cronus had confined in Tartarus. . . . Cronus and all the defeated Titans, except Atlas, were banished to a British island in the farthest west.*

The generations of Greek gods relate to one another in terms of competition, oppression/rebellion, and lust for power. Succession occurs when the young vanquish and replace the old. In these myths, power is not added or created; it is snatched and usurped. This process of violently overthrowing the older generation is characteristic of the pre-civilized mythic world. William Graham

Sumner claimed that ancient Greek mortals imitated the mythic gods, "treating the old with neglect and disrespect."[4] This lends credence to the idea that myths were vehicles through which people could project their feelings. The Greeks attributed parricide to the gods, who were privileged to act in ways that mortals could not fully carry out.

The Oedipal myth reiterates these themes of the parental oppression of offspring and the son's need to kill his father in order to acquire power:[5]

Laius, son of Labdacus, married Iocaste, and ruled over Thebes. Grieved by his prolonged childlessness, he secretly consulted the Delphic Oracle, which informed him that this seeming misfortune was a blessing, because any child born to Iocaste would become his murderer. He therefore put Iocaste away, though without offering any reason for his decision, which caused her such vexation that, having made him drunk, she inveigled him into her arms again as soon as night fell. When, nine months later, Iocaste was brought to bed of a son, Laius snatched him from the nurse's arms, pierced his feet with a nail and, binding them together, exposed him on Mount Cithaeron.

Yet the Fates had ruled that this boy should reach a green old age. A Corinthian shepherd found him, named him Oedipus because his feet were deformed by the nail-wound, and brought him to Corinth, where King Polybus was reigning at the time (with Queen Periboea). One day, taunted by a Corinthian youth with not in the least resembling his supposed parents, Oedipus went to ask the Delphic Oracle what future lay in store for him. "Away from the shrine, wretch!" the Pythoness cried in disgust. "You will kill your father and marry your mother!"

Since Oedipus loved Polybus and Periboea, and shrank from bringing disaster upon them, he at once decided against returning to Corinth. But in the narrow defile between Delphi and Daulis he happened to meet Laius, who ordered him roughly to step off the road and make way for his betters; Laius, it should be explained, was in a chariot and Oedipus on foot. Oedipus retorted that he acknowledged no betters except the gods and his own parents.

"So much the worse for you!" cried Laius, and ordered his charioteer Polyphontes to drive on. One of the wheels bruised Oedipus' foot and, transported by rage, he killed Polyphontes with his spear. Then, flinging Laius on the road entangled in the reins, and whipping up the team, he made them drag him to death.

Laius had been on his way to ask the Oracle how he might rid Thebes of the Sphinx. This monster was a daughter of Typhon and Echidne or, some say, of the dog Orthrus and the Chimaera, and had flown to Thebes from the uttermost part of Ethiopia. She was easily recognized by her woman's head, lion's body, serpent's tail, and eagle's wings. Hera had recently sent the Sphinx to punish Thebes for Laius' abduction of the boy Crysippus from Pisa and, settling on Mount Phicium, close to the city, she now asked every Theban wayfarer a riddle taught her by the Three Muses: "What being, with one one voice has sometimes two feet, sometimes three, sometimes four, and is weakest when it has the most?" Those who could not solve the riddle she throttled and devoured on the spot.

Oedipus, approaching Thebes fresh from the murder of Laius, guessed the answer. "Man," he replied, "because he crawls on all four as an infant, stands firmly on his two feet in his youth, and leans upon a staff in his old age." The mortified Sphinx leaped from Mount Phicium and dashed herself to pieces in the valley below. At this the grateful Thebans acclaimed Oedipus king, and he married Iocaste, unaware that she was his mother.

This particular myth, however, represents a step beyond the unrestrained competition expressed in Greek creation myths. First, there is the fact that Laius does not kill Oedipus but abandons him to die. Second, the murder of Laius takes place by accident, despite Oedipus's intentions. The entire story hinges on a series of tragic misunderstandings, secrets, unexplained punishments, and deception. Feelings were no longer linked directly to actions. And actions represented feelings other than the ones characters thought they had. Ambivalence began to be expressed, both by parents toward their children and children toward their parents.

The Extension of the Greek Model in Psychoanalytic Theory

As is well known, Freud believed that the myth of Oedipus, with its central patricidal act, represented a universally experienced desire of sons vis-à-vis their fathers. (Freud developed the Oedipal ideas primarily in terms of men's lives rather than women's, although it is women who served as his chief set of patients and who furnished him with material about seduction by a parent of the opposite sex. Freud did not analyze women's apparent desire to kill their mothers.) Even if patricide seemed unintentional in the myth, Freud defined it as an essential element of the human psyche. To support the idea of universal Oedipal wishes, Freud posited that there had been a primal patricidal creation event:[6]

One day the brothers [of the primal horde] who had been driven out came together, killed and devoured their father and so made an end of the patriarchal horde. . . . In the fact of devouring him they accomplished their identification with him, and each one of them acquired a portion of his strength. . . . After they had got rid of him, had satisfied their hatred and had put into effect their wish to identify themselves with him, the affection [for him] which had all this time been pushed under was bound to make itself felt. It did so in the form of remorse. . . .

The dead father became stronger than the living one had been— for events took the course we often see them follow in human affairs to this day. What had up to then been prevented by his actual existence was thenceforward prohibited by the sons themselves, in accordance with the psychological procedure so familiar to us in psycho-analysis under the name of "deferred obedience." They revoked their deed by forbidding the killing of the totem; and they renounced its fruits by resigning their claim to the women who had now been set free. They thus created out of their filial sense of guilt the two fundamental taboos of totemism, which for that very reason inevitably corresponded to the two repressed wishes of the Oedipus complex.

Freud's notion of this primal patricide is psychologically more complex than the Greek creation myth, however, because in Freud's view, the original sons experienced guilt. Paradoxically, Freud believed that the sons who committed the primal patricide first experienced it as necessary (in order to acquire power) and then regretted it as immoral. The themes of abuse and regret, hate and love, honor and contempt were collapsed in one deed, parricide by the primal fraternal horde. Ambivalence toward elders was given clear expression.

One source of Freud's idea that adults harbor murderous hostility against their parents was his discovery that large numbers of people dream about the death of their parents. Freud claimed that this patricidal dream represents an unconscious wish, and that moral considerations during the waking hours make it impossible for the individual to act on, or even acknowledge, this wish. Freud believed people would deny the wish when confronted with his interpretation. People would say, "This is the last wish that we could credit ourselves with harboring. . . . such a wish would never occur to us even in a dream . . ."[7]

A second source of Freud's patricidal creation idea was Darwin's theory of human origins, based on his studies of animals and plants. In 1871 Darwin described the probable social condition of primal man:[8]

The most probable view is that he aboriginally lived in small communities, each with a single wife, or if powerful, with several, whom he jealously guarded against all other men. Or he may not have been a social animal, and yet have lived with several wives, like

> *the gorilla, for all the natives . . . agree that but one adult male is seen in a band; when the young male grows up, the contest takes place for mastery, and the strongest, by killing and driving out the others, established himself as the head of the community.*

In Freud's view this primal experience became embedded in all adult sons' attitudes toward their elders. In order to understand the human psyche, Freud also examined himself. His self-analysis uncovered patricidal wishes concerning his own father, which Freud interpreted as additional evidence of the primal patricide experience. Freud's unconscious hostility toward other important senior men in his life was a fact that provided him with further evidence. Historian Edwin Wallace relates this incident:[9]

> *Freud suffered two faints in the presence of Jung which Freud himself related to death wishes toward Jung. Jung asserted of Freud that "the fantasy of father-murder was common to both cases". . . . Freud was alternately the murdered father (slain by Jung) and the murdering son (slaying his father and Jung).*

The hostility of sons toward their fathers is sometimes disguised by behavior that appears to be the opposite. This duality is expressed in many artistic products that sublimate or sometimes reiterate people's feelings. For example, two Freudians analyzed the painting of a man wielding a two-edged hatchet. The artist, Richard Dadd, had recently killed his father. Poised precariously over the outstretched neck of his victim, the twin-bladed hatchet was interpreted as an expression of the war between love and hate that the artist experienced toward his own father.[10]

The Biblical Model

To support his theory that there is a universal structure in the human psyche, Freud drew both on Greek myths and the Bible. It is important to understand, however, that there is a major contradiction between these two sources. For his theory of the universality of the patricidal wish to be consistent, there would have to be at least a hint of patricidal acts, wishes, intentions, or accidents in the Bible. Yet, surprisingly, there are none. Nearly every other human act does take place—murders of all sorts, near sacrifices of one's own child, a father unwittingly impregnating his daughter-in-law, two daughters conspiring to become pregnant by their father, and more. Incest is a motif in the Bible, but not patricide. Although Otto Rank wrote about incest in the Bible as a literary and cultural motif, the patricide and elder abuse motifs have not received much attention.[11] The lack of patricide in the Bible becomes even more interesting when examined in the light of attitudes toward parents that are advocated in the Bible.

Two explanations of this surprising omission seem plausible. First, by the time the Bible was written, repugnance against the idea of patricide might have developed to such an extent that it could not even be mentioned. This repugnance is hinted at in the Oedipal myth, which depicts patricide as unintentional and guilt-inducing. In this vein, one can understand the Bible's deliberate omission of stories about patricide (in contrast with Greek creation myths) as the positing of a different, superior morality for the Hebrews. The Bible does not even mention the heinous act that characterized the mythical birth of other nations.

Second, one can argue, from a Freudian perspective, that the omission of patricidal stories in the Bible represents a thorough repression, as strong in its reaction as the strength of the patricidal wish itself. God may have been represented as omnipotent in order to reinforce an absolute deterrence to this patricidal tendency.[12] From this point of view, the Hebrews could be seen not as different from, but simply as repressing, what the Greeks acted out.

In the Bible, sons don't kill fathers; they kill each other. The first murder occurs in the second generation—the fratricide of Cain and Abel. True, Biblical sons outwit their fathers and dream of outshining them. Jacob deceived his old father Isaac, and Joseph dreamt that he, the sun son, was superior to his father. But Biblical sons do not kill parents actually or accidentally, nor do they even express wishes about their death. The near murder of Isaac by Abraham not only undermined the loyalty between parent and child, and trust between child and parent, but also cemented the loyalty between Abraham and his symbolic father, God. In this story the Bible stressed that loyalty to one's parent (Isaac to Abraham, Abraham to God) surpassed the loyalty one might feel even toward one's own child or to oneself. This near abandonment of one's own offspring in the face of a commandment from one's father (God) is remarkable given the socio-biological imperative to reproduce and protect life. (The horror of being forced to sacrifice one's own offspring is the secret theme of William Styron's *Sophie's Choice*. The horror of that deed tormented the mother until she killed herself.)

The omission of patricidal stories in the Bible coincides with the model of love, fear, and respect for God the father that the Bible encourages and demands. Relations between a people and God, as developed in the Bible, are the opposite of the Greek mythical model. The Biblical model of respect and obedience to God has become the basis for civilization itself.

In succinct form, the Bible's definition of civilization is contained in the Ten Commandments. One commandment prohibits all murder, including, by implication, patricide. Another commandment contains a single rule for behavior toward parents, thereby suggesting that this, too, is an essential ingredient of civilization. The Hebrews were commanded to show respect toward parents, regardless of the son's needs, of the elder's behavior, and of any other principles. The treatment due parents by their offspring stems exclusively from their ascriptive role as parents. As evidenced in the following passage, there is no ambivalence expressed in the commandment; we are required to show unconditional respect:[13]

> *"Honor thy father and thy mother, that thy days may be long upon the land which the Lord thy God giveth thee." One expresses honor by showing them respect, obedience and love. Each parent alike is entitled to these. . . . And this obligation extends beyond the grave. . . . Respect to parents is among the primary human duties; and no excellence can atone for the lack of such respect. Only in cases of extreme rarity (e. g., where godless parents would guide children toward crime) can disobedience be justified. Proper respect to parents may at times involve immeasurable hardship; yet the duty remains. Shem and Japhet threw the mantle of charity over their father's shame; only an unnatural child gloats over a parent's disgrace or dishonor. The greatest achievement open to parents is to be ever fully worthy of their children's reverence and trust and love.*

The Bible reinforces this commandment by suggesting that honoring one's parents will more or less ensure that one's own children will neither abuse nor abandon one in old age. In contrast with the Bible's view of how old people can expect to be treated, the Greek laws of Solon commanded that only if fathers teach their sons a useful trade do they have the legal right to receive support in old age. The Bible implies that if relations between generations are honorable, everyone will benefit in old age, and civilization will persist. In addition, if one does not honor one's parents, a terrible punishment—stoning—must be meted out, either by the parents themselves or by the entire community. Note the following passage from the Book of Deuteronomy in the Old Testament:[14]

> *If a man have a stubborn and rebellious son that will not obey the voice of his father or the voice of his mother, and that, when they have chastened him, will not harken unto them; Then shall his father and his mother lay hold on him, and bring him out unto the elders of his city. This, our son is stubborn and rebellious, he will not obey*

our voice; he is a glutton and a drunkard. And all men of his city
shall stone him with stones, that he shall die; so shalt thou put evil
away from among you; and all Israel shall hear, and fear.

Rites and Ceremonies

Sir J. G. Frazer documented rites and ceremonies that can be
assumed to represent the collective mind in a way that parallels the
dream's representation of the individual mind. In this way, his
work was understood during his time as the history of the whole
range of human thought. In his massive work, *The Golden Bough*,
considerable space is devoted to initiation rites that mark the
transition from childhood to adulthood. Initiation rites express the
emotional ties between the generations. During initiation, youths
are compelled to be physically separated from the parent so as to
symbolize a change in attitude.[15]

> *In the cruel rites which are so often inflicted on the novices by the*
> *elder members of the community it is possible to see a manifestation*
> *of that fear and hatred which fathers often feel towards their sons*
> *and which mothers often feel towards their daughters—feelings*
> *which often correspond in nature to the equivalent emotions in the*
> *children themselves; the pretended killing or death of the novice*
> *being frequently of the nature of a punishment on the talion*
> *principle for the thoughts of parricide or matricide which the*
> *children may themselves have entertained towards their parents.*
> Before initiation youths are often not allowed to carry arms, proba-
> bly because of the fear that they may be tempted to hurt or kill the
> father; *sometimes, however, before they can be admitted to the full*
> *privileges of maturity, they must have killed a man—in order,*
> *probably, to work off their hostile feelings on some third person who*
> *may serve as a substitute for the father who was the original object*
> *of these feelings. [Emphasis added.]*

During these cruel ceremonies boys are usually made to suffer
physical harm or punishment and are encouraged and/or forced to
engage in sexual intercourse. These practices can be compared to
contemporary hazing or stag parties that accompany the change of
status in males from outsider to insider, youth to adult.

Parallel to these initiation rites that bring in the young was the
widespread practice of putting kings to death when they became
old. Frazer documents customs in which a king whose health was
waning, who was no longer pleasing, or who simply had grey hairs,
wrinkles, or some missing teeth, was simply put to death:[16]

> *If the high gods, who dwell remote from the fret and fever of this*
> *earthly life, are believed to die at last, it is not to be expected that a*

god who lodges in a frail tabernacle of flesh should escape the same fate. The danger is a formidable one; for if the course of nature is dependent on the man-god's life, what catastrophes may not be expected from the gradual enfeeblement of his powers and their final extinction in death? There is only one way of averting these dangers. The man-god must be killed as soon as he shows symptoms that his powers are beginning to fail and his soul must be transferred to a vigorous successor before it has been seriously impaired by the threatened decay.

Numerous types of euthanasia were practiced on these aging kings or priests—stabbing, strangling, bludgeoning, hanging, starving, suffocating, burying alive, poisoning, and forced suicide. When the elder had lost his power or even while he was at the peak of his power, Frazer tells us that he had to be put to death so that the group would not be ruled by an incompetent who would endanger them all:[17]

Some people appear to have thought it unsafe to wait for even the slightest symptom of decay and have preferred to kill the king while he was still in the full vigor of life. Accordingly, they have fixed a term beyond which he might not reign, and at the close of which he must die, the terms fixed upon being short enough to exclude the probability of his degenerating physically in the interval.

The practice of regicide may represent an ancient foundation to the contemporary practices of forced retirement and limiting the terms of office of rulers.

Elder Abuse and Respect in Primitive Societies

William Graham Sumner, the 19th century sociologist, argued that the two themes, destruction and honor, underpin different cultures. Sumner claimed that the two types of societies socialize the young differently: There are those that teach respect for the aged and those that teach that the aged are "societal burdens which waste the strength of the society." In pre-civilized societies, the elderly were killed so that the strength of younger adults could be maximized. Examples of such societies were the Teutons in which "the father could expose or sell his children under age, and the adult son could kill his aged parents." Among nomadic peoples it was common for the elderly to "drop out by the way and die from exhaustion" so that "to kill them . . . is perhaps kinder" and "the old sometimes request it from life weariness or from devotion to the welfare of the group."[18] Native American tribes forced their elderly members to labor to the point of exhaustion; other elderly members were deserted when the tribe became too hungry to support them.

Other examples come from South America, Melanesia, Africa, and the Indo-European peoples. It was usually a response to extreme hardships that sometimes characterized the normal conditions of a society. When economic conditions and technology advanced, these practices could be abandoned, and compassion for the elderly could be cultivated. The Hudson Bay Eskimo "strangle the old who are dependent on others for their food, or leave them to perish when the camp is moved. They move in order to get rid of burdensome old people without executing them." Just as in the case of the nomadic groups, elderly Eskimos may ask to die in an altruistic manner in order to assure the survival of the group. In these societies the old were killed in order to conserve resources, and mores were developed for the young to be cruel to the elderly so that the elderly would want to die: "The central Eskimo kill the old because all who die by violence go to the happy land; others have not such a happy future."[19]

From a Darwinian point of view, the elderly represented a burden in these societies. From this perspective, protecting one's parents after reaching maturity is nonadaptive, as it only contributes to overpopulation which endangers the species. The sociobiological position asserts that it is important to protect only one's ability to procreate and shelter one's offspring. It may also be functional to protect those who can help protect one's offspring, or who can ward off attacks from other groups. In a world of scarcity, the protection of parents interferes with the hoarding of resources to protect own's genes. From a selfish point of view, the only reason to protect parents is to ensure access to their resources as an asset for one's own offspring. The injunction to honor one's parents—that is, civilized morality—runs counter to self-interest. The task of civilized societies was to develop mores that would interfere with this "adaptive" response of wanting to do away with one's elders and with the desire of the elderly themselves to die for the sake of social welfare. The pre-civilized approach of patricide for the sake of survival contrasts with the civilized post-Biblical approach of sustaining and honoring one's elders.

Fairy Tales

Fairy tales speak both to morality and to wishes. They conclude with morals that the child is encouraged to live by, and they fascinate children since they apparently express what children would like to do. Fairy tales are stories that have endured for many generations and have sprung up in virtually identical form in numerous cultures. This suggests that they speak to widespread human concerns. Since fairy tales are not connected with any particular ideology or religion, anyone can feel free to identify with the characters.

What do fairy tales have to say about the idea of killing one's parents? Bruno Bettelheim shows that "many stories begin with the death of a mother or father" and end with our understanding that we cannot "escape separation anxiety and death anxiety by desperately keeping our grasp on our parents [for] we will only be cruelly forced out, like Hansel and Gretel." The child learns to go out into the world and upon so doing, finds the one with whom he or she will be able to live happily ever after.[20]

Bettelheim suggests that the underlying structure of fairy tales begins with an acknowledgment of the child's fear of being left without his/her parents. The fairy tale then creates a situation in which this very horrifying circumstance exists. To make the situation bearable, the good parent is converted into a bad one, and the child then vanquishes mother or father. The child also learns, subliminally perhaps, to express rage at and do away with the elders.

The "giants" who populate fairy tales and stand in for parents are also vanquished by the daring deeds of little children. The child feels the thrill of doing away with the big, bad parent and recognizes that it might not be terrible to be big, free, and whole. In order to justify this horrible deed, however, the parent must first be made bad or not a real parent after all—a stepparent, perhaps, or a wolf in grandma's clothing. Fairy tales revolve around simple principles of justice, they protect the lives of the good characters rather than introducing elements of fate, and they even assure perpetual pleasure (the children live happily ever after).

Fairy tales are pseudo-civilized stories. Unlike the Bible, which broaches no ambivalence, fairy tales imply that children may kill their parents if the parents are evil. Thus Hansel and Gretel kill the cruel witch who originally had fed them sweets. Because they are written with children as characters, they offer a particularly clear picture of ambivalence toward one's elders. Interestingly, clinical material about adolescents who have killed their parents suggests that their parents were bad in deed, not simply in the imagination of their children. Adolescent parricide seems to occur when physical or sexual abuse of the child by the parent is so extreme that murder is the only avenue the child has to save his or her own life. Apparently, this type of murder does not form the foundation of a life of criminal activity. Rather, it is a discrete event, and these children no longer have any trouble with the law.[21]

Shakespeare

Just as myths, customs, fairy tales, and the Bible express human wishes, so too have Shakespeare's works earned a prominent place in illuminating the psyche. Ernest Jones was very explicit in this regard. He argued that to understand the human mind, one must examine *Hamlet*: "The play is almost universally considered to be the chief masterpiece of one of the greatest minds the world has known." It is a play which both reveals Shakespeare himself, and has moved the minds and hearts of millions. "More has been written about Hamlet than about any other character of fiction; more, it has been said, than about anyone who actually lived with the exception of Jesus Christ, Napoleon, and of course Shakespeare himself." This universal appeal suggests that its theme "contains something to which the heart of mankind in general reverberates, and there is little doubt that this resides in the personality of the hero."[22]

Among other things, *Hamlet* is a portrait of intergenerational relations. As is well known, the theme around which *Hamlet* revolves closely parallels the Oedipal conflict. The adult son, Hamlet, burns with a desire to kill his uncle/stepfather who has usurped his mother's love. In addition, Hamlet believes his stepfather is responsible for his father's death. Nevertheless, Hamlet vacillates. On the surface, his patricidal impulse is blocked by his stepfather's communion with God, but on a psychoanalytic level, his inability to kill his stepfather stems from guilt, because his stepfather has only done what Hamlet himself wished. Thus, killing his stepfather would be like killing himself.

Just as Freud's patricidal creation myth might mirror Freud's own ambivalence toward his father, Shakespeare's *Hamlet* has been interpreted as a reflection of the ambivalence he felt toward his father. Freud himself suggested this interpretation. Apparently Shakespeare composed *Hamlet* in 1601 a few months after the death of his father, "that is to say, when he was still mourning his loss, and during a revival, as we may fairly assume, of his own childish feelings in respect of his father."[23] Freud believed that the "death of the father is perhaps the most important event in men's lives; the moment when a man succeeds, i.e. replaces, his father may revive the forbidden wishes of his infancy."[24] One may also interpret Hamlet's two fathers (the murder victim and the murderer; the good and bad father) as the representation of the son's ambivalence toward the father figure.

Shakespeare's play *King Lear* also expresses the intense passions between adult children and their parents. Goneril and Regan are the symbols of evil children (daughters) who conspire to rob their father, King Lear, of his possessions while pretending that they love him. Cordelia, his third daughter, on the other hand, maintains her dignity and separateness in the face of her father's humiliating requests, but reunites with him in a display of "honor" and love before their death.

Whereas the plotting Hamlet might have appeared to be "natural," the plotting daughters are considered so unnatural that they are portrayed as nonhumans—that is, devils, monsters, animals, fiends:[25]

> *What have you done?*
> *Tigers, not daughters, what have you perform'd?*
> *A father, and a gracious aged man,*
> *Whose reverence even the head-lugg'd bear would lick,*
> *Most barbarous, most degenerate! have you madded.*

King Lear, the father, gave them everything he had, and yet "they conspired together to insult, humiliate and, finally, to kill him. . . . First they grudge him maintenance and seek to reduce his train of hundred knights to which they had agreed at the time of the transfer of power." They wanted to save the expense of supporting him. They infuriated, insulted, and humiliated him, even pushing him out of doors bareheaded during a furious storm. Their filial ingratitude actually drove King Lear mad. "He is crazed by the unnaturalness of their conduct . . ."[26]

In contrast to *Hamlet* where the *son* appears maddened by the strained intergenerational relations, in *King Lear*, the *father* is maddened by the strain. Also, in contrast to *Hamlet*, in which there are multiple fathers or father figures, in *King Lear* there are multiple children, expressing the ambivalence of love and hate vis-à-vis the parent. As a pair, the plays make a statement that the relationship between adult offspring and their elders is rife both with love and hate.

Actual Cases of Parricide

When a parent (or parent surrogate) is "bad," a child may hit, strike, or bite her or him. An adult, on the other hand, is expected to be better socialized (i.e., civilized) than the child and to be able to suppress this wish for revenge against badness. If an adult attempts physically to harm a parent, the adult is likely to be considered a child, an idiot, mentally ill, or utterly inhuman.

Historians of medieval peasant societies that practiced primogeniture have long believed that this system led to severe tensions between the eldest son and his father as well as to rivalry between siblings. By barring the eldest son from obtaining land until his father died, the father's longevity effectively delayed his son's marriage. "The effect of this long wait . . . is that men marry older and spend part of their youth on fantasies of parricide."[27] Whether or not this actually occurred is currently being debated among historians with some critics arguing that sons were allowed to marry even if they had no land. Perhaps fathers recognized the danger to themselves from their oldest son and thus attempted to reduce the antagonism from the younger ones by allowing them to marry even without land.

A son who stands to inherit his father's property may also develop murderous wishes against others who are depleting this inheritance. In most instances the wish is not acted upon, but Michel Foucault has edited an account of a matricide case in 1835 in which the wish was realized.[28] The murderer was a 20-year-old French peasant, Pierre Riviere. The victims of his premeditated murders were his approximately 40-year-old mother, who was 6 months pregnant, his 18-year-old sister, and his 8-year-old brother. Immediately after the murders, Pierre Riviere explained that he deliberately axed his family members in order to end the tribulations they caused his father. At his interrogation and in a lengthy memoir, Riviere claimed that the three were in league to persecute his father.

According to Foucault, "cases of parricide were fairly common in the . . . courts in that period—ten to fifteen yearly, sometimes more."[29] Although not uncommon, parricide was considered to be the most horrible crime, and therefore deserving of the most horrible punishment. The reason for this was to discourage regicide (the killing of a king), which meted out the same punishment as parricide.[30] The "most horrible punishment" consisted of mutilating the prisoner first by cutting off his hand, and then executing him. There was no other crime for which mutilation preceded execution.

Why were parricide and regicide considered the most horrible of crimes, "more heinous and more total even than premeditated murder, infanticide, or poisoning, all of which, however, were punishable by death"? The answer is that the "Penal Code complemented the Civil Code, which established the paternal authority and consecrated the family . . ." Parricide was considered the crime of crimes since it destroyed the sanctity of the family and the rule of the father, both of which were the foundation of civilization and religion. Its perpetrator was seen as so far outside normal society as to be considered capable of all other atrocities.[31]

In an indirect way, it is possible that this judgment also stemmed from the fact that there was no mention of parricide in the Bible. When Riviere attempted a defense based on religion, he lamely tried to vindicate himself with the story of God's slaying the worshipers of the Golden Calf. He argued that matricide was justified by his mother's material greed. But this analogy was ridiculed and disallowed by the court. There was no Biblical analogue for parricide; there could be no excuse.

About 50 years later a case of possible double parricide occurred in the industrial New England mill town of Fall River.[32] The trial of Lizzie Borden for the murder of her father and stepmother became famous overnight and has remained an enigma. No murderer was ever convicted. The Lizzie Borden case seems to have aroused a great deal of anxiety, as evidenced by all the associated limericks that have entered our culture. Perhaps these events have become a way of expressing repressed unspeakable wishes.[33]

Although Lizzie Borden was a 32-year-old adult, she lived with her sister, father, and stepmother. At the time of their deaths Andrew Borden, her father, was 69 and Abby Borden, her step-mother, was about 64. Lizzie despised her stepmother, in part because the woman's relatives were receiving portions of Andrew Borden's wealth. Since Lizzie Borden did not defend herself at her trial, her motivations can only be inferred. If Lizzie did indeed kill her parents, her motive was probably greed. Her father was an extremely wealthy man, and Lizzie wanted as great a share of the inheritance as possible. Her other motive—hatred of the step-mother—harkens back to the fairy tales discussed earlier.[34]

Despite the double motive for the double murder and the overwhelming evidence against Lizzie Borden, the court acquitted her of parricide. She was acquitted in part because it was consid-ered inconceivable that a God-fearing woman *could* do such a thing. The court had a hard time believing that anyone, let alone a woman, could defy morality and civilization itself with such a heinous crime. Realizing that her greatest defense was having people believe that her act was inconceivable, Lizzie kept minis-ters at her side after her arrest to bolster her reputation of being God-fearing. Her lawyers emphasized that she was engaged in religious and charitable enterprises, had an unimpeachable reputa-tion, and was therefore "incapable of committing the crimes."[35] By

the time of the Lizzie Borden case, therefore, the old idea embedded in Greek myths that parricide is natural had been turned
completely on its head. Stories about people who kill their parents
continue to be bestsellers.[36]

Elder Abuse, Parricide, and Parricidal Wishes in Modern Literature

In our present society, the family has lost much of its definition,
authority, and function. Increased mobility, industrialization,
urbanization, liberation movements of oppressed peoples including women, and increased longevity have coalesced to diminish
the rule of parents. When society is anomic, anything becomes
possible, including abuse of elders. Contemporary literature rarely
depicts elders as larger than life. Rather, they are frequently
presented in scenes where they are made to look depressed or
ridiculous.[37] In television commercials, for example, elderly people who speak as if they were young and assertive seem to strike
people as being particularly comical.

Literature often depicts children striking out against "offensive
elders" or amusing themselves with helpless, childlike elders. For
example, in Guy De Maupassant's short story, "A Family," two
friends are reunited after a 15-year separation during which one of
them has married, fathered five children, and taken in his wife's
grandfather. The man who remained single considers himself a
refined gentleman. The married friend is portrayed as having lost
his dignity by marrying and becoming a family member in which
vicious interactions prevail. Whereas once the two friends shared
the same sentiments, now they have become completely polar-
ized. The husband and wife with their five children amuse themselves by tormenting the old grandfather. They deny him food
under the guise of "protecting his health" and laugh at his frenzied,
useless struggle for sweets.[38]

Making fun of the elderly is perhaps a means of disguising the
desire to get rid of them, while still preserving the sense that one
has not really done it. Philip Roth's *Portnoy's Complaint* is a telling
literary example. Roth spends pages ridiculing his father's consti-
pation, incompetence, and ineffective rage. As the tale unwinds,
however, he realizes that only when his father (whom he also
dearly loves) dies, will Portnoy be a man:[39]

> *Good Christ, a Jewish man with parents alive is a fifteen-year-old
> boy, and will remain a fifteen-year-old boy till they die! . . . Doctor!*

Doctor! Did I say fifteen? Excuse me, I meant ten! I meant five! I meant zero! A Jewish man with his parents alive is half the time a helpless infant!

It is not just Jewish men who feel this way, of course. Florence Nightingale, a Christian woman, for example, took to bed for years in part as a means for achieving independence from her mother. When her mother died, Nightingale left her sickbed permanently.[40]

Modern literature rarely represents elders as unconditionally loved by virtue of their ascriptive role. Rather, they are treated as anyone else, anomically or according to some impartial rules. When people are equals in families, authority based on age has no place,[41] and children can try to punish "offensive" elders. One literary example of this attitude can be found in Joyce Carol Oates's novel about the life of poor whites in Detroit at the time of the riots. Interestingly, this vignette shows an abusive girl expressing anal fantasies while striking her "evil" grandmother. The grandmother had been criticizing her own daughter, the mother of two teen-aged girls, Betty and Maureen. These two girls symbolize divergent attitudes toward elders. Betty represents "vindictive justice" and Maureen "self-destructive humility." Interestingly, neither is attractive.[42]

She and her grandmother stared at each other, nearly the same height. Betty snickered like a boy.

"One of you two help me now—I got to go in the bathroom."

Maureen went obediently to her grandmother and helped her walk. The old lady leaned upon her. She said, "You wouldn't stand around telling your grandmother to go to hell if your father was still alive. You'd see what was what then. Or if your mother didn't run around with every man she could find, anything in pants—"

"Shut up," Betty said.

"—if she didn't stay out all hours of the night running around in cars and getting drunk!"

Maureen went to open the bathroom door, but Betty got there before her. She slammed the door to and held onto the knob. "Don't let the old bag in! You're always letting her boss you around!"

"Betty!"

"Let her go in her pants! She's all dirty anyway, the old bag, the old bitch! Or let her go out in the yard like the dogs, shove her out here, here!" Betty opened the back door wide. She was shouting. "Come on! Shove her out the back door! She ain't no better than a dog! Come on, Maureen! Let go of her!"

"Betty, are you crazy?"

"I had enough, I ain't taking any more! She ain't going to push me around, let me tell you! This door is standing wide open and she can

*climb right down the steps here and do her business in the back
yard, she thinks she's so smart. Come on! Come on!"*

*While their grandmother cried out, Maureen and Betty struggled
over her. Betty seized the old woman's wrist and began yanking her
toward the door. Maureen pulled her back. . . . Betty yanked her
forward and Maureen had to let go. "Now go outside! Go on! You do
what I tell you 'cause I am now your boss!" Betty screamed. When
the old lady grabbed hold of the door frame, Betty raised her foot
and brought her knee back, like a man, and gave her a hard solid
kick right in the small of the back.*

*The old woman fell forward onto the top of the back steps, then
over the steps and down a few yards to the ground.*

They looked down at her. She lay writhing in silence.

"Come on, get up! You ain't hurt!" Betty screamed.

The old woman's silence terrified them. Maureen could not move.

*"She's just pretending, she fell on purpose! You saw her fall on
purpose!" Betty said. "I ain't taking nothing more from her or from
nobody! Nobody is going to push me around! Let her lay there and
die! Let her! You saw yourself she fell on purpose to get me put in
jail! You saw it!"*

In other works of literature, elderly parents are portrayed as
having insatiable needs for company from their children. In an
anomic society without strong social supports, elders are unable to
let go of their adult children. Childhood is perpetuated ad infini-
tum, and the adult child is enraged. In Harold Pinter's play, "A
Night Out," for example, 28-year-old Albert violates his mother's
ritual of playing cards with him on a Friday night when he attempts
to tell her he is going out. Pinter presents the mother, Mrs.
Stokes, as completely unable to tolerate even the slightest "abandonment" by her son. Her smothering becomes so unbearable that
Albert finally takes a clock and tries to kill her by smashing her
head. His murder attempt fails as miserably as all of his other
attempts to get away from the "evil mother":[43]

> *Mother:* "Albert, I'll tell you what I'm going to do. I'm going to
> forget it. You see? I'm going to forget all about it. We'll have our
> holiday in a fortnight. We can go away."
> She strokes his hand.
> "We'll go away together."
> Pause.

When parents hold on so tightly, then children, even adult children, have to push them away in order to be free. This pushing
away, given the Biblical injunction to honor one's parents, may be
experienced as guilt. When guilt is present, then even small-scale
separation can be experienced as murder. In another bestseller,

Nancy Friday wrote about women's relations with their mothers: "Most of us need to get over the fear that separation is going to kill her."[44] If separation feels like abuse, then an adult offspring who is trying to decide whether or not a parent should live in a nursing home may be tortured by guilt.

Conclusion

It should be apparent by now that the relations of adult children and their parents as depicted in various cultural products are complex. According to Greek creation myths, patricide is intentional and necessary. In the Oedipus myth, on the other hand, patricide is unintentional and associated with guilt and misunderstanding. In the Bible, patricide is not even mentioned, and the "patricidal wish," thought by Freud to be universal, is not even acknowledged. Only "dishonoring" is alluded to. The requirement to love parents is likened to the requirement to love God. Fairy tales give voice to the separation-murder wish among children and allow it to take place in order to restore good.

When youths kill their parents they usually do so in order to free themselves from abuse, while adults who kill their parents seem to do so in order to gain power, and more specifically, to gain wealth. Clinical cases of adolescent parricide have the quality of self-defense; adult parricide cases have the quality of robbery. In the past, the murder of parents was seen as an analogue of the murder of kings—in precarious societies with scarce resources, both are tolerated or encouraged. In more resource-rich societies, parents are more likely to be respected, although respect may not be linked to access to productive roles. Although it is correct to link different attitudes toward the elderly with specific cultural attributes (e.g., values, family forms),[45] it is also important to recognize that polar attitudes exist within the same individual and within the same culture. In other words, from a social psychological perspective, the ambivalence of individuals is mirrored in the ambivalence within cultures.

Although the patricidal wish might be part of the "collective unconscious" and de-repressed both in mass culture and in great literature, contemporary behavior is more in keeping with the Fifth Commandment to honor one's parents than to the Greek myth of overcoming them. In general and despite their ambivalence, adult offspring provide time, energy, finances, emotional support, and other resources to their parents. In one study of American families, 90 percent of the elders sampled received gifts,

70 percent received direct physical assistance when ill, 45 percent received financial help; 34 percent received help with errands, and 27 percent were helped fixing things around the house. Many other studies report that the care provided by family members is the predominant source of care to disabled elders, although in many instances the care is primarily in the hands of the spouse or the daughter or daughter-in-law. Family members are willing to tolerate severe burdens in caring for the aged. They delay the admission of their elders to institutions and sustain them in the community. In lower-income families, the adult children are even more likely to provide physical care than in middle-income families where others are hired to provide the necessary care. In both cases, adult children do not abandon elders, but rather provide them with substantial support.[46]

Yet lurking underneath this outward display of commitment is the wish and possibility of abuse, expressed and sporadically enacted throughout the ages. As in the past, this tension is sustained in a vast array of cultural products such as ageist humor and stereotypic advertising. To be civilized is to keep these feelings in check; to be human is to acknowledge that they exist.

Endnotes

1. See Richard Slotkin, *The Fatal Environment: The Myth of the Frontier in the Age of Industrialization, 1880–1890* (New York: Atheneum, 1985).
2. Robert Graves, *The Greek Myths*, vol. 1 (New York: George Brazilier, 1957).
3. Ibid., pp. 9–10.
4. William Graham Sumner, *Folkways: A Study of the Sociological Importance of Usage, Manners, Customs, Mores, and Morals* (New York: The New American Library, 1906; reprinted in 1960), p. 282.
5. Graves, *The Greek Myths*, pp. 37–44.
6. Sigmund Freud, *Totem and Taboo*, trans. A. A. Brill (New York: New Republic, 1913), pp. 141–43.
7. Sigmund Freud, *The Interpretation of Dreams*, trans. A. A. Brill (New York: Carleton House, 1931), p. 165.
8. Freud, *Totem and Taboo*, pp. 218–19. For this quote, Freud cites: Dr. Savage in the *Boston Journal of Natural History*, vol. 5, pp. 1845–47. Dr. Savage, in turn, cites: Charles Darwin, *The Origin of Man*, vol. 2, pp. 603–04.
9. Edwin Wallace, "The Primal Parricide," *Bulletin of the History of Medicine*, 54, no. 2 (1980), pp. 162–63.
10. This painting is discussed in Charles N. Lewis and John Arsenian, "Murder Will Out: A Case of Parricide in a Painter and His Paintings," *Journal of Nervous and Mental Disease* 164, no. 4 (1977), pp. 273–79.

11. Otto Rank, *Das Inzest-Motif in Dichtung and Sage: Grandzuge einer Psychologie des dichterischen Schaffens* (Vienna and Leipzig: Deuticke, 1912, 1926).

12. Personal communication, Prof. Gordon Fellman, Dept. of Sociology, Brandeis University, September 1985.

13. J. H. Hertz, ed., *The Pentateuch and Haftorahs* (London: Soncino Press, 1961).

14. Deut. 21:18–21.

15. Quoted in J. C. Flugel, *The Psychoanalytic Study of the Family* (London: Hogarth Press, 1960), p. 83. By quoting Frazer, Flugel is demonstrating the extent to which themes in ancient practices were considered relevant to contemporary family life.

16. Sir James Frazer, *The Golden Bough: A Study in Magic and Religion*, abridged ed., ed. Thomas Gaster (London: Macmillan, 1955), p. 130.

17. Ibid., p. 132.

18. Sumner, *Folkways*, pp. 277, 279.

19. Ibid., p. 280.

20. Bruno Bettelheim, *The Uses of Enchantment: The Meaning and Importance of Fairy Tales* (New York: Vintage Books, 1977), pp. 8, 11.

21. Shelley Post, "Adolescent Parricide in Abusive Families," *Child Welfare* 61, no. 7 (1982), pp. 445–55; Billie F. Corder et al., "Adolescent Murder," *American Journal of Psychiatry* 133, no. 8 (1976), pp. 957–61.

22. Ernest Jones, *Oedipus and Hamlet* (Garden City, N.Y.: Doubleday and Anchor, 1954), pp. 24, 25.

23. Ibid., p. 40.

24. Freud, *The Interpretation of Dreams*, p. 164.

25. William Shakespeare, *King Lear*, Act 4, Scene 2, lines 39–43.

26. G. B. Harrison and Robert F. McDonnell, *King Lear: Text, Sources, and Criticism* (New York: Harcourt, Brace and World, 1962), pp. 186, 187.

27. Barbara Hanawalt, *The Ties That Bound: Peasant Families in Medieval England* (New York: Oxford University Press, 1986), p. 96.

28. Michel Foucault, ed., *I, Pierre Riviere, Having Slaughtered My Mother, My Sister, and My Brother . . . A Case of Parricide in the 19th Century* (New York: Pantheon Books, 1975).

29. Ibid., p. viii.

30. For an extensive set of examples demonstrating the connection between regicide and parricide, see Frazer, *The Golden Bough*, and Flugel, *The Psychoanalytic Study of the Family*, pp. 129–132.

31. Foucault, *I, Pierre Riviere*, p. 220.

32. Unlike Foucault's claim that parricide was common in France at that time, Sullivan claims that parricide was and is rare in the United States. See Robert Sullivan, *Goodbye Lizzie Borden* (Brattleboro, Vt.: Stephen Greene Press, 1974), p. 1.

33. The morbid appeal of parricide is expressed in grotesque humor. An example can be found in Rosten's dictionary of Yiddish terms where an analogue of the Lizzie Borden case is used to define the word "chutzpah": "After killing his (sic) parents, he had the chutzpah to ask for clemency on the grounds of being an orphan" (Leo Rosten, *The Joys of Yiddish* [New York: McGraw-Hill, 1968], p. 92). Another example of humor: Someone asked Lizzie Borden what time

it was. She said, "I don't know, I'll axe my father." Some limericks: "Lizzie Borden took an ax; and gave her mother forty whacks; when she saw what she had done she gave her father forty-one!" or "Andrew Borden, he is dead; Lizzie hit him on the head." Edmund Pearson claims to have seen these limericks printed all over the world, including Australia and Natal (Edmund Pearson, ed. *Trial of Lizzie Borden* [Garden City, New York: Doubleday and Anchor, 1937], pp. 44–45).

34. The complete transcript of her trial plus an interpretive introduction are contained in Pearson, *Trial of Lizzie Borden*.
35. Sullivan, *Goodbye Lizzie Borden*, p. 144.
36. See, for example, Shana Alexander, *Nutcracker* (Garden City, N.Y.: Doubleday and Anchor, 1985); Jonathan Coleman, *At Mother's Request: A True Story of Money, Murder and Betrayal* (New York: Atheneum, 1985).
37. See Mary Sohngen and Robert J. Smith, "Images of Old Age in Poetry," *The Gerontologist* 18, no. 2 (1978), pp. 181–86; Gladys Blue, "The Aging as Portrayed in Realistic Fiction for Children 1945–1975," *The Gerontologist*, 18, no. 2 (1978), pp. 187–92; David Peterson and Elizabeth Karnes, "Older People in Adolescent Literature," *The Gerontologist* 16, no. 3 (1976), pp. 225–31; K.E.M. Kent and Peggy Shaw, "Age in *Time*: A Study of Stereotyping," *The Gerontologist* 20, no. 5 (1980), pp. 598–601.
38. Guy de Maupassant, "A Family," in *Short Stories of the Tragedy and Comedy of Life* (Akron, Ohio: St. Dunstan Society, 1903).
39. Phillip Roth, *Portnoy's Complaint* (New York: Random House, 1967), p. 113.
40. See Myra Stark's introduction in Florence Nightingale's *Cassandra* (1852; reprint ed., Old Westbury, N. Y.: The Feminist Press, 1979).
41. See Emmanuel Todd, *The Explanation of Ideology: Family Structures and Social Systems* (New York: Basil Blackwell, 1985).
42. Joyce Carol Oates, *Them* (New York: Fawcett Crest, 1969), pp. 148–50.
43. Harold Pinter, "A Night Out," in *Complete Works* (New York: Grove Press, Random House, 1977), p. 87.
44. Nancy Friday, *My Mother, My Self* (New York: Dell, 1977), p. 457.
45. See Donald O. Cowgill, *Aging Around the World* (Belmont, Calif.: Wadsworth Publishing Company, 1986).
46. This literature is reviewed in Mary Ann Wilner, "Predictors of Outcome Among Frail Elders Receiving Home Care for One Year" (Ph. D. diss., Heller School, Brandeis University, 1985), pp. 25–32.

Chapter 3

THE HELPING RELATIONSHIP
AND FAMILY NEGLECT
IN LATER LIFE

by Victor G. Cicirelli

Family members providing physical and psychological care or help to each other is fundamental to maintaining the family as a unit throughout the life cycle. This interaction is also one of the sources of emotional satisfaction for family members. During much of the adult life cycle, there is a mutual exchange of help between adult children and their elderly parents. In later life, however, the balance of exchange can shift when the dependency needs of older parents increase. Once the elderly parents require a great deal of help, the helping relationship often becomes a source of conflict, negative or hostile feelings, and considerable burden or strain on the part of the adult child caregiver. In some cases, the helping relationship can deteriorate into its opposite: abuse and/or neglect of the elderly.

This chapter attempts to show how the dynamics of the helping relationship can help to explain neglect of the elderly by their adult child caregivers. By understanding the factors that lead to neglect, we may be able to prevent such neglect or more easily remedy it when it occurs.

What Constitutes Neglect?

We are going to focus on neglect rather than on other forms of abuse. Before discussing reasons for this focus, we need to specify what is meant by "neglect." Family abuse is a recent area of study that had its origins in the concerns of various practitioners who encountered instances of abuse. The field has been troubled by the difficulty in defining such terms as "violence," "abuse," and "neglect." Gelles refers to violence and abuse as "pejorative, emotion-charged terms used to call attention to behavior called deviant."[1] Previous attempts at definition have not only involved considerable variation, but also a great deal of ambiguity.

Part of the difficulty in defining these terms lies in the fact that abuse and neglect are behaviors that are not typically observable by others outside the family; thus one must rely on verbal reports after the fact (in cases where there is no compelling physical evidence). A further difficulty arises from the great variety of behaviors to be included, from physical assault to exploitation of resources to neglect. Other considerations are the intentions of the perpetrator to inflict harm or distress on the victim and the seriousness of the effects of abuse. Above and beyond all of these problems, Gelles and Pedrick-Cornell believe that the ultimate source of the difficulty in formulating a satisfactory definition is the varying cultural and subcultural views on the acceptability of certain behaviors.[2]

Although the efforts to define violence and neglect are continuing, it is not our intent to review the definitions extant in the literature here. For the purposes of this chapter, we will adopt the definition/taxonomy advanced by Wolf, Strugnell, and Godkin.[3] One of the strengths of their definition is that it identifies five distinct types of abuse and neglect. The three types of abuse include *physical abuse* (infliction of physical pain or injury), *psychological abuse* (mental anguish), and *material abuse* (exploitation of resources). The two types of neglect are *active neglect* ("refusal or failure to fulfill a caretaking obligation, including a conscious and intentional attempt to inflict physical or emotional distress on the elder") and *passive neglect* ("refusal or failure to fulfill a caretaking obligation, excluding a conscious and intentional attempt to inflict physical or emotional distress on the elderly").[4] Examples of active neglect are abandonment and deliberate denial of food and health needs. Examples of passive neglect include nonprovision of food or health needs because of inadequate knowledge, laziness, or other nondeliberate reasons. Although the definitions fail to deal with the severity of the caregiving lapse and also depend on a judgment of the intention of the caregiver, they represent a step forward in the field by clarifying the different types of abuse and neglect.

As stated previously, this chapter will focus on neglect rather than on the three types of abuse, for several reasons. First, neglect is a highly prevalent form of mistreatment of the elderly. In a small study of disabled elderly, it was the most common form of abuse/neglect.[5] Hickey and Douglass, in a survey of 228 professionals working with vulnerable elderly, found that nearly all professionals had encountered cases of passive neglect.[6] Verbal and/or emotional abuse was next most familiar to these professionals, followed by active neglect and physical abuse. In another small study, 10 percent of abuse victims reported "physical neglect."[7] Block and Sinnott reported frequencies of various types of abuse behavior; they found lack of personal care in 38 percent of the cases in their sample, lack of supervision in 38 percent, and lack of food in 19 percent.[8] These percentages were not as great as those reported for various forms of psychological abuse (46 to 50 percent), but were greater than for types of direct physical abuse (4 to 31 percent). Finally, in the recently completed model projects study, neglect was sustained by 56 to 58 percent of the cases studied.[9] Although such percentages were less than those reported for psychological abuse, they are in the same range as those reported for physical and material abuse. The conclusion to be drawn from these data is that neglect of the elderly is in itself worthy of study, since neglect is involved in a large percentage of abuse/neglect cases.

A second reason for focusing on neglect in this chapter is that cases of neglect tend to be concentrated more heavily among the oldest and most dependent elderly, in contrast to the other types of abuse.[10] Thus, victims of neglect are more likely to be quite old and cognitively and/or physically impaired; they are a highly vulnerable group in need of care by family or other caregivers—in other words, neglect appears to occur most frequently within the family caregiving situation.

Finally, recent findings indicate that the various types of abuse and neglect cannot be described by a single set of factors or explained by any one theory.[11] Neglect seems to be related to stress and burden in the caregiving situation. By contrast, physical abuse and psychological abuse seem to be related to poor mental health and interpersonal pathology of victim and perpetrator, and material abuse may be explained by the financial needs of the perpetrators. If this is indeed the case, then the different types of abuse and neglect arise from different causal factors and should be studied separately. Thus we have decided to concentrate on neglect here. We will examine the caregiving relationship of adult children to their elderly parents and present a model of the helping relationship that will suggest possible causes of elder neglect.

Conflict in the Parent-Child Relationship

Since conflict with the parent is an important variable, both in the model of the helping relationship and in relation to family abuse, some preliminary clarification of the concept is desirable. Different writers in the field have used various definitions of the term, without any clear agreement in the field.

We have chosen to use the definition advanced by Peterson: "Conflict is an interpersonal process that occurs whenever the actions of one person interfere with the actions of another."[12] "Actions" involve verbal and physical actions, as well as cognitive and affective accompaniments to these actions. Conflict can occur in relation to a specific behavior of one person or the other, to norms or rules governing the two parties, or to personal dispositions (e.g., traits) of one or both. Overt conflict (argument, physical actions) is precipitated when there is criticism of one person by another (whether intended or merely interpreted as such), when one makes a demand on the other that is considered unfair or unjust, when one rejects or rebuffs the other, or when there is annoyance due to the cumulative effect of several small actions. For the event to lead to actual conflict, at least one of the parties must feel that the conflict will lead to a favorable outcome of some kind (more power in the situation, inflicting some costs upon the other person, etc.).

Once begun, the conflict can be ended in several ways. One or both may withdraw from the interaction, thus avoiding further conflict. Or, one person may simply submit to the arguments of the other, who is left in a more dominant position than before. Alternatively, the conflict can be handled by negotiation and compromise between the two persons so that each gains something as a result. Finally, the conflict can simply terminate in a "standoff" without any kind of resolution; the two may simply agree to disagree and stop further arguing.[13] In a study of younger families, Vuchinich found withdrawal to be rare, compromise in only about one in ten conflicts, submission in one in four conflicts, and standoff in about two of every three conflicts.[14] Whatever the outcome, every conflict becomes part of the history of the relationship; effects of previous conflicts determine the nature of future conflicts.

Opinions differ as to whether conflicts fulfill a positive or negative function in the relationship. One view is that conflict is the means by which relationships grow and change and by which new rules and goals are formulated. By engaging in conflict and working it through to a mutually satisfying resolution, the affection and understanding of the two people involved in the conflict deepen, and their relationship becomes stronger. The avoidance of conflict to preserve harmony is regarded as destructive to the relationship; each person withdraws from certain topics of discussion or areas of activity until little of mutual concern remains to hold the relationship together. Without conflict to stimulate growth, the relationship becomes an outwardly harmonious but sterile shell.[15] When conflict is avoided or denied, the latent conflict may resurface in another form (e.g., displacement); basic issues may need to be confronted at a later date.[16]

The alternative view is that each conflict leaves a negative affect. Close personal relationships are characterized by an emotional investment that can be very strong. When conflicts are accompanied by criticism, threats, coercions, deception, and the like, the negative feelings are often quite intense. Angry withdrawal of one person in the interaction, or submission to a more dominant partner, or agreeing to disagree do not offer the possibility for reconciliation and reduction of the negative feelings. Often, after an argument things are never the same. These residues of conflict accumulate over time, and in themselves predispose the two persons to further conflict and a generally deteriorating relationship.

Probably both views of the functions of conflict in a relationship have an element of truth. Negotiated settlements of conflict can lead to increased understanding, while the negative affect accompanying conflict can lead to a deteriorating relationship or even its termination. However, family relationships do persist over long periods of time, and nearly all are accompanied by conflict in varying degrees.

A bipolarity on ambivalence in close relationships has been suggested by several investigators to account for relationships in which both love and hate (or affection and hostility) are displayed by the same person on different occasions.[17] Hostile conflict can erupt at times, but an underlying bond of affection keeps the two persons together. Evidence in support of such bipolarity is mixed, yet the concept remains popular to explain the persistence of otherwise puzzling relationships.[18]

Existence of Parent-Child Conflict

Conflicts with parents appear to exist throughout adult life.[19] In an analysis of conflicts reported by men and women from 20 to 60 years of age, conflicts with parents (as a percentage of all conflicts) were highest in the twenties, as young adults were establishing independence from parents. However, conflicts with parents remained fairly stable through the remaining decades, with women reporting a slightly increasing percentage in their forties and fifties. For both men and women, there were more conflicts with parents than with their own children. Overall, a bigger percentage of women's conflicts was with parents (17 percent) than was the case for men (13 percent).

In a study of adult children's relationships with their elderly parents, we found that 64 percent of adult children reported some frequency of conflict with their elderly fathers and 61 percent reported some degree of conflict with elderly mothers.[20] However, only 6 percent reported frequent or continual conflicts with fathers, and 5 percent reported such conflicts with mothers. Since most of the adult children studied did not share a residence with the parent, they were also asked to predict the extent of conflict should the parent come to live with them. Both men and women expected an increase in conflict; this increase was greater in regard to elderly mothers than in the case of fathers. Indeed, 4 percent expected conflict with the father to be so severe that living together would never work out, while 11 percent expected conflict that severe with the mother. Adult children expected conflict with mothers to extend into more different topical areas than for fathers.

Finally, we asked about the topical areas around which conflicts with the elderly parents occurred. Areas in which the largest number of children reported conflicts centered on the parent's health, things the child felt that the parent should do, and the parent's temperament. Other areas of conflict were the parent's criticism of the child (or the child's family or friends), parent intrusiveness into the child's life, parent demands, and the way one parent treated the other. Conflict revolving around areas external to the family were reported in a relatively low percentage of cases.[21] Another study reported that conflicts with grandmothers centered on family and interpersonal issues, while conflicts with grandfathers tended to involve general social issues.[22] Since the two studies asked different questions and used different categorization systems, it is difficult to explain the varying findings.

Steinman distinguished three types of conflicts that occur in later life when parents need support from adult children: continuing conflicts, reactivated conflicts, and new conflicts.[23] *Continuing conflicts* are those that have always been present between parent and child and are still going on. *Reactivated conflicts* are those that were never settled in earlier years but were disregarded during the years when the parent and adult child lived more independently; these reappear when contact becomes more frequent during the process of giving help. *New conflicts* concern issues in relation to problems of the parent's aging. Unless such conflicts can be resolved or otherwise dealt with, difficulties in the relationship can be expected when the elderly parent needs help.

The Helping Relationship in Later Life

In the sociological tradition, the help that adult children give to their elderly parents in time of need can be explained in terms of cultural expectations or exchange theory (the need to repay the parent for care and help given earlier in life). However, the psychological tradition may be of value in understanding more complex motivations toward helping behavior.

Attachment theory as the basis for a model explaining adult children's helping behavior is not a new concept; this author has used it elsewhere.[24] Originally, the concept of attachment was used to describe an infant's relationship to the mother; however, it can be applied to relationships later in life as well. Attachment is an emotional or affectional bond between two people. It involves being identified with, in love with, and having the desire to be with the other person. Attachment is a stable internal state within the individual that is inferred from the individual's tendency to seek proximity and contact with the attached figure. In infancy, periods of exploratory behavior alternate with proximity seeking to restore contact with the mother. Later, protective behavior develops; it is concerned with preserving or restricting the threatened existence of the attached figure rather than merely maintaining or restoring proximity.[25]

According to Bowlby, attachment does not end in early childhood but continues through the entire life span, along with its related proximity-seeking, exploratory, and protective behavioral systems.[26] Separation from the parent is inevitable as the child establishes independence as an adult and develops new multiple attachments with others.[27] To resolve the conflict inherent in such a separation, the child learns to experience closeness and contact with the parent on a symbolic level, using the mechanism of identification. By incorporating parts of the parent's personality, the child is able to symbolize the parent. This view of attachment implies that feelings of closeness and perceived similarity to the parent can be used as criteria of attachment in adulthood in addition to evidence of proximity behavior.

Attachment Behaviors

Attachment behavior in adulthood is defined as a class of behaviors, including the interaction via communication over distance to maintain psychological closeness and contact, as well as periodic visits to the parent to reestablish physical closeness. Attachment behaviors include living near the parent, telephoning, letter writing, sending messages through others, and actual visiting.

Helping Behaviors

The protective behaviors that are related to attachment to the parent are manifested in old age by the adult child's helping and caregiving behaviors to the elderly parent. Perceiving that the attachment bond is threatened by the parent's illness or incapacity, the adult child who is attached will provide help and care to maintain the survival of the parent and to preserve the emotional bond. Attachment behaviors are regarded as occurring prior to protective behaviors, since some contact or communication must occur for the child to become aware of the parent's needs for help before any helping can take place.

The Attachment Model

The causal path model of adult children's helping behavior that has been developed in our earlier work consists of a network of variables that predict adult children's present helping behaviors to their elderly parents and their commitment to provide further help in the future (see Figure 3–1).[28] In addition to feelings of attachment and attachment behaviors, variables in the model include the adult child's filial obligation, parent dependency, and interpersonal conflict with the parent. The child's sense of filial obligation represents the extent to which the child accepts cultural normative expectations regarding help to aging parents. Some adult children may feel very little attachment to their parents but be motivated to visit and help parents because it is expected by the society in which they live. According to the model, the adult child's attachment behaviors to the parent are a function of the adult child's feelings of attachment, the parent's dependency, and the child's sense of filial obligation. That is, the adult child will visit and communicate more with the parent when the feelings of attachment and the sense of filial obligation are stronger and when the parent's dependency is greater. The child's helping behavior to the parent is a function of the child's attachment behaviors and the

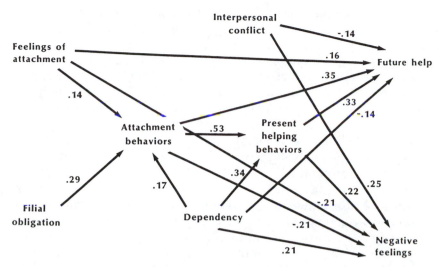

Figure 3-1 Path Diagram of Adult Children's Present Helping Behaviors and Future Help to Elderly Mothers. (Path Coefficients are Standardized Partial Regression Coefficients.) (Source: "Adult Children's Attachment and Helping Behavior to Elderly Parents: A Path Model," by Victor G. Cicirelli, *Journal of Marriage and the Family* 45, 1983, p. 821. Copyright 1983 by *Journal of Marriage and the Family*, National Council on Family Relations. Reprinted by permission of the National Council on Family Relations.)

parent's dependency, with more help the greater the parent's dependency and the more frequent the attachment behaviors. Feelings of attachment and filial obligation have only an indirect effect on present helping behaviors through their effect on attachment behaviors. Unexpectedly, conflict is not related to present help to the parent.

The adult child's commitment to help the elderly parent in the future is a function of all prior variables in the model other than filial obligation, which has an indirect effect through its effect on attachment behaviors. Thus, there is a greater commitment to provide future help the more help that is given at the present time, the more attachment behaviors are displayed, the stronger the feelings of attachment, and the less the conflict with the parent. Parent dependency has a somewhat paradoxical effect on commitment to provide future help. The direct effect of parent dependency is to reduce commitment to help in the future, while its indirect effect (through its effect on attachment behaviors and present help) is to increase the commitment to help in the future as dependency increases. The net effect of these opposing tendencies is a very weak positive influence of dependency on commitment to future help.

A secondary portion of the model is concerned with variables associated with negative feelings generated in the adult child who is giving help or care to the elderly parent. Negative feelings refer to an unpleasant emotional state—for example, impatience, frustration, irritation, bitterness, resentment, anger, and so on. Negative feelings are a function of adult children's present helping behaviors, parent dependency, conflict with the parent, feelings of attachment, and attachment behaviors. Negative feelings are greater as helping behaviors increase, as parent dependency increases, and as conflict increases. On the other hand, negative feelings are lessened when the adult child's feelings of attachment are stronger and as attachment behaviors increase. Thus, strong feelings of attachment to the parent and established patterns of visiting and communication act to temper any negative feelings that arise as a result of conflicts with the parent, the parent's dependency, or the burden of helping. Negative feelings are not related to commitment to help in the future, although such a relationship was originally hypothesized in the model.

Implications of the Attachment Model for Parent Neglect

The attachment model of helping has a number of implications for the study of the causes of parent neglect. First of all, the negative effects of the adult child's present help, the parent's dependency, and the parent-child conflict on commitment to future help have a direct bearing on the question of parent neglect. If commitment to help cannot be maintained over time, then the adult child will be less likely to give help or care in response to the parent's needs. Parent-child conflict, known to be a precursor of abuse and neglect, is part of this model of helping and is particularly salient.

The model also indicates that conflict, dependency, and present help all contribute to negative feelings on the part of the adult child who is acting as caregiver. We have already shown how negative feelings are part of a cycle of continuing conflict in a relationship. The fact that parent dependency and present helping behavior also contribute to these negative feelings suggests that a cycle of conflict may be especially likely in a caregiving situation with a dependent elderly parent.

The model underscores the value of a strong bond of attachment between the parent and the adult child, for not only does the child's attachment to the parent motivate attachment behaviors of visiting and telephoning, but it also leads to such protective behaviors as giving help to dependent parents when needed and a commitment to help in the future. Further, a strong attachment bond appears to temper the effects of conflict on commitment to future help and the development of negative feelings in the caregiving situation. Such a model may help to explain why some family caregivers sustain a high level of commitment to give care under an objective burden that is very great without perceiving the burden to be great or finding the parent's demands or difficult behaviors to be upsetting.[29]

According to the model, filial obligation has only a small indirect effect (if any) on the adult child's commitment to future help or on the reduction of negative feelings. Thus it would seem that if the adult child's helping behavior is motivated only by a sense of obligation, the commitment to future help would be more easily subject to erosion by the hardships of helping, the parent's dependency, and the conflict cycle. Some support for this position is given in the work of Adams, who distinguished between affection and obligation in relationships to parents, concluding that relationships based on obligation alone are likely to be perfunctory in comparison to the qualitatively richer interactions of affection-based relationships.[30] Certainly, cultural norms and expectations do play an important part in shaping adult children's behaviors toward their elderly parents, but without the closeness of an attachment bond in addition, obligation alone is likely to result in a minimal caregiving effort.

According to Steinman, adult children who are involved in conflicts with elderly parents can take several possible courses.[31] One is that of "an overzealous approacher," who continues in the caregiving situation and the cycle of conflict, enduring a great deal of stress and negative feelings in the process. Another type is the "active avoider," who avoids both the conflict with parents and the caregiving situation by hiring someone else, letting siblings or other relatives give care, or doing nothing. A third type is a "vacillator," who has a classic approach-avoidance reaction to parent care. The vacillator gives care for a while, but as the conflicts and the negative feelings build up, this adult child switches to avoiding the caregiving situation. Eventually, the avoidance reaction subsides, and the child approaches again. The final type is the "constructive approacher," who recognizes the conflict with the parent for what it is and takes steps to resolve the problem. Parent caregiving when there is conflict is less likely to lead to neglect by the constructive approacher or the overzealous approacher, although the overzealous approacher may experience burnout symptoms at some point and be unable to continue caregiving duties.

The active avoider may neglect the parent by simply walking away from the conflict-ridden caregiving situation and ignoring the parent's needs. If there is no one else to assume care, this kind of neglect can be quite serious. The vacillator would seem to be more likely to become involved in a continuing series of neglect incidents, neglecting the parent during the avoidance phase when the effects of conflicts and caregiving pressures become too great but returning to caregiving during the approach phase.

Based on the model, an adult child with a strong bond of attachment would be expected to be either a constructive approacher or an overzealous approacher; in either case there would be a strong commitment to the caregiving relationship in spite of conflicts. A child with a very weak attachment bond would be more likely to be active avoider, while one with a moderate attachment bond would be more likely to be a vacillator, caught in a cycle of approach and avoidance in response to the conflict. Unfortunately, not all children assuming a caregiving role have a strong affectional bond with the parent.[32] Sometimes none of the adult children in a family is close to the parent; in other cases, the child who is closest to the parent is unable to give care. Thus, the caregiving role often falls to a child who is not the one preferred by the parent and who has only a moderate bond of attachment to the parent. Such children are often those with unresolved conflicts with the parent from the past, and the stage is set for further conflict.

From a different perspective, Hickey and Douglass hypothesize that when the personal relationship with the aging parent has been poor, the adult child (or other family member) develops means of coping, which include various self-protective mechanisms and a tendency to avoid the problem situation.[33] Thus, when the parent needs care and a conflict develops, the adult child may handle the problem by simply neglecting the parent and walking away. From this view, as well as our own, the adult child's response to parent conflict in the caregiving situation is determined by the history of the relationship.

Other Factors Related to Conflict in the Helping Relationship

Several other factors that are related to conflict with the parent in the helping situation are not included in the model of helping but should be mentioned here.

Perception of Parent's Needs

When adult children perceive their parent's needs for care as being less than legitimate, conflict tends to result when the parent requests or demands help in satisfying these needs.[34] This makes the parent more vulnerable to neglect, since an adult child caregiver will feel justified in not responding to parent requests that the child considers inappropriate.

We found that elderly parents and adult children do have differing perceptions of the relative importance of various needs.[35] The top four needs as rated by the elderly were for protection, transportation, bureaucratic mediation, and reading materials. Adult children listed transportation, personal care, home health care, and psychological support as being most important. If a child caregiver attempts to force a service on a parent who thinks it is unimportant, or if the child disregards or ridicules a need that the parent considers important, conflict and negative feelings result.

Perception of Parent's Traits

We have already noted that conflict frequently involves the dispositions or traits of the people involved.[36] We examined adult children's perceptions of their elderly parents' personality traits (fair, selfish, envious, affectionate, etc.) in relation to variables of interest here. Those who viewed their parents' traits more positively had a closer bond of attachment to them, while those who viewed their parents' traits more negatively reported more conflict and negative feelings. Such negative trait perceptions, not surprisingly, were related to a lower commitment for future help, particularly in such crucial areas as homemaking, personal care, and home health care.

Sibling Relationships

When adult children and their siblings have a rivalrous, conflict-filled relationship, there are implications for the helping relationship to parents. If the parent played a part in fostering sibling rivalry in childhood and adolescence, feelings of ambivalence toward the parent can remain throughout life. When help is needed, parents can prefer one child's help and reject another's, play one child against another, and use a poor sibling relationship as a basis for manipulation. Adult siblings involved in conflict are unable to work cooperatively for a parent's care, and there is little sibling support of the adult child who takes on the primary caregiving role. In a situation in which an adult child is divorced or widowed, that child is more likely to wish to leave parent care to siblings, thus exacerbating any problems caused by poor relationships.[37]

Conflict Resolution Techniques

Those parents and adult children who are involved in a cycle of conflict tend to have less effective means of resolving conflicts when they arise. In a study of conflict resolution among adult children and their dependent elderly parents, Steinmetz and Amsden found that screaming and yelling on the part of both parent and child were frequently used.[38] Parents frequently withdrew and pouted, or attempted to manipulate others, impose guilt, and use their disabilities to gain sympathy. Adult children, although they frequently tried to talk things through or sought advice from others, indicated that they also used threats, used force or coerced the parent, or withheld food. While some of these methods were used to achieve the adult child's caregiving aims in spite of the parent's wishes, they illustrate how easily force or neglect can be resorted to in the conflict situation. Steinmetz and Amsden's findings also illustrate the part that the parent plays in the conflict cycle. These parent tactics are similar in many ways to parent strategies that we found were ineffective ways of soliciting help from adult children.[39] Problems in the parent-child relationship appear to have many effects on the helping process.

Changes in the Elderly

In addition to the physical disabilities and mental impairments that frequently accompany aging, other changes and adjustments have a bearing on the helping relationship. One is an increasing egocentrism. Older people often become absorbed in their own concerns and needs and show less interest in others, including other family members. They become less able to see the perspective of the other person and thus less able to negotiate a compromise solution to a conflict situation. A second trend, at least for many elderly, is toward increasing disinhibition of certain negative behaviors that were repressed or otherwise controlled during earlier years—for example, screaming and yelling, name calling, and hitting. Such behavior not only makes conflict more likely, but also increases the negative feelings generated in the caregiver. Another change that occurs for the elderly who do not have considerable material resources is the loss of power that accompanies aging. As power erodes in the wider community, parents may increase their efforts to maintain or regain control and authority over adult children, thereby increasing conflict and negative feelings.[40] Adult children who can understand some of the changes that their parents have to face in the late stages of life may be able to reduce the conflict that would otherwise occur within the helping relationship.

Caring for Parents with Senile Dementia

For the elderly parent who has dementia (any of various forms of global and progressive impairment of cognitive functioning), providing care places the adult child at risk for a great deal of conflict with the parent.[41] The unreasonable nature of the parent's demands, numerous behavior problems, and the physically stressful nature of the around-the-clock care that is often needed are all contributing factors to a most difficult caregiving situation. In addition, the demented parent offers the child few of the rewards gained in a normal human relationship. The adult child's affection may not be returned, there are no longer shared memories, and so on. Under these circumstances, it is difficult for adult children to maintain the commitment to continue giving care, and the elderly parent becomes highly vulnerable to neglect and abuse.

Conclusion

In this chapter, we have presented a model of adult children's helping behavior in order to suggest how neglect of a dependent elderly parent can occur within a seemingly normal family situation. However, it may not be easy to take advantage of the model to prevent neglect. One cannot hope to create a strong attachment to a parent if this kind of bond was not formed early in life. At best, one can try to strengthen an existing bond by helping to resolve conflicts between parent and child. Since many of these conflicts are continuing or are reactivated from childhood and adolescence, a counselor would need to go far back into the past to understand the basis of the conflicts and of the games that parents and children play. It might also be possible to reduce some of the negative feelings associated with the activity of helping a dependent parent by bringing adult children to a better understanding of their own problems in attempting to give care. If one can identify adult children whose feelings of attachment to the parent are at a moderate level, but who have a history of conflict with the parent, it may be possible to work with such caregivers to prevent neglect. In the absence of such an approach, the remaining alternative is to reduce the care load of family caregivers through supplemental household help, respite care, day care, and other formal services.

Endnotes

1. Richard J. Gelles, "An Exchange/Social Control Theory," in *The Dark Side of Families: Current Family Violence Research*, eds. D. Finkelhor, R. J. Gelles, G. T. Hotaling, and M. A. Straus (Beverly Hills, Calif.: Sage Publications, 1983), p. 155.
2. Richard J. Gelles and Claire Pedrick-Cornell, *Intimate Violence in Families* (Beverly Hills, Calif.: Sage Publications, 1985).
3. Rosalie S. Wolf, Cecile P. Strugnell, and Michael A. Godkin, "Preliminary Findings from Three Model Projects on Elderly Abuse" (Worcester, Mass.: University of Massachusetts Medical Center, University Center on Aging, 1982).
4. Ibid., p. 25.
5. Joanne Steuer and Elizabeth Austin, "Family Abuse of the Elderly," *Journal of the American Geriatrics Society* 28 (1980), pp. 372–76.
6. Tom Hickey and Richard L. Douglass, "Neglect and Abuse of Older Family Members: Professionals' Perspectives and Case Experiences," *Gerontologist* 21 (1981), pp. 171–83.
7. Mary C. Sengstock, Sara Barrett, and Robert Graham, "Abused Elders: Victims of Villains or of Circumstances" (Paper presented at the Thirty-fifth Annual Meeting of the Gerontological Society of America, Boston, Mass. November 1982).
8. Marilyn R. Block and Jan D. Sinnott, "The Battered Elder Syndrome: An Exploratory Study" (College Park: University of Maryland, Center on Aging, 1979), pp. 67–84.
9. Wolf et al., "Preliminary Findings from Three Model Projects on Elderly Abuse."
10. Rosalie S. Wolf, Michael A. Godkin, and Karl A. Pillemer, "Elder Abuse and Neglect: Final Report from Three Model Projects" (Worcester: University of Massachusetts Medical Center, University Center on Aging, 1984).
11. Ibid.
12. Donald R. Peterson, "Conflict," in *Close Relationships*, eds. H. H. Kelley et al. (New York: W. H. Freeman & Co., 1983), p. 365.
13. Ibid.; Samuel Vuchinich, "Arguments, Family Style," *Psychology Today* 19, no. 10 (1985), pp. 40–46.
14. Vuchinich, "Arguments, Family Style."
15. Ellen Berscheid, "Emotion," in *Close Relationships*, eds. H. H. Kelley et al. (New York: W. H. Freeman and Co., 1983), pp. 110–68.
16. Martin Deutsch, *The Resolution of Conflict: Constructive and Destructive Processes* (New Haven: Yale University Press, 1973).
17. Clifford H. Swensen, Jr., *Introduction to Interpersonal Relations* (Glenview, Ill.: Scott, Foresman, 1973); Lillian Troll and James Smith, "Attachment

Through the Life Span: Some Questions About Dyadic Bonds Among Adults," *Human Development* 19 (1976), pp. 156–70.

18. Peterson, "Conflict."
19. Ursula Lehr, "The Role of Women in the Family Generation Context," in *Intergenerational Relationships*, eds. V. Garms-Homolova, E. M. Hoerning, and D. Schaeffer (Lewiston, N.Y.: C. G. Hogrefe, 1984), pp. 125–32.
20. Victor G. Cicirelli, *Helping Elderly Parents: Role of Adult Children* (Dover, Mass.: Auburn House, 1981).
21. Ibid.
22. Gunhild O. Hagestad, "Multigenerational Families: Socialization, Support, and Strain," in *Intergenerational Relationships*, eds. V. Garms-Homolova, E. M. Hoerning, and D. Schaeffer (Lewiston, N.Y.: C. J. Hogrefe, 1984), pp. 105–14.
23. Lynne A. Steinman, "Reactivated Conflicts with Aging Parents," in *Aging Parents*, ed. P. K. Ragan (Los Angeles: University of Southern California Press, 1979), pp. 126–53.
24. Cicirelli, *Helping Elderly Parents;* Victor G. Cicirelli, "Adult Children's Attachment and Helping Behavior to Elderly Parents: A Path Model," *Journal of Marriage and the Family* 45 (1983), pp. 815–25.
25. Mary D. Ainsworth, "Attachment and Dependency: A Comparison," in *Attachment and Dependency*, ed. J. L. Gewirtz (New York: John Wiley & Sons, 1972), pp. 97–137; John Bowlby, *The Making and Breaking of Affectional Bonds* (London: Tavistock Publications, 1979); John Bowlby, *Attachment and Loss*, vol. 3, *Loss: Stress and Depression* (New York: Basic Books, 1980).
26. Bowlby, *Attachment and Loss*.
27. Troll and Smith, "Attachment Through the Life Span."
28. Cicirelli, "Adult Children's Attachment and Helping Behavior to Elderly Parents."
29. Steven H. Zarit, "New Directions," *Generations* 10, no. 1 (1985), pp. 6–8.
30. Bert N. Adams, *Kinship in an Urban Setting* (Chicago: Markham Pub. Co., 1968).
31. Steinman, "Reactivated Conflicts with Aging Parents."
32. Deborah Bookin and Ruth E. Dunkle, "Elder Abuse: Issues for the Practitioner" (Paper presented at the Thirty-sixth Annual Meeting of the Gerontological Society of America, San Francisco, Calif., November 1983).
33. Hickey and Douglass, "Neglect and Abuse of Older Family Members."
34. Ibid.; Victor G. Cicirelli, "Effects of Divorce, Widowhood, and Remarriage on Adult Children's Relationship and Services to Elderly Parents," Report to the AARP Andrus Foundation (1981).
35. Cicirelli, *Helping Elderly Parents*.
36. Peterson, "Conflict."
37. Victor Cicirelli, "Marital Disruption and Adult Children's Perceptions of Their Sibling's Help to Elderly Parents," *Journal of Family Relations* 33 (1984), pp. 613–21.
38. Suzanne K. Steinmetz and Deborah J. Amsden, "Dependent Elders, Family Stress, and Abuse," in *Family Relationships in Later Life*, ed. T. H. Brubaker (Beverly Hills, Calif.: Sage Publications, 1983), pp. 173–92.
39. Cicirelli, "Effects of Divorce, Widowhood, and Remarriage."

40. Steinmetz and Amsden, "Dependent Elders, Family Stress, and Abuse."
41. Elaine M. Brody, "The Informal Support System and Health of the Future Aged," in *Aging 2000: Our Health Care Destiny*, vol. 2, *Psychological and Policy Issues*, ed. C. M. Gaitz (New York: Springer, 1985); Nancy L. Mace and Peter V. Rabins, *The 36-Hour Day: A Family's Guide to Caring for the Person with Alzheimer's Disease, Related Dementing Illness, and Memory Loss in Later Life* (Baltimore: Johns Hopkins University Press, 1981).

Chapter 4

CAREGIVER BURDEN: CONFLICT BETWEEN NORMS OF RECIPROCITY AND SOLIDARITY

by Linda K. George

It is now widely recognized that the majority of supportive services received by older persons are provided by family members. In fact, informal sources of social support are the largest component of the long-term care delivery system in the United States. There is also increasing awareness that providing care to an impaired older adult is a taxing responsibility that can cause potentially serious problems for the caregiver.[1] "Caregiver burden" is the term frequently used to refer to the physical, psychological, financial, and emotional problems that can affect persons who provide services to an impaired older adult. Emotional or mental health problems are the most common difficulties experienced by family caretakers,[2] but problems can and do arise in a variety of other areas. In spite of compelling evidence concerning the prevalence of caregiver burden, surprisingly little research has attempted to identify the reasons why caregiving places caregivers at risk for negative outcomes.

The absence of explanations for the negative impact of caregiv-

Note: The research reported in this chapter was supported by grants from the AARP Andrus Foundation. I am most grateful for their support. I also wish to thank Elizabeth Colerick for insightful comments on an earlier version of this chapter.

ing upon family providers is, perhaps, an oversight. Many investigators undoubtedly believe that the reasons for caregiver burden are obvious. After all, the physical demands of caring for an impaired adult are substantial; it is emotionally stressful to observe a loved one experience pain or disability; and the time commitments required for care can undermine social participation and create competing role demands (e.g., employment, other family relationships). Some of the factors that affect the severity of caregiver burden, however, may be less obvious.

One potential explanatory factor—and the focus of this chapter—is the role of social norms in creating the stress associated with family caregiving. That is, certain widely accepted norms concerning responsibilities of family members toward each other may set the stage for conflict, ambiguity, and/or discomfort concerning appropriate caregiving behavior in the family context. The potential importance of normative expectations in the development of caregiver burden has been implied by Brody.[3] In attempting to account for the guilt and anguish experienced by adults caring for their aged parents, Brody hypothesizes the existence of a widely accepted norm that offspring should provide their aged parents with care of comparable quality and quantity as that which they received from their parents during childhood. Brody concludes that subscribing to this norm results in inevitable disappointment and guilt because the norm is an unattainable ideal.

This chapter examines the normative context surrounding family caregiving more broadly. The central thesis is that an important factor underlying the stress of caregiving involves the conflict between two norms characteristic of interpersonal relationships in our society: (1) the norm of *reciprocity,* which holds that members of a relationship should experience equitable levels of profit and loss and (2) the norm of *solidarity,* which suggests that family members should be given as much help as they need, without concern for a return on one's investment in the relationship. In most family situations, these norms, which are somewhat contradictory in the abstract, can be balanced such that potential normative conflict is not realized. Providing care to a chronically ill older adult, in contrast, leads to a long-term imbalance in adherence to these norms and creates personal discomfort and the conclusion that one has behaved badly—regardless of which norm is adhered to most strongly.

The chapter begins with a theoretical background concerning the norms of reciprocity and solidarity within the context of interpersonal relationships, especially family relationships. Subsequent sections relate the norms of reciprocity and solidarity specifically to family caregivers of demented older adults. The final section of the chapter places the findings into a broader context.

Theoretical Background of Norms of Reciprocity and Solidarity

The Norm of Reciprocity

The norm of reciprocity stipulates that members of a relationship should experience equitable levels of profit and loss. This norm has an honored status in the social sciences, having proved to be of critical theoretical importance in anthropology, psychology, and sociology. Substantively, the norm of reciprocity has been used to explain such wide-ranging phenomena as status and power,[4] non-verbal behavior,[5] altruism and pro-social behavior,[6] interpersonal attraction,[7] marital choice,[8] and marital dissolution.[9] The norm of reciprocity has been useful in understanding both the "starting mechanisms" that initiate social structure and the dynamics that enable social structures to persist over time.[10] Indeed, two major meta-perspectives of sociology—functional theory and conflict theory—which generally are contradictory rather than complementary, recognize the norm of reciprocity as an integral component of social life.[11] In short, there is consensus that the norm of reciprocity is a fundamental and universal guiding principle of human behavior.

Although it has been valuable to several theoretical perspectives, the norm of reciprocity is most closely identified with two theoretical traditions: exchange theory and equity theory. Moreover, the links between the norm of reciprocity and family life are best articulated in these two theoretical frameworks.

Exchange Theory. Social exchange theory begins with a simple assumption about human nature: that people desire to maximize their profits and minimize their losses.[12] The crux of this proposition can be summarized by a straightforward equation: Profit equals rewards minus the sum of actual costs and foregone rewards.[13] It should be noted that the debits charged against rewards are of two types: (1) the actual costs incurred in the transaction and (2) the foregone rewards that could have been gained had the individual engaged in an alternative transaction. Thus, exchange theory has a rational, economic foundation.

Economic exchange is, of course, a common occurrence and quantitative calculations of monetary profit and loss are relatively straightforward. Social exchange is more complex than economic exchange for several reasons. First, there is no single medium of social exchange—the process can involve a broad array of rewards such as instrumental assistance, reassurance, self-esteem enhancement, and companionship. Second, there is no objective, quantifiable system for determining the value of the resources exchanged.[14] How does one impute a value to a word of reassurance or an act of tangible assistance? Third, unlike economic exchanges, social exchanges are not assumed to involve reciprocation of the same resource.[15] For example, you may owe a person a favor because she provided you with transportation when your car was being repaired, but you can redeem your obligation in ways other than providing her with transportation. For these reasons, social exchanges are characterized by greater ambiguity than economic exchanges.

The ambiguities of social exchanges have both positive and negative repercussions for social relationships. On the positive side, these ambiguities result in considerable flexibility. For example, because one need not repay a reward with the same resource received, individuals often can meet their responsibilities with those resources that are most available and least costly to them. But, the uncertainties of social exchange also can be problematic because conclusions about the equality and timeliness of exchanges are ultimately subjective. Consequently, partners in a relationship may disagree about the degree to which exchange principles are being upheld.

If people engage in interaction for the purpose of maximizing profits, how does the norm of reciprocity fit into the picture? In fact, the two concepts are not as contradictory as they appear at first glance. If an individual attends only to maximizing his own profits, others will not engage in ongoing relationships with him. That is, relationships can develop and be sustained only if both members find interaction profitable. If one of the individuals does not realize profits, motivation for continuing the relationship is reduced or eliminated. Thus, if one wishes to receive profits on a long-term basis, it is necessary to insure that one's partner receives rewards in the interim. The norm of reciprocity helps to sustain relationships so that both participants realize reasonable levels of profits in the long run, because both know that rewards given now will be reciprocated in the future. Beyond the fact that rewards are to be exchanged (rather than flow in a unidirectional fashion), the norm of reciprocity stipulates that a reward should be repaid with a benefit of equivalent value.[16]

Obviously, we neither have nor desire the same kinds of relationships with all people. There is a strong association between the level of intimacy in a relationship and the nature of its patterns of exchange. The more intimate the relationship, (1) the longer the acceptable interval between receipt of rewards and repayment of them, (2) the wider the acceptable discrepancy between the nature of the rewards given and those received in reciprocation, (3) the greater the value of the resources exchanged, and (4) the longer an imbalance in the value of rewards given versus received will be tolerated. Thus, intimacy is characterized by a trust that the relationship will involve equitable exchanges over the long run and periodic departures from reciprocity will be tolerated.

Gouldner has contributed to our understanding of the norm of reciprocity in several important ways. Of particular relevance to this chapter are his insights regarding social roles and the norm of reciprocity. Gouldner notes that sociologists typically describe roles as involving complementary or reciprocal rights and duties—implying that complementarity and reciprocity are synonymous when, in fact, these terms have distinct and consequential meaning. If two roles are complementary, then the right of one role incumbent is an obligation to the other. For example, if there is social consensus that minor children have a right to financial support from their parents, then parents have a complementary duty to provide financial support to their minor children. But, thus far, there is no evidence that these two roles are reciprocal because reciprocity implies that giving and receiving are mutually contingent.[17] In the same example, if social consensus does not dictate that children somehow repay their parents for the financial support they receive, then the parent and child roles are not reciprocal (though they are complementary). On the other hand, if social consensus dictates that children owe their parents respect because of (that is, in return for) parental financial support—and the parents' obligation to provide support is contingent upon reciprocal respect—the two roles are reciprocal. As shown later, this subtle distinction between complementarity and reciprocity is relevant to our understanding of family caregiving for impaired older adults.

Gouldner alerts us to another important issue concerning the link between social roles and the norm of reciprocity. Regardless of whether the rights and duties of a social role are complementary or reciprocal, they are limited in scope to that role relationship. Consequently, role obligations cannot provide guiding principles for all behavior or all situations. In contrast, the norm of reciprocity is a generalized value or principle, mandating that, at a minimum, people should help those who have helped them and should not injure those who have helped them. Thus, the norm of

reciprocity guides human behavior outside of formal role relationships as well as reinforcing exchanges within role relationships.[18]
Consequently, if we observe reciprocal exchanges within role
relationships, in the absence of other information we cannot know
whether this pattern of exchanges represents reciprocal role obligations or adherence to the generalized norm of reciprocity.

   Equity Theory.   Equity theories are direct descendants of exchange theories and focus specifically on the dynamics of social
relationships, particularly the conditions under which relationships are stable and satisfying. The most popular equity theory—
and one that is appropriate for our purposes—is that of Walster and
her colleagues. This model defines an equitable relationship as one
in which the participants perceive that they are receiving equal net
gains from the relationship. Individuals assess the equity of their
relationships by examining the ratio of inputs to outcomes, where
inputs are defined as the individual's contributions to the partner,
and outcomes are the costs and rewards received from the partner.[19] Similar to social exchange theory, net gains (or losses) equal
outcomes minus inputs. Three types of relationships are possible:
(1) both perceive net gains to be equitable for themselves and their
partners, (2) overbenefited individuals perceive their net gains to
be greater than those of their partners, and (3) underbenefited
individuals view their net gains as smaller than those of their
partner.

   Equity theory predicts that individuals participating in inequita-
ble relationships will be distressed and that the amount of distress
will be directly proportional to the degree of inequity.[20] Overbenefiters and underbenefiters, however, are expected to experience
different kinds of distress. Overbenefiters will experience a sense
of guilt as a result of their excess rewards and unmet obligations.
Underbenefiters, in contrast, will experience anger and resentment as a result of their excess contributions. The norm of
reciprocity receives less explicit attention in equity theories than
in exchange theories. Nonetheless, the norm of reciprocity underlies expectations about the relationship between equity and satisfaction or distress.

   There are obvious similarities between equity and exchange
theories, but there also are some relevant differences. On the one
hand, equity theories offer two insights relatively undeveloped in
exchange theories. First, equity theory articulates the differential
consequences of overbenefiting versus underbenefiting—an important contribution that has been empirically verified in many
studies. Second, the theory explicitly notes that equity is a perceptual rather than an objective phenomenon. This is not only an

important conceptual point (e.g., because two individuals observing the same relationships might come to different conclusions concerning the level of equity), but also greatly facilitates research (i.e., by focusing on members' perceptions rather than objective assessments of equity).

On the other hand, however, equity theories fail to incorporate two important insights of exchange theories. First, equity theories do not acknowledge foregone rewards—a factor which considerable research has shown to explain situations that could not otherwise be explained by exchange perspectives. Second, equity theories fail to distinguish between role obligations and the norm of reciprocity. The neglect of this distinction probably has been consequential: Although most research supports the hypothesized relationships between satisfaction and equity, a significant number of studies have failed to support these propositions. A careful review of these "deviant cases" (i.e., in which overbenefiters do not feel guilty and/or underbenefiters do not feel angry) suggests that they may reflect situations in which role obligations override the norm of reciprocity.

The Norm of Solidarity

The norm of solidarity has received far less attention and theoretical development than the norm of reciprocity. The norm of solidarity dictates that we provide our loved ones with all the support and assistance they need, without concern for a return on our investments or for the emotional distress consequent to inequity of benefits given versus those received. Indeed, the crux of the norm of solidarity is that it involves an intensity of commitment sufficient to override the self-concerns that underpin the norm of reciprocity.[21] Most authors describe the norm of solidarity as involving a commitment to a relationship that supercedes attention to individual contributions and rewards, rendering distinctions between "me" and "my partner" irrelevant.

The norm of solidarity is much narrower in scope than the norm of reciprocity. Although the norm of reciprocity is a general backdrop for most human interaction, the norm of solidarity applies to only a few types of relationships—primarily romantic or conjugal love and the commitments of parents for their offspring.[22] As is true for the norm of reciprocity, however, one must understand the distinction between role obligations and the norm of solidarity. As noted previously, role complementarity involves situations in which the rights of one role incumbent are obligations to the incumbent of the complementary role. Thus, role complementarity also can override the norm of reciprocity by creating a situation in which one individual must perform duties for another person without expectation of reciprocal benefits. Consequently, if we observe a unidirectional flow of resources in a relationship, in the absence of other information we cannot know whether this pattern represents complementary role obligations or results from the norm of solidarity.

Like the norm of reciprocity, the norm of solidarity is characterized by ambiguities that complicate human interaction. First, assessment of the need for support or assistance is the responsibility of the individuals involved and is ultimately a subjective evaluation. This ambiguity may result in individuals receiving "bonus benefits" that they would not have received as a result of interaction based on role obligations or the norm of reciprocity. Unfortunately, the opposite also may occur—that is, situations in which needy individuals do not receive assistance because significant others do not recognize those needs. Another source of ambiguity concerns just how much sacrifice an individual is expected to incur as a result of adhering to the norm of solidarity. The norm of solidarity clearly implies that, at a minimum, one should contribute to significant others without expectations that the contribution will necessarily be repaid. The maximum sacrifice that can be expected under the auspices of the norm of solidarity is poorly articulated, however. Does one continue to meet the needs of loved ones even when those contributions take a major toll on one's own well-being? As will be noted later, ambiguities concerning the norm of solidarity are reflected in the context of family caregiving for impaired older adults.

The norm of solidarity has important social consequences. Many problems cannot be managed on the basis of obligations that others owe us or by institutional solutions (i.e., formal helpers). The availability, therefore, of one or more significant others who are ready and willing to provide assistance in accordance with the norm of solidarity can be crucial. The nature of the norm permits and encourages problem solving within the context of informal relations rather than institutional resources. In such situations, the norm of solidarity functions as a safety net that benefits individuals served by the adherents of the norm and conserves collective social resources.

Some theorists contend that no norm of solidarity is distinct from the norm of reciprocity. These theorists view what might appear as behaviors generated by the norm of solidarity as in fact behavior spurred by the norm of reciprocity. They point out that intimacy implies a long-term perspective and that individuals currently making contributions far in excess of the rewards they are receiving either are paying back previous debts (of which we are unaware) or expect to receive repayment in the future. Consensus on this issue has not been achieved—or at least no position exists that satisfies both those who do and do not believe that there is a norm of solidarity. Resolution of this issue, however, is not critical to our examination of normative conflict in the context of family caregiving for impaired older adults.

Relationship Between the Norms of Reciprocity and Solidarity

It is tempting to conclude that the norms of reciprocity and solidarity apply to different relationships. Under this assumption, individuals simply change gears, so to speak, matching their behaviors and expectations to the interaction context—operating in an exchange mode in most situations, but switching to a solidarity mode when interacting in the narrow limits of truly intimate relationships. Under these circumstances, the probability of conflict between these norms would be quite low. There are at least three reasons, however, why this notion that the norms of reciprocity and solidarity operate in exclusive spheres of interaction is overly simplistic.

First, as Schwartz and Merton note, exchange perspectives and solidarity perspectives are more accurately viewed as "modes of consciousness" than as properties of particular relationships.[23] That is, all relationships of more than minimal duration and/or of more than the most formal nature involve both exchange and solidarity perspectives. Thus, for example, participating in even relatively superficial relationships involves sufficient trust to offer a reward with the knowledge that it may not be repaid. Conversely, considerable evidence indicates that even marriage, the most intimate of relationships, involves patterns of exchange.[24] Consequently, it is more accurate to conceptualize relationships as lying along a continuum, with one end representing an almost exclusive concern with exchange and the other end representing a preponderance of concern with solidarity. But few if any relationships involve a single mode of consciousness. Instead, relationships typically are characterized by complex and ongoing efforts to achieve an appropriate balance of exchange and solidarity behaviors.

Second, relationships are dynamic—they develop and change over time. Relationships that begin as relatively superficial and are almost exclusively oriented toward social exchange may, over time, become more intimate and, hence, come to include a greater emphasis on solidarity. Conversely, some relationships may experience a "cooling out," in which concern over solidarity lessens and exchange principles come to dominate interaction. As relationships move along the continuum of exchange and solidarity, modes of consciousness are adjusted and renegotiated.

Third, relationships inevitably involve more than one person, and there is no guarantee that all participants will define the relationship in the same way. One partner in a dyad may define the relationship as more intimate than the other partner. Consequently, the first person may perform a service for the second in order to express solidarity, without expecting that the service be repaid. The second partner may interpret that service as an exchange obligation, however, and feel either obliged to repay it or guilty because of being overbenefited. Indeed, because all relationships involve some ratio of exchange to solidarity expectations, misinterpretations can occur even when both partners share a general consensus concerning the level of intimacy in the relationship.

Thus, there is an interaction between the norms of reciprocity and solidarity; one cannot simply interact with most people in a purely exchange mode and with significant others in a purely solidarity mode. Because all relationships involve both exchange and solidarity concerns, the possibilities of conflict are numerous. Efforts to establish and sustain an appropriate balance between exchange and solidarity perspectives therefore comprise a tension characteristic of most interpersonal relationships. Although appropriate balances between exchange and solidarity usually are maintained quite successfully in interpersonal relationships, most of us also recall times when imbalances became the focus of either interpersonal conflict or personal feelings of guilt or resentment.

Reciprocity and Solidarity in the Caregiving Context

Before considering the issue of family caregiving for impaired older adults, it is necessary to note briefly that three kinds of ties bind family members to each other. First, like all relationships, family relationships involve ties based on social exchange principles. There is ample evidence that relationships between spouses, between parents and children, and between siblings all involve the norm of reciprocity.[25] Even in our most intimate family relationships, we expect rewards and resources to flow in both directions, and we count on family members to repay acts of kindness and assistance. We may attribute such exchanges to family loyalty rather than to obligations owed, but expectations of exchange exist. Because of the intimacy characteristic of family relationships, we may accept more unequal exchanges or tolerate imbalances for a longer period of time, but exchange expectations are clearly characteristic of family life.

Second, because of their intimate character, family relationships also involve ties based on the norm of solidarity. If a family member needs assistance that cannot be repaid, we believe that we should provide that assistance. Unlike other relationships that we can terminate if the solidarity mode of consciousness is required beyond what we consider to be appropriate limits, family relationships are characterized by willingness to operate in the solidarity mode frequently and/or for long periods of time. And, it is clear when we operate in the solidarity mode that we are not resentful at the prospect of providing excess rewards and we do not want the recipient of those rewards to experience guilt as a result of being overbenefited.

Third, family members are bound together by role rights and obligations—a factor that distinguishes family ties from more informal relationships. Some of the role obligations in the family are reciprocal, while others are simply complementary. Interestingly, the distinction between reciprocal and complementary role duties is vague, not only in social science, but also in the ongoing dynamics of family life. For example, one of the common tensions between adolescents and their parents concerns the issue of whether parental support and adolescent respect for parental rules are mutually contingent. Adolescents often contend that their parents should not try to enforce behavioral regulations or value preferences on their children just because the parents have provided material support for them—a claim of noncontingency. Parents, on the other hand, frequently attempt to persuade their children that parental rules should be followed because they are providing the material comforts of the home—a claim of mutual contingency. Thus, even when there is consensus that family roles involve obligations, it frequently is not clear whether those obligations are reciprocal or complementary.

Because family relationships involve three distinct kinds of ties, it is extremely difficult to determine which type of bond accounts for a particular behavior. Consider the example of an adolescent son, John, who washes his mother's car without being asked to do so. One possibility is that John is hoping to transform this favor into an exchange—perhaps his mother now will honor his request to use the car that evening. Alternatively, John's behavior may reflect the norm of solidarity—his mother is unusually burdened because of deadlines at work and the impending arrival of out-of-town guests, and he decides to pitch in and make her life easier with no expectation of repayment. Or, John may view this kind of chore as one of the obligations that accompany his role as son. In fact, John may not be totally conscious of his motivation in washing his mother's car. Further, John may have intended his contribution to represent one type of behavior (e.g., an exchange behavior), and his mother may attribute it to another motivation (e.g., a role obligation).

The crucial point in this discussion is that family members may contribute rewards to one another for very different reasons—reasons that often are not made explicit by the person contributing the rewards, reasons that have different implications for the recipient of the reward, and reasons that may be attributed to other motivations by the reward recipient. Obviously, ambiguities concerning the motivation for providing and receiving rewards have the potential to generate tension or conflict within families. Fortunately, under normal circumstances, family relationships involve complex behaviors reflecting all three types of ties, thus permitting family members to be more comfortable with the dynamics of their family relationships. That is, family members typically engage in numerous and complex interactions, generating an acceptable mix of exchange, solidarity, and role behaviors. Moreover, by providing explanations for their behaviors, family members often settle misunderstandings after the fact. Thus, for the most part, family members give and receive benefits sufficient to insure general satisfaction with the nature and quality of their kinship ties.

Although most family relationships involve an acceptable blend of benefits given and received, some circumstances challenge this delicate balance. Any substantial departure from the comfortable mix of exchange, solidarity, and role behaviors can be distressing and threaten the stability of family relationships. Strict adherence to formal role obligations and/or an excessive preoccupation with equity can lead family members to question levels of family intimacy and the solidarity safeguards that should characterize family life. Alternatively, unwillingness or inability to provide reciprocal rewards to family members can result in those family members feeling betrayed and exploited by those persons on whom they depend the most. An inappropriate mix of exchange, solidarity, and role behaviors is especially destructive if it persists over time; indeed, it is precisely this kind of long-term imbalance that characterizes family caregivers for chronically ill older persons.

Caregiving for Impaired Older Adults: A General Scenario

Caregiving for impaired older adults may be defined as a situation in which, because of incapacitating chronic disease, an older person is no longer able to function independently, and one or more family members take responsibility for providing care to compensate for the older person's disability. The amount of care required depends on the nature and extent of the older family member's illness. The degree to which care involves instrumental assistance versus decision making—for example, about place of residence, daily activities, etc.—also depends on the nature and extent of the older person's disability. Almost certainly, however, the care required is long term, because chronic diseases typically result in permanent disability and full recovery is unlikely. In addition, many chronic diseases are progressive, and some are terminal. In such cases, caregiving is not only a long-term proposition, but also one that will require increasing effort and responsibility.

Caregiving for the chronically ill is considerably different than care provided to a family member experiencing an acute illness from which full recovery is expected. Acute illnesses often result in short-term imbalances in the mix of exchange, solidarity, and role behaviors among family members. During acute illness episodes, the sick family member must suspend most exchange behaviors and formal role obligations; other family members, in turn, must operate almost exclusively in the solidarity mode. The imbalance will be corrected, however, as the ill family member gains functional ability and ultimately returns to normal family life. Moreover, the recovered family member will be available to offer similar services to other family members should the need arise. In contrast, the chronically ill older adult will never regain normal functional status, and the normative imbalance is permanent. Thus, chronic illness of an older family member results in permanent suspension of normal exchange and role behaviors and continuing excess contributions by other family members—contributions that can, at least initially, be conceptualized as repayments for past services but that ultimately become justified solely on the basis of the norm of solidarity.

Permanent imbalance in normal family ties is difficult for both the caregiver and the care recipient. For the caregiver, although the norm of solidarity is meaningful, it is difficult not to feel distressed, as previous role relationships and accustomed modes of exchange are no longer possible. Despite feelings of distress, however, it is also difficult to contemplate refusing further caregiving effort, for to cease caregiving would violate the norm of solidarity, which suggests that significant others deserve our assistance, without expectation of repayment, as long as they legitimately need help. For the care recipient, the inability to repay contributions, with no prospect of being able to in the future, can generate feelings of helplessness and guilt.

Not all family members are equally involved in caregiving responsibilities. Typically, one family member is identified as the impaired older adult's primary caregiver.[26] This key figure provides most of the day-to-day assistance to the impaired older adult and also holds the most power in terms of decision making for him or her (depending on the level and nature of disability, however, the impaired older person may retain considerable decision-making power). There is disagreement about the stability of the primary caregiver status. Johnson reports that primary caregivers change frequently over time and that serial caregiving is very common.[27] Our own longitudinal study, in contrast, indicates overwhelming stability of primary caregivers for impaired older adults.[28] Some impaired older adults also obtain assistance from secondary caregivers, who provide unreciprocated assistance beyond that typically found in family relationships, and whose major contributions consist of helping the primary caregiver (e.g., providing relief to the primary caregiver at specified times or performing specific but limited tasks). In our research, family members displayed overwhelming consistency in identifying those individuals who are primary caregivers, secondary caregivers, and family members who are not involved in caregiving on an intense regular basis.[29]

As several authors have noted, primary caregivers are not randomly selected from the available network of family members.[30] Instead, there is a kind of hierarchy or pecking order of potential primary caregivers for impaired older adults.[31] If the impaired older adult is married and the spouse is healthy, the spouse will always serve as the primary caregiver. If a spouse is unavailable, children are the primary caregivers of choice, especially daughters. Indeed, if there is no spouse and the only child available is a son, the daughter-in-law rather than the son typically provides the majority of caregiving assistance.[32] After spouses and children, siblings and grandchildren are the most likely to serve as caregivers, although this is uncommon. Other family members (e.g., cousins, nieces) are occasionally identified as primary caregivers, but such cases are very rare.

Thus, two principles seem to guide the process of primary caregiver selection. First, the primary caregiver will usually be the closest relative to the impaired older person—a pattern that Cantor has termed the principle of centrality.[33] Second, within a kinship category (e.g., among adult children), caregiving responsibilities typically are assigned to or assumed by women, presumably because the tasks involved in caregiving are more compatible with the traditional female sex role. In contrast to primary caregivers, secondary caregivers appear to be recruited from all kinship categories, and the principle of centrality is much less relevant.

Normative Conflict in the Caregiving Context

As noted at this chapter's outset, the majority of services received by older persons are provided by family members rather than by formal service agencies. Consequently, there is no doubt that the norm of solidarity is practiced in fact as well as subscribed to in theory. Nonetheless, there also is evidence that caregiving takes its toll on those family members who shoulder caregiving responsibility—with decrements in well-being most commonly experienced in the domain of emotional symptoms or psychic distress. At least part of the reason for this psychic distress is the normative conflict generated by a long-term imbalance in the usual mix of exchange, solidarity, and role behaviors in the family. In this section of the chapter, the nature and distribution of these normative tensions are examined in greater detail.

Data from a longitudinal study of family caregivers of older persons suffering from Alzheimer's disease or a related dementing disorder are used to illustrate the nature of these normative conflicts. Before turning to the data, however, the background of the caregiver study will be briefly described (more detailed descriptions of the methods and results of the caregiver study are available[34]). The purpose of the study was to examine the well-being of family caregivers of demented older adults in four dimensions: financial resources, physical health, mental health, and social participation. More specifically, we wished to (1) determine the extent to which caregivers experience decrements in well-being compared with non-caregiver age peers, (2) identify the correlates of well-being within the sample of caregivers, and (3) examine the dynamics of caregiver well-being over time.

More than 500 family caregivers participated in the study (n = 510). The sampling frame for the study consisted of the mailing list of the Duke University Family Support Program, a statewide technical assistance program for the caregivers of demented older adults. Although the sampling frame did not generate a random sample of community caregivers, the sample was large and demographically diverse.

Participants completed two surveys, administered a year apart. The majority of the survey consisted of standardized scales and forced-choice questions concerning the four dimensions of caregiver well-being, demographic characteristics of caregivers and their patients, the patients' symptoms and levels of functioning, and services the caregiver received from both formal (i.e., agencies, paid helpers) and informal (i.e., family and friends) sources. The standardized questions did not focus on normative conflict. Also included in the surveys, however, were open-ended questions asking respondents to describe the specific problems they encountered in caring for their demented relatives and to provide any additional information that they believed would advance our understanding of their caregiving experiences. The vast majority of respondents provided detailed information about issues of concern to them. Indeed, although we had provided an entire page for their responses, more than one-third of the caregivers attached additional pages of comments.

The data reported in this chapter are taken from caregivers' responses to the open-ended questions. Caution must be used in interpreting these data because information is available only from those caregivers who volunteered comments about normative conflicts they experienced. Consequently, no epidemiological conclusions are offered or intended. The data are useful, however, for illustrating the normative conflicts that underpin the caregiving experience. In line with our previous findings,[35] as well as the research of others,[36] it is important to distinguish caregivers in terms of two characteristics: (1) the relationship between the caregiver and the impaired older adult and (2) whether the caregiver is a primary or secondary caregiver.

Spouse Caregivers. Without exception, the spouse caregivers in our sample defined themselves as the older adults' primary caregivers. Overall, spouse caregivers do not experience normative conflict or tension consequent to providing services—often full-time care—to their demented husbands and wives. Interestingly, however, the comments of these spouse caregivers indicated that they explain their commitments to caregiving in very different ways. More specifically, some caregivers describe their commitments from an exchange perspective, while others explain their behavior in terms of role obligations; still others indicate that caregiving is a way of demonstrating family solidarity.

These different styles of accounting for caregiving commitments are best demonstrated by examining three representative quotes by spouse caregivers. In the first example, the respondent clearly offers an explanation based on the role obligations that exist between spouses.

> *He's my husband and it is my job to take care of him. My children keep telling me to put him in a [nursing] home. But I can't do that. Not yet anyways. When I married Ed, I promised that it was for sickness and for health. Now I just have to do the best I can.*

A caregiving husband offers an explanation that is couched in terms of social exchange:

> *We've been together 42 years. She was always a wonderful wife and mother. She took care of us and the house and always gave her best. Now I guess it is my turn to take care of her.*

Still another spouse caregiver describes her caregiving in terms of the norm of solidarity:

> *Jim was a wonderful man. Everyone liked him and he made people happy just to be with him. When you love someone, you just do what needs to be done.*

Note that the last caregiver described her husband in the past tense, although he was alive and living with her at the time of the study. This grammatical pattern is very common among family members of demented patients—in essence, the demented person is seen as "someone different" from the person who used to occupy that body.

The important point here is that regardless of what mode of consciousness the spouse caregiver used, the conclusion was the same: One should care for one's spouse, even when the illness is a long and tremendously debilitating one. The comments of these caregivers thus indicate that substantial long-term imbalances in the conjugal relationship do not necessarily lead to distress or tension. This is a critical point in that much of the marital research based on an exchange perspective suggests that violations of exchange principles are highly likely to lead to marital instability or dissolution.[37] These comments should not be viewed as evidence that spouse caregivers do not experience burden—they clearly do as shown in our own and in previous research. But the problems they experience are not a result of normative tension or conflict.

Adult Child Caregivers. The distinction between primary and secondary caregivers is highly relevant when considering adult child caregivers. In our sample, about one-third of the adult child caregivers described themselves as primary caregivers; the remainder described themselves as secondary caregivers. None of the adult child secondary caregivers lived with the demented adults. Instead, they reported helping another relative—usually a parent, but occasionally a sibling—to care for the older adult. Regardless of whether they described themselves as primary or secondary caregivers, more than 90 percent of the adult child caregivers were women, similar to distributions reported in previous studies.[38]

The comments of adult child primary caregivers indicate some areas of normative tension or conflict. Consider the following quotations, all offered by female adult child caregivers who lived with their demented parents and described themselves as primary caregivers:

> *I'm not sure how much longer I can go on. The doctor says [that] Mom could live for years yet. I think children should help their parents, but there are limits to everything.*

> *You never think that this will happen to you. Mom and I always helped each other. We'd shop together, do gardens together. Now it's like I'm her mother and she's a little baby. I never thought it would be like this, with me doing everything for her.*

> *I want to take care of Dad, but I have my own family too. My husband doesn't say much, but I know he wonders when it will end. My kids are coming to hate old people. They don't understand why Grandpa screams and won't call them by their names. If I put Dad in a nursing home, I'll be miserable. But I'm miserable now too.*

> *We need programs to help us. It isn't fair to expect us, with our own families, to do everything.*

These quotations illustrate several themes that pervade the comments of adult child primary caregivers. The first caregiver suggests that there must be a stopping point—that it is legitimate to think about the limits that can appropriately be placed on children's contributions to their parents. The second caregiver obviously yearns for a time in which there was a more balanced and bi-directional flow of rewards. That same quotation provides another common theme expressed by adult child caregivers—the sense of surprise that their parents could ever require such a tremendous level of assistance. The third caregiver very poignantly raises two issues common among adult child primary caregivers: (1) the conflicting loyalties to one's parents versus one's own spouse and children and (2) the sense that there is no escape from feelings of guilt—that one will be miserable no matter what. The last and very straightforward comment reiterates the competing demands posed by one's family of procreation and also acknowledges normative tension in a very direct manner: "It isn't fair."

Adult child primary caregivers thus experience normative conflict concerning the level of caregiving that they can and should provide to their impaired parents. They recognize an imbalance and express a preference for operating on the basis of the norm of solidarity. At the same time, they are not sure that the norm of solidarity can carry them through the entire illness or that it is fair to expect an indefinite commitment on the basis of family solidarity.

The normative conflicts experienced by the adult children who describe themselves as secondary caregivers are quite different. Again, four illustrative quotes set the stage for a discussion of the tensions experienced by this set of caregivers:

I try to help Mom take care of Dad. I know she has it rough but she doesn't make it easy for me either. I never do things just like she wants them. Then she tells me that it's pretty bad when you can't even count on your own children for help. After that, I stay away for a while. Later on I'll go back and try it again.

I know I should help Dad [the caregiver] more than I do. He never complains but he looks tired and worn out. But he's always so busy that he doesn't seem to want my company. And I can tell he doesn't like it when I bring Donna [respondent's wife] and the kids.

I know my sister [primary caregiver] thinks I don't do enough. But she isn't "Queen for a Day" either. She wants to make all the decisions and then have me do it. She is very bossy about it.

I try to go by Mother's house every day. I usually give Dad his bath and I try to take Mom something or do a little something for her too. What makes me mad is that my brother never helps. When he does visit Mom he expects to be treated like a guest. If everyone helped it wouldn't be so bad. But it seems like everything falls on one or two.

As these comments demonstrate, although there is less labor involved with being a secondary caregiver, this position has its own problems. One common theme, indicated in the first and third quotes, is that secondary caregivers feel that if they contribute to care, they also should have some say in decisions about patient care. From these caregivers' perspectives, primary caregivers are reluctant to relinquish appropriate levels of decision-making power. Another problem that these caregivers have is balancing the secondary caregiver role against the role of normal family member. Both the second and fourth quotes suggest that it is difficult to achieve this balance (as seen in the themes of family member as guest and concerns about the desirability of a normal family visit complete with grandchildren). Secondary caregivers, more than any other subgroup, also express concern about equity—asking questions like, Why am I doing more than other family members? And why does she think that she can tell me what to do? There is a common issue underlying these themes: The normative tensions and conflicts surrounding the role of secondary caregiver center on the relationship between the secondary caregiver and other family members rather than that between the secondary caregiver and the patient. Thus, the reports of secondary caregivers highlight the dynamics of the broader family network as they face a caregiving situation.

Daughters-in-Law. Daughters-in-law have a unique and unenviable position in the caregiving hierarchy. When caregiving responsibility falls on a son, the major time commitments and caregiving duties tend to be passed on to the patient's daughter-in-law. Although the duties of caregiving are given to the daughter-in-law, however, the son remains the individual formally viewed as the primary caregiver. More than 90 percent of the daughters-in-law in our sample, for example, provided the major caregiving services to their patients but nonetheless described themselves as secondary caregivers.

Many of the comments of the daughters-in-law in our sample were similar to those of adult child caregivers, involving questions about the number and/or duration of contributions that adult children (and their spouses) should provide to impaired older adults. In addition, the issue of care providing versus decision making is highly salient for daughters-in-law. Interestingly, however, the daughters-in-law have mixed feelings about the extent to which they should be involved in the decisions being made. Some of the daughters-in-law believe that their levels of effort justify a greater influence on decision making—a perspective highly compatible with social exchange principles. The following quote reflects this perspective.

> *I spend most of my time caring for Bill's mother. It's a lot of work, but we get by. But when we are with Bill's family no one ever asks my opinion about how to handle things. That's the thing that gets me the most. If I am the one who changes her diapers, I should be able to have a say in things.*

Other daughters-in-law, however, purposely avoid participation in decision making—perhaps believing it to be a no-win proposition. Consider this comment by a daughter-in-law who reports spending 85 hours a week caring for her father-in-law:

> *Robert will have to decide about a nursing home. He asks me what I want, but I just keep quiet and don't say anything. It's his father and he will have to live with the decision.*

Thus, although daughters-in-law are aware of their limited role in decision-making, they have mixed reactions to it.

One unique theme emerged from the comments offered by daughters-in-law. A number of these caregivers wonder whether their husbands would be as amenable to the disruptions of caregiving if it were her parents rather than his—and some know they would not be.

> *My mother was in the hospital for eight weeks before she died. Gerald let me know that he did not appreciate my almost living there [at the hospital] then. Now his mother has been here for two years and is very hard to handle. I don't nag Gerald about it, but once or twice I let him know that I decided to handle things different than he did.*

Final Thoughts

From a theoretical perspective, there is reason to expect that caregiving for an impaired older adult would be stressful, in part, because of normative conflicts or tensions. The demands of caregiving involve a long-term imbalance in the exchange, solidarity, and role obligations between family members—a situation that is likely to lead to distress, especially feelings of guilt or resentment. Our limited data suggest that such normative conflicts occur in the caregiving context, especially for adult child caregivers, daughters-in-law who provide caregiving services, and secondary caregivers (regardless of their relationship to the impaired older adult). However, these data also suggest several important qualifications to the expectation of normative conflict.

First, caregiving spouses apparently experience little normative conflict in committing themselves to the role of primary caregiver. The comments of spouse caregivers indicate that exchange, solidarity, and role obligations are all relevant modes of consciousness. But, regardless of the mode of consciousness, the conclusion is the same—spouses should provide care for each other. For spouses then, the long-term imbalances in normal conjugal relationships do not necessarily involve perceptions of inequity or resentment. This does not mean, however, that the lives of spouse caregivers are free of normative conflict. Several adult children who were secondary caregivers attempting to provide assistance to their parents indicated at least occasional disagreements with their parents who were serving as primary caregivers. In addition, 52 percent of the spouse caregivers in our sample indicated that they wanted more help from their children and other relatives.[39] Thus, for spouses, the normative conflicts characteristic of the caregiving situation focus on relationships with other members of the support network, rather than with concerns about the demands generated by the impaired spouse.

Issues of equity arise most frequently in the comments of adult child caregivers. For adult child primary caregivers, concerns about caring for an impaired parent must be balanced with responsibilities for one's own family of procreation. This conflict leads to a fairly explicit concern about the limits of responsibility. For adult child secondary caregivers, issues of equity arise frequently in the context of comparison of self to other potential secondary caregivers (for example, that all are siblings shouldering equal levels of responsibility). In addition, secondary caregivers frequently desire a reasonable balance between caregiving effort and the power to make decisions about the impaired older adult. This perceived inequity reflects the concern of the secondary caregiver; in all likelihood, the primary caregiver could make a persuasive argument for retaining primary decision-making power.

Daughters-in-law have a unique position in the caregiving hierarchy. These caregivers frequently provide a majority of caregiving services to the impaired older adult. Nonetheless, they describe themselves as secondary caregivers. Consequently, daughters-in-law express the same concerns reported by both primary and secondary adult child caregivers: concerns about the limits of responsibility (a concern shared by adult child primary caregivers) and perceptions of a lack of input in decision making (a concern shared by adult child secondary caregivers). In addition, it is perhaps natural that daughters-in-law would compare the contributions made to their husbands' parents with those that have been or might in the future be offered to their own parents.

The data used to illustrate the normative conflicts and tensions that can arise in the caregiving context are not without limitations. First, participants in the study were individuals who had some level of involvement in providing care to an impaired older adult. Consequently, those persons who are unwilling to participate in any level of caregiving for their impaired older relatives were not present in the sample. Second, and more consequential, questions specifically about normative conflict were not included in the survey. All data reported here were elicited from open-ended and nonspecific questions about the problems of caregiving and from a general request that respondents tell us anything else that we needed to know about their experiences. Consequently, no conclusions can be made about the prevalence of specific types of normative conflicts or the representativeness of the issues raised in these volunteered comments. It may be that those respondents who commented on normative issues were those most bothered by them or were the most articulate participants. Moreover, a systematic set of questions about these issues might have uncovered types of normative tensions not volunteered on the basis of a nonspecific stimulus.

Finally, the data obtained may be highly influenced by the fact that all of the caregivers in the study were providing services to a demented older adult. Caring for a demented patient is unique in at least two ways. First, Alzheimer's disease and related disorders generate a unique set of behavioral problems and functional limitations. Second, because of the severity of the cognitive impairment, the patient has little input into decisions made about his or her care. Many other chronic diseases that are very disabling lead to a need for significant levels of family care but leave the impaired person mentally intact. In such situations, the impaired person will be an active participant in caregiving decisions and the patient-caregiver relationship may become an arena for normative conflict of a type not visible in this study. Conversely, normative conflict may be less likely when the impairment is due to a condition other than dementia because there is some evidence suggesting that family members find mental impairments more difficult to cope with than purely physical infirmities.[40]

Normative conflict in the context of family caregiving clearly merits more systematic examination. Nonetheless, there is sufficient evidence to state, with confidence, that the norm of solidarity is highly effectual. One cannot look at the statistics concerning the contributions of family members to their impaired older relatives without being impressed with just how far this form of commitment takes us. Nor can one study a sample of caregivers such as that reported in this chapter without a sense of awe in the face of the powerful commitments forged by bonds of solidarity and affection. Moreover, questions that caregivers raise—and sometimes fail to raise because of their intense commitments—concerning the limits of solidarity are important issues for social science and public policy. Caregiving often entails severe social, psychological, and physical costs—costs which, if they become too great, can be counterproductive in that they lead to functional problems among caregivers.

There must be limits on the norm of solidarity. Those limits are needed not because family members must have an equitable outcome from their interpersonal investments, but because the failure to define acceptable limits leads to unwarranted human suffering—both the functional problems that can result from caregiving that is pushed beyond healthful limits and the psychic scars that result from guilt. Thus, although this chapter is intended to elucidate the normative conflicts that serve as a backdrop against which caregiving occurs, our greatest risk is not that solidarity is somehow losing out to concerns of equity. Rather, our greatest risk is that family members will not place limits on solidarity such that their own well-being can be sustained.

Perhaps there is no better way to end this chapter than with the words of a caregiver—a caregiver who illustrates just how powerful the norm of solidarity can be. These words were sent to us, at our follow-up survey, by a woman who took her demented mother into her home and cared for her on a full-time basis for more than four years.

> *Mom passed away last month. We had to put her in a nursing home for the last few weeks because she could no longer swallow and was racked by terrible seizures. They say she didn't know us, but she responded when I held her hand or hugged her. Sometimes she even smiled. My job as a caregiver is done. I walk around the house most days with nothing to do. I don't remember how I filled the time before Mom was with us. I miss her so much.*

Endnotes

1. Elaine M. Brody, " 'Women in the Middle' and Family Help to Older People," *The Gerontologist* 21, no. 5 (1981), pp. 471–80; Linda K. George and Lisa P. Gwyther, "Caregiver Well-Being: A Multidimensional Examination of Family Caregivers of Demented Adults," *The Gerontologist* (in press); S. Walter Poulschock and Gary T. Diemling, "Families Caring for Elders in Residences: Issues in the Measurement of Burden," *Journal of Gerontology* 39, no. 2 (1984), pp. 230–39; Steven H. Zarit, Karen E. Reever, and Julie Back-Peterson, "Relatives of the Impaired Elderly: Correlates of Feelings of Burden," *The Gerontologist* 20, no. 6 (1980), pp. 649–55.
2. Brody, " 'Women in the Middle' and Family Help to Older People"; George and Gwyther, "Caregiver Well-Being."
3. Elaine M. Brody, "Parent Care as a Normative Family Stress," *The Gerontologist* 25, no. 1 (1985), pp. 19–29.

4. Peter M. Blau, *Exchange and Power in Social Life* (New York: John Wiley & Sons, 1964).

5. Cecilia H. Solano and Mina Dunnam, "Two's Company: Self-Disclosure and Reciprocity in Triads Versus Dyads," *Social Psychology Quarterly* 48, no. 2 (1985), pp. 183–87.

6. Blau, *Exchange and Power in Social Life*.

7. David A. Kenny and Lawrence La Voie, "Reciprocity of Interpersonal Attraction: A Confirmed Hypothesis," *Social Psychology Quarterly* 45, no. 1 (1982), pp. 54–58.

8. F. Ivan Nye, "Choice, Exchange, and the Family," in *Contemporary Theories About the Family*, vol. 2, *General Theories/Theoretical Orientations*, eds. Wesley R. Burr, Reuben Hill, F. Ivan Nye, and Ira L. Reiss (New York: The Free Press, 1979), pp. 1–41.

9. Ibid.

10. Alvin W. Gouldner, "The Norm of Reciprocity: A Preliminary Statement," *American Sociological Review* 25, no. 2 (1960), pp. 161–78.

11. Ibid.

12. Blau, *Exchange and Power in Social Life*.

13. Ibid.

14. Ibid.; Gouldner, "The Norm of Reciprocity."

15. Ibid.

16. Gouldner, "The Norm of Reciprocity."

17. Ibid.

18. Ibid.

19. E. Walster, G. Walster, and E. Berscheid, *Equity: Theory and Research* (Boston: Allyn & Bacon, 1978).

20. Ibid.

21. Gary Schwartz and Don Merton, *Love and Commitment* (Beverly Hills, Calif.: Sage Publications, 1980).

22. Ibid.; John Cuber and Peggy Harroff, *Sex and the Significant Americans* (Baltimore: Penguin, 1965).

23. Schwartz and Merton, *Love and Commitment*.

24. Nye, "Choice, Exchange, and the Family"; R. O. Blood, Jr. and D. M. Wolfe, *Husbands and Wives: The Dynamics of Married Living* (Glencoe, Ill.: Free Press, 1960).

25. Nye, "Choice, Exchange, and the Family."

26. George and Gwyther, "Caregiver Well-Being."

27. Colleen Leahy Johnson, "Dyadic Family Relations and Social Support," *The Gerontologist* 23, no. 4 (1983), pp. 377–83.

28. Linda K. George and Lisa P. Gwyther, *The Dynamics of Caregiver Burden*, final report to the AARP Andrus Foundation (Durham, N.C.: Duke University Center for the Study of Aging and Human Development, 1984).

29. Ibid.

30. Marjorie H. Cantor, "Strain Among Caregivers: A Study of Experience in the United States," *The Gerontologist* 23, no. 6 (1983), pp. 597–604; Charlotte Ikels, "The Process of Caretaker Selection," *Research on Aging* 5, no. 4 (1983), pp. 491–509; Ethel Shanas, "The Family as a Social Support System in Old Age," *The Gerontologist* 19, no. 2 (1979), pp. 169–74.

31. Shanas, "The Family as a Social Support System in Old Age."
32. Brody, " 'Women in the Middle' and Family Help to Older People"; Cantor, "Strain Among Caretakers."
33. Cantor, "Strain Among Caretakers."
34. George and Gwyther, "Caregiver Well-Being"; George and Gwyther, *The Dynamics of Caregiver Burden*.
35. George and Gwyther, "Caregiver Well-Being."
36. Cantor, "Strain Among Caregivers"; Shanas, "The Family as a Social Support System in Old Age."
37. Nye, "Choice, Exchange, and the Family"; Blood and Wolfe, *Husbands and Wives*.
38. Cantor, "Strain Among Caregivers"; Shanas, "The Family as a Social Support System in Old Age."
39. George and Gwyther, "Caregiver Well-Being."
40. Peter Sainsbury and Jacqueline Grad de Alarcon, "The Effects of Community Care on the Family of the Geriatric Patient," *Journal of Geriatric Psychiatry* 1, no. 1 (1970), pp. 23–41.

Chapter 5

GRANDFATHERS, FATHERS, AND SONS: INTERGENERATIONAL RELATIONS AMONG MEN

by Andrew M. Boxer, Judith A. Cook,
and Bertram J. Cohler

Over the course of the past two decades, there has been increased study of women's lives, a trend generally believed to be a reaction to the previous virtually exclusive concern with the lives of men. It is perhaps more accurate to say that the study of the lives of both men and woman has been neglected by a social science literature more concerned with the measurement of dispositions or traits than with the course of adult lives, including factors associated with differences in adjusting to the role strains and normative and eruptive life events of adulthood. Models of growth and change in adulthood have been criticized on the grounds that they represent only the experience of men. Many students of personality have recognized women as more sensitive to context[1] and more willing to acknowledge the interdependencies of their lives than men.[2] In

Note: Portions of the research reported in this paper were supported by the following: National Institute on Aging (POL-AG-123); National Institute of Mental Health (T32-MH14668-10); The Ohio Department of Mental Health, Office of Program Evaluation and Research; Children's Hospital of Columbus, Ohio; and the National Research and Information Center, Evanston, Illinois. Portions of the data in this paper have been presented at the Annual Meeting of the Gerontological Society of America, New Orleans, Louisiana, November 1985.

fact, there has been very little study of family relations among men. Much of the work reported to date has focused on men at work and has not examined the interrelations of work and family.[3] In striking contrast, women's work lives have been underappreciated, generally tied to concerns with parenthood and family and typically concerning the investigation of the impact of women's work on their children's development.

Among men in our society, self-definitions and evaluations are, indeed, closely tied to the world of work. Through the roles of worker and provider, self-assessments are made with regard to how well one is succeeding in such other roles as husband and father. There is no doubt that work has a major impact on life-style, values, habits, and interpersonal relations across a large portion of the life course. Perhaps owing to the centrality and rigidity of work commitments required of them, men commonly perceive cues in the work situation as life course markers. Even among younger workers, self-assessment is tied to subjective evaluation of competence in the workplace. Neugarten has pointed out that life line and career line are perceived as closely related for middle-aged men. Consistent with this emphasis on the centrality of work, Gilligan has pointed out that "power and separation secure the man in an identity achieved through work, but they leave him at a distance from others who seem in some sense out of his sight."[4]

This singular emphasis on men's work roles has been accompanied by underevaluation of men's relationships with other men, both at home and at work. It is interesting to note that until recently, the study of men has been highly focused on those within middle-class families. To the extent that there has been research on men's relationships, studies have been organized around the connection of work and other nonfamilial role contexts. Unique exceptions include Abramson's study of patterns of identification across two generations of men in the family, which resulted in a variety of psychosomatic problems; the six-volume compilation by Mahl regarding the daily experience and dreams reported by undergraduate men regarding their fathers; and the recent edited volume, *Father and Child*, by Cath, Gurwitt, and Ross, which focuses on fathers' relations in the family but at the exclusion of understanding the intermeshing of work and family.[5]

The interrelations of work and family appear to have been typically underestimated among men and overestimated among women. To date, then, little is known of the experiences and ties that men have to one another as grandfathers, fathers, and sons. Understanding of the conflict, satisfaction, and support that may be engendered by these ties is conspicuously missing. In the report that follows, we first review the literature that enables us to understand men's familial relations within the context of their work experiences, as well as from the point of view of men's own definitions of the nature and meaning of their relationships with other males in the family. By avoiding an implicit "female model" of family relations and by using literature on men's own perceptions, we hope to begin to uncover new, previously unrecognized aspects of male intergenerational ties. One implicit assumption underlying these notions is that there is more to men's relationships than has generally been discussed in social science research, and that much of the previously conducted research has used a deficit model in viewing men's interpersonal lives, including an implied feminine standard of what constitutes a "close" or "nurturant" bond.[6]

In the second part of this chapter we present data on men's intergenerational family relations with one another and, in particular, we focus on reports of family conflict among three generations of male family members. Our framework for this investigation is designed to examine the extent to which male family members' relationships are characterized by conflict or whether dimensions of support are discernible. Secondarily, we explore whether work plays a role in these conflicts, as an impediment or support to men's interpersonal familial relationships. Our intent is to gain further knowledge about men's family relationships and to enhance our understanding of intergenerational conflict and support.

Background of the Research: Men, Work, and Family

Early Experiences of Attachment in Men's Lives

As already noted, men's roles are defined as occupationally based and as nonfamilial in contemporary American society. While some investigators have turned their attention toward the reciprocal effects of work and family on men's lives, not much work has been based on an intergenerational approach. One line of reasoning found in the literature is that the nature of both work and familial realms in men's adult years is influenced by early childhood experiences with separation and attachment. Because male infants' pre-oedipal attachment is to a female figure, coupled with the remoteness of the masculine figure in infancy, boys are faced with more stringent separation tasks at an earlier age than girls.[7] This early construction of highly impermeable intrapsychic barriers

through repression of maternal identification and resulting "symbi-
osis anxiety"[8] leads to men's later tendencies to engage in denial of
affect and to experience fear of interpersonal connectedness.[9]
These tendencies, in turn, are related to men's extensive involvement (and apparent success) in occupational spheres, along with
their concomitant avoidance of (and relative failure within) the
familial realm. For example, the predominance of men's concern
with protecting rights over providing nurturance can be viewed as
a result of preparation for workplace relationships, in which instrumental requirements supersede expressive ones.[10] Chodorow argues that pressure on boys to reject femininity creates a sense of
masculine superiority that prepares men for competition in a
capitalist workplace.[11] Similarly, Rubin proposes that since men
find they operate best in a cognitive-rational mode, parenting does
not become a deeply internalized part of the self for most fathers;[12]
men turn instead to their work for validation.

This early construction of rigid superego boundaries is reinforced by later cultural socialization, particularly that involving the
male gender role. One of the major facets of this normative set of
prescriptions and expectations for men is inexpressiveness—the
tendency to suppress outward expressions of private thoughts and
emotions.[13] Using an index to measure the extent to which people
reveal personal information to interactional partners, Jourard
found that men disclose little personal information about themselves to others, and that others, in turn, disclose far less to men
than to women.[14] The masculine ban on expressions of caring and
affection carries over to men's relations with their children, creating a view in which close and spontaneous father-child relationships are viewed with suspicion, as "unmanly."[15]

Interestingly, this definition is held by those surrounding the
father as well. For example, Lein's research on father-child interaction discovered not only that men were embarrassed to
express affection to their children in front of observers, but also
that the observers confirmed this evaluation by regarding men as
"odd" or "different" when they did display close paternal bonds.[16]
Male avoidance of the fathering role is further documented in
studies of children, in which large proportions say they wish their
fathers would spend more time with them, and in which children
of divorce report not seeing their fathers on any regular basis.[17]

The Impact of Men's Work on their Family Life

Other investigators have turned their attention to two issues:
studying the ways in which men's work experiences influence their

family lives and exploring the effects of familial factors on male occupational performance. Consistent with the emphasis on the primacy of men's breadwinner role,[18] however, the bulk of this already sparse literature focuses on the former rather than the latter relationship.

This first line of research, then, explores the ways in which men's occupational roles condition their familial participation. This involves the recognition that the structure of organization at work forms men's sense of themselves and their opportunities.[19] Since the managerial point of view stresses rationality and efficiency, men may paradoxically feel more "at home" in the workplace, since they are better prepared to operate in the cognitive-rational mode. Further, since male bonds rest more on "shared activities" than on "shared intimacies," men may find workplace relationships with co-workers and superiors easier to manage than familial relationships.[20]

Another influence of work on men's familial experiences is that emotion management (requiring "deep acting" or the creation of feelings to fit the situation in a utilitarian fashion) is easily and unconsciously transferred from the workplace to the familial setting.[21] Thus, the workers in Hochschild's study of bill collectors and airline personnel questioned how much of their personality was actually their own and how much was "company policy." If emotional management techniques learned on the job are brought home by men, it is likely that they will duplicate the "managerial ethic" that stresses nonintuitive, nonemotional styles of relating to others.[22]

Another feature of the effects of work on family life is evident in research linking occupational performance to familial participation among men. For example, in their review of this literature, Aldous, Osmond, and Hicks propose that men in middle-level occupations with less severe time demands than those in higher- or lower-level occupations participate most in their families.[23] In another study suggesting that men compensate for lack of occupational achievement through greater than average familial involvement, Rychlak found that those managers rated as less successful professionally were those who spent more time with wives and children.[24]

Interestingly, men who have reached both highest and lowest levels of occupational attainment may be those least likely to exhibit familial involvement.[25] Thus, the importance of the family realm may be determined for men by their occupational experiences, with professional success leaving little time for kinship ties and occupational failure leading to either a man's embarrassed avoidance of wife and children,[26] their angry rejection of him as a failed breadwinner, or some combination of the two.

The Impact of Men's Family Life on Workplace Experience

The second issue investigated in the literature concerns the ways in which men's family lives influence their workplace experiences. There are few studies in this area, although some authors have pointed out that the perception of a worker as a "family man" (married, preferably with children) leads to evaluation of him as a more stable, reliable employee.[27] There is one study by Kantor in which familial ties appear to condition, or at least supersede, occupational commitments. Her survey of the sales force of a multinational corporation, in which the majority of executives asked to name the most important things in their lives listed family (66 percent) over career (17 percent), suggests that familial commitment may delimit a man's investment in work.[28]

Summary of Men, Work, and Family

The preceding studies, although limited in their relevance to male intergenerational family relations, do raise some important and interesting questions about the nature of men's familial experiences and how they are reciprocally related to their occupational situation. On the one hand, avoidance of attachments stemming from early separation experiences, and inexpressiveness internalized as part of the male role, would both suggest that men exhibit rather distant, uninvolved familial bonds. Given men's particular avoidance of intimate disclosure to other *men*, it is even less likely that sons, fathers, and grandfathers would exhibit highly charged, intimate, and close connections or interpersonal ties. This is further supported by the notion that emotion management strategies learned at work carry over into the home environment, especially for men who are more comfortable managing instrumental rather than nurturant relationships. Finally, the proposal that shared activities rather than intimacies bond males together also supports the idea that male familial ties are weaker, especially in cases where sons are too young to share an employed status and grandfathers are in their retirement years. Therefore, one conclusion that can be drawn from the literature reviewed thus far is that men's intergenerational family relations are conditioned by their work experiences in such a way that the bonds are narrowly defined and low in their intensity and significance.

On the other hand, some of the literature indicates that men's familial relations are actually wide in scope and deep in their levels of attachment. Evidence can be drawn from the study of sales executives who viewed "family" as more important than "career," as well as research showing heavy familial involvement for at least some types of employed men (generally those in middle-level positions). Thus, there is also support in the literature for the idea that men (or at least some types of men) do engage in meaningful relations with family members, including other males, and also that these relationships exhibit variation in the forms they may take.

Man to Man: Intergenerational Relationships in the Workplace

The perspective proposed here, in which men's lives are organized around work, affecting family life, is apparent in the paucity of available knowledge of just how men do relate to one another in their families. Given the primacy of work, it is not surprising that much has been made of the mentoring relationship across generations in the workplace. Levinson and his associates have discussed the mentor relationship as a mixture of friend and teacher.[29] A good mentor acts as a guide for a young man, ushering him into the adult world, and acts as a teacher, sponsor, and friend. At the same time, it was noted that the mentor relationship was rarely smooth and frequently ended painfully. Feelings of exploitation, envy, and competition often emerged to override the positive aspects of these relationships. In Levinson's study of men, friendships in general were often absent. In fact, the organization and structure of work life have been seen as so central to men's intimacy that in a recent reconceptualization of adult life, Vaillant and Milofsky concluded that to master the capacity for intimacy, career consolidation is a necessary requisite.[30] Such consolidation may require the internalization of mentors and the transformation of self-preoccupations. Thus, one can become the mentor for another, younger than oneself, as part of one's generativity.

The question can be posed as to whether men's capacities for intimacy are structurally inadequate, or whether the expression of care and connectedness is simply in a different form from that of women. Lewis has pointed out that while men appear to report more same-sex friendships than women, most of these are neither intimate, very close, nor characterized by high levels of self-disclosure.[31] A number of studies have demonstrated that throughout the life course American males have often not engaged in close male friendships, at least not without some anxieties and guilt, and that self-disclosure as a dimension of intimacy is quite low between males.[32] Hess has suggested that middle-class men, in particular, look to their marriages and to their wives for all of their interpersonal needs and for sources of support.[33]

Intergenerational Relations in the Family

In their 1982 review, Troll and Bengtson pointed to the increasingly large body of research that gives evidence to the maintenance of parent-child bonds over the life course. ". . . parent-child solidarity appears to represent consistently an important interpersonal bond in contemporary American culture."[34] Of course, as has been pointed out now by many authors, we know little about the quality of intergenerational ties; what we do know is largely focused on women in their kin-keeping role. Thus, perspectives on intergenerational relations in the family are largely organized around women's bonds to other family members.

Intergenerational studies of men's relations within the family are largely absent. Ties between mothers and daughters have been seen as the closest dyad in the family.[35] Much of this literature has been focused on exchange, and the more material aspects, including goods and services as well as monetary support. This tendency to focus on material exchange at the expense of study of the quality of bonds, as well as an emphasis on the mother as kin-keeper, has resulted in the theme that fathers are seen as largely uninvolved with the family, even though they may rate their bonds with other family members as greater than ratings made by women (see, for example, Snow[36]). Fathers, then, are seen as contributors to the maintenance of bonds in a material sense more than in an emotional one. Less likely to be confronted with strains associated with the everyday relations within the family, men may also be less likely to express negative feelings about their family relations. In addition, men may feel more constraint, in particular, when discussing other male family members than when discussing their wives, daughters, or mothers.

Paradoxically, several investigators have observed increased levels of affection and attachment between fathers and their children following separation from the family; generally these studies are of middle-class families, in which sons and daughters are at college.[37] Sullivan and Sullivan, for example, report that boys who go away to college report significantly higher levels of affection for and from their parents, as compared with their preseparation report and as compared with boys who stay at home to attend college.[38] Curiously, fathers whose sons moved more than 200 miles away perceived their sons as significantly more dependent than fathers whose sons lived at home and commuted to college. Absence and distance did seem to make the heart grow fonder. Men may also feel more comfortable expressing their feelings at a distance than in direct interaction with other males. Further examination of variations in patterns of affection and social status is clearly needed.

Current conceptions of the father's role in the family delineate a set of activities that are largely supportive and supplementary to those of a mother. Fathers are an important support but not the main ingredient in family life.[39] Fathers are viewed as models for their sons and as providers. A likely exception may be the case of single fathers and of men who become primary caretakers when their wives work full time outside of the home; these cases, however, are clearly small groups of men.

During the past decade fatherhood has gained increasing attention.[40] Typically, this literature has focused on the ways in which fathers affect their children's development, and little attention has been paid to the reciprocal influences of offspring on fathers.[41] Previous conceptions of fathers' relationships have often been based on the reports of others, most notably mothers. Viewed in this light, it may be that a female standard of attachment and connection has shaped our views of men's difficulties in the interpersonal domain. Ironically, there appears to have been more study of the impact of fathers' absence than of any understandings we have of fathers' presence in the family.

Some of the constraints that may operate in preventing men from achieving intimate, nonconflictual relationships with other men have been examined by Lewis.[42] These include feelings of competition, homophobia (fears of being or appearing homosexual), socially conditioned aversion to vulnerability and openness, and a lack of role models by which to model expressive behavior. This suggests that men's sentiments about each other are expressed, but in quite different idioms than those of women.

Summary of Men's Intergenerational Relationships

The research on men's intergenerational relations with each other indicates that, on the one hand, men form meaningful, intense, and important relationships in the workplace, similar in some respects to what Hagestad has called "cement and dynamite."[43] However, these relationships were subject to abrupt endings or disruptions. Other research on men's friendships, though, suggests that men have difficulty in experiencing highly intimate, self-disclosing interchange. In other words, they may feel close to other men, but they do not express it. The intergenerational family literature, to add another line of evidence, informs us of the maintenance of men's family ties over the life course, although these relationships have been examined more in terms of instrumental exchange than in terms of intimate connection or emotional support. In addition, when examined from the point of view of an outside observer, the portrait of men's relationships in the family that emerges is that men are invested but not necessarily highly involved, particularly with other males. In contradistinction, when using self-report measures, men tend to perceive/evaluate their bonds with others at high levels of affection and closeness—at times higher than women's reported levels of affection and bondedness to other family members.

Relations Among Men in the Family of Adulthood: Two Research Studies on Social Support and Conflict Across Generations

The review of existing literature, then, presents an interesting ambiguity. Many of the findings suggest that men's intergenerational familial relations are of low intensity and have a relatively lesser sense of importance than those of the workplace. Literature on boys' early separation experiences, masculine gender role training, and the imperatives of male labor force participation all suggest that such is the case. Yet, other studies point to different features in men's relations with their own fathers and male offspring. For example, familial considerations may override the importance of work for some men. Moreover, men may experience closeness with other men that is not expressed verbally or may be manifested in a more aggressive manner. This raises the question of whether some of the difficulty in understanding existing literature is related to the frameworks used for viewing male relationships. By unquestioningly imposing a "female model" of interpersonal relationships on men's experiences, investigators may be missing relevant information in this area. Male bonds may require more subtle measurement techniques and may manifest themselves in ways or in settings that are different from women's bonds.

With these issues in mind, the following four research questions were formulated to guide the present analysis:

1. How important are men's intergenerational family relations with other males?

2. What are some of the salient features of support and conflict in the bonds between men of different generations?
3. What place does generational position play in a male's experience of these bonds?
4. How is work related to conflict and support as it is manifested in male intergenerational relationships?

By addressing these four lines of inquiry we are aiming for an understanding that emerges from men's own accounts of how they relate to other men across generations. In particular, we are interested in how aspects of support and conflict appear in intergenerational ties and what part these two processes play in shaping men's interpersonal bonds to one another.

In order to examine these issues empirically, we have drawn on a data set that enables us to examine the kinds of conflicts and difficulties reported by grandfathers, fathers, and sons. This allows us to examine men's own views on the difficulties and conflicts they see arising in their relationships. In addition, from their own point of view, we are able to examine the salience of men's occupations and work situations as these may affect their intergenerational bonds with other males in the family.

Findings from a Study of Three-Generation Urban American Families: Conflict Among Men in the Family of Adulthood

Method. In order to examine how men manage their relationships with each other, we have found it useful to examine conflict areas across generations in the family. The data set being used is from a larger study of three-generation urban American families conducted in Chicago by Gunhild Hagestad, Bertram Cohler, and Bernice Neugarten.[44] Four members from each of 148 white families were interviewed: one young-adult child, the middle-aged mother and father, and one grandparent. In total, there were 592 respondents. The present analysis is principally concerned with the experiences of the males—that is with the 40 grandfathers, 81 middle-aged fathers, and 81 young-adult sons.[45]

The sample as a whole would be classified as middle class. In every family the middle-aged parents had an intact marriage (Table 5–1). The median age of the grandfathers was 80, the middle-aged fathers, 50, and the young-adult sons, 21. Respondents were interviewed privately in their homes. The interview, which allowed for open-ended responses to structured questions, focused on the relationships between various intergenerational pairs of family members.

Table 5-1 Characteristics of the Total Sample (in %)

	Grandfathers (N=40)	Grandmothers (N=108)	Fathers (N=148)	Mothers (N=148)	Grandsons (N=81)	Granddaughters (N=67)
Age range	66–92	59–96	39–75	35–65	16–35	17–33
Median	80	76	50	49	21	22
Marital Status						
single	0	0	0	0	71	70
married	68	32	100	100	26	27
widowed	28	64	0	0	0	0
divorced	3	5	0	0	2	3
Religious Preference						
Protestant	55	33	36	36	16	34
Catholic	23	32	30	34	25	26
Jewish	10	24	19	20	18	14
Other	12	11	15	10	41	26
Education (highest level)						
not h.s. graduate	33	38	7	5	4	4
h.s. graduate	10	32	17	21	8	19
some college	10	17	23	28	52	44
college graduate or more	47	13	59	46	36	33
Living arrangements						
alone	20	64	0	0	4	9
with spouse only	63	16	61	61	26	28
coll. dorm or roommate	0	0	0	0	35	30
institution	2	2	0	0	0	0
with grandparents	—	—	7	7	1	2
with parents	5	8	—	—	26	30
with children	2	1	29	29	—	—
all three generations	3	2	2	2	3	1
other	5	7	1	1	5	0

104

We asked each family member, with regard to one another, what issues or topics tend to make things more difficult between them, and what methods or strategies they use to deal with or resolve these difficulties. Responses were coded for the types of conflict reported, the ways people deal with these difficulties, and to which family member they had attributed these difficulties. A wide range of topics—sixteen—were reported, which we grouped into four thematic areas: health and instrumental concerns (work, education, and money); views on sociopolitical issues; interpersonal and life-style issues; and a miscellaneous group. The methods of managing conflict were grouped according to process—that is, forms of discussion (such as influence attempts and confrontation) and avoidance. We also looked at outcomes that included the respondents' perception of whether resolution of the reported conflict had occurred or whether it remained unresolved. Finally, we coded these responses according to the focus of the reported difficulties—that is, whether the differences reported had to do with the decisions, problems, or habits of the younger as contrasted with the older member of each intergenerational pair.

Findings.   In order to consider adequately the complex social forces in operation within the families, we shall consider the findings at two very different but related levels of analysis: (1) as aggregates of individuals grouped by generational position—that is, the grandfather generation, the middle-aged fathers, and the young-adult sons; and (2) as aggregates of intergenerational pairs, such as grandfathers discussing their grandsons or middle-aged fathers discussing their young-adult sons.

At the generational level (Table 5–2), grandfathers in over half of their reports said there were *no conflicts* in the relationships with other family members. As one grandfather reported:

> *No difficulties for us. Blood is very thick with the family. Everybody sticks together. All is one and one is all. We don't have differences.*

Table 5–2   Conflict Topics by Generational Location (percentage)

Question: What kinds of issues or topics tend to make things more difficult between the two of you?

	N*	Nothing	Health	Work, Education, Money	Views on Issues	Interpersonal Relations & Style of Life	Other
Grandfathers	(84)	54	5	7	7	16	11
Fathers	(355)	8	5	15	9	46	17
Sons	(298)	9	5	23	7	47	9

*N always refers to number of reports.

Another grandfather talked about his middle-aged son and put it this way:

> *No arguments between us. We are like two peas in a pod. I really can't think of anytime we differed on anything.*

While the older generations were generally less likely to report conflict, grandfathers, in fact, reported a significantly higher level of conflict-free relationships ($p<.001$) when compared with the oldest female generation. The younger generations were much more willing to discuss and report on conflict. The fathers and sons reported a wide range of topics around which they may engage in arguments. However, issues related to work, education, and money seemed to be themes that were more frequently subject to argument than among other family members. Fathers and sons also reported difficulties with each other over issues dealing with interpersonal relations and life-style. These issues included the use of free time, whom to date and marry, relationships with other family members and friends, feelings about life-styles, and dealing with responsibilities.

Chi square analyses revealed some interesting differences among grandfathers, fathers, and sons ($p<.10$). In particular, the young-adult sons reported more conflicts in the areas of work, education, and money. Grandfathers who did report family conflicts reported markedly few difficulties in the areas of interpersonal relations and life-style issues when compared with the two younger male generations.

Of those men who did report conflict, nearly a majority of grandfathers avoided or dropped any attempts at conflict resolution (Table 5-3). Attempts at resolution were, on the other hand, quite high among fathers and sons. Comparing men in their conflict management strategies across generations, chi square analyses revealed significant differences ($p<.01$) between generations, with grandfathers avoiding conflict resolution, as well as reporting a great deal more unresolved conflict, than either the middle or younger male generations.

Table 5-3   Conflict Resolution (Process and Outcome) by Generational Location (percentage)

		Process			Outcome		
	N	Avoid	Discussion	Other	Resolved	Unresolved	Other
Grandfathers	(29)	48	45	7	14	76	10
Fathers	(247)	21	72	6	41	49	11
Sons	(203)	20	75	5	29	50	21

Thus far this report has focused on respondents as generational groups. Let us change perspectives now and discuss pairs or dyads in these families. When grandfathers and the middle-aged fathers discussed one another (Table 5–4), there was a small range of topics around which they reported having difficulties. The two most frequently reported conflict areas were "views on sociopolitical issues" and "interpersonal relations and life-style issues." It is interesting to note that "work, education, and money" were not salient between the two eldest generations. In addition, grandfathers appeared reluctant to argue about these issues with their grandsons, the young-adult generation. From the perspective of the young-adult sons, all of the conflict topics were more frequently reported as problem areas. In contrast, when fathers and sons discussed one another, they were much more likely to report conflict areas, with "interpersonal relations and life-style issues" being the most frequent topic of contention. The themes of work, money, and education were also key in many father-son conflicts. One father described a conflict with his young-adult son about a summer job:

> *I told him if he didn't get an outside job for the summer he would have to paint and work around the house. He felt I was being unreasonable. I felt irritated and disgusted with him.*

At the dyadic level, when grandfathers discussed the processes of resolution and outcome—that is, whether the conflict was resolved or not—they were much more likely to report avoidance of discussion with both the middle-aged fathers and the young-adult sons (Table 5–5). The grandfathers also reported that more than half of these conflicts remained unresolved in interactions with both the middle and younger generations. However, conflict resolution between the middle-aged fathers and their young-adult sons was quite different. A majority of respondents from both sides of this dyad reported discussion as part of the conflict resolution process. In contrast to the grandfathers, less than a quarter of fathers and sons reported engaging in avoidance as part of the process. Half of the fathers reported these conflicts as having been resolved. The sons were less likely to perceive the conflicts with their fathers as having been resolved. In fact, more than half of them believed their disagreements were unresolved.

Do two individual family members discussing each other agree on the nature of their conflicts? An examination of these pairs (Table 5–6) reveals that less than a third of any dyad (i.e., fathers discussing sons, etc.) across our sample had similar perceptions about the topics of their conflicts or the mode of resolution and the

Table 5–4   Dyadic Perceptions of Conflict by Topic (percentage)

Dyad	N	Nothing	Health	Work, Education, and Money	Views on Sociopolitical Issues	Interpersonal Relations and Life-Style	Other
Grandfathers discussing fathers	(21)	43	5	5	19	19	9
Fathers discussing grandfathers	(48)	10	6	17	25	23	19
Grandfathers discussing sons	(20)	35	5	10	5	10	35
Sons discussing grandfathers	(22)	14		23	32	22	9
Fathers discussing sons	(100)	1	5	25	7	43	19
Sons discussing fathers	(102)	7	4	29	6	45	11

Table 5–5 Dyadic Perceptions of Conflict Resolution (percentage)

		Process			Outcome		
Dyad	N	Avoid	Discussion	Other	Resolved	Unresolved	Other
Grandfathers discussing fathers	(10)	50	30	20	30	60	10
Fathers discussing grandfathers	(33)	36	61	3	24	70	6
Grandfathers discussing sons	(7)	71	29	—	—	100	—
Sons discussing grandfathers	(16)	44	51	6	25	63	13
Fathers discussing sons	(74)	11	80	9	53	33	14
Sons discussing fathers	(69)	13	86	6	29	52	19

Table 5–6 Congruence of Perceptions on Difficult Topics and Process and Outcome (percentage)

Dyad	N	Topic		Process		Outcome	
		Congruent	Noncongruent	Congruent	Noncongruent	Congruent	Noncongruent
Grandfathers discussing fathers	(20)	30	70	15	85	15	85
Grandfathers discussing sons	(19)	5	95	16	84	21	79
Fathers discussing sons	(81)	15	85	31	69	16	84

outcome of the conflict. Slightly less than a third of the grandfathers and middle-aged fathers had congruent perceptions about the topic of their conflict. Markedly few pairs between grandfathers and grandsons or grandfathers and middle-aged sons were in agreement about the topic of their disagreement. With regard to processes of conflict management, the middle-aged fathers and young-adult sons were more likely to be congruent in their perceptions of strategies of conflict management. However, even within this dyad, only 31 percent agreed on the nature of their negotiation. There was much less agreement between the other dyads. When comparing the dyads with regard to the outcome of the conflict resolution process, few were in agreement with each other as to whether or not the conflicts were resolved.

Finally, we asked who is the focus of the disagreement between pairs of family members—that is, are the differences reported attributed to the decisions, problems, or habits of the younger as contrasted with the older member of each intergenerational pair (Table 5–7)? Grandfathers and the middle-aged fathers discussing one another tended to attribute the focus of their difficulties to each other. This is not the case between the grandfathers and the young-adult sons. The grandfathers, when discussing their grandsons, tended to attribute the focus of their difficulties to the grandsons. The grandsons, however, from their perspective, were much less likely to do so. They tended to attribute the difficulty to themselves, to the relationship with their grandfathers (i.e., both parties), or to a third party. Between the middle-aged fathers and their young-adult sons the focus was much more likely to be attributed to the younger generation. Even from the perspective of the young-adult sons, slightly more than half of them attributed the focus of their difficulties to themselves. When examining the congruence of perceptions among dyads (Table 5–8), there was little agreement between each pair of family members as to the focus of their difficulties. There was, however, some agreement between the middle-aged fathers and the young-adult sons (38 percent) as to who is the focus of their disagreements.

Discussion. Conflict appears to be part of a normative process of family relationships among the two younger generations in these intact and relatively bonded families. Conflict may serve the function of reinforcing family ties and be part of the cohesion and cement of family relationships. It may be true that, as others have suggested, there is a dialectic within relationships: a source of conflict may turn into an object of cohesion.[46]

Conflict resolution is an ongoing process among family members, particularly the middle and younger generations. Since few

Table 5–7 Dyadic Perceptions of Focus of Differences (percentage)

	N	Focus on Respondent	Focus on Alter	Focus on Dyad	Focus on 3rd Party
Grandfathers discussing fathers	(11)	9	55	36	—
Fathers discussing grandfathers	(32)	19	47	13	19
Grandfathers discussing sons	(12)	8	83	8	—
Sons discussing grandfathers	(16)	31	13	25	31
Fathers discussing sons	(74)	7	76	7	11
Sons discussing fathers	(70)	53	21	17	9

Note: *Focus of Difference is as follows: Focus on Respondent* = respondent's decisions, problems, habits, etc.; *Focus on Alter* = other's decisions, problems, habits, etc.; *Focus on Dyad* = interpersonal relations within the dyad; and *Focus on Third Party* = issue or event.

Table 5–8   Congruence of Perceptions on Focus of Difference (percentage)

	N	Focus	
		Congruent	*Noncongruent*
Grandfathers discussing fathers	(20)	10	90
Grandfathers discussing sons	(19)	21	79
Fathers discussing sons	(81)	38	62

of our family members actually reached consensus regarding resolution, perhaps it is best to characterize these ongoing dialogues as conflict or relationship management.[47] While families may pick their fights, they also choose when not to have them and concomitantly the ways in which to maintain and restructure family ties.[48] Conflict is one of the important processes through which relationships are reshaped in the context of developing individuals and the fluid worlds in which they live.

In an earlier analysis of these data with regard to influence patterns, Hagestad found that grandfathers and fathers made distinctions in their relations with sons and daughters and grandsons and granddaughters.[49] That is, typical "expressive"/relational issues were discussed among females, while work, money, and education issues were discussed among men. The reports of conflict that were discussed previously also attest to the fact that features of work and workplace were carried over into the family relations of males among each other, while the perception and expression of conflicts themselves were affected by the generational position of the family member. Interpersonal and life-style issues were particularly salient for middle-aged fathers and their young-adult sons. In addition, males discussing one another did not report higher levels of conflict than the females in our sample did when discussing either other females or male family members.

Of course, a number of the young adults in our study—members of the third generation—were in a stage of transition with regard to career status, marriage, and financial independence. It seems likely that these transitions are related to the fact that family members tend to attribute the focus of their differences to the younger generation when they are discussing one another.

It has been suggested that individuals of different generational positions have different types or degrees of investment in sustaining ties to their families.[50] And now a growing number of studies point to the fact that the older generations appear to have the highest estimate of their bonds to other family members; when compared with other family members, they report the most favorable relationships with their families.[51] This trend was apparent in the present analysis, with grandfathers reporting the fewest diffi-

culties with other family members. These grandfathers may exem-
plify those who are most concerned with relationship maintenance.

On the other hand, grandparents may play less actively involved
roles in the lives of the middle and younger generations, and this
may in truth occasion fewer possibilities of conflict. Therefore,
grandfathers may be highly invested but not necessarily highly
involved. The grandfathers' relationships with other family members also happen to be asymmetrical, in the sense that most of the
young-adult sons in our study have fewer grandparents alive than
the grandfathers have grandchildren. There may be less opportunity or reason for the old to express conflict with a particular
grandchild when they have ties to a number of grandchildren.

Negotiation is an important process during which individuals
learn from and react to one another.[52] Thus, the content of family
members' disagreements may not be as important as the negotiation process itself—that is, whether or not conflicts are acknowledged and whether or not resolutions are attempted. Perhaps it
does more justice to these families to regard these difficulties as
points of friction rather than major disruptions.

It should be noted that extremely charged or hot issues that may
thematically infuse family perceptions are possibly avoided due to
the threat to relationship maintenance and of disaffiliation such
interactions would arouse. The real trouble may be where *no*
conflicts are reported. Hagestad has discussed, in another analysis,
the existence and maintenance of "demilitarized zones"—that is,
shared perceptions of issues or topics that are mutually avoided.
What we have reported in the present study are the acknowledged
differences; future research needs to further address the less easily
examined but more sensitive areas between family members that
may be more difficult to report and investigate.

As Wilen has pointed out, respondents from the older generations prefer to regard their intergenerational relationships as
smooth and stable.[53] For the grandfathers to acknowledge conflict
with another family member may be tantamount to reporting the
entire relationship as unsatisfactory. In addition, family ties may
come to be highly valued as a source of psychological support and
sustenance. The older generation's value of family bonds may
override the more difficult issues that might arise between them
and other family members. In this sense, their stake in family
relations is not so much a "developmental" one, but rather what
Neugarten has called a "survivor stake."

The grandfathers in this study were typically the oldest living
generation in their families, and the young-adult sons were the

youngest. The active investment and emotional bonds of these grandfathers were toward those younger than themselves, while the young-adult sons' family ties were all up the generational line. Grandfathers, as stated previously, may have been reluctant to report conflict so as not to rock the boat; however, they may also have been more actively in touch with new forms of emotional relatedness. Formerly devalued and "unmasculine" aspects of the self may be embraced in later life, as men begin to discover changing patterns of emotional relatedness,[54] as well as experience a reawakening of the sensual and aesthetic aspects of their personalities. In their cross-sectional study, Feldman and her associates found that compassion increased in an almost linear fashion for men from young adulthood to grandfatherhood.[55] Conflict may be less salient to the grandfathers, though when they are discussing their grandsons, as contrasted with their granddaughters, they consider work, money, and education as important areas of their concern.

Clearly for respondents of the middle generation, conflict may reflect their stake in the young-adult sons as well as the responsibilities they feel toward their own parents. A middle-aged father discussed an argument he had had with his son about saving money for the future:

> He is realizing that I am right to help him save money. I have told him that he has to reevaluate his thoughts so he can save for the future.

For the young-adult sons, conflict may be a manifestation of their transition and launching into adult life. Many of these young adult sons are often perplexed and irritated by the constraints they perceived the older generations have thrust upon them. In the present analysis, the meaning, expression, and management of conflict varied vertically with the generational position of family members, but formed part of an overall configuration of family process. That these men had maintained a high degree of mutual affection and coherence may attest to the idea that these friction areas impart further strength and vitality to family ties, as well as develop increased problem-solving abilities for the family negotiating the life course of its members.

Conclusion

The results of our analysis suggest that men's relationships with each other must be understood on their own terms, avoiding comparisons that use implicit female criteria and apply a "deficit model" to male intimacy. The men in our sample did report meaningful ties to other men in their families—meaningful in the sense of the men's own self-definitions. Large proportions of men in the intergenerational sample cared enough about their relations with a male relative to report and describe disagreements over issues such as interpersonal relations, life-style, work, education, and money. These men were able to identify not only the nature but also the outcome of disagreements and how these were resolved. Overall, men's relations with other male family members appear to be highly salient to their life experiences.

Male-to-male ties were not only salient; they were also influenced by a man's position in the generational hierarchy. Grandfathers in the three-generation sample consistently exhibited responses that diverged from the middle-aged sons and grandsons. Grandfathers perceived less conflict in relations with their sons and grandsons and were more likely to describe avoidance as a means of dealing with familial conflict. On the other hand, grandsons often seemed to be the focus of disagreement as described by those in all three generational positions, with the grandsons themselves being least likely to view these conflicts as having been resolved. While patterns were apparent in the data, there was little actual cross-generational agreement on these patterns. In other words, although the men did experience and express familial conflicts, they did not appear to have common perceptions of these patterns. The fact that male kin did not always agree on what they were arguing about or on the outcome of the argument is consistent with other studies of discrepancies in interpretations of family relationships such as the work of Bernard or of Bengtson and associates.[56]

Finally, the significance of work is demonstrated by results from these data. For the three-generation sample, the salience of work was evident in the frequency with which it arose as an issue in the disagreements of male family members. A male's choice of occupation, decisions about whether to take or leave a job, and strategies for maintaining employment were all concerns in the lives of male relatives. As such, it is not surprising that male employment serves as a major source of both conflict and support in male-to-male relationships. The fact that employment looms large in men's lives gives it a doubly significant role in relationships when both partners are men, since each is likely to have strong opinions and preferences regarding occupational issues.

To summarize, even though patterns of attachment and emotional relatedness may change over the course of life, men across all generations are able to report dimensions of significance in their ties to other males. These relationships appear to be more diverse and less homogeneous than previously recognized, and are shaped both by vertical position in the family and by position in the life course. Generational location in the family has an effect on the perception and expression of conflict and the experience and use of social support. The oldest and youngest generations in the family may be at some disadvantage in terms of power or access to resources, and this may also differentially affect the expression and management of family conflict. The "survivor stake" of the oldest males may place them in a position necessitating minimization of conflict in order to maintain their investment in an increasingly limited number of primary relationships. Such a position, along with increased acceptance of "feminine" qualities such as emotionality and nurturance, may also account for the high levels of support and help offered by this generation.

The youngest generations may have less of a "developmental stake" in the maintenance of ties to their fathers and grandfathers, and thereby may be more willing than their fathers and grandfathers to discuss the difficult issues in their relationships. The notion that men tend to idealize aspects of their relationships seems to be the case primarily for the oldest males in the family. The other generations seem to manifest more varied and heterogeneous patterns of conflict management and resolution. Social changes since the beginning of the 1950s may make it more acceptable than previously for men to engage in homosocial relationships,[57] although how one's social status may affect patterns of emotional relatedness is an issue clearly in need of investigation. Men's interdependencies on each other may only be really understood when they are investigated in the terms and concepts meaningful to men. To do this, we must investigate how men do relate to one another, rather than examine how they may be deficient when compared with a feminine ideal.

Endnotes

1. N. Chodorow, *The Reproduction of Mothering: Psychoanalysis and the Sociology of Gender* (Berkeley: University of California Press, 1978); B. J. Cohler and H. Grunebaum, *Mothers, Grandmothers, and Daughters: Personality and Child Care in Three-Generation Families* (New York: John Wiley & Sons, 1981); C. Gilligan, *In a Different Voice: Psychological Theory and Women's Development* (Cambridge, Mass: Harvard University Press, 1982); and D. McClelland, "Wanted: A New Self-Image for Women," in *The Women in America,* ed. R. J. Lifton (Boston: Houghton-Mifflin, 1965), pp. 175–191.
2. B. J. Cohler, "Autonomy and Interdependence in the Family of Adulthood: A

Psychological Perspective," *The Gerontologist* 23 (1983), pp. 33–39; B. A. Pruchno, F. C. Blow, and M. Smyer, "Life Events and Interdependent Lives," *Human Development* 27 (1984), pp. 31–41.

3. D. M. Bray, R. J. Campbell, and D. L. Grant, *Formative Years in Business: A Long-Term AT&T Study of Managerial Lives* (New York: John Wiley & Sons, 1974); S. D. Osherson, *Holding On or Letting Go: Men and Career Change at Midlife* (New York: The Free Press, 1980); S. B. Sarason, *Work, Aging and Social Change: Professionals and the One Life-One Career Imperative* (New York: The Free Press, 1977); K. Soddy and M. C. Kidson, *Men in Middle Life* (London: Tavistock Publications, 1967); L. Tamir, *Men in Their Forties* (New York: Springer, 1982).

4. A. Kornhauser, *Mental Health of the Industrial Worker: A Detroit Study* (New York: John Wiley & Sons, 1965); Bernice L. Neugarten, "The Awareness of Middle Age," in *Middle Age*, ed. R. Owen (London: British Broadcasting Co., 1967). Reprinted in B. L. Neugarten, ed., *Middle Age and Aging: A Reader in Social Psychology* (Chicago: University of Chicago Press, 1968), pp. 93–98; Gilligan, *In a Different Voice*, p. 163.

5. H. A. Abramson, *Psychological Problems in the Father-Son Relationship: A Case of Eczema and Asthma* (New York: October House, 1969); G. Mahl, "Fathers and Sons, Source Material, vol. 2: Reminiscences by a Son and His Father About Each Other," *Catalog of Selected Documents in Psychology* 4 (1974), Mns. 623; S. B. Cath, A. R. Gurwitt, and J. M. Ross, *Father and Child: Developmental and Clinical Perspectives* (Boston: Little, Brown & Co., 1982).

6. J. A. Cook, "Emotional Factors in the Experience of Men Following Their Children's Death" (Paper presented at the Annual Meeting of the American Sociological Association, Washington, D.C., 1985).

7. Chodorow, *The Reproduction of Mothering*.

8. R. Stoller and G. Herdt, "The Development of Masculinity: A Cross-Cultural Contribution," *Journal of the American Psychoanalytic Association* 30 (1982), pp. 29–59.

9. L. Rubin, *Intimate Strangers: Men and Women Together* (New York: Harper Colophon Books, 1983).

10. Gilligan, *In a Different Voice*.

11. Chodorow, *The Reproduction of Mothering*.

12. Rubin, *Intimate Strangers*.

13. J. Baleswick and C. Peek, "The Inexpressive Male and Family Relationships During Early Childhood," *Sociological Symposium* 4 (1970), pp. 1–12; J. Baleswick and C. Peek, "The Inexpressive Male: A Tragedy of American Society," *Family Coordinator* 20 (1971), pp. 363–68; and J. Baleswick, "The Effect of Spouse Support on Employment Success," *Journal of Marriage and the Family* 32 (1970), pp. 212–15.

14. S. Jourard, "Some Lethal Aspects of the Male Sex Role," in *The Transparent Self*, ed. S. Jourard (New York: Van Nostrand Reinhold, 1964).

15. J. Dubbert, *A Man's Place: Masculinity in Transition* (Englewood Cliffs, N.J.: Prentice-Hall, 1979).

16. L. Lein, "Male Participation in Home Life: Impact of Social Supports and

Breadwinner Responsibility in the Allocation of Tasks," *Family Coordinator* 28 (1979), pp. 489–95.

17. L. Pogrebin, "Are Men Rediscovering the Joys of Fatherhood?" *Ms* 10 (1982), pp. 41–46.

18. W. Goode, "Why Men Resist," in *Rethinking the Family: Some Feminist Questions,* eds. B. Thorne and N. Yalom (New York: Longman, 1982).

19. R. M. Kanter, *Men and Women of the Corporation* (New York: Basic Books, 1977).

20. Rubin, *Intimate Strangers.*

21. A. Hochschild, *The Managed Heart: Commercialization of Human Feeling* (Berkeley: University of California Press, 1983).

22. Kanter, *Men and Women of the Corporation.*

23. J. Aldous, M. Osmond, and M. W. Hicks, "Men's Work and Men's Families" in *Contemporary Theories About the Family,* vol. 1, eds. W. R. Burr and F. I. Nye (New York: Free Press, 1979), pp. 227–56.

24. J. F. Rychlak, "Life Themes: Enlargers and Enfolders," in *Formative Years in Business: A Long-Term AT&T Study of Managerial Lives,* eds. D. M. Bray, R. J. Campbell, and D. L. Grand (New York: John Wiley & Sons, 1973), pp. 82–128.

25. Aldous et al., "Men's Work and Men's Families."

26. G. R. Elder, Jr., *Children of the Great Depression* (Chicago: The University of Chicago Press, 1974).

27. P. Stein, *Single* (Englewood Cliffs, N.J.: Prentice-Hall, 1976).

28. Kanter, *Men and Women of the Corporation.*

29. D. Levinson, C. Darrow, E. Klein, M. Levinson, and G. McKee, *Seasons of a Man's Life* (New York: A. Knopf, 1978).

30. G. Vaillant and E. Milofsky, "Natural History of Male Psychological Health: IX. Empirical Evidence for Erikson's Model of the Life Cycle," *American Journal of Psychiatry* 137 (1980), pp. 1348–59.

31. R. A. Lewis, "Emotional Intimacy Among Men," *Journal of Social Issues* 34 (1978), pp. 108–21.

32. B. B. Hess, "Sex Roles, Friendship and the Life Course," *Research on Aging* 1 (1979), pp. 494–515; Jourard, "Some Lethal Aspects of the Male Sex Role"; M. Komarovsky, "Patterns of Self-Disclosure Among Male Undergraduates," *Journal of Marriage and the Family* 36 (1974), pp. 677–86; A. Komarovsky, *Blue Collar Marriage* (New York: Random House, 1976); K. Olstad, "Brave New Men: A Basis for Discussion," in *Sex: Male/Gender: Masculine,* ed. J. Petras (Port Washington, N.Y.: Alfred Publishing Corp., 1975), pp. 160–78; J. Pleck, "Male-Male Friendship: Is Brotherhood Possible?" in *Old Family/ New Family: Interpersonal Relationships,* ed. N. Glazer-Malbin (New York: Van Nostrand Reinhold, 1975), pp. 229–44; E. A. Powers and G. L. Bultena, "Sex Differences in Intimate Friendships and Old Age," *Journal of Marriage and the Family* 38 (1976), pp. 739–47.

33. Hess, "Sex Roles, Friendship, and the Last Course."

34. L. E. Troll and V. L. Bengtson, "Intergenerational Relations Throughout the Life Span," in *Handbook of Developmental Psychology,* ed. B. Wolman (Englewood Cliffs, N.J.: Prentice-Hall, 1982), p. 907.

35. Ibid.; B. Adams, *Kinship in an Urban Setting* (Chicago: Markham, 1968); E. Bott, *Family and Social Network*, 2nd ed. (London: Tavistock, 1971); H. Gans, *The Urban Villagers: Group and Class in the Life of Italian-Americans* (New York: Free Press, 1962); and M. Young and P. Wilmott, *Family and Kinship in East London* (London: Routledge & Kegan Paul, 1964).

36. R. B. Snow, "Middle-Aged Persons' Perceptions of Their Intergenerational Relations" (Ph.D. diss., Committee on Human Development, The University of Chicago, 1980).

37. L. D. Levi, H. Stierlin, and R. J. Savard, "Fathers and Sons: The Interlocking Crisis of Integrity and Identity," *Psychiatry* 35 (1973), pp. 48–56; E. B. Murphey et al., "Development of Autonomy and Parent-Child Interaction in Late Adolescence," *American Journal of Orthopsychiatry* 33 (1963), pp. 643–52; H. Stierlin, *Separating Parents and Adolescents* (New York: New York Times Book Co., 1974); H. Stierlin, L. D. Levi, and R. J. Savard, "Parental Perceptions of Separating Children," *Family Process* 10 (1971), pp. 411–27.

38. K. Sullivan and A. Sullivan, "Adolescent-Parent Separation," *Developmental Psychology* 16 (1980), pp. 93–99.

39. R. Rapoport, R. Rapoport, and N. Strelitz, *Fathers, Mothers and Society* (New York: Basic Books, 1977).

40. Cath et al., *Father and Child*; M. Lamb, "The Role of the Father: An Overview," *The Role of the Father in Child Development*, 2nd ed., ed. M. E. Lamb (New York: John Wiley & Sons, 1981) pp. 1–63; S. Price-Bonham, "Bibliography of Literature Related to Roles of Fathers," *Family Coordinator* 25 (1976), pp. 489–512.

41. J. A. Cook and B. J. Cohler, "Reciprocal Socialization and the Care of Offspring with Cancer and with Schizophrenia," in *Life-Span Developmental Psychology: Intergenerational Networks*, eds. N. Datan, A. L. Greene, and H. W. Reese (Hillsdale, N.J.: L. Erlbaum and Associates, 1986).

42. R. A. Lewis, "Emotional Intimacy Among Men," *Journal of Social Issues* 34 (1978), pp. 108–121.

43. G. O. Hagestad, "Role Change and Socialization in Adulthood: The Transition to the Empty Nest" (Unpublished manuscript, Committee on Human Development, The University of Chicago).

44. See also, G. O. Hagestad, "Problems and Promises in the Social Psychology of Intergenerational Relations," in *Aging: Stability and Change in the Family*, eds. R. W. Fogel et al. (New York: Academic Press, 1981).

45. For comparisons of males and females, see A. Boxer, "Intergenerational Conflicts in Three-Generation Families," (M.A. diss., The University of Chicago, Committee on Human Development, 1983).

46. K. Riegel, "From Traits and Equilibrium Toward Developmental Dialectics," in *Nebraska Symposium on Motivation 1975*, eds. J. K. Coe and W. J. Arnold (Lincoln: University of Nebraska Press, 1976); A. Foner, "Age Stratification and the Changing Family," *American Journal of Sociology* 84 (1978), pp. 340–65.

47. J. Sprey, "Conflict Theory and the Study of Marriage and the Family," in *Contemporary Theories About the Family: vol. 2*, eds. W. R. Burr et al. (New York: The Free Press, 1979), pp. 130–59; G. O. Hagestad, "Patterns of

Communication and Influence Between Grandparents and Grandchildren in a Changing Society" (Paper presented at the World Congress of Sociology, Uppsala, Sweden, 1979).

48. L. Troll, "The Family of Later Life: A Decade Review," in *A Decade of Family Research and Action,* ed. C. Broderick (Minneapolis: National Council on Family Relations, 1971).

49. Hagestad, "Problems and Promises."

50. V. L. Bengtson and J. A. Kuypers, "Generational Differences and the Developmental Stake," *International Journal of Aging and Human Development* 2 (1971), pp. 249–60.

51. V. L. Bengtson, "Perceptions of Inter-Generational Solidarity: Attitudes of Elderly Parents and Middle-Aged Children," *Proceedings of the 10th International Congress of Gerontology,* vol. 1, Jerusalem, Israel, June 22–27, 1975; S. Horowitz, "Perceptions of Bondedness in Intergenerational Pairs of Adults" (Paper presented at the Annual Meeting of the Gerontological Society of America, Washington, D.C., November 26, 1979); and Snow, "Middle-Aged Persons' Perceptions."

52. Sprey, "Conflict Theory"; J. G. Cross, "Negotiation as a Learning Process," *Journal of Conflict Resolution* 21 (1967), pp. 581–606.

53. J. B. Wilen, "Changing Relationships Among Grandparents, Parents, and Their Young-Adult Children" (Paper presented at the Annual Meeting of the Gerontological Society of America, Washington, D.C., November 27, 1979).

54. H. Peskin and N. Livson, "Uses of the Past in Adult Psychological Health," in *Present and Past in Middle Life,* eds. D. Eichhorn et al. (New York: Academic Press, 1981), pp. 153–81.

55. S. Feldman, Z. Biringen, and S. Nash, "Fluctuations in Sex-Related Attributions as a Function of Stage of Family Life Cycle," *Developmental Psychology* 17 (1981), pp. 24–35.

56. J. Bernard, *The Future of Marriage* (New York: Bantam Books, 1972); V. L. Bengtson and O. Black, "Intergenerational Relations: Continuities in Socialization," in *Life Span Developmental Psychology: Personality and Socialization,* eds. P. B. Baltes and K. W. Schaie (New York: Academic Press, 1973); Bengtson and Kuypers, "Generational Differences."

57. B. Enrenreich, *The Hearts of Men: American Dreams and the Flight from Commitment* (Garden City, N.Y.: Anchor Press/Doubleday, 1983).

Part Two

EMPIRICAL AND THEORETICAL PERSPECTIVES ON ELDER ABUSE

Chapter 6

ELDER MISTREATMENT: CURRENT RESEARCH

by Margaret F. Hudson

The American family has historically been viewed as a sacrosanct institution for care of the individual—the inviolate haven of love, safety, and protection. Growing awareness of family violence, however, has shown this view to be faulty, first with the "discovery" of child neglect and abuse in the 1960s, followed by spouse abuse in the 1970s, and, most recently, by elder neglect and abuse. Some people believe that family violence, in general, and elder mistreatment, specifically, have probably existed since the beginning of human history.[1]

Acceptance of these historical facts as evidence, however, depends on one's definition of elder mistreatment. The likelihood of disagreement is considerable, since this concept is value-laden and typically triggers emotional responses before logical thought. Further, our society is now beginning to change its parameters of acceptable and unacceptable violence, especially with regard to violence within the family. For example, spouse abuse used to be an acceptable norm; now it is not. The norms for mistreatment of elders are just now developing. To illustrate this point, one study found that some professionals viewed certain forms of elder neglect and abuse as benign and somewhat normal; for example, they demonstrated very little concern about isolation or loneliness of elders.[2]

Although mistreatment of elders is probably not a new phenomenon, our awareness that some elders are mistreated by their own families and academic interest in examining the problem are novel. People in Great Britain seemed to recognize elderly abuse before

Americans did. In 1975 Burston wrote of "granny bashing," but few Americans seemed to note or respond to his concern, even though child abuse and spouse abuse were recognized societal concerns.[3] In 1978, when Steinmetz, an American sociologist, shared her "discovery" of battered elders, disbelief and denial were not atypical responses.[4]

In the late 1970s, the number of articles on elder abuse began to increase significantly. The earliest lay and professional literature teemed with sensational comments and unsupported opinions, as well as stories of adult children and other relatives beating up, robbing, and abandoning elderly parents. The negative impact of these publications produced alarm and misinformation, which led to cries for solving the elder neglect and abuse problem before it was adequately defined or understood. The positive impact included public and professional consciousness-raising, and investigations by researchers and Congress. As with earlier forms of family violence, acknowledgment of elder mistreatment led to discovery of an increasing number of cases, which in turn led to a greater awareness that elder mistreatment is a problem. Researchers soon began to investigate ways of identifying its nature and extent. With similar goals in mind, the House Select Committee on Aging began a series of public hearings around the country. Awareness continues to grow, but unfortunately our knowledge has been unable to keep pace.

Problem Significance

Contrary to popular perceptions, at any given time only 5 percent of persons 60 years or older reside in institutions. Most live in the community, either in their own homes or in the homes of relatives. Approximately 75 percent of older adults are physically, psychologically, and financially independent, despite the fact that 85 percent of them have at least one chronic illness. The other 20 percent of older adults are disabled to some degree but are still able to live in the community. In most cases they are cared for by their own families. There is evidence that most family members treat their older relatives with love and respect.[5] Therefore, it was surprising to find in the early research studies that most abusers (and neglectors) of older persons were members of the victim's family.

The climate of concern about older adults and their caregiving families is heightened by knowledge of current and projected demographic and societal changes. America's older adult population has rapidly grown, both in absolute numbers and in percentage of the total population. Alarmingly, the greatest increase is in persons 75 years of age and older. At the same time, the rapid entrance rate of women into the work force has greatly diminished the number of available family caregivers. These factors, combined with an apparent increase in disability (not wholly associated with advanced age) and rising expectations of politically mobilized aged consumer groups, have led to a growing need and demand for long-term care.[6] Realization has dawned that 80 percent of long-term care of elders is provided by family members. However, the extended family is changing to a more mobile nuclear family with fewer children; and with the rising divorce rate, to a single parent family. Thus, family resources are as finite as outside material resources.

These trends raise serious concerns about future long-term care for older adults. Our society, in general, and the federal government, specifically, expect families to care for their dependent members with minimal outside support.[7] Most families have responded by giving loving and effective care to their elders even without preparation, training, support, or recognition of the long-term burden they carry. However, the existence of elder mistreatment by relatives is a potential obstacle to these expectations, which focus on continued development of the family unit as a major support system for older adults. The question needs to be raised as to whether elder mistreatment is a symptom of American society's and families' unpreparedness for coping with the increasing number of older adults who need long-term care.

Certainly, the need to gain knowledge about aging and older adults has been recognized and partially met. But insufficient attention has been given to family elder care, especially to the identification of the social, psychological, physical, and economic costs such families incur.[8] The stage is set and the needs are obvious for research-based public policies that will address both the dilemma of long-term care for older adults by families and the problem of elder mistreatment. The development of such policies and resolution of these issues will be complex and difficult, for they require the joint efforts of state and federal governments and legal, judicial, and health care systems, as well as practitioners and researchers.

Early researchers on elder mistreatment were understandably hampered in their investigations by the "newness" of this phenomenon, the inviolate nature of the family, and the difficulty in obtaining data about sensitive, value-laden issues. These researchers and their findings were also impaired by the lack of clarity as to what constituted elder mistreatment. Thus, currently there is a need to be clear regarding what is known and unknown about elder mistreatment and to gain some degree of definitional consensus about related elder mistreatment concepts which need further investigation. The goal of this paper is to clarify some of these issues by reviewing the status of existing research. This review focuses on elder mistreatment within the family; it includes an analysis and summary of the currently available studies, a synthesis of the current status of knowledge, an evaluation of progress to date, and identification of future needs for research and practice.

Analysis of the Research Literature

The research efforts to date (identified in Table 6–1) have been primarily exploratory, descriptive studies. The typical objective has been to examine the extent and nature of elder neglect and abuse among adults age 60 or older who live alone or with family members, friends, or other relatives and caretakers in the community. Respondents have included paraprofessionals, professionals, elders, and caregivers. The scope of the samples ranged from a single agency to a metropolitan area, to several counties in a state, to an entire state, to a nationwide state-by-state survey. Most were retrospective studies that used convenience samples and were dependent on voluntary responses; the results were relatively low response rates and unrepresentative information. Data were gathered by a variety of methods, including retrospective case analysis, mailed questionnaires, telephone interviews, and personal interviews.

The differences in sampling and data collection make it impossible to compare these studies systematically. In addition, there is little agreement as to what is meant by elder neglect and abuse, so that findings yield particular rather than generalizable information. Other limitations include lack of control groups, lack of control for duplication of cases, solicited opinions from uninformed respondents, and retrospective data based on respondents' memories. However, despite these severe limitations on the utility of the findings, these studies have uncovered an important fact about elder neglect and abuse—it is primarily a family affair. Therefore, any effort to identify it, determine causal factors, or develop treatment options should be done in the context of family dynamics.

(Text continues on p. 150.)

Table 6–1   Research Studies on Elder Mistreatment

Study, Date, and Location	Type of Research	Purpose(s)	Research Techniques	Findings
O'Malley et.al (1979) Massachusetts	Exploratory descriptive survey.	Provide preliminary data on the nature of elder abuse. Raise the awareness of professionals and paraprofessionals on the subject of elder abuse.	Mailed questionnaire. Findings controlled for male-female ratio and for dependency rate in the general older adult population.	Most professionals knew of cases of abuse, with visiting nurses, social service workers, and home care staff accounting for the majority of citings. Third-party observation tended to be the primary means of identifying cases—70%. Physical trauma constituted over 41% of the reported injuries. Other types of abuse included verbal harassment, malnutrition, financial mismanagement, unreasonable confinement, over sedation, and sexual abuse. Victims were likely to be 75 years of age and older and female (80%). Most (75%) victims had a mental or physical disability, lived with the abuser (75%). Abuse tended to be a recurring rather than a single event: 78% occurred twice or more. Most (75%) abusers were experiencing some form of stress and were relatives of the abused (84%). Often (63%) the victim was a source of stress to the abuser. A wide variety of intervention strategies were reported. 70% of respondents indicated some barrier to service provision.

Table 6–1 *continued*

Study, Date, and Location	Type of Research	Purpose(s)	Research Techniques	Findings
Lau & Kosberg (1979) Cleveland, Ohio	Exploratory, descriptive case analysis.	Determine the incidence and nature of abuse in cases accepted by the Chronic Illness Center.	Retrospective review of case records of all clients over 60 years old, for a 12-month period.	77% of abused were women, 75% were white, 54% were widowed, and 66% lived with relatives. Most (82%) abusers were relatives of the victims. Most (94%) victims experienced two or more forms of abuse, and most (75%) had at least one major physical or mental impairment. Types of abuse: physical 75%, psychological, 51%, material 31%, and violation of rights 18%. Victims: 46% were institutionalized, 26% refused assistance.
Beachler (1979) Brasoria County, Texas	Exploratory, descriptive survey.	Document the existence, kinds, and frequency of elder mistreatment. Determine the underlying associated factors, how mistreatment is identified, and the actions taken.	Mailed questionnaire to all individuals and agencies whose practices involved contact with older persons—physicians, social service, home health agencies, attorneys, police, and funeral homes.	Four causal factors from the literature included in questionnaire were: dependency, developmental disorder of the abuser, situational crisis of abuser (least frequent) or victim, long-term environmental conditions (most frequent). Some 92% of 26 respondents who identified mistreatment did so through interviews with the victim or persons close to the victim; 8% observed signs of mistreatment. Actions included referral to mental health services (50%), nursing home placement (8.3%), and other options. No cases referred to law enforcement agencies. Responses from the six professional groups involved in the survey did not differ significantly.

Study	Design	Purpose	Methods	Findings
Block & Sinnott (1979) Maryland	Exploratory inferential survey, 3 parts.	Determine feasibility of methods for investigating the national incidence of maltreatment of older persons. Seek preliminary estimates of the prevalence.	Retrospective case analysis of records from public agencies. Mailed questionnaire to elders and professionals.	Most victims were "old-old," female (81%), Protestant (61%), middle class (51%), white (88%), lived with relatives (76%), and physically or mentally impaired (96%). Most abusers were 40 to 60 years old (53%), female (56%), middle class (65%), white (88%), a relative of the victim (80%), and under some form of stress. Types of abuse: Psychological (most common) (58%), physical (38%), and material (46%). 95% of cases were reported to some authority, but help seemed not to be obtained.
Douglass, Hickey & Noel (1980) Michigan	Exploratory survey.	Determine if elder neglect and abuse was of sufficient magnitude to justify investment of resources. Identify its characteristics and potential case finding procedures. Relate the findings to the psychosocial literature on domestic violence.	Personal interview with semistructured interview schedule and analysis of records. Geographical areas were randomly selected.	Passive neglect was the most prevalent and physical abuse the least. No single explanation for mistreatment emerged as predominant. Most respondents attributed cases to multiple causes. Domestic mistreatment of elders was familiar to most professionals interviewed. Most respondents indicated there were no established procedures for dealing with or following up mistreatment cases. Over half reported nothing was done.

Table 6–1 *continued*

Study, Date, and Location	Type of Research	Purpose(s)	Research Techniques	Findings
McLaughlin, Nickell & Gill (1980) Maine and New Hampshire	Exploratory descriptive survey, 2 phases.	Document elder abuse in selected areas of Maine and New Hampshire.	Telephone interviews with unstructured schedule of statewide health and social service personnel. Questionnaire to community health nurses and home health aids.	Estimated prevalence rate of 4.5% of clients over 65 years old sustained some degree of neglect or abuse over the past 18 months. Five categories of abuse found. Most abused elders were female over 75 years old, functionally disabled, roleless, dependent for some basic survival need, lonely, fearful, and lived with the abuser. Abuse was cyclical and precipitated by stress. Most abusers were relatives of the victim and experienced a variety of stressors. In most cases there were no other incidences of violence or abuse in the immediate family of the abuser. 79% of respondents indicated resolution of the "problem."
Boydston & McNairn (1981) San Diego, Calif.	Exploratory survey.	Seek preliminary estimates of the prevalence of elder abuse in San Diego.	Mailed questionnaire.	Most abused elders were women (73%) between ages 70 & 84 (62%) who were disabled (76%). Physical abuse occurred in 62% of the citings, and psychological abuse in 85%. Most citings indicated more than one type of abuse. The abuse was a recurrent event and most often by male family members who lived with the victim. The elder was a source of stress to the abuser, who was experiencing a variety of stressors. Third-party observation accounted for most citings, and a wide variety of interventions were employed, with barriers occurring frequently (76%).

132

Chen et al. (1981) Boston, Mass.	Exploratory survey, 3 phases.	Explore the etiological and prevalent conditions which contribute to elder abuse. Effects of abuse on abused and abusers. Identify forms of interventions.	Interviews with experts: telephone, in-person, and written. Questionnaire to practitioners.	The abused was typically a widowed white female of the low socioeconomic class with low income, less than a high school education, with a mean age of 70 years. The abuser was a married or single white male of the low socioeconomic class and typically a blue collar worker with less than a high school education, a relative of the victim with a mean age of 50 years. These families were under stress 80% of the time, with the elderly person being the scapegoat for the caregivers' frustrations. Lack of resources and lack of understanding of the aging process with unrealistic expectations of the victim were also frequent issues. The public at large was unaware of and unconcerned about the elderly victims of abuse.
Hageboeck & Brandt (1981) Scott County, Iowa	Descriptive assessment of cases, survey.	Call attention to elder abuse by documenting cases, patterns of abuse, and barriers to service. Recommend policies.	Case studies, community based system of multidisciplinary assessment of and care planning for functionally dependent adults, most over age 60.	Of the 41 cases of abuse found, 21 involved physical abuse, 19 neglect, 32 psychological abuse, and 16 financial abuse. Some victims reported the abuse on interview, other cases picked up by assessor. Abuse is a reoccurring event, and victim usually lives with the abuser, who is often a close relative—42.5% children, 32.5% spouse. Some 41% of abuse by children was financial; spouses usually committed physical abuse or neglect usually due to caregiver breakdown after long-term care. Abused: 18 male, 23 female; usually impaired and dependent for long time. Abuse found in rural, urban, and suburban areas; number of cases increased with age.

Table 6–1 *continued*

Study, Date, and Location	Type of Research	Purpose(s)	Research Techniques	Findings
				Patterns of abuse included: • families with histories of family violence, long-standing conflict or mental health problems. • long-term family care of dependent elder with increasing dependency and exhaustion of caregiver. Major barrier to intervention was victim or abuser refusal.
Pepper & Oakar (1981)	Exploratory survey.	Estimate national incidence of elder abuse, exploitation, and neglect. Explore what is known about elder abuse and its causes. Explore prevention and intervention strategies.	Questionnaire to all state human service depts. Chiefs of police, visiting nurses associations (D.C., MD. & N.J.), interviews with experts. Telephone surveys with 1/3 of state Human Service Depts. Library research, case histories, hearings reviewed all state studies.	Many states had no data with which to answer questionnaire. Elder abuse is less likely to be reported than child abuse—only one out of six cases reported. The "typical" abused elder was a dependent woman of 75 + years. The "typical" abuser was a male caretaker, who was under great stress—drug, alcohol, marriage, or financial. The abuse was recurrent rather than being a single incident. One million elders (4%) may be abuse victims. Physical violence was the most common form, then financial and psychological abuse. Those abused as children were more likely to abuse their parents. Elder abuse is a full-scale national problem (4% of pop.) is slightly less frequent than child abuse and is increasing. 26 states have adult protective service laws which vary widely in scope, only 16 with mandatory reporting, 20 more states have bills sponsored. No one theory explains causes of elder abuse.

Crouse et al. (1981) Illinois	Exploratory survey, 2 phase.	Study the incidence and characteristics of elder neglect and abuse in Illinois. Study legislation dealing with elder abuse. Make policy recommendations.	State divided into five strata from which seven units were randomly drawn. Interviewers talked with people (in seven communities) about elder abuse and list of service providers. Second questionnaire sent if respondent knew of abuse.	Elder abuse and neglect is a problem of the magnitude of child abuse and neglect. All six types of abuse and neglect existed in each of the communities studied. Differences found in different communities—e.g., greater crime in urban areas. Passive neglect and verbal/emotional abuse were the most prevalent. Urban and rural areas had the highest incidence, suburban areas the least. Estimate 4% incidence, with neglect representing 80% of these cases. Medical emergency room staff, police, and clergy were the leaders in reporting cases. The family situation was seen as a major factor contributing to maltreatment.
Wolf, Strugnell & Godkin (1982) Boston and Worcester, Mass.	Community survey, 2 part.	Determine the nature and extent of elderly abuse in a geographic area. Assess the effectiveness of education/training/information activities. Measure the impact of the intervention model.	Mailed questionnaire with attached individual case report forms to human service agencies.	Physical abuse likely found where victim is female and lives with abuser who suffers from substance abuse or mental illness & is financially dependent on elder. Psychological abuse occurs when abused is dependent on abuser for help with activities of daily living. Material abuse occurs when abuser is financially dependent on elder but does not live with elder and abused is not a source of stress. The profile of the abused: white female, 70 years or older with physical or mental impairments, lives with and is dependent on abuser/caretaker for ADL, companionship and finances, and is a source of stress. The profile of the abuser: a male relative under age 60 with a history of mental illness, alcohol or drug abuse, or medical problems and who had become somewhat financially dependent on the elder. 66% of abuse is recurrent. Elder abuse is intimately tied to the family.

Table 6–1 *continued*

Study, Date, and Location	Type of Research	Purpose(s)	Research Techniques	Findings
				Psychological abuse was most common, with physical abuse and general neglect equally reported. Material abuse reported the least.
Department of Aging (1982) Pennsylvania	Descriptive survey	Collect information on elder abuse: (1) occupation of those reporting abuse; (2) characteristics of the abused elder and the abuser; (3) agency's response to the abuse report; (4) the nature of the abuse incidence.	Mailed questionnaire to agencies and individuals providing service to elders. Given to all representatives of small agency or group. Used random selection with large agencies or groups (example—police). One follow-up.	Elder abuse is occurring at a significant rate in Penn. Abusers: 52% were male, 58% married, 67% were under stress (drug, alcohol, financial or medical problem), and 75% were relatives of the abused. In 61% of cases the abused elder was a source of stress. Abused: 76% were female, most were 70 years of age or older, 88% were physically disabled, 71% had a mental disability, and 69% lived with the abuser. APS workers, homemakers, home health aids, and social workers noted abuse most often. Most cases of abuse were repetitive (85%). In 90% of cases, the victim required either medical treatment or protective services. Physical abuse was involved in 44% of the cases, psychological abuse 38%, material abuse 13% and violation of rights 4%. Agency responses to reported cases were diverse.
Sengstock & Liang (1982) Detroit, Michigan	Descriptive survey, multistage.	Five research questions re (1) the profile of abused, abusers and family situa-	Mailed questionnaire to agencies, then interviews of personnel, followed by inter-	Abused: 33% were 80 years of age or older, 74% were female, with physical and emotional impairment 22%, with incomes of $10,000 or less (80%). Abusers: 49% were children of the victim (sons 26% & daughters 23%).

136

Study	Design	Purpose	Method	Findings
		tions; (2) dynamics of elder abuse; (3) methods of identification; (4) treatment and prevention.	ventions with 20 abused elders. Last, interviews with 50 non-abused elders.	Psychological abuse occurred most often (82%), financial 55%, physical 43%.
Levenberg et al. (1983) West Virginia	Exploratory descriptive survey	Determine the extent and nature of abuse, and provide recommendations for elder abuse prevention and protection in West Virginia.	Mailed questionnaire to individuals or agencies thought to be involved with problem of elder abuse in the state of West Virginia.	The most frequently reported cause of elder abuse was "frustration of the caregiver due to change in lifestyle and burden of the elder" accounting for 34% of the open-ended responses. Neglect was the most frequently reported type of abuse, followed by mental cruelty, economic abuse, medication abuse, and physical abuse. The most common relationship of the abuser to the victim was child (son or daughter), followed by spouse and other relatives. Improving services included education of the public and professionals regarding the incidence of abuse; more "explicitly defined" law to protect both the elderly and the professional; more staff; better follow-up; and better interagency coordination. Those who were most at risk for elder abuse were females between ages of 60 and 75.
Gioglio and Blakemore (1983) New Jersey	Exploratory survey.	Study the nature of elder abuse in New Jersey.	Personal interview of elders with a questionnaire: 4 vignettes and an attitude	Financial abuse: occurred in 50% of all cases cited and occurred with other forms of abuse. Physical abuse: least reported form of mistreatment. 74% of elders reporting abuse had first-hand knowledge of it.

Table 6–1 *continued*

Study, Date, and Location	Type of Research	Purpose(s)	Research Techniques	Findings
			scale. Mailed questionnaire to resistive respondents. Sample of persons 65 years of age and older living in the community (noninstitutionalized). Abused's initials or name requested to control duplication of citings. Questionnaire pretested with elders and professionals.	Abused: 70% were female, 56% were 75 years of age or older, 87% reported in poor general health, 47.8% had greatly limited activity, 35% lived with their abuser, and 60.9% of victims did not seek help. 70% of those financially abused did not live with their abuser. Abusers: 72% were males, with ages evenly divided from 16–69 years, 61% were in victim's immediate family, and 13% in extended family. 25% of cases reported as involving more than one type of abuse. Patterns: • financial abuse—victim was older female, unmarried, with fair to poor health. • psychological abuse—victim was under 75, female, widowed, with fair to poor health but not limited by health status. • physical abuse—victim was an older female, in fair to poor health, greatly limited in health status.
Phillips (1983) Arizona	Ex post facto correlational descriptive survey.	To test two hypotheses which predicted the nature of differences between the two groups and four hypotheses which predicted the	Subjects referred from active caseloads of public health nurses working in one public health and two home health agencies.	The significant differences between the good relationship and abusive/neglectful relationship groups included: • Lower expectations among the abused subjects for their caregivers. • Lower perceptions among the abused subjects of their caregiver's actual behavior. • The abused group had significantly fewer friends

	Type	Purpose / Sample	Methods	Findings
(continued)			magnitude and direction of theoretically deduced causal relationships. Elders separated into abused and nonabused groups and compared. Elders interviewed in own home by one of three trained data collectors with a blind interview technique. 90% interrater and intercoder reliability rates on instruments used. Multiple regression analysis used.	who call on the phone, people who correspond and people to call in times of trouble. • More depression in the abused group. None of the six hypotheses were supported—no support for previous research findings of dependency, social networks, stress, etc.
Gray Panthers of Austin, Texas (1983)	Exploratory descriptive statewide survey.	To determine the extent, location, kinds, frequency, and underlying factors of elder abuse. Questionnaire mailed to agencies and individuals whose practice involves elderly throughout Texas. Sample of a random number of each category of agencies and provider.		Hospital social workers and health care nurses comprised the highest return rates. Encountered elder abuse in their work—61.9% yes, 29.6% no, 8% unsure. Hospital social workers and home health services reported the greatest percentage. Elder abuse occurred in all areas of Texas. Percentage of types of abuse encountered by respondents—self-neglect 82%, exploitation 75%, verbal/emotional abuse 72%, physical abuse 62%, and actual neglect 50%. Most frequent cause of abuse was reported as long-

Table 6–1 *continued*

Study, Date, and Location	Type of Research	Purpose(s)	Research Techniques	Findings
			Respondents given definitions of types of abuse to guide them in answering questionnaire.	term environmental conditions, such as crowded living quarters, extreme poverty, and marital conflict. Respondents with consistent, regular contact with the elderly recognized more abuse than providers without consistent contact. Recommendations—a centralized, structured system for case finding and reporting, public and professional education on elder abuse, and intensive family counseling for elder care.
Steinmetz (1983) Delaware	Exploratory descriptive survey.	To ascertain the stresses, conflicts, abuse and maltreatment experienced in families who cared for an elderly parent.	Structured format, taped interviews of volunteer adult children presently caring for elderly parent or had done so within past three years. Volunteers screened by telephone to see if met criteria. Interview questions on three topics. Tasks performed for elders, caretaker stress expe-	Majority of caregivers (90%) and of vulnerable elderly (more than 82%) were women. Caregivers were often elderly (60 or older) themselves and caring for a still older dependent. Double direction violence found in these generationally inversed families—slapped, hit with object, or shook elder by adult child caregiver once, adult child caregiver by elder 18%. Violence by elders on their adult children has remained hidden. Caregivers were often caught in the middle between two or more generations. Caregiving tasks—housekeeping tasks done for elder most (for 90% of elders) frequently, with social/emotional task second (66%) in frequency, help in mental health tasks (57%), financial management and personal health care (both over 50%) and mobility tasks (43%).

rienced from these tasks, how often caretaker and elder used certain techniques to resolve problems or carry out their wishes.

Caretaker stress from tasks—mental health dependency tasks produced the greatest stress, social/emotional dependency tasks (2nd most frequently performed) also produced an extremely high degree of stress, instrumental/housekeeping tasks produced little stress. Methods of resolving conflicts: Technique most frequently used by elders was to pout or withdraw (61%), followed by imposing guilt (53%), manipulation (43%), crying (37%) and using their disability to gain sympathy (33%), i.e. 71% used some form of psychological manipulation to impose guilt or sympathy. Screaming also frequently used by adult children (40%) and elder parent (36%).

85% of adult children reported talking out problems, many with a raised voice or loud tone; they also sought advice of a third party (65%), considered alternate housing (20%) and threatened to send elder to a nursing home (7%).

Abusive and neglectful methods of control often became the method of last resort. About 10% of elderly had experienced one or more acts of violence or a threat by their adult child while 18% of elders slapped, hit with an object, or threw something at their adult child.

Data suggest services most likely to reduce stress and relieve burden faced by generationally inversed families would be those such as friendly visiters, day care and respite care, elder "sitters," and support groups for adult children who are doing elder care.

Table 6–1 *continued*

Study, Date, and Location	Type of Research	Purpose(s)	Research Techniques	Findings
Pratt, Koval & Lloyd (1983) Oregon	Exploratory descriptive survey.	To assess service providers' and physicians' intervention responses to hypoethical cases of elder abuse	Mailed questionnaires in which participants responded to vignettes which described four levels of abuse (verbal abuse, pushing, hitting and severe beating) and gave data on own experience with abuse cases in last year.	Severe abuse—referral, especially to police and safe housing and personal interventions and counseling referrals. Physicians more likely to intervene personally or recommend counseling, while social workers more likely to refer to another agency. Supervisors and physicians almost twice as likely to report recent experience with elder abuse. Most common type of abuse reported was verbal abuse; physicians reported more experience with physical abuse. The victim's age did not significantly affect the chosen interventions, but the abuser's relationship to the victim did.
Hall & Andrew (1984) San Antonio, Texas	Exploratory descriptive survey.	Provide more systematic information on a statewide basis from validated maltreatment cases.	Retrospective content analysis of case records.	Neglect and self-neglect were common forms of elder mistreatment. The typical elders were females age 70 or older; 65% were Anglo, and 35% were black. 44% of maltreatment was reported by immediate and extended family members of Mexican Americans, while third parties report it for black and Anglos. Exploitation is more common among Mexican-Americans and Anglo females.

				33% of mistreated elders denied a problem existed of the 67% acknowledging a problem, 32% were reluctant to accept services and 18% refused services. Multiple maltreatment was more common for old-old women and self-neglect was more common for men.
Andrew & Hall (1984) San Antonio, Texas	Exploratory descriptive case analysis.	Examine alcohol use in elder mistreatment situations. Identify emerging characteristics of the elder, types of maltreatment, interventions and outcomes.	Retrospective content analysis of case records indicating elder mistreatment and alcohol use.	Alcohol use by elder ($N = 25$): Elder profile—Anglo (72%), widowed (56%), female (60%), live alone (44%), in communities of 25,000 or less (40%) or rural areas (32%), low income without bank accounts, confusion, and recent memory deficit (63%), and no contact with others (50%). Medical abuse and self-neglect were main forms of mistreatment. 64% of elders did not have a designated caregiver. Alcohol use by others ($N = 41$): Elder profile—Anglo (67%), widowed (50%), female (82%), living with relatives (52%), in communities of 25–100,000, 74–85 year old (46%), confused (51%), and living in dirty and cluttered homes (46%). Multiple mistreatment (46%), exploitation (43%), and physical abuse (27%) were the main forms of mistreatment. Alcohol use by both the elder and others ($N = 10$): Elder profile—black (70%), male (60%), living with relatives (70%), in rural areas (70%), without telephones (90%), or bank accounts (60%), and with recent memory deficits (56%). Medical abuse, self-neglect, neglect, and material neglect/abuse were the major problem areas.

Table 6–1 *continued*

Study, Date, and Location	Type of Research	Purpose(s)	Research Techniques	Findings
Rounds (1984) Austin, Texas	Descriptive survey.	To investigate the internal and external environments in which elder abuse occurs. Look at the physical, psychological and financial variables in the abuse situation.	Retrospective case review by use of a structured schedule (Elder Abuse Report form).	Neglect and self-neglect were the most frequently occurring forms of mistreatment and violation of rights the least common. The descriptive characteristics of the abusers were inconsistent, although most were relatives and had no form of support. The elderly victims were typically widowed females age 70–79 years. Ethnicity was equally divided between blacks and whites. Most lived alone, had chronic illnesses and low income. The mistreatment was typically reported by a neighbor.
O'Brien, Hudson and Johnson (1984) North Carolina and Michigan	Exploratory descriptive survey.	Experience, knowledge, identification, and intervention of elder abuse by primary care physicians and nurse practitioners.	Mailed questionnaire with two follow-ups.	Preliminary: Fifty-one percent of primary care physicians and nurse practitioners have seen a case of elder abuse. Some 84% of the respondents considered detection difficult. Only 5% of respondents used a standard protocol in detection and among them no respondent reported having a written instrument. Most respondents were not familiar with state legislation on reporting of cases. Approximately 50% did not know whether their community had any programs which especially addressed elder abuse. Some 92% reported that they probed for reasons for the abuse. 80% discussed the abuse with the abused and 57% discussed the abuse with the abuser.

Study	Design	Purpose	Method	Findings
				54 percent of health care providers reported that they went beyond medical treatment in their assistance in elder abuse cases and most families were willing to accept assistance.
Dozier (1984) Georgia	Prospective field test of assessment instrument on 52 clients.	Study: To design an assessment tool that was sensitive enough to distinguish abused, neglected from non-abused, nonneglected elderly. To train APS workers of the Dept. of Family & Children Services in implementing the tool. To evaluate the two processes. To determine the relevance, extent and implication of elder neglect and abuse in the Atlanta region. Tool: To assess the demographic, psychological & social circumstances of elderly clients.	Assessment tool & evaluation form sent to county supervisors. In each unit every case worker was assigned at least one case of referred elder neglect and abuse. Assessment tool used in investigation of referred cases.	Self-neglect, especially among the elderly living alone, is a major problem. Over 46% of the cases listed it as the primary problem. Self-referral is very rare in cases of elder neglect and abuse; in only 4 of 52 cases was the victim the person making the referral. Referrals came from many different sources, but few were from physicians or clergy. Increase in single-person household, especially among the elderly, and a related lack of needed health care was one of the largest concerns of clients. Many of the elderly were fearful of change; services were refused in 23% of the 52 cases. More than 90% of the clients had one or more chronic mental or physical conditions, and needed help in transportation, shopping and cooking. Where caregiver abuse was alleged, the most frequent abuser was a relative; exploitation was a very common type of abuse by the caregiver. Some abusers were noncaregiver relatives. Some of the most important stressers were alcohol abuse (41%) and mental illness (26%) found among both the abusers and their victims. Greatest finding—was the need for further and more extensive study of elder neglect and abuse. Case workers felt the tool was too long, its questions too intensive and that its use hampered the client-worker relationship.

Table 6–1 *continued*

Study, Date, and Location	Type of Research	Purpose(s)	Research Techniques	Findings
Elderly Abuse Task Force (1984) Toledo, Ohio	Exploratory survey.	Research incidence of elderly abuse in Lucas County. Determine present response of professionals. Determine response of community and knowledge of resource(s).	Professional survey: Mailed questionnaire to preselected group of professionals mandated by law to report elderly abuse. Community Survey: Telephone interviews of Toledo area residents. Respondents asked to define elder abuse, and assessed their knowledge of instances of abuse, abusers, sources of help, familiarity with relevant agencies and the mandatory reporting law.	Professional Survey: Over 70% of victims in each category were female. Neglect is main problem (55%). Abuse seen by 48% of professionals. Exploitation seen by 38% of professionals. Females are predominant victims (70% +). Person causing elder neglect and abuse is usually related to victim. Victim is usually responsible for own neglect. If residence status is known, victim usually lives alone. Major motivation of abusers were stress and financial problems. 57% of respondents referred to an appropriate agency. A significant number of respondents did not know what action resulted from referral. Community Survey: 12% reported knowing of case of elder neglect and abuse. In 64% of the cases help was sought. 18% reported knowing of case of exploitation. Person exploiting was usually a relative.

146

| Giordano & Giordano (1984) Florida | Exploratory descriptive case analysis. | Determine specific patterns of individual and family circumstances which tended to be present in substantiated cases of physical, psychological, financial, and multiple abuse and neglect. Develop a profile of the abused elder. | Retrospective review of cases reported to Adult Service units in six Fla. counties between Jan. 1976 and Jan. 1982. Sample divided into abused (N = 600) and non-abused (N = 150) categories. Structured schedule and cross-validation of data used. | Distinct profile found for each type of mistreatment. Physical: Abused—66–83 years old, white, and female, with income ≤ $7,000/year and lives with abuser. Abuser—white, married male with income ≤ $7,000/year. Psychological: abused—66–83 years old, white, female, with income ≤ $7,000/year and lives with abuser. Abuser—white, married male with income ≤ $7,000/year. Neglect: victim—72–89 years old, white female with income ≤ $7,000/year and lives with abuser. Perpetrator—white male or female. Financial exploitation: victim—72–89 years old, white widower with income ≤ $7,000/year and lives with abuser. Abuser—white male or female. Multiple Abuse: abused—66–83 years old, white female with income ≤ $7,000/year and lives with abuser. Abuser—white male or female with income ≤ $7,000 & lives with abuser. Spouse abuse was a dominant variable in abuse. |
| Pillemer (1985) New York, Rhode Island, Massachusetts | Case-control study, part of ongoing research project (See Wolf 1982). | Test hypothesis that: (1) Physically abused older persons will be more socially isolated than members of a matched control group. (2) The increased dependency of an older | Researcher did personal interviews with the abused and non-abused elders using open-ended questions and a tape recorder. Control group matched by sex | Hypothesis was supported—abused elders tended to have fewer social contacts and to be less satisfied with these contacts. The abused elders were more likely to report that their relationship with the abuser had had a negative impact on their contacts with others. The elder found the erratic and antisocial behavior of the abuser to be threatening. Elderly victims were not likely to be more dependent, but were instead more likely to be supporting the |

Table 6–1 *continued*

Study, Date, and Location	Type of Research	Purpose(s)	Research Techniques	Findings
		person causes stress for relatives who then respond with physical violence. (3) The increased dependency of the abusive relative leads to maltreatment.	and living arrangements.	dependent abuser. There is a strong association between dependency of the perpetrator and physical abuse. The typical abused elder was an older woman supporting a dependent child or a disabled spouse. The abused elders were no more likely to be seriously ill than the controls. The same was true for recent hospitalizations and functional vulnerability. The control group elders were significantly more likely to be dependent than the abused elders. Less than 36% of the abusers were financially independent of their victims. Physically abused elders are more likely to be depended upon than to be dependent. The familial relationship and few options were reasons given for staying in the abusive relationship.
Phillips & Rempusheski (1985) Arizona	Exploratory survey.	To formulate a conceptual model to describe the decision-making processes that health care providers use to identify and intervene in poor quality elder-caregiver relationships.	Grounded theory technique. Personal interviews using a tape recorder and open-ended questions.	These health care providers assessed the quality of the care-giving situations and not the quality of the elder/caregiver relationships when making decisions about abuse and neglect. A four-stage model of decision making was formulated from the data. The association between the intervention decision and the diagnostic decision was surprisingly low. The type and strength of intervention strategy chosen often did not match the diagnostic decision.

148

References for Table 6-1

Andrew, S. R., and Hall, P. A. 1984. "Alcohol Use and Elder Mistreatment: An Exploratory Study." Unpublished manuscript, San Antonio, Texas.

Beachler, M. A. 1979. "Mistreatment of Elderly Persons in the Domestic Setting." Unpublished manuscript, Brasoria County, Texas.

Block, M. R., and Sinnott, J. D., eds., 1979. "The Battered Elder Syndrome: An Exploratory Study." College Park: University of Maryland, Center for Aging.

Boydston, L. S., and McNairn, J. A. 1981. "Elder Abuse by Adult Caretakers: An Exploratory Study." In *Physical and Financial Abuse of the Elderly*. Pub. No. 97–297, U.S. House of Representatives, Select Committee on Aging, San Francisco.

Chen, P.N.; Bell, S. Dolinsky, D. Doyle, J.; and Dunn, M. 1981. "Elderly Abuse in Domestic Settings: A Pilot Study." *Journal of Gerontological Social Work*, (4): 3–17.

Crouse, J. S.; Cobb, D. C.; Harris, B. B.; Kopecky, F. J.; and Poertner, J. 1981. "Abuse and Neglect of the Elderly in Illinois: Incidence and Characteristics, Legislation and Policy Recommendations." Unpublished manuscript, State of Illinois, Department of Aging.

Douglass, R. L.; Hickey, T.; and Noel, C. 1980. "A Study of Maltreatment of the Elderly and Other Vulnerable Adults." Unpublished manuscript, University of Michigan.

Dozier, C. 1984. "Report of the Elder Abuse and Neglect Assessment Instrument Field Test." Atlanta, Georgia: The Atlanta Regional Commission.

Elderly Abuse Task Force. 1984. "Elderly Abuse in the Toledo Area." Unpublished manuscript, Toledo, Ohio.

Gioglio, G. R., and Blakemore, P. 1983. "Elder Abuse in New Jersey: The Knowledge and Experience of Abuse Among Older New Jerseyans." Trenton: New Jersey Department of Human Services.

Giordano, N. H., and Giordano, J. A. 1984. "Individual and Family Correlates of Elder Abuse." Unpublished manuscript, Bradenton, Florida.

Gray Panthers of Austin. 1983. "A Survey of Abuse in the Elderly in Texas." Unpublished manuscript, Austin, Texas.

Hageboeck, J., and Brandt, K. 1981. "Characteristics of Elderly Abuse." Unpublished manuscript, Scott County, Iowa.

Hall, P. A., and Andrew, S. R. 1984. "Minority Elder Maltreatment: Ethnicity, Gender, Age, and Poverty." Unpublished manuscript, San Antonio, Texas.

Lau, E., and Kosberg, J. I. 1979. "Abuse of the Elderly by Informal Care Providers." *Aging*, Sept.-Oct.: 11–15.

Levenberg, J.; Milan, J.; Dolan, M.; and Carpenter, P. 1983. "Elder Abuse in West Virginia: Extent and Nature of the Problem." In *Elder Abuse in West Virginia: A Policy Analysis of System Response*, ed. Leroy G. Shultz. Morgantown: West Virginia University.

McLaughlin, J. S.; Nickell, J. P.; and Gill, L. 1980. "An Epidemiological Investigation of Elderly Abuse in Southern Maine and New Hampshire." In *Elder Abuse*, Pub. No. 68–463, U.S. House of Representatives, Select Committee on Aging.

O'Brien, J. G.; Hudson, M. F.; and Johnson, T. F. 1984. "Health Care Provider Survey on Elder Abuse." Unpublished manuscript, East Lansing, Michigan.

O'Malley, H.; Segars, H.; Perez, R.; Mitchell, V.; and Knuepfel, G. 1979. "Elder Abuse in Massachusetts: A Survey of Professionals and Paraprofessionals." Boston: Legal Research and Services for the Elderly.

Pennsylvania Department of Aging, Bureau of Advocacy. 1982. "Elder Abuse in Pennsylvania."

Pepper, C., and Oakar, M. R. 1981. "Elder Abuse: An Examination of a Hidden Problem." Pub. No. 97–277, U.S. House of Representatives, Select Committee on Aging.

Phillips, L. R. 1983. "Abuse and Neglect of the Frail Elderly at Home: An Exploration of Theoretical Relationships." *Journal of Advanced Nursing* 8: 379–92.

Phillips, L. R., and Rempusheski, V. F. 1985. "A Decision-Making Model for Diagnosing and Intervening in Elder Abuse and Neglect." *Nursing Research,* 34 (3): 134–39.

Pillemer, K. A. 1985. "Domestic Violence Against the Elderly: A Case-Control Study." Ph.D. diss., Brandeis University, Waltham, Massachusetts.

Pratt, C. C.; Koval, J.; and Lloyd, S. 1983. "Service Workers: Responses to Abuse of the Elderly." *Social Casework,* March: 142–53.

Rounds, L. R. 1984. "A Study of Selected Environmental Variables Associated with Non-Institutional Settings Where There Is Abuse or Neglect of the Elderly." Ph.D. diss., University of Texas at Austin.

Sengstock, M., and Liang, J. 1982. "Identifying and Characterizing Elder Abuse." Unpublished manuscript, Wayne State University, Institute of Gerontology, Detroit.

Steinmetz, S. K. 1983. "Dependency, Stress, and Violence Between Middle-Aged Caregivers and Their Elderly Parents." In *Abuse and Maltreatment of the Elderly,* ed. J. L. Kosberg. Littleton, Mass.: John Wright - PSG, Inc.

Wolf, R. S.; Strugnell, C. P.; and Godkin, M. A. 1982. "Preliminary Findings from Three Model Projects on Elderly Abuse." Worcester: University of Massachusetts Medical Center, Center on Aging.

(Text continued from page 128.)

These pioneering studies can now provide a springboard for future research efforts. Many key questions still need to be answered, including the following:

1. What factors differentiate neglectful or abusive families from nonneglectful and nonabusive ones?
2. What factors distinguish neglected or abused elders from elders who are not mistreated?
3. What are the circumstances in family settings that generate elder neglect and abuse?
4. How can families at risk for elder neglect and abuse be identified?
5. How can families be helped to prevent or control neglectful and abusive situations effectively?

In general, existing studies have not been able to determine the causes of elder neglect and abuse. Thus, the findings document the existence and forms of mistreatment, but they do not provide clear or consistent information on the antecedents, causes, or consequences of such mistreatment or on the characteristics of the abuser or abused. For example, a recurrent finding has been that both the abused elder and the abusive caregiver experienced excessive stress. But it is not yet clear whether stress is an antecedent or a consequence of mistreatment. The studies only indicate that stress is linked with neglect and abuse in some manner. However, stress could easily mask the discovery of other significant contributing or causative factors. Stress does seem to be an intensifier of potential mistreatment, but it is not a clear predictor, since most families providing elder care experience stress and yet do not mistreat their elders. Therefore, researchers need to identify how abusive (and neglectful) families and abused (and neglected) elders differ from nonabusive families and nonabused elders with regard to stressors and coping skills.

Many of the earliest researchers identified functional disability, impairment, or dependence as common correlates or implied antecedents of elder mistreatment.[9] Some researchers found that most abused elders were functionally impaired (physically or mentally) 75-year-old and older women who could not fully care for themselves.[10] The O'Malley study found that significant disability and being female cut across all subcategories of age and appeared to be present in a much higher percentage of the abused population than of the elder population as a whole.[11] Yet Phillips's study does not support these correlations,[12] and Pillemer found that a significant percentage of abusers were dependent on the elders and the victims were no more likely to be seriously ill than the nonabused control group elders.[13] Thus, the consistency of these antecedents has not yet been established.

Not much research has focused on the consequences of elder

mistreatment, except for descriptions of physical injuries, monetary losses, and the like, which are typically mentioned only as examples within extrinsic definitions. Only Phillips has addressed this issue.[14] She found that abused elders were more depressed and had fewer friends in their support systems than their non-abused counterparts, but it is not clear whether the depression and reduced support system are antecedents or consequences of the mistreatment. It is quite likely that many effects of elder mistreatment are as yet unrecognized or undiscovered. This area seems to be a fertile ground for future research.

Many of the early studies attempted to discover the characteristics of the typical abuser and abused elder. However, the findings are equivocal and inconsistent. Some studies found that the typical abuser was a woman;[15] others found that the abusers tended to be male.[16] The only consistency was that the abuser was typically a relative of the abused and usually was also the caregiver.[17] Other characteristics of the abuser that were addressed were too diffuse from study to study to form any helpful pattern; age, sex, race, alcoholism, mental illness, retardation, resentment of caregiver role, and physical illness were among these characteristics. These problems make it impossible to prepare a profile of the typical abused elder, especially in light of the fact that the characteristics identified by early researchers were rarely compared with the characteristics prevalent in the general older adult population.

Incidence Estimates

Although various studies have held that the percentage of elders who are abused ranges between 1 and 10 percent, there are as yet no accurate statistics because of (1) a lack of uniformity in state reporting laws and record keeping and (2) definitional, sampling, and methodological differences in current research. The House Select Committee on Aging estimates that 1 million, or 4 percent, of our older population are abused by relatives, but only one of every six cases of elder abuse comes to the attention of the authorities;[18] thus the committee views current estimates as the tip of the iceberg. Block and Sinnott also estimate 1 million cases of elder abuse and believe it is probably less frequent than spouse abuse but at least as frequent as child abuse.[19] Crouse et al. estimate a 4 percent abuse rate for Illinois elders.[20] Steinmetz estimates that 10 percent of the U.S. older adult population (2.5 million) are abused.[21] According to Lau and Kosberg, 9.6 percent of all older adult clients seen at their agency in one year had been abused.[22] Gioglio and Blakemore, however, report a much lower figure: Approximately 1 percent of the respondents in their random sample survey reported some form of abuse.[23] Elder neglect estimates exceed those for elder abuse. The incidence and prevalence of elder mistreatment still need to be better documented. In particular, the methodological weaknesses in many of these studies, which have hindered the generalizability of any of the incidence figures, must be overcome.

Identification

Definitions

Basic questions are still unanswered regarding what is, and is not, elder neglect or abuse. Several of the studies provided extrinsic definitions (typologies) without formulating an intrinsic definition (conceptualization). Thus, they begin with illustrations of the concept without having first defined it. The assumption seems to be that the intrinsic meanings of elder neglect and abuse are understood. However, this creates a tautology: Elder neglect and abuse are often lumped together and defined as elder neglect and abuse. In addition, studies that begin without an intrinsic definition provide no information on which to evaluate the characteristic behaviors. For example, is strapping an elder to a chair abusive? What about the family who has always had unhygienic personal habits? Can we say that they are neglectful toward the older member if they apply the same standards to themselves? Other studies reported in Table 6–1 provide some kind of intrinsic definition. However, these definitions often suffer from vagueness of meaning, circularity, or clarity obscured by mixing intrinsic and extrinsic components in the same definition.

O'Malley et al. define elder abuse as "the willfull infliction of physical pain, injury or debilitating mental anguish, unreasonable confinement or deprivation by a caretaker of services which are necessary to the maintenance of mental and physical health."[24] This definition has been utilized by four other researchers. However, the O'Malley et al. definition narrowly circumscribes elder abuse. It applies the label of abuse only when it is clear that the caregiver intended to do harm. It also assumes that the older person is dependent—an assumption that effectively excludes independent elderly who may also fall victim to abuse.

Recently, O'Malley et al. altered their intrinsic definition, changing "willful infliction" to "active intervention," and the

"maintenance of mental and physical health" to "unmet needs";
they also simplified the kinds of abuse conditions to "physical,
psychological or financial injury" and developed a new definition
for neglect: "the failure of a caretaker to intervene to resolve a
significant need despite awareness of available resources."[25] In
sum, O'Malley et al. now distinguish abuse from neglect on the
basis of intent. Abuse seems to be an act of commission and neglect
an act of omission. The incorporation by O'Malley et al. of the
concepts of "unmet needs" and "significant needs" helps to clarify
what the intrinsic definition of elder neglect and abuse should
contain.

In contrast to the relative lack of intrinsic definitions, most of the
studies in Table 6–1 present some kind of extrinsic behavioral
typology, which may be applied to the neglect and abuse situation.
The extrinsic categories of neglect/abuse in the studies range from
2 to 6, with most also including illustrations for each category.
Physical and psychological mistreatment are consistently included,
while separate classifications of neglect (active and passive), financial or material abuse, self-neglect, violation of rights, sexual
abuse, and medical abuse vary from study to study. On the surface,
these categories appear to be easily synthesized. However, a closer
look reveals that the categories are not illustrated in the same way.
Thus, some researchers refer to "withholding of personal care" as
psychological neglect; others call it physical abuse or active neglect.[26]

This lack of uniformity in the application of the extrinsic behavioral categories may also explain why there are contradictions in
the incidence of types of abuse. Some researchers found physical
abuse to be the most common form;[27] others found psychological
abuse to be the most frequently identified type.[28] Crouse et al. and
Douglass et al. claimed passive neglect to be the most common
form, and Gioglio and Blakemore stated that financial abuse was
most frequently reported in their study.[29] Later studies found self-
neglect to be most prevalent.[30] Of course, such differing results
could be accounted for by variations in sampling techniques and
other discrepancies in research design. However, when typologies
are defined differently, this particularization constitutes a sufficient
cause of incongruity among the findings of research studies.

Detection

A major part of identification is detection. This refers to the
method used by professionals to determine whether older persons
have been mistreated. The method may be an unwritten individual

assessment, a list of guidelines, or a more formal systematic detection protocol. Many factors complicate detection. Signs of physical, psychological, and material abuse can readily be attributed to normative changes that result from aging, and challenging this attribution can be very difficult.[31] For example, visual, hearing, and circulatory impairments and changes in the skin, soft tissue, blood vessels, and bones that occur with aging can result in bruises and pathological fractures with everyday living. Thus, proving that the elder was slapped, pushed, or hit can be difficult. Patterns of injuries must be considered as well. Detection is also complicated by the fact that psychological abuse can cause confusion and a failure to thrive syndrome, but so can dementia, delirium, drugs, and chronic illness; and loss of money or possessions can occur due to early dementia, stress on the elder, or coercion by caregivers.

Reluctance of criminal justice agencies to incorporate elder abuse as a distinct category of mistreatment reduces the available data and thus awareness of the problem.[32] Lack of awareness of elder abuse and its signs and symptoms decreases the frequency of recognition,[33] as does the lack of legislation in some states to protect the frail older adult.[34] Further, the public belief that the family protects its loved ones and does not mistreat them tends to hamper recognition. Investigators often hesitate to depend on second-hand data about elder mistreatment and are uncomfortable with the lack of guidelines for what constitutes sufficient evidence.[35]

Based on research reports, standardized methods of detection used by professional respondents are generally either nonexistent or not consistent from case to case. When Wolf et al., O'Brien et al., and Levenberg et al. inquired whether professionals had written "procedures" or "protocols" for detection, less than a third in each study said that they had.[36] This observation, coupled with an average response rate of 40 percent from those studies reporting detection protocol information, really does not provide substantial data on which to base definitive conclusions about elder abuse and neglect.

A number of writers in the general elder mistreatment literature have proposed methods of detection ranging from formal protocols to guidelines.[37] Some of these methods are applicable only in hospitals, while others can be used in any setting. Most are multidimensional assessment tools that elicit data on both the elder and the caregiver, pointing to the fact that family dynamics are a key factor in neglect and abuse. Now that a number of tools are available, two subsequent steps need to occur. First, any effective assessment tool needs to be based on a definition about which there is consensus. Second, the tool's validity and reliability need to be documented.

Reporting

Detection is closely intertwined with reporting. Reporting may precede or follow detection by professionals, since undetected abuse can be reported by lay persons involved in the abuse situation or acknowledged following detection. When reporting does not occur, detection is often impeded. The assumption has been that professionals are more likely to become involved in severe abuse cases and in cases where families use health care services, thus distorting the profile of the nature and extent of elder mistreatment. Recognizing the limitation of using only professionals to identify elder neglect and abuse, Block and Sinnott, Gioglio and Blakemore, Phillips, Sengstock and Liang, Steinmetz, and Pillemer decided to interview caregivers or elders residing in the community. Some of their subjects included respondents from abusive and nonabusive families. Their objective was to gain primary data on the dynamics of elder neglect and abuse. The general findings from both the professional and community respondent surveys seem to be similar.[38]

The literature is consistent about self-reporting of elder neglect and abuse. The abused elder characteristically tends to deny (consciously or unconsciously) that abuse has taken place, or refuses to report it for a number of reasons, including (1) fear of retaliation, abandonment, or being removed from the home or family setting; (2) belief that the abuse was deserved; (3) sense that there is nowhere else to go or that nothing can be done to help; or (4) shame in admitting such treatment by one's own children. For example, Beck and Ferguson observe that elders wish to protect their image as good parents.[39] If their children have abused them, then, as some elders believe, it must have been their own fault.

There is also the elders' fear of institutionalization; many would rather be at home and abused than in a nursing home. Indeed, most elders choose to stay in the abusive situation rather than face an unknown situation.[40] Steinmetz believes abused elders are in a double bind since they also feel dependent on the abuser for survival or have feelings of love and kinship for him or her.[41]

The older adult may be unable to recognize or report neglect or abuse because of severe illness, depression, immobility, or dementia. Further, the myth of "senility" may cause older adults to hesitate to report abuse and risk having their credibility questioned when they do try to report it. In either instance, elders' fear of retaliation may be reinforced.[42] The privacy and intimacy norms of the family result in members' reticence to share information about abuse,[43] and strangers hesitate to violate these norms in pursuit of evidence. Relatives, neighbors, and friends are also reluctant to report suspected abuse out of fear, anxiety about how to handle the problem, or ambivalence about becoming involved.[44]

There is evidence that victims and abusers rarely seek outside help. Neglect and abuse usually occur without witnesses, and in few cases is abuse reported to the authorities or help sought.[45] O'Malley et al. found that outside (third-party) observation tended to be the primary (70 percent) means of identifying cases of abuse.[46] Yet only one out of every five cases was reported to some authority by persons involved in the situation. In contrast, in Block and Sinnott's study, 95 percent of their 26 cited cases were reported to some authority, apparently unsuccessfully.[47] This raises the question of whether elder neglect and abuse are really under-reported by elders and other lay persons, or whether professionals are not recognizing clues or not reporting the abuse because of lack of witnesses, proof, legal guidelines, or interventions. It appears that accurate reporting of cases is mired in both personal and professional quandaries and is likely to remain that way until all parties can be convinced that reporting is protective rather than punitive.

In summary, the task of identification involves developing comprehensive working definitions of the various elder mistreatment concepts, a standardized procedure for detection, and a reporting system that is responsive to the maintenance of the quality of life for caregivers and elders instead of the label of family deviance and the prognosis of family deterioration. Effective identification is fundamental to successful treatment.

Treatment

Treatment is another dimension of elder neglect and abuse that needs to be explored. As there is limited information about what constitutes and causes elder neglect and abuse, it is difficult to talk about effective treatment. All researchers can do at this point is to propose possible courses of action. Treatment or intervention consists of protection and prevention. Several studies found that some kind of protective action has been taken in cases of elder neglect and abuse. In the Lau and Kosberg study, 46 percent of the 39 abused elders were institutionalized, 26 percent refused assis-

tance, and 28 percent accepted community agency assistance.[48]
O'Malley et al. reported that removal of the elder from the abusive
situation was the most typical protective intervention, although in-
home services and counseling of the elder and family were also
utilized.[49]

An interesting feature of these and other reports of direct action
is that such resolutions were not fully satisfactory. O'Malley et al.
reported that 45 percent of the cases were resolved, 36 percent
were not, and 20 percent were not determined.[50] Block and
Sinnott concluded that 95 percent of their cases were not satisfactorily resolved.[51] In the Chen et al. study, 70 percent of the 30
professional respondents sampled reported that intervention was
ineffective.[52] In the McLaughlin et al. study, professionals reported that 39 percent of the cases had been resolved, but an
almost equal number (36 percent) had not been resolved.[53] In the
three model projects studied by Wolf et al., some 45 percent of the
cases cited by professionals had not been resolved.[54] However, the
questions of what constitutes resolution and to whose satisfaction
have not been addressed.

The apparent lack of success in treating cases of elder neglect
and abuse is the result of a number of understandable circumstances. First, even when assistance is offered, the records show
that many elders or families refuse the help.[55] In the Boydston and
McNairn study and the O'Malley et al. study, 58 percent of the
victims and/or families refused help.[56] In the Wolf et al. study, the
refusal rate was 46 percent for victims and 32 percent for abusers.[57]
Second, if service is given, it is often inadequate or inappropriate
to the family's needs. Finally, follow-up of the abused and abuser is
not likely to be undertaken, especially in cases in which the older
person is institutionalized. The family tends to fade out of the
picture, with few supports made available to them.

At the community level, Crouse et al. have identified three
treatment models in cases of elder abuse: the child abuse model,
the domestic violence model, and the advocacy model.[58] In the
child abuse model, treatment is protective, reporting is mandatory, authority in problem resolution rests with the helping
agency, assistance is involuntary, and the victim loses his or her
rights to determine the action to be taken. The domestic violence
model is a short-term protective intervention strategy that focuses
on crisis resolution in the family setting by treating symptoms
rather than causes. Authority in the intervention is given to law
enforcement personnel—the police, the courts, and so forth.
Finally, the advocacy model is oriented toward both prevention

and protection. Treatment is not attached to any service delivery system, and authority rests with the older person. His or her rights are paramount. Both Crouse et al. and Gioglio and Blakemore observe that all three models can be useful in treating the older person and the family because there must be a balance between the elder's and the family's needs, and between the family's and the state's obligations to ensure the well-being of older citizens.[59]

Preventive treatment is becoming recognized as an important aspect of the problem-solving component of elder neglect and abuse. On a personal level, O'Malley et al. advise health care providers to use a family systems approach rather than the medical model in treating the patient.[60] This approach allows health care providers to observe family dynamics, and by consulting with the caregivers, as well as the patient, health care providers may be able to pick up early signs of stress and conflict.

Several studies recommend better training of professionals, with a strong educational component on the aging process and cues for detecting potential neglect and abuse.[61] Wolf et al. found that four out of five professionals believed that training needs exist.[62] Preventive care must also include education of families of older adults. It has been observed that older persons who are victims of Alzheimer's disease, Parkinson's disease, or stroke are at high risk for abuse because of the emotional toll they take from their caregivers.[63] Therefore, public education needs to include not only information, but also recommendations for community and family support services to alleviate feelings of loss and isolation.

Finally, Chen et al. and the Pennsylvania Department of Aging study encourage professional researchers to devote more effort to the problem of elder mistreatment.[64] Problem solving will, of course, be more effective with more information. Researchers should address the whole spectrum of elder mistreatment—physical, psychological, social, and legal issues. Practitioners in the social services are asked to develop more elder care support programs. The legal system is asked to evaluate the caregiver's and elder's human rights, and physical and mental health systems to provide more effective counseling and guidance to families who are facing elder care. When addressing the issue of long-term elder care, all of these human service providers need to confront realistically the family's and elder's needs, and the family's and society's responsibilities. Such an assessment is important, for if the family is incapable of elder care or is expected to carry too much of the burden without reasonable support and guidance, then the family will be set up for failure and guilt and the elders for mistreatment.

Summary and Conclusion

The studies just reviewed tell us that elder mistreatment occurs in various forms and is often inflicted on older women by relatives who are in a caregiving role. Yet, the studies' findings are insufficient to document the prevalence or to identify the causes. Given our concern about elders and their families, further research is needed—research that is guided by consideration of some priority issues.[65]

Three of these issues are particularly important. First, we need to define our terms. What is, and is not, elder abuse? Elder neglect? Exploitation? Self-abuse? Who should define these terms? Since one's professional orientation has a major impact on one's perceptions, will we see what we expect to see when confronted with a possible mistreatment situation? Is elder abuse a legal problem, a criminal act, or a symptom of our society's lack of preparation for care of our old? Research needs to address ways in which society can prepare itself to care for the increasing population of older citizens. Second, as researchers and practitioners, we need to be clear about our own motives and incentives for focusing on elder mistreatment. Are our interests self-serving or other-serving? How can we each most effectively help our elders and their families and thus prevent the occurrence of elder mistreatment? Third, we need public and professional education that provides accurate information about aging, elder care, community resources, and elder mistreatment and that counterbalances mass media's misleading accounts.

These issues all suggest appropriate future directions for research on elder mistreatment. The time has come not only for definitional consensus but also for building on our existing research base. Some of our most current research efforts are leading the way in that they are (1) identifying and focusing on distinct entities of elder mistreatment, such as physical abuse or self-neglect, rather than on the global concept of elder mistreatment and (2) testing specific hypotheses. Even if these appropriate research directions are followed, much more has to be done before we can begin to answer questions relevant to the previously mentioned family elder care and elder mistreatment issues. Some pertinent research questions include the following:

1. How are elder care decisions made and by whom?
2. What factors affect the making of such decisions so that the decision is appropriate to the individuals involved?
3. What are the effects of family elder care on the nuclear

family unit, the primary caregiver, and the care-receiving elder?

4. What are the antecedents and consequences of elder abuse? Elder neglect? Exploitation? Self-neglect? Multiple abuse and neglect?[66]

5. Are there differences in the abuser and/or victim in different types of elder mistreatment?[67]

6. What forms and type of support do elder caregiving families most need and want? What about care-receiving elders?

7. Are there ethnic/cultural[68] or socioeconomic differences with regard to elder mistreatment?

8. How do the various service and health care professionals respond to and intervene with families doing elder care and with abusive family situations?[69] Neglectful situations?

9. How can existing elder care resources be allocated to maximize effective utilization?

10. What barriers deter effective identification of and interventions for family elder care issues and elder mistreatment situations?

11. Do the dynamics and causes vary with different elder mistreatment situations? For example, how much of elder abuse is spouse abuse,[70] how much is child abuse revisited on the elder, and how much of it is a distinct phenomenon?

12. What are the most specific and sensitive signs and symptoms of the various forms of elder mistreatment?

13. What is the relationship between alcohol abuse and elder mistreatment?[71]

Obviously, many other such questions can be generated and addressed by research. It is important at this time to conduct research that will allow our society to respond to elder maltreatment in reasonable ways, so that societal costs will not exceed benefits. In particular, research on the causes of abuse and neglect rather than on the symptoms can assist in the identification of at-risk persons and in the development of preventive programs. Such programs may in the long run be more effective than laws that inappropriately decrease family privacy and control.

Endnotes

1. M. A. Straus, R. J. Gelles, and S. Steinmetz, *Behind Closed Doors: Violence in the American Family* (Garden City, N.Y.: Anchor Press/Doubleday, 1980); see also, Chapters 1 and 2 in this volume by Peter Stearns and Shulamit Reinharz.

2. R. L. Douglass, T. Hickey, and C. Noel, "A Study of Maltreatment of the

Elderly and Other Vulnerable Adults" (University of Michigan: Institute of Gerontology, 1980).

3. G. R. Burston, "Granny-Battering," *British Medical Journal*, September 6, 1975, p. 592.

4. S. K. Steinmetz, "The Politics of Aging, Battered Parents," *Society* (July-August 1978), pp. 54–55.

5. Douglass et al., "A Study of Maltreatment of the Elderly"; S. K. Steinmetz, "Elder Abuse," *Aging* (January-February 1981), pp. 6–10.

6. J. J. Callahan, "Elder Abuse Programming—Will It Help the Elderly?" *Urban Social Change Review* 15, no. 2 (Summer 1982), pp. 15–19; L. R. Faulkner, "Mandating the Reporting of Suspected Cases of Elder Abuse: An Inappropriate, Ineffective and Ageist Response of the Abuse of Older Adults," *Family Law Quarterly* 16, no. 1 (1982), pp. 69–91

7. E. Rathbone-McCuan and J. Hashami, "Isolated Elders: Health and Social Intervention" (Rockville, Md.: Aspen Systems Corporation, 1982); S. K. Steinmetz, "Dependency, Stress, and Violence Between Middle-aged Caregivers and Their Elderly Parents," in *Abuse and Maltreatment of the Elderly*, ed. J. L. Kosberg (Littleton, Mass.: John Wright-PSG, 1983).

8. Kosberg, *Abuse and Maltreatment of the Elderly*.

9. Douglass et al., "Maltreatment of the Elderly"; C. Dozier, "Report of the Elder House and Neglect Assessment Instrument Field Test" (Atlanta, Ga.: The Atlanta Regional Commission, 1984); H. O'Malley et al., "Elder Abuse in Massachusetts: A Survey of Professionals and Paraprofessionals" (Boston: Legal Research and Services for the Elderly, 1979); J. Stever and E. Austin, "Family Abuse of the Elderly," *Journal of the American Geriatrics Society* 28, no. 8 (1980), 372–76.

10. M. R. Block and J. D. Sinnott, "The Battered Elder Syndrome: An Exploratory Study" (College Park: University of Maryland, Center for Aging, 1979); G. R. Gioglio and P. Blakemore, "Elder Abuse in New Jersey: The Knowledge and Experience of Abuse Among Older New Jerseyans" (Trenton: New Jersey Department of Human Resources, 1983); P. Hall and S. R. Andrew, "Minority Elder Maltreatment: Ethnicity, Gender, Age and Poverty" (Unpublished manuscript, San Antonio, Texas, 1984); E. Lau and J. I. Kosberg, "Abuse of the Elderly by Informal Care Providers," *Aging* (September-October 1979), pp. 11–15; O'Malley et al., "Elder Abuse in Massachusetts"; L. R. Rounds, "A Study of Selected Environmental Variables Associated with Noninstitutional Settings Where There Is Abuse or Neglect of the Elderly" (Ph.D. diss., University of Texas at Austin, 1984); Stever and Austin, "Family Abuse of the Elderly"; R. S. Wolf, C. P. Strugnell, and M. A. Godkin, "Preliminary Findings from Three Model Projects on Elderly Abuse" (Worcester: University of Massachusetts Medical Center, Center on Aging, 1982).

11. O'Malley et al., "Elder Abuse in Massachusetts."

12. L. R. Phillips, "Abuse and Neglect of the Frail Elderly at Home: An Exploration of Theoretical Relationships," *Journal of Advanced Nursing* 8 (1983), pp. 379–92.

13. K. Pillemer, "The Dangers of Dependency: New Findings on Domestic Violence Against the Elderly" (Paper presented at the Annual Meeting of the American Sociological Association, 1985).

14. Phillips, "Abuse and Neglect of the Frail Elderly at Home."
15. Block and Sinnott, "The Battered Elder Syndrome"; N. H. Giordano and J. A. Giordano, "Individual and Family Correlates of Elder Abuse" (Unpublished manuscript, Bradenton, Fla., 1984); Steinmetz, "Dependency, Stress, and Violence"; Stever and Austin, "Family Abuse of the Elderly."
16. P. N. Chen et al., "Elderly Abuse in Domestic Settings: A Pilot Study," *Journal of Gerontological Social Work* 4 (Fall 1981), pp. 3–17; Gioglio and Blakemore, "Elder Abuse in New Jersey"; Giordano and Giordano, "Individual and Family Correlates of Elder Abuse"; Pennsylvania Department of Aging, Bureau of Advocacy, "Elder Abuse in Pennsylvania," 1982; C. Pepper and M. R. Oakar, "Elder Abuse: An Examination of a Hidden Problem," U.S., Congress, House, Select Committe on Aging, Pub. No. 97-277 (Washington, D.C.: U.S. Government Printing Office, 1981); M. Sengstock and J. Liang, "Identifying and Characterizing Elder Abuse" (Detroit: Wayne State University, Institute of Gerontology, 1982); Wolf et al., "Preliminary Findings from Three Model Projects on Elderly Abuse."
17. Block and Sinnott, "The Battered Elder Syndrome"; Douglass et al., "Maltreatment of the Elderly and Other Vulnerable Adults"; Dozier, "Report of the Elder Abuse and Neglect Assessment Instrument Field Test"; Gioglio and Blakemore, "Elder Abuse in New Jersey"; Lau and Kosberg, "Abuse of the Elderly by Informal Care Providers"; J. Levenberg et al., "Elder Abuse in West Virginia: Extent and Nature of the Problem," in *Elder Abuse in West Virginia: A Policy Analysis of System Response*, ed. G. Leory (Morgantown: West Virginia University, 1983); J. S. McLaughlin, J. P. Nickell, and L. Gill, "An Epidemiological Investigation of Elderly Abuse in Southern Maine and New Hampshire," U.S., Congress, House, Select Committee on Aging, Pub. No. 68-463, June 11, 1980; O'Malley et al., "Elder Abuse in Massachusetts; Steinmetz, "Elder Abuse."
18. "Abusing the Aged: The Unreported Crime," *U.S. News and World Report* 10 (1981), p. 10; "Elder Abuse Becoming a National Problem," *Geriatrics* 36, no. 7 (1981), p. 32; Pepper and Oakar, "Elder Abuse."
19. Block and Sinnott, "The Battered Elder Syndrome."
20. J. S. Crouse et al., "Abuse and Neglect of the Elderly in Illinois: Incidence and Characteristics, Legislation and Policy Recommendations" (Report prepared for the State of Illinois, Department of Aging, October 1981).
21. Steinmetz, "Elder Abuse."
22. Lau and Kosberg, "Abuse of the Elderly by Informal Care Providers."
23. Gioglio and Blakemore, "Elder Abuse in New Jesrey."
24. O'Malley et al., "Elder Abuse in Massachusetts."
25. T. O'Malley et al., "Identifying and Preventing Family-Mediated Abuse and Neglect of Elderly Persons," *Annals of Internal Medicine* 98, no. 6 (1983), pp. 998–1004.
26. Lau and Kosberg, "Abuse of the Elderly by Informal Care Providers"; Douglass et al., "Maltreatment of the Elderly and Other Vulnerable Adults"; Wolf et al., "Preliminary Findings from Three Model Projects on Elderly Abuse"; Sengstock and Liang, "Identifying and Characterizing Elder Abuse."
27. Lau and Kosberg, "Abuse of the Elderly by Informal Care Providers"; McLaughlin et al., "An Epidemiological Investigation of Elderly Abuse";

O'Malley et al., "Elder Abuse in Massachusetts"; Pennsylvania Department of Aging, "Elder Abuse in Pennsylvania"; Pepper and Oakar, "Elder Abuse."

28. Block and Sinnott, "The Battered Elder Syndrome"; L. S. Boydston and J. S. McNairn, "Elder Abuse by Adult Caretakers: An Exploratory Study," *Physical and Financial Abuse of the Elderly*, U.S., Congress, House, Select Committee on Aging, Pub. No. 97-297, April 3, 1981; C. C. Pratt, J. Koval, and S. Lloyd, "Service Workers: Responses to Abuse of the Elderly," *Social Casework* (March 1983), pp. 142–53; Sengstock and Liang, "Identifying and Characterizing Elder Abuse"; Wolf et al., "Preliminary Findings from Three Model Projects on Elderly Abuse."

29. Crouse et al. "Abuse and Neglect of the Elderly in Illinois"; Douglass et al., "Maltreatment of the Elderly"; Gioglio and Blakemore, "Elder Abuse in New Jersey."

30. Dozier, "Report of the Elder House and Neglect Assessment Instrument Field Test"; Hall and Andrew, "Minority Elder Maltreatment"; Rounds, "A Study of Selected Environmental Variables."

31. Block and Sinnott, "The Battered Elder Syndrome"; C. M. Long, "Geriatric Abuse," *Issues in Mental Health Nursing* 3 (1981), pp. 123–35.

32. Long, "Geriatric Abuse."

33. Block and Sinnott, "The Battered Elder Syndrome."

34. Long, "Geriatric Abuse"; M. Mancini, "Adult Abuse Laws," *American Journal of Nursing* 80, no. 4 (1980), pp. 739–40.

35. E. Rathbone-McCuan, "Elderly Victims of Family Violence and Neglect," *Social Casework* 61, no. 5 (1980), pp. 296–304.

36. Wolf et al., "Preliminary Findings from Three Model Projects on Elderly Abuse"; J. G. O'Brien, M. F. Hudson, and F. F. Johnson, "Health Care Provider Survey on Elder Abuse" (Unpublished manuscript, East Lansing, Michigan, 1984); Levenberg et al., "Elder Abuse in West Virginia."

37. C. J. Anastasio, "Elder Abuse Identification and Acute Care Intervention" (Paper delivered at the First National Conference on Abuse of Older Persons, March 23–25, 1980); Dozier, Report of the Elder House and Neglect Assessment Instrument Field Test; D. Falcioni, "Assessing the Abused Elderly," *Journal of Gerontological Nursing* 8, no. 4 (1982), pp. 208–12; D. Ferguson and C. Beck, "H.A.L.F.—A Tool to Assess Elder Abuse Within the Family," *Geriatric Nursing* 4, no. 5 (September-October 1983), pp. 301–04; T. Fulmer, "Elder Abuse Detection and Reporting," *Massachusetts Nurse* (May 1982), pp. 10–12; D. Johnson, "Abuse of the Elderly," *Nurse Practitioner* 6, no. 1 (January-February 1981), pp. 29–34; O'Malley et al., "Elder Abuse in Massachusetts"; E. Rathbone-McCuan and B. Voyles, "Case Detection of Abused Elderly Patients," *American Journal of Psychiatry* 139, no. 2 (1982), pp. 189–92; S. K. Tomita, "Detection of Elder Abuse and Neglect in a Medical Setting" (Paper presented at the First National Conference on Abuse of Older Persons, San Francisco, April 1–3, 1981).

38. Block and Sinnott, "The Battered Elder Syndrome"; Gioglio and Blakemore, "Elder Abuse in New Jersey"; Phillips, "Abuse and Neglect of the Frail Elderly at Home"; Sengstock and Liang, "Identifying and Characterizing Elder Abuse"; Steinmetz, "Dependency, Stress, and Violence"; Pillemer, "The Dangers of Dependency."

39. C. M. Beck and D. Ferguson, "Aged Abuse," *Journal of Gerontological Nursing* 7 (1981), pp. 333–36.

40. C. L. Anderson, "Abuse and Neglect Among the Elderly," *Journal of Gerontological Nursing* 7, no. 2 (1981), pp. 77–85; R. T. Bahr, Sr., "The Battered Elderly: Physical and Psychological Abuse," *Family and Community Health* 4, no. 2 (1981), pp. 61–69; T. Hickey and R. L. Douglass, "Mistreatment of the Elderly in the Domestic Setting: An Exploratory Study," *American Journal of Public Health* 71, no. 5 (1981), pp. 500–07; T. Hickey and R. L. Douglass, "Neglect and Abuse of Older Family Members: Professionals' Perspective and Case Experiences," The Gerontologist 21, no. 2 (1981), pp. 171–76; L. R. Kinsey, R. R. Tarbox, and D. F. Bragg, "Abuse of the Elderly—The Hidden Agenda, the Caretakers and the Categories of Abuse," *Journal of American Geriatrics Society* 29, no. 10 (October 1981), pp. 465–72; Lau and Kosberg, "Abuse of the Elderly by Informal Care Providers"; Long, "Geriatric Abuse"; O'Malley et al., "Elder Abuse in Massachusetts"; J. Renvoize, *Web of Violence: A Study of Family Violence* (London: Routledge and Kegan Paul, 1978); Steinmetz, "The Politics of Aging, Battered Parents."

41. Steinmetz, "The Politics of Aging, Battered Parents."

42. Long, "Geriatric Abuse."

43. Ibid.

44. Lau and Kosberg, "Abuse of the Elderly by Informal Care Providers."

45. Ibid.; O'Malley et al., "Elder Abuse in Massachusetts."

46. O'Malley et al., "Elder Abuse in Massachusetts."

47. Block and Sinnott, "The Battered Elder Syndrome."

48. Lau and Kosberg, "Abuse of the Elderly by Informal Care Providers."

49. O'Malley et al., "Elder Abuse in Massachusetts."

50. Ibid.

51. Block and Sinnott, "The Battered Elder Syndrome."

52. Chen et al., "Elderly Abuse in Domestic Settings."

53. McLaughlin et al., "An Epidemiological Investigation of Elderly Abuse."

54. Wolf et al., "Preliminary Findings from Three Model Projects on Elderly Abuse."

55. J. Hageboeck and K. Brandt, "Characteristics of Elderly Abuse" (Unpublished manuscript, Scott County, Iowa, June, 1981).

56. Boydston and McNairn, "Elder Abuse by Adult Caretakers"; O'Malley et al., "Elder Abuse in Massachusetts."

57. Wolf et al., "Preliminary Findings from Three Model Projects on Elderly Abuse."

58. Crouse et al., "Abuse and Neglect of the Elderly in Illinois."

59. Ibid.; Gioglio and Blakemore, "Elder Abuse in New Jersey."

60. O'Malley et al., "Identifying and Preventing Family-Mediated Abuse."

61. Anastasio, "Elder Abuse"; Bragg et al., "Abuse of the Elderly"; Chen et al., "Elderly Abuse in Domestic Settings"; Gray Panthers of Austin, "A Survey of Abuse of the Elderly in Texas" (Unpublished manuscript, Austin, Texas, February 1983).

62. Wolf et al., "Preliminary Findings from Three Model Projects on Elderly Abuse."

63. D. M. Beck and L. R. Phillips, "Abuse of the Elderly," *Journal of Geronto-logical Nursing* 9, no. 2 (1983), pp. 97–101; S. E. Goldstein and A. Blank, "The Elderly: Abused or Abusers?" *Canadian Medical Association Journal* 127, no. 6 (1982), pp. 455–56; O'Malley et al., "Identifying and Preventing Family-Mediated Abuse."

64. Chen et al., "Elderly Abuse in Domestic Settings"; Pennsylvania Depart-ment on Aging, "Elder Abuse in Pennsylvania."

65. Callahan, "Elder Abuse Programming."

66. Phillips, "Abuse and Neglect of the Frail Elderly at Home"; Pillemer, "Social Isolation and Elder Abuse"; Pillemer, "The Dangers of Dependency."

67. Giordano and Giordano, "Individual and Family Correlates of Elder Abuse."

68. Hall and Andrew, "Minority Elder Maltreatment."

69. L. R. Phillips and V. F. Rempusheski, "A Decision-making Model for Diagnosing and Intervening in Elder Abuse and Neglect," *Nursing Research* 34, no. 3 (19), pp. 134–39.

70. Giordano and Giordano, "Individual and Family Correlates of Elder Abuse."

71. S. R. Andrew and P. A. Hall, "Alcohol Use and Elder Mistreatment: An Exploratory Study" (Unpublished manuscript, San Antonio, Texas, 1984).

Chapter 7

CRITICAL ISSUES IN THE DEFINITION OF ELDER MISTREATMENT

by Tanya Johnson

Researchers and clinicians have been involved in the study, detection, and treatment of elder abuse for about a decade. Over the course of these ten years, important steps have been taken by human service professionals to help prevent and protect older persons from mistreatment. Since 1980, surveys on elder mistreatment have increased from 4 to approximately 30, and identification instruments have expanded from 1 to at least 15. Consciousness has been raised at the national level through House and Senate Select Committee Hearings on Elder Abuse, President Reagan's Task Force on Family Violence, and federal legislation passed in October 1984 (H.R. 1904) to establish a family violence center that would include elder abuse as well as other forms of family violence. In August 1985, $6 million was appropriated for the family violence portion of H.R. 1904. Guidelines for spending this money are being established by the Department of Health and Human Services. Eighty percent of these funds are going directly to the states in the form of competitive demonstration grants.

These and other advances in the state of the art in elder abuse research, policy, and practice demonstrate the scope and speed with which knowledge, evaluation, and treatment strategies are growing. With all of this activity, it is surprising and a matter of

Note: This research has been supported by the National Institute of Mental Health Adult Development grant 5-T32MH14660.

concern that there is no uniform, comprehensive definition of the term "elder abuse." Critical reviews of elder abuse literature consistently point out this flaw when research and detection instruments are compared.[1] It is impossible to evaluate or build knowledge in the field in the absence of a common definitional frame of reference. In order to address this need, it is the intent of this chapter to develop a more universal definition so that we can proceed to the tasks of theory development and measurement of the effectiveness of various treatment strategies.

The important areas in which the definition of elder abuse plays a critical role include research studies that have focused on the nature and scope of elder abuse and detection protocols used by human service professionals to determine what is and is not elder abuse. These two areas show a lack of uniformity in the conceptualizations and classification systems used to identify the behavioral manifestations of elder abuse. Tables 7–1 and 7–2 illustrate the variations in the classification of abuse.

Differences in terminology and meaning make it impossible to compare research findings, to collaborate on detection instruments, or, in the broader context, to establish a national forum for preparing a standard definition in order to develop public policy on the subject of elder abuse. In addition, until we can adopt a standard definition of elder abuse, causal theory cannot be explored. Theory building relies on a clearly defined, measurable proposition with a consistent definition.

Pedrick-Cornell and Gelles contend that the subject of elder abuse began on the wrong footing by focusing on ex-post facto cases of abuse rather than on the concept:[2]

> *The concept of elder abuse has become a political/journalistic concept, best suited for attracting public attention to the plight of the victims. But while elder abuse may be a fruitful political term, it is fast becoming a useless scientific concept.*

It is important to reverse this orientation and move in the direction of scientific meaning. To do this, some fundamental dimensions of the defining process need to be explored.

The specific objectives of this chapter are to (1) present a paradigm that outlines the essential parameters necessary for the development of a valid definition, (2) identify the major problems that have developed in previous efforts to define elder abuse, and (3) propose a definition for elder mistreatment, based on the paradigm, that is designed to correct some of the problems currently existing in definitions of elder abuse.

Paradigm for the Development of the Meaning of a Concept

Defining is the procedure used to specify the meaning of phenomena.[3] The assignment of meaning to a concept is perhaps the most challenging aspect of research, policy, and practice. First, we must set up the parameters on what elder abuse means and distinguish it from what it does not mean. Since elder abuse can be a life-threatening situation, practitioners and policy makers must scrutinize what is and is not elder abuse very carefully.

Four steps that are critical to the formulation of a meaningful definition of elder abuse are (1) conceptualizing the variable, (2) specifying behavioral manifestations, (3) measuring observable events, and (4) distinguishing the act from the cause. Each of these steps constitutes a discrete task having a unique function, with each step building on the prior defining procedure. Any effort to combine functions or skip any of the procedures will result in vagueness and potential distortion in the meaning of the concept. In the next section, current definitions of research, detection, and legislation will be analyzed in terms of these four steps. Following clarification of the meaning of the four steps, an evaluation will be made of definitions currently operating in the available research, detection protocols, and legislation. (See Tables 7–1 and 7–2.)

Conceptualizing

The first procedure in the defining process is the development of an intrinsic definition (or what some have called a nominal definition). The primary function of the intrinsic definition is to conceptualize the variable by targeting the linguistic meaning of the construct rather than by identifying observable events. The essential ingredients for the intrinsic definition include (1) the condition or conditions that occasion the necessity for the construct in the first place and (2) the identification of the parties involved in those conditions.

Intrinsic definitions are conspicuously absent from the elder mistreatment literature. Why researchers, policy makers, and practitioners have steered clear of intrinsic definitions is not clear. We could speculate, however, that since the formulation of an intrinsic definition requires abstraction, such a definition becomes all the more removed from the applied setting. It appears to be a philosophical and semantic enterprise with little relevance or impact on reality. In reality, however, this level of naming or

(Text continues on page 177)

Table 7–1 Definitions of Elder Mistreatment Used in Survey Research

Surveys	Abuse	Neg-lect	Active Neglect	Pass. Neglect	Physical Abuse	Physical Neglect	Psych-ological Abuse	Psych-ological Neglect	Verbal/ Emotional Abuse	Mater-ial Abuse	Medi-cal Abuse	Exploi-tation	Viola-tion of Rights	Other
Andrew/Hall (1985)										X	X		X	• physical assault • verbal/psycho-logical violence • personal care/living area
Beachler (1982)			X	X	X				X			X		
Chen et al. (1982)					X		X							• sexual abuse • social/environ.
Crouse et al. (1981)			X	X	X				X					• severe neglect • severe physical abuse
Douglass et al. (1980)			X	X	X				X					
Gioglio/Blakemore (1983)			X		X		X							• financial abuse
Giordano/Giordano (1984)					X		X							• financial abuse • multiple abuse
Gray Panthers (1983)			X		X				X			X		• self-neglect
Hageboeck/ Brandt (1981)			X		X		X							• financial abuse
Hall/Andrew (1984)	X		X									X		• self-neglect, multiple forms
Lau/Kosberg (1979)					X		X			X		X		
Levenberg et al. (1983)	X				X						X			• mental cruelty • economic abuse

Study									Additional categories
McLaughlin et al. (1980)	X	X							
O'Brien et al. (1984)	X		X				X	X	• self-abuse • abandonment
O'Malley et al. (1979)	X	X	X					X	• abandonment
Pennsylvania Dept. of Aging (1982)			X				X	X	
Pepper/Oakar (1981)			X	X			X	X	• sexual abuse • financial exploitation • self-abuse • neglect
Phillips (1985)			X	X	X	X	X		• emotional abuse • emotional neglect • emotional deprivation • sexual exploitation/assault • verbal assault • neglect of environment
Rounds (1982)	X		X	X			X	X	• active physical abuse • self-abuse
Sengstock/ Liang (1982)			X	X	X	X			
Wolf et al. (1982)	X	X	X	X			X		

References for Table 7–1

Andrew, Sylvia R., and Hall, Phillip A. 1985. "Alcohol Use and Elder Mistreatment: An Exploratory Study." Unpublished manuscript, Our Lady of the Lake University, Worden School of Social Service, San Antonio, Texas.

Beachler, Mary Ann. 1982. "Mistreatment of Elderly Persons in Domestic Settings." Unpublished manuscript, Brazoria County, Texas.

Chen, Pei; Bell, Sharon; Dolinsky, Deborah; Doyle, John; and Dunn, Moire. 1982. "Elderly Abuse in Domestic Settings: A Pilot Study." *Journal of Gerontological Social Work* 4 (1): 3–17.

Crouse, Joyce; Cobb, Deborah; Harris, Britta; Kopecky, Frank J.; Poertner, John. 1981. "Abuse and Neglect of the Elderly in Illinois: Incidence and Characteristics, Legislation, and Policy Recommendations." Sangamon State University and Illinois Department on Aging, Springfield, Illinois.

Douglass, Richard; Hickey, Tom; and Noel, Catherine. 1980. "A Study of Maltreatment of the Elderly and Other Vulnerable Adults." Ann Arbor: University of Michigan, Institute of Gerontology.

Gioglio, Gerald, and Blakemore, Penelope. 1983. "Elder Abuse in New Jersey: The Knowledge and Experience of Abuse Among Older New Jerseyans." New Jersey Department of Human Resources, Trenton.

Giordano, Nan Hervig, and Giordano, Jeffrey A. 1984. "Individual and Family Correlates of Elder Abuse." Unpublished manuscript, Bradentown, Florida.

Gray Panthers of Austin. 1983. "A Survey of Abuse of the Elderly in Texas." Unpublished manuscript, Austin, Texas.

Hageboeck, Helen, and Brandt, Karen. 1981. "Characteristics of Elderly Abuse." Unpublished manuscript, Scott County, Iowa.

Hall, Philip A., and Andrew, Sylvia R. 1984. "Differentiating Self-Neglect in Elder Mistreatment Situations." Unpublished manuscript, Our Lady of the Lake University, The Worden School of Social Science, San Antonio, Texas.

Lau, Elizabeth, and Kosberg, Jordan. 1979. "Abuse of the Elderly by Informal Care Providers." *Aging*, Sept.-Oct.: 10–15.

Levenberg, Jud; Milan, Judith; Dolan, Mary; and Carpenter, Pamela. 1983. "Elder Abuse in West Virginia: Extent and Nature of the Problem." In *Elder Abuse in West Virginia: A Policy Analysis of System Response*, ed. Leory G. Shultz. Morgantown: West Virginia University.

McLaughlin, J. S.; Nickell, J. P.; Gill, L. 1980. "An Epidemiological Investigation of Elderly Abuse in Southern Maine and New Hampshire." In *Elder Abuse*. San Francisco: U.S. House Select Committee on Aging.

O'Brien, James G.; Hudson, Margaret F.; and Johnson, Tanya F. 1984. "Health Care Provider Survey on Elder Abuse." Unpublished manuscript, East Lansing, Michigan.

O'Malley, Helen; Segars, Howard; Perez, Ruben; Mitchell, Victoria; and Knuepfel, G. 1979. "Elder Abuse in Massachusetts: A Survey of Professionals and Paraprofessionals." Boston: Legal Research and Services for the Elderly.

Pennsylvania Department of Aging. 1982. "Elder Abuse in Pennsylvania." Harrisburg: Pennsylvania Department of Aging, Bureau of Advocacy.

Pepper, Claude, and Oaker, Mary Rose. 1981. *Elder Abuse: An Examination of the Hidden Problem*. Washington, D.C.: U.S. Government Printing Office.

Phillips, Linda R., and Rempusheski, Veronica F. 1985. "A Decision-Making Model for Diagnosing and Intervening in Elder Abuse and Neglect." *Nursing Research* 34 (3): 134–39.

Rounds, Linda Raedene. 1982. "A Study of Selected Environmental Variables Associated with Non-Institutional Settings Where There Is Abuse or Neglect of the Elderly." Ph.D. diss., University of Texas at Austin.

Sengstock, Mary, and Liang, Jersey. 1982. "Identifying and Characterizing Elder Abuse." Wayne State University, Institute of Gerontology, Detroit.

Wolf, Rosalie; Strugnell, Cecile; and Godkin, Michael. 1982. "Preliminary Findings from Three Model Projects on Elder Abuse." Worcester: University of Massachusetts Medical Center, University Center on Aging.

Table 7–2 Definitions of Elder Mistreatment Used in Detection Protocols

Protocols	Abuse	Neglect	Physical Abuse	Physical Neglect	Psycho-logical Abuse	Psycho-logical Neglect	Mate-rial Abuse	Medi-cal Abuse	Exploi-tation	Vio-lation of Rights	Other
Anastasio (1981)	X	X									• mistreatment
Atlanta Regional Commission (1984)			X	X					X		• abusive social circumstances • caregiver neglect • societal neglect • self-neglect • self-abuse
Block/Sinnott (1979)					X	X	X	X			
Daiches (1983)	X	X							X		• self-endangering behavior • environmental hazards • intelligence impairment
Falcioni (1982)			X		X		X			X	
Ferguson/Beck (1983)											• health status • attitudes on aging • living arrangements • finances
Fulmer/Cahill (1984)					X	X	X	X			
Jacobs (1983)		X	X		X						
Johnson (1981)					X	X	X	X			
Kosberg (1983)										X	• passive neglect • active neglect • verbal abuse • emotional abuse • physical attacks • material theft

Rathbone-McCuan/Voyles (1982)

Category	Rathbone-McCuan/Voyles (1982)	Sengstock/Hwalek (1985)	Tomita (1982)	Villmoare/Bergman (1981)	Wolf/Pillemer (1984)
financial dependency and exploitation		X	X	X	X
withholding basic life resources		X	X	X	
not providing care to physical dependent		X	X	X	
active physical assault		X	X	X	
verbal and psychological assault		X	X		
misuse of money/property or theft		X	X	X	
forced entry into nursing home		X			
misuse and abuse of drugs		X			

Sengstock/Hwalek (1985)
- sexual abuse/assault

Tomita (1982)

Villmoare/Bergman (1981)
- financial abuse

Wolf/Pillemer (1984)
- emotional abuse
- abusive actions
- evidence of serious neglect
- neglectful actions
- financial exploitation

References for Table 7–2

Anastasio, Charlotte. 1981. "Elder Abuse: Identification and Acute Care Intervention." Paper delivered at the National Conference on Abuse of Older Persons, Cambridge, Massachusetts.

Atlanta Regional Commission. 1984. *Report of the Elder Abuse and Neglect Assessment Instrument Field Test*, Atlanta, Georgia.

Block, Marilyn, and Sinnott, Janice. 1979. "The Battered Elder Syndrome: An Exploratory Study." College Park: University of Maryland, Center on Aging.

Daiches, Sol. 1983. "Protective Services Risk Assessment: A New Approach to Screening Adult Clients." New York: Human Resources Administration.

Falcioni, Denise. 1982. "Assessing the Abused Elderly." *Journal of Gerontological Nursing* 8 (4): 208–12.

Ferguson, Doris, and Beck, Cornelia. 1983. "H.A.L.F.—A Tool to Assess Elder Abuse Within the Family." *Geriatric Nursing* 4 (5): 301–04.

Fulmer, Terry, and Cahill, Virginia. 1984. "Assessing Elder Abuse: A Study." *Journal of Gerontological Nursing* 10 (12): 16–20.

Jacobs, Marilyn. 1983. "The Protocol for the Treatment and Referral of Adult and Elderly Abuse Victims." Unpublished manuscript, The Family and Child Abuse Prevention Center, Toledo, Ohio.

Johnson, Douglas. 1981. "Abuse of the Elderly." *Nurse Practitioner* 6 (1): 29–34.

Kosberg, Jordan. 1983. *Abuse and Maltreatment of the Elderly: Causes and Intervention*. Littleton, Mass.: John Wright, PSG.

Rathbone-McCuan, Eloise, and Voyles, Barbara. 1982. "Case Detection of Abused Elderly Parents." *American Journal of Psychiatry* 139 (2): 189–92.

Sengstock, Mary, and Hwalek, Melanie. 1985. "Comprehensive Index of Elder Abuse." Paper presented at Gerontological Society of America, Nov., 1985, New Orleans.

Tomita, Susan. 1982. "Detection and Treatment of Elderly Abuse and Neglect: A Protocol for Health Care Professionals." *Physical and Occupational Therapy in Geriatrics* 2 (2): 37–51.

Villmoare, Edwin, and Bergman, James. 1981. "Elder Abuse and Neglect: A Guide for Practitioners and Policy Makers." In *Physical and Financial Abuse of the Elderly*. San Francisco: Hearing of the Select Committee on Aging, House of Representatives.

Wolf, Rosalie, and Pillemer, Karl. 1984. "Working with Abused Elders: Assessment, Advocacy, and Intervention." Worcester: University of Massachusetts Medical Center, University Center of Aging.

defining must indeed be abstract in order to be inclusive of all of the circumstances that constitute elder mistreatment.

There is also the tautological problem of using the word to define itself, which often occurs in the naming of a phenomenon. But, of course, this circularity confuses meaning rather than clarifies it. An example of this problem can be found in Chen et al., in their definition of elder abuse. They state that it is ". . . an abusive action inflicted by the abusers on adults 60 years of age or older."[4] Gioglio and Blakemore define elder neglect and abuse as "a generic term that refers to the neglect and/or physical, psychological or financial abuse of the older person."[5] Even though forms are distinguished, neglect and abuse are basically defined as neglect and abuse.

The recognition that there are categories of behavior which fall under the heading of abuse raises another question. Tables 7–1 and 7–2 show a whole range of terms—"abuse," "neglect," "exploitation," "abandonment," and so on. We cannot say that abuse may be classified into abuse, neglect, or exploitation. Another concept is needed as the umbrella term. Several writers have solved the dilemma by using the term "elder mistreatment" rather than "elder abuse." In this way, the concept of abuse is free to take its place as a form of mistreatment. The concept of *elder mistreatment* protects against the tautological trap that has just been described. The broader category of elder mistreatment rather than elder abuse will be used in the material that follows.

Specifying Behavioral Manifestations

Once an intrinsic meaning has been established, the defining procedure can move to a clarification of behavioral manifestations of the phenomenon. There is a difference between the meaning of the construct and the identification of observable events.[6] Extrinsic definitions facilitate observations by specifying concrete behaviors that relate to the conditions identified in the intrinsic definition. There are two types of extrinsic definitions: real and operational. A real definition, according to Norman Denzin, "gives meaning to a concept by resolving it into its constituent elements."[7] The development of a real definition is what comprises the second step in the defining process. The operational definition is the third step in the development of the definition. In contrast to intrinsic definitions, most of the research studies and detection protocols contain lists of behavioral manifestations or the designation of observable events. The number of categories ranges from two to six. Common constituent elements include physical abuse, psychological abuse, material abuse, exploitation, and neglect. As Tables 7–1 and 7–2 show, it would appear that the same or similar categories could be synthesized to achieve greater uniformity among definitions. However, categories are not represented in the same way. For example, Lau and Kosberg call "withholding of personal care" physical abuse. Douglass et al. and Wolf et al. call withholding of personal care active neglect; Rounds calls it physical neglect; and Sengstock and Liang consider this circumstance a representation of psychological neglect.[8]

This lack of uniformity in the application of the extrinsic behavioral categories may also explain why there are contradictions in the prevalence of different types of abuse. Some researchers found physical abuse to be the most common form.[9] Others found psychological abuse to be the most common.[10] On the other hand, Crouse et al.[11] and Douglass et al. found passive neglect to be the most common form. Gioglio and Blakemore, by contrast, reported that financial abuse was the most frequently reported form in their study. Of course, these contradictory results could also be explained by variations in sampling techniques and other differences in research design. Nevertheless, when typologies are defined differently, we run the risk of ending up with different conclusions.

Measuring Observable Events

The operational definition constitutes the third dimension of the defining process. It converts the elements identified at the level of real definition into measurable units that can be analyzed systematically.[12] This definitional level is applied to the empirical situation by means of variables that can be measured. Operational definitions should be found at the level of detection of elder mistreatment so that practitioners will have clear discriminators of what is elder mistreatment and what is not. The detection protocols that have been developed thus far represent a broad range of subject matter and different methods of assessing observable events. These include protocols that call for descriptive information,[13] the professional's personal observation in the in-home setting,[14] Likert-type scaling of behavioral manifestations to measure severity,[15] a mix of forms,[16] and an instrument to assess elders who may be at risk for elder abuse now or later.[17]

Distinguishing Act from Cause

A final defining procedure involves the separation of the act that culminates in mistreatment from intent to harm. Does the act of tying the older person to a chair constitute elder mistreatment?

What if tying the older person to a chair is a method to protect the older person from injury due to falling? What about the older person who is malnourished because of the poor eating habits of the caregiving family? Can we say that a family is neglectful of the older member's nutritional needs if they apply the same standards to themselves? Is the older person who appears anxious signaling mistreatment from others or a personality characteristic peculiar to that individual? The inclusion of intent to harm in definitions of elder mistreatment raises a number of questions that have no easy answers. Should families who are unaware that they are being neglectful be counseled by professionals in the same way as those who have knowingly left the older person unattended? If the effect is elder neglect, how important is the cause?

Elder mistreatment must be approached at two levels—identification and intent to mistreat the older person. Combining both identification and intent in the same definition includes some cases that should be excluded and excludes some that should be included. The function of identification, which is determined by the operational definition, is to establish whether, in fact, this mistreatment has occurred. Although a relative may have been ignorant of the fact that his or her overmedication of the older person has caused harm or mistreatment, we should not allow the condition to persist. Indeed, serious harm can occur with the best of intentions. If these cases fall through the net because the acts were not deliberate, we are not helping the elder or the caregiver. On the other hand, there are cases in which the caregiver has deliberately intended to overmedicate in an effort to control a serious health problem the older person is experiencing. Would we consider this act mistreatment?

The issues raised by intent and deliberate acts do not fall into the identification mode. Rather they present factors that are appropriate to intervention and treatment. Combining identification and intent in the same definition confounds both detection and treatment. If elder mistreatment has occurred, even if unintentional, some type of intervention needs to take place to prevent the recurrence. The identified condition is either a case of elder mistreatment or it is not. Intent to harm is an issue that is more appropriately situated in the treatment phase. Treatment calls for a different set of propositions, a different purpose—not determining whether mistreatment has taken place, but once elder mistreatment has occurred, assessing what must be done to prevent future episodes.

Effective identification, protection, and prevention against elder mistreatment cannot be achieved until we develop discrete levels of the defining procedure. What follows will be a proposed four-stage definition of elder mistreatment that will include the definition of the concept, behavioral manifestation, a system for measuring observable events, and a method for determining cause.

A Proposed Definition of Elder Mistreatment

The remainder of this chapter will be devoted to a proposed four-stage systematic definition of elder mistreatment, based on the paradigm presented in the preceding section. The four stages include an intrinsic definition of elder mistreatment, an extrinsic definition that is divided into two parts—a real definition and an operational definition—and finally a causal definition. The following definition of elder mistreatment includes these four sequential stages:

- Stage 1: a state of self- or other-inflicted suffering unnecessary to the maintenance of the quality of life of the older person.
- Stage 2: identified as one or more behavioral manifestations, categorized as physical, psychological, sociological, or legal circumstances.
- Stage 3: measured by determining the intensity and density of the behavioral manifestations.
- Stage 4: treated on the basis of whether the cause is the result of passive neglect, active neglect, passive abuse, or active abuse.

The Intrinsic Definition

Elder mistreatment is conceptualized as self- or other-inflicted suffering unnecessary to the maintenance of the quality of life of the older person. Each of the key words work together to define elder mistreatment.

The intrinsic definition includes the whole spectrum of mistreatment and therefore must include self-inflicted elder mistreatment as well as other-inflicted mistreatment. Research on self-inflicted elder mistreatment has been conducted in England by Baker and by Clark.[18] They have called self-neglect the "Diogenes syndrome." Thibault, and Hall and Andrew[19] have studied this phenomenon in the United States. Even though we are just beginning to study systematically self-inflicted elder mistreatment, we recognize that it is just as potentially harmful as other-inflicted elder mistreatment. Although they represent different phenomena, both sources of elder mistreatment should be included in the intrinsic definition.

Other-inflicted elder mistreatment is, of course, not setting-specific. It includes mistreatment in both the institutional as well as the noninstitutional setting. In addition to the older person himself or herself, those who may perpetrate the mistreatment include strangers, family members, friends, acquaintances, and professionals involved in some way in the life of the older person.

Suffering is generally understood to mean intense and sustained pain and anguish. For elder mistreatment to be considered pain or anguish, the older person must have experienced more than one episode of suffering. An occasional "shove" of the older person in a fit of frustration or a "slanderous" name-calling episode does not constitute suffering, although, indeed, both circumstances may cause pain and anguish. Another aspect of suffering has to do with the degree of pain or anguish sustained in a single episode.

In order to determine whether, in fact, the elder mistreatment is superficial or severe in a single episode, we need to look more closely at the nature of interaction in the residential and social settings in which the older person is involved. For some older persons, teasing may cause mental anguish; for others it may be the usual mode of interaction. The distinctions of "normal violence" and "abusive violence" developed by Gelles and Pedrick-Cornell may be helpful in clarifying situation-specific interaction.[20] These writers hold that normal violence may be typified by behaviors some families have modeled their whole life and thus may be their usual method of relating to one another. If quips, barbs, sarcasm, banter, or teasing are typical ways of communicating with one another, then these behaviors toward the older person would not constitute a sufficient condition for suffering. On the other hand, Gelles and Pedrick-Cornell contend that "abusive violence" is an act that has a high potential for injury or what we have called suffering because it falls outside the repertoire of expected noninjurious violent behavior. If, for example, shouting is a typical way of relating for the older person and neither pain nor suffering ensue, then the nature of relating produces normal violence, which is absorbed and disregarded. However, when shouting is defined by the parties as sufficiently intense to cause some degree of pain or anguish, we are speaking about abusive violence that is not superficial. In this latter case it is severe enough to warrant intervention. To distinguish normal from abusive violence, one must look beyond the act to the shared meaning of the situation of which the elder is a part.

A final dimension of suffering is identified as the density of the elder mistreatment, or the numbers of behavioral manifestations that have occurred in the elder mistreatment situation. The wider the range of forms, the more complex the suffering. Suffering encompasses two dimensions—*intensity* (frequency of occurrence of pain and/or anguish and the severity of the mistreatment in single episodes) and *density* (the scope of the behavioral manifestations of elder mistreatment measured by the number and variety of observable events).

One last qualification must be made when we evaluate the meaning of suffering. The designation of suffering applied to an older person's condition need not be an indicator of elder mistreatment. We recognize that intense pain and anguish may be very much a part of one's everyday life, but we would not wish to identify this circumstance as elder mistreatment. Those who are victims of stroke, Alzheimer's disease, or Parkinson's disease may be found in the category of sufferers. In addition, there are times when physical restraint or involuntary medication is necessary to protect the older person from falls, anxiety, or self-inflicted mistreatment. Under some circumstances, suffering may occur to achieve some greater good in the process of maintaining the quality of life of the older person. Oversedation, undersedation, overmedication, undermedication, social isolation, or shouting at the older person does not, in itself, mean that unnecessary suffering has occurred. To the contrary, suffering may be necessary to the overall well-being of the older person in order to prevent mistreatment. But who decides whether the suffering is justified? This determination would need to be made by the older person if able, the family members or caregivers if there are such in the situation, and third-party professionals who are aware of the mental, social, and physical conditions of the older person. In sum, the critical issue is whether the suffering is necessary to maintain the overall quality of life to which the older person has been accustomed. In order to make this determination, both a subjective and objective evaluation are needed.

Maintaining the quality of life of the older person also requires subjectivity as well as objectivity similar to the concept of suffering. Some professionals may believe that if the older person has no friends, that person's quality of life is diminished. Consequently, the older person may be identified as being at risk for mistreatment. But there is more to the story than the objective assessment. While no one would argue against the premise that social stimulation retards the aging process and enriches one's life, one cannot gauge the evaluation of elder needs on an ideal. It may be that the older person has a history of reclusiveness, has had few friends in his or her lifetime, and prefers solitude. Can we say in this instance that the quality of life of the older person is threatened? An objective third party would have to have a convincing argument for changing this pattern of behavior on the part of the older person.

A comprehensive assessment of elder needs must be based on both the subjective and objective evaluation. Just as we had to know about the nature of life course experiences of the older person before determining whether the older person is experiencing pain or mental anguish, in like manner with the issue of the quality of life, the life course of the older person must be taken into consideration before we determine whether, indeed, his or her experiences have changed significantly from what they had been before the mistreatment took place. If an observable shift has occurred, the evidence may point to elder mistreatment. Forcing the older person to stay awake when all that person wants to do is sleep during the day, or requiring the elder to get up and walk in order to maintain muscle tone may be signs of love rather than mistreatment.

The concept "older person" is difficult to quantify. Even though chronological age is probably the most straightforward way to decide who is old and who is not, there are some serious problems with this form of stratification. Some 75-year-olds may be young "olds," and others may be old "olds" in terms of their overall health and conduct. Therefore, age itself is not really an adequate indicator of being an older person. Once again, we must acknowledge a subjective element when we talk about the meaning of older person. Being old is a state of mind and body, and the definition of the term "older person" varies from individual to individual.

Distinctions regarding mistreatment made on the basis of age imply that age is a significant correlate. Mistreatment must be different for different age cohorts. But is not mistreatment really mistreatment no matter what one's age? Is it not the case that distinguishing mistreatment by age is arbitrary and artificial? To argue with this hypothesis would be difficult. The intrinsic definition could just as accurately read: "Mistreatment is the state of self- or other-inflicted suffering unnecessary to the quality of life of the person." Age need not be a criterion. Mistreatment is mistreatment for all that, at least in principle. However, it is important to designate age as a critical variable in practice.

There are three reasons for including age in the intrinsic definition. First, those of us in the field of elder mistreatment research, policy, and practice must still answer the question of whether "age" is a factor in family violence. We continue to struggle with the question of whether elder mistreatment is different from other age-related types of mistreatment. Does it constitute an independent variable? If age is a critical factor in mistreatment, we cannot have a universal intrinsic definition of mistreatment. Until we can demonstrate that age has no bearing on the nature and scope of mistreatment, we must continue to distinguish among the areas of child mistreatment, adult mistreatment, parent mistreatment, spouse mistreatment, and elder mistreatment.

Second, it behooves us as social scientists to adapt to the current system of specialization in the life course in order to gain maximum recognition for our contributions. As long as we separate human development by age, then gerontologists and geriatricians must continue to focus on this particular age group. Inevitably, this recognition will bring us closer to the needs of older people. Aging in the eighties is a significant enough area of specialization in research and policy that it is in the best interest of the older person to call attention to this special group when addressing the issue of mistreatment.

Finally, our political and economic social institutions are powerful influences over our perceptions of the life course. Our society has a clear delineation of the legal transition into the status of being old. The establishment of a rite of passage by this means provides for the formation of a social group that can be studied from a sociological point of view. Retirement, social security, pension, medicare, medicaid, loans, and life insurance separate the category of older person from the rest of society. For this and the other reasons mentioned above, it is important to make mistreatment age-specific at this stage of our development in the human sciences. In keeping with the arbitrary age of retirement set up in the legal-political system, age 70 is proposed as the age at which one becomes an "older person." Therefore, for our purposes in clarifying the definition, a person has become a victim of *elder* mistreatment if he or she has reached the age of 70 at the time of the first episode.

The Extrinsic Definition

The extrinsic real definition calls for the naming of behaviors that may be classified as elder mistreatment. The definition proposed states that elder mistreatment is identified as one or more behavioral manifestations categorized as physical, psychological, sociological, or legal circumstances. Labeling the categories facilitates the identification process. While the intrinsic definition signifies the parameters of the circumstances of elder mistreatment and

who qualifies as a victim and perpetrator, the extrinsic real definition names the concrete behaviors within the designated parameters.

Specifying Behavioral Manifestations

Table 7–3 provides an outline of the four-part classification
scheme. First, behaviors are divided into the categories of physical, psychological, sociological, and legal. Then, within categories
there is a threefold subclassification system. These subcategories
are distinguished by means of specific behavioral circumstances.
Physical mistreatment means that the victim's body or bodily
functions are suffering some level of pain. This pain may stem from
behaviors involved in medical health maltreatment (either or both
medication and health care), bodily impairment, or actual bodily
assaults of various kinds. Medical health maltreatment may be the
consequence of not receiving or being refused medication when it
is needed, receiving too much or too little medication, or receiving
medication irregularly or improperly. Problems in health care can
be categorized using the same typology. Health care may be
unavailable when needed or available to an excessive degree, or
irregular, improper, inadequate, or duplicated in some way; or, if
the older person refuses health care, the refusal may lead to self-
inflicted mistreatment. Bodily impairment pertains to the body's
lack of basic needs for survival. These deficits are manifest in
malnutrition, dehydration, emaciation, poor hygiene, drug addic-
tion, sleep/rest disturbance, unexplained fatigue, failure to thrive,
hypo/hyperthermia, and improper ventilation. One, some, or all of
these unmet needs for bodily maintenance can be identified as
elder mistreatment. The last subcategory of physical mistreatment
is designated as bodily assaults. It refers to the varieties of injuries
to which older persons may fall victim, either at their own hands or
the hands of others. These include burns, abrasions, bruises,
fractures, dislocations, welts, wounds, rashes, sores, sprains, internal injuries, suicidal behavior, sexual assaults, and physical restraint.

Psychological mistreatment encompasses suffering that may be
characterized as mental anguish. The three subcategories in the
context of psychological mistreatment include humiliation, harassment, and manipulation. Humiliation is identified by three forms:
(1) making the older person feel ashamed of his or her behavior; (2)
blaming the older person for certain attitudes, actions, or events so
that the older person is made to feel guilty; and (3) ridiculing the
older person for his or her conduct. Harassment is a category of

Table 7–3   The Extrinsic Definition of Elder Mistreatment (Behavioral Manifestations)

Physical	Psychological	Sociological	Legal
I. Medical Health Maltreatment (medication/care)	I. Humiliation	I. Isolation	I. Material Exploitation
• absence	• shaming	• involuntary withdrawal from social interactions	• misuse of money
• excessiveness	• blaming	• voluntary withdrawal from social interaction	• misuse of property
• irregularity	• ridicule	• inadequate supervision	• misuse of possessions
• improperness		• improper supervision	• misuse of insurance
• inadequacy		• inadequate social support	• blocking access to money
• duplication			• blocking access to property
• refusal			• blocking access to possessions
			• blocking access to insurance
II. Bodily Impairment	II. Harassment	II. Role Confusion	II. Exploitation of Person
• malnutrition	• name calling	• role conflict	• denial of rights to self-determination of competent elderly
• dehydration	• intimidation	• role dispersion	• denial of rights to self-determination of incompetent elderly
• emaciation	• threats	• role inversion	• involuntary servitude
• poor hygiene	• instilling fear	• role dissolution	
• drug addiction	• shouting		
• sleep/rest disturbance			
• unexplained fatigue			
• hypo/hyperthermia			
• improper ventilation			
• failure to thrive			

III. Bodily Assaults
- burns
- abrasions
- bruises
- fractures
- dislocations
- welts
- wounds
- rashes
- sores
- sprains
- internal injuries
- suicidal behavior
- sexual assaults
- physical restraint

III. Manipulation
- information withheld
- falsified information
- unreasonable dependence
- interference with decision making

III. Life-style Incompatibility
- lack of privacy
- household disorganization
- unsafe environment
- poor allocation of space
- abandonment

III. Theft
- stealing money
- stealing property
- stealing possessions
- stealing insurance
- extortion of property
- extortion of possessions
- extortion of insurance

mental anguish in which the older person is bullied in some way—
either through being called names, being intimidated, being
threatened, being made to have fear for his or her health and well-
being, or being shouted at in episodes of anger. Finally, mental
anguish may be manifest in manipulative behavior. Manipulation
can be experienced by an elder in a variety of ways—being denied
access to information, being given false information, being forced
to rely on others so that a situation of unreasonable dependence is
created, or having others interfere with such decision making
activities as deciding where to live or what groceries to buy.

Sociological mistreatment represents suffering as a consequence
of not being integrated into the primary group setting as a result of
the elder's resistance or coercion on the part of others. Each of the
three subcategories of sociological mistreatment identifies the
varieties of social circumstances that lead to an unhealthy relationship with others in the group setting with whom the older person is
most likely to interact on a regular basis. The subcategory of
isolation identifies those circumstances that prevent the older
person from having meaningful associations with others. These
include the involuntary withdrawal from the group, voluntary
withdrawal, inadequate or improper supervision (under conditions
when the older person is incapacitated or declared incompetent),
and, finally, inadequate social support from friends, family, or
others.

Role confusion refers to the part or parts one plays in the
dynamics of association with others that is essential for maintaining
personal identity. The roles of grandmother, retired postman, and
choir member, for example, have built-in functions that serve to
integrate the person into the group. Without role identification,
one is defined as useless—a burden to the group—and runs the
risk of being disregarded. Within the context of role confusion,
there are four varieties of behaviors. Role conflict means that the
older person may be competing for roles in the household or
institutional setting. Unresolved conflict can lead to suffering. Role
dispersion refers to the older person's being forced to take on a
number of roles for which he or she feels unsuited. Role inver-
sions, or what Suzanne Steinmetz[21] calls "generational inversion,"
go a step beyond infantilization[22] (treating the older person like an
infant or child). In role inversion, another has taken over the role
of the elder as *adult* and forced the older person to behave as a
child. Consequently, the older person loses his or her right to
perform the role of adult. Finally, role dissolution means that
either the older person has become roleless (does nothing at all as a
function-performing human being) or has been forced by others to

relinquish any roles. The third subcategory is life-style incompatibility. Conditions in this subcategory include the lack of privacy for the older person, a disorganized household that could make the older person confused, anxious, agitated, or physically ill; unsafe conditions in the household or institutional setting; the poor allocation of space for the older person's daily living; or simply being abandoned by caregivers.

Legal mistreatment is the last category of behavioral manifestation. This type of mistreatment has its roots in the legal system that protects individuals against various kinds of theft and exploitation. There are three subcategories of mistreatment: material exploitation, exploitation of the person, and theft. Material exploitation comes in two forms—misuse of the older person's money, property, possessions, or insurance by the older person or others; and blocking access to these four material goods. Exploitation of the person includes denying the rights of the competent elder; denying the rights of the incompetent (when guardianship is indicated); and involuntary servitude wherein the older person is treated like a slave—being forced to perform tasks that are inappropriate or inhumane. The last subcategory of legal mistreatment is theft, of which there are two forms: (1) blatant theft through stealing the older person's money, property, possessions, and insurance, and (2) extortion, which consists of bilking the older person out of his or her money, property, possessions, or insurance.

Table 7–3 serves to hone the specific behaviors that we may classify as mistreatment. The next step is to construct a method for measuring the observable events that provide the substance of the behavioral manifestations. This brings us to the second level of extrinsic definition—the operational definition.

Measuring Observable Events

The behaviors identified in Table 7–3 need to be brought into sharper focus at this level of operational definition. At this stage in the defining process, one needs to decide whether the suffering is unnecessary to the maintenance of the quality of life of the older person, and, when it is, how we are to assess the severity of the mistreatment. Determining the severity informs us about the degree to which the mistreatment is life-threatening and how difficult it will be to alter mistreatment. This third state of defining elder mistreatment is measured by the intensity and density of the behavioral manifestations. The determination as to whether the suffering is necessary or unnecessary can be established by an objective assessment of what is needed to maintain the quality of life of the older person in combination with an objective assessment of the subjective life-style and daily dynamics taking place between the older person and others with whom he or she is associated. If this evaluation concludes that the suffering being experienced by the older person is unnecessary, then some form and degree of mistreatment are taking place. Once mistreatment is established, we have already identified the behavioral manifestations. What remains is to measure the severity of the observable events, a task that can be accomplished by using the variables of intensity and density.

Intensity measures depth, and density measures scope. Intensity consists of two measures—the frequency of occurrence of the mistreatment and the severity of the typical episode. Density is determined by the number of forms of mistreatment that can be identified in a single case. The greater the intensity the more potentially harmful the mistreatment; the greater the density the more entrenched the suffering and the more complicated the corrective measures.

The frequency of occurrence provides one measure of the severity of the mistreatment. A proposed method to secure this information is to ask a three-part question—how many times has mistreatment occurred in the last month, the last three months, and the last six months? The question would be asked of all parties or witnesses to the mistreatment. Averaging the number stated among the reporters in each of the three time frames would provide a good gauge of the frequency of occurrence. The second measure of intensity would be the severity of the mistreatment. This measure would need to be assessed objectively but only after a clear understanding of the nature of the dynamics operating among parties in the alleged mistreatment. What the professional may define as mistreatment the participants may not. On the other hand, what the participants may not define as mistreatment may actually be mistreatment that requires some kind of outside interpretation. In a single case of mistreatment, each of the specified behaviors under the subcategories in Table 7–3 would need to be evaluated as either mild, moderate, or severe mistreatment. When severity of behaviors is combined with the frequency of occurrence, we can predict the intensity of the mistreatment.

Density may be measured by the degree to which the various categories overlap in actual cases of mistreatment. Figure 7–1 presents a set theory arrangement of the four categories of elder mistreatment. The overlapping circles come together at varying levels until in the very center of the circle all four categories occur together. The greater the number of behavioral forms of mistreat-

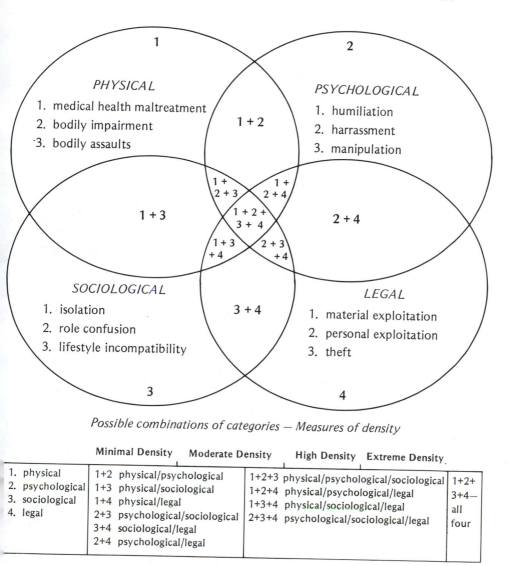

Figure 7-1 The Extrinsic Behavior Manifestations of Elder Mistreatment (The Measurement of Observable Events)

ment, both within and across categories, the more complex the problem and the more difficult to unravel. If the professional is unable to identify the complexity of the situation by examining the layers of behavior represented in Figure 7–1, the treatment areas become more explicit. As the key states at the base of Figure 7–1, one category of behavior represents minimal density, any combination of two may be labeled moderate density, three categories would be considered high density, and all four would signify extreme density. This schematic representation indicates the breadth of intervention techniques needed as well as the scope of the helping services required. Once we have clarified who is the most appropriate agent to provide help, and in what areas, we can move to the next stage of the defining process. Measuring the observable events forms the backdrop for the causal definition.

The Causal Definition

Elder mistreatment is treated on the basis of whether the cause is the result of passive neglect, active neglect, passive abuse, or active abuse. The term "treated" refers to professional intervention. Cause in this final stage of the definitional process refers to the immediate cause, not the roots or origin of the mistreatment. In the case of the latter, we may be talking about a long-standing resentment over many years. In the case of the former, we are speaking of the immediate precipitating circumstances for the particular episode or episodes. Learning the immediate provoking cause precedes getting at the roots. Root causes for elder mistreatment constitute another defining process and thus are not relevant here. This last stage of the defining process for elder mistreatment includes only the immediate cause of the mistreatment.

The immediate cause may come from two sources: neglect or abuse. *Neglect* refers to the omission of an act or actions, the consequence of which is elder mistreatment. On the other hand, *abuse* is the commission of an act or actions whose consequence is elder mistreatment. Neglect occurs in either of two situations: when the appropriate parties do not know any better—are innocently ignorant about how to care for the older person—and when the appropriate parties do, in fact, know better—are aware of how to care for the older person—but because of limited time and other resources can do no better. Abuse may be the result of two interpretations of the situation. In the first instance, the abuser believes that the older person needs to be better disciplined so the abuse is designed to be instructive; in the second instance, the abuser wishes to retaliate against the older person by truly making the person suffer. This latter is a deliberate act of malice, whereas the first type of abuse is interpreted as "teaching a lesson" to improve the character of the elder. The two types of neglect are best efforts in bad situations. These distinctions may be illustrated in the case of malnutrition. The family who neglects the older person unintentionally may typically buy junk foods for the whole family and thus prevent the older person from receiving the proper nutrition as a consequence of food-purchasing habits. In the other circumstance—intentional neglect—it may be that the older person is cared for by someone who has other legitimate demands. The caregiver may be too busy to keep the shelves stocked in the older person's home or provide the kinds of foods the elder needs. With regard to abuse, the older person may be denied the proper food because the caregiver wants to teach that person a lesson— you cannot eat until you get up to use the bathroom. Finally, food may be withheld from the older person because the abuser may wish to see the older person suffer. This may be a strategy to show the older person how much suffering the caregiver has gone through in looking after him or her. In each instance, the behavioral manifestation is the same—that is, malnutrition. What is different is the cause or the intent behind the behavioral manifestation.

Two major benefits are to be derived from the causal definition. First, it informs the mental or physical health care professional about the level of cooperation among the parties in the mistreatment when corrective measures are initiated. In the case of both types of neglect, it is possible for there to be a mutually supporting relationship. It is less likely in lesson-learning abuse for there to be a wholesome relationship, and it is least likely in retaliatory abuse. Knowing the nature of the motives for or cause of mistreatment will be useful in developing protective measures for the victim. A second benefit to be derived from determining the cause is to know how to counsel the perpetrators. In each type—unintentional neglect, neglect due to limited time and resources, lesson-learning abuse, and retaliatory abuse—different intervention strategies will need to be employed. Unless we know the specific cause, we cannot proceed to the treatment phase. One can see the folly of treating all elder mistreatment perpetrators in the same way. This cause-sorting scheme provides a systematic method for determining whether education, community support resources, therapy, or other corrective measures are the best fit for a particular case of elder mistreatment.

Conclusion

The field of elder mistreatment is at a critical turning point. Over the last ten years, we have made impressive strides in research, policy, and practice in elder mistreatment. But a great deal of work remains to be done in each of these areas. We can remain splintered within our various disciplines, professions, perspectives, and definitions of the situation, or we can mobilize our resources to develop a multidisciplinary yet unified approach to elder mistreatment. Several investigators are very much involved in the development of a systematic definition of elder mistreatment which can be utilized in the applied setting. The recent work of Phillips and Rempusheski provides a good illustration.[23] The proposed definition of elder mistreatment that we have presented here is an attempt to continue the efforts made toward a uniform definition of the situation. This definition is a proposal and must be understood at that level of development. It will need to be reviewed and revised as others in research, policy, and practice evaluate its utility. One wonders what the next ten years will look like. How will we define elder mistreatment at the end of this period? The challenge before us is to work very hard to make the definition of elder mistreatment more meaningful over the course of the next decade.

Endnotes

1. Margaret O'Rourke, "Elder Abuse: The State of the Art" (Paper presented, National Conference on Abuse of Older Persons, Cambridge, Mass., 1981); Terrence O'Malley et al., "Identifying and Preventing Family-Mediated Abuse and Neglect of Elderly Persons," *Annals of Internal Medicine* 98, no. 6 (1983), pp. 998–1004; James J. Callahan, "Elder Abuse Programming—Will It Help the Elderly?" *Urban Social Change Review* 15, no. 2 (1983), pp. 15–19; Claire Pedrick-Cornell and Richard Gelles, "Elder Abuse: The Status of Current Knowledge," *Family Relations* 32, no. 3 (1982), pp. 457–65.
2. Pedrick-Cornell and Gelles, "Elder Abuse," p. 459.
3. Abraham Kaplan, *The Conduct of Inquiry* (San Francisco: Chandler Publishing Company, 1964).
4. Pei Chen et al., "Elderly Abuse in Domestic Settings: A Pilot Study," *Journal of Gerontological Social Work* 4, no. 1 (1982), pp. 3–17.
5. Gerald Gioglio and Penelope Blakemore, "Elder Abuse in New Jersey: The Knowledge and Experience of Abuse Among Older New Jerseyans" (Trenton: New Jersey Department of Human Resources, 1983).
6. Claire Selltiz et al., *Research Methods in Social Relations* (New York: Holt, Rinehart & Winston, 1967).
7. Norman K. Denzin, *The Research Act* (Chicago: Aldine, 1970).
8. Elizabeth Lau and Jordan Kosberg, "Abuse of the Elderly by Informal Care Providers," *Aging* 299–301 (1979), pp. 10–15; Richard Douglass, Tom Hickey, and Catherine Noel, "A Study of Maltreatment of the Elderly and Other Vulnerable Adults" (Ann Arbor: University of Michigan, Institute of Gerontology, 1980); Rosalie S. Wolf, Cecile P. Strugnell, and Michael A. Godkin, "Preliminary Findings from Three Model Projects on Elder Abuse" (Worcester: University of Massachusetts Medical Center, University Center

on Aging, 1982); Linda Raedene Rounds, "A Study of Selected Environmental Variables Associated with Non-Institutional Settings Where There Is Abuse or Neglect of the Elderly" (Ph.D. diss., University of Texas at Austin, 1982); Mary Sengstock and Jersey Liang, "Identifying and Characterizing Elder Abuse" (Detroit: Wayne State University, Institute of Gerontology, 1982).

9. "Elder Abuse in Pennsylvania" (Harrisburg: Pennsylvania Department of Aging, Bureau of Advocacy, 1982); J. S. McLaughlin, J. P. Nickell, and L. Gill, "An Epidemiological Investigation of Elderly Abuse in Southern Maine and New Hampshire," *Elder Abuse* (Washington, D.C.: U.S. Government Printing Office, 1980); Helen O'Malley et al., "Elder Abuse in Massachusetts: A Survey of Professionals and Paraprofessionals (Boston: Legal Research and Services for the Elderly, 1979); Claude Pepper and Mary Rose Oaker, *Elder Abuse: An Examination of the Hidden Problem* (San Francisco: House Select Committee on Aging, Pub. No. 97-277, 1981).

10. Marilyn Block and Janice Sinnott, "The Battered Elder Syndrome: An Exploratory Study" (College Park: University of Maryland, Center on Aging, 1979); Linda Boydston and James McNairn, "Elderly Abuse by Adult Caretakers: An Exploratory Study," in *Physical and Financial Abuse of the Elderly*, ed. (San Francisco: House Select Committee on Aging, 1981).

11. Joyce Crouse et al., "Abuse and Neglect of the Elderly in Illinois: Incidence and Characteristics, Legislation, and Policy Recommendations" (Springfield, Ill.: Sangamon State University and Illinois Department on Aging, 1981).

12. George Theodorson and Achilles Theodorson, *A Modern Dictionary of Sociology* (New York: Thomas Y. Crowell, 1969).

13. Charlotte Anastasio, "Elder-Abuse: Identification and Acute Care Intervention" (Paper delivered at National Conference on Abuse of Older Persons, Cambridge, 1981); Denise Falcioni, "Assessing the Abused Elderly," *Journal of Gerontological Nursing* 8, no. 4 (1982), pp. 208–12; Douglas Johnson, "Abuse of the Elderly," *Nurse Practitioner* 6, no. 1 (1981), pp. 29–34; Mary Sengstock and Melanie Hwalek, "Comprehensive Index of Elder Abuse" (Paper presented at Annual Meeting of the Gerontological Society of America, New Orleans, November 1985); Susan Tomita, "Detection and Treatment of Elderly Abuse and Neglect: A Protocol for Health Care Professionals," *Physical and Occupational Therapy in Geriatrics* 2, no. 2 (1982), pp. 37–51; Edwin Villmoare and James Bergman, "Elder Abuse and Neglect: A Guide for Practitioners and Policy Makers," in *Physical and Financial Abuse of the Elderly* (San Francisco: House Select Committee on Aging, 1981).

14. Eloise Rathbone-McCuan and Barbara Voyles, "Case Detection of Abused Elderly Parents," *American Journal of Psychiatry* 139, no. 2 (1982), pp. 189–92.

15. Sol Daiches, "Protective Services Risk Assessment: A New Approach to Screening Adult Clients" (New York: Human Resources Administration, 1983); Doris Ferguson and Cornelia Beck, "H.A.L.F.—A Tool to Assess Elder Abuse Within the Family," *Geriatric Nursing* 4, no. 5 (1983), pp. 301–04; Terry Fulmer and Virginia Cahill, "Assessing Elder Abuse: A Study," *Journal of Gerontological Nursing* 10, no. 12 (1984), pp. 16–20.

16. Rosalie Wolf and Karl Pillemer, "Working with Abused Elders: Assessment,

Advocacy, and Intervention" (Worcester: University of Massachusetts Medical Center, University Center on Aging, 1984); *Report of the Elder Abuse and Neglect Assessment Instrument Field Test* (Atlanta, Georgia: The Atlanta Regional Commission, 1984).

17. Jordan Kosberg, "The Cost of Care Index" (Paper presented at the Southern Gerontological Society, Knoxville, Tenn., May 1984).

18. A. A. Baker, "Slow Euthanasia—Or, She Will Be Better Off in Hospital," *British Medical Journal* 2, no. 6,035 (1976), pp. 571–72; A. N. C. Clark. "The Diogenes Syndrome," *Nursing Times* 71, no. 21 (1975), pp. 800–02.

19. Jane M. Thibault, "A Developmental Research Design for the Clinical Treatment of Indirect Life-Threatening Behaviors in Elderly Patients" (Paper presented at the Fifth Annual Meeting of the Southern Gerontological Society, Knoxville, Tenn., May 1984); Philip A. Hall and Sylvia R. Andrew, "Differentiating Self-Neglect in Elder Mistreatment Situations" (Unpublished manuscript, Our Lady of the Lake University, the Worden School of Social Science, San Antonio, Texas, 1984).

20. Richard J. Gelles and Claire Pedrick-Cornell, *Intimate Violence in Families* (Beverly Hills, Calif.: Sage Publications, 1985).

21. Suzanne Steinmetz, "Dependency, Stress, and Violence Between Middle-Aged Caregivers and Their Elderly Parents," in *Abuse and Maltreatment of the Elderly: Causes and Interventions*, ed. Jordan Kosberg (Littleton, Mass.: John Wright, PSG, 1983).

22. M. I. Gresham, "The Infantilization of the Elderly: A Developing Concept," *Nursing Forum* 15, no. 2 (1976), pp. 195–210.

23. Linda R. Phillips and Veronica F. Rempusheski, "A Decision-Making Model for Diagnosing and Intervening in Elder Abuse and Neglect," *Nursing Research* 34, no. 3 (1985), pp. 134–39.

Chapter 8

THEORETICAL EXPLANATIONS OF ELDER ABUSE: COMPETING HYPOTHESES AND UNRESOLVED ISSUES

by Linda R. Phillips

As Peter Stearns points out in Chapter 1, the history of elder abuse predates by many years its "discovery" in the 1970s. When social phenomena have long traditions in society and short scientific histories, the initial theories derived to explain their existence are often blends of tradition, social myth, conventional wisdom, folklore, and the best fit that theoreticians and clinicians can make with the existing scientific knowledge at the time. In the search for remedies, assumptions are made and concepts are borrowed from other areas; some fit, but many do not. Such has been the case with elder abuse. Although currently many theoretical explanations for elder abuse have been suggested and accepted, few have been subjected to the rigor of empirical testing. The purpose of this chapter is to explore three of the competing theories that have been advanced to explain elder abuse and to examine the fit between these theories and some of the available empirical data. In addition, attention will be directed at identifying some of the issues currently underlying theory development and testing in this area.

Overview of Competing Theoretical Explanations of Elder Abuse

The Situational Model

The "situational model" is the explanatory base that was the earliest devised to explain elder abuse. It also appears to be the most widely accepted at this time. Derived from the theoretical base associated predominantly with child abuse and less strongly with other forms of intrafamily violence, this model has considerable intuitive appeal. In addition, among clinicians, this model has popular support, since its basic premise fits easily within an intervention framework.

Very simply, the basic premise of the situational model is that as the stress associated with certain situational and/or structural factors increases for the abuser, the likelihood increases of abusive acts directed at a vulnerable individual who is seen as being associated with the stress. The situational variables that have been linked with abuse of the elderly have included (1) elder-related factors such as physical and emotional dependency, poor health, impaired mental status, and a "difficult" personality;[1] (2) structural factors such as economic strains, social isolation, and environmental problems;[2] and (3) caregiver-related factors such as life crisis, "burn-out" or exhaustion with caregiving, substance abuse problems, and previous socialization experiences with violence.[3]

Theoretical support for the situational model has come from a number of diverse sources. First, the model simply appears to "make sense" based on conventional wisdom. Even before any research was published on elder abuse, at about the time that the popular media discovered its existence, this model was provided as a primary explanation for the phenomenon. For example, in 1977 when George Maddox, then director of Duke University's Center for the Study of Aging, was asked by a journalist for his explanation of elder abuse, he stated: "Older parents can be a genuine burden on their children; for instance, when they are bedridden for months or even years, it can be a terrible strain for even strong families."[4] With the large amount of recently derived research data that describes the high levels of stress, strain, and burdens experienced by informal caregivers in the course of elder caring,[5] popular support for this explanatory base is abundant, at least for those forms of elder abuse associated with poor caregiving.

The second source of support for the situational model arises from the child abuse and intrafamily violence literature and the empirical evidence that supports those roots. Gelles, for example, derived a social-psychological model of the causes of child abuse and a model of intrafamily violence, the central features of which are situational or structural stress and socialization experiences of the abusers.[6] Both of these models rely to a certain degree on frustration-aggression theory, which views violence as a learned reaction that is displayed by an aggressor when goals are blocked or frustrated,[7] and social learning theory, which views violence as behavior that is learned through emulation of parental role models within the confines of the primary socialization unit—the family. The empirical data from which both of these models were derived provide convincing support for the argument that, at least between parents and children and between spouses, situational stress and the socialization experiences of the abusers are key variables in the occurrence of abuse. Although these variables may not be sufficient to produce abuse independently, they appear (from Gelles's work and that of other researchers) to be essential for explaining child abuse and intrafamily violence within a multicausal system.

The third source of support for using the situational model to explain elder abuse arises from its effectiveness in explaining child abuse and other intrafamily violence and the obvious similarities among these other forms of abuse and elder abuse. Finkelhor and Pillemer, for example, note that child abuse and elder abuse are similar to the extent that (1) both involve the relationship between a vulnerable individual as abused and, sometimes, a frustrated caregiver as abuser; and (2) both share the social context of having first been identified and publicized by professionals who were specifically responsible for care of the two populations—that is, they were "medicalized," and the locus of responsibility for intervention and amelioration was set within the domain of public welfare agencies.[8] Spouse abuse and elder abuse, according to Finkelhor and Pillemer, are similar to the extent that (1) a certain portion of elder abuse actually is spouse abuse and (2) both situations involve consensual relationships between independent adults. For both spouse abuse and elder abuse, the relationships have usually been in existence for many years and involve emotional and, often, economic dependence but certainly less dependence than is evidenced in child abuse situations. As a result of these obvious similarities, the logic of borrowing concepts from the situational model as an explanation for elder abuse is hard to resist.

The final source of conceptual support for the utility of the situational model in explaining elder abuse arises from its association with a simple intervention model for prevention and intervention. If the situational model is true, then at least a partial solution to both prevention and intervention is the reduction of situational and/or structural stress, particularly that stress associated with caregiving burdens and strain. The appeal of the situational model for clinicians is evidenced by the number of intervention models for elder abuse that have a strong component involving efforts to reduce the burdens and strains of the caregiver through means such as respite services.[9] Similarly, prevention models designed by clinicians often contain a component that involves teaching caregivers to reduce the stresses associated with caregiving before the situation becomes untenable or volatile. Admittedly, not all portions of the model are equally amenable to intervention. For example, it is difficult after the fact to remedy the socialization experiences of the caregiver. Similarly, reducing economic burdens may be beyond the scope of our current intervention systems. Nevertheless, clinicians who are looking for immediate answers for often overwhelming problems find the appeal of the situational model hard to resist if it is assumed that reducing stress in one part of the family system will lower the overall abuse potential by decreasing the total amount of pressure within the system.

In addition to the conceptual support for the situational model, some studies of elder abuse have provided empirical support for the model as well. Pillemer's study, for example, showed a relationship between social isolation and elder abuse in that abused elders had significantly less contact with others and significantly less satisfaction with their social relationships than did nonabused elders. While Phillips found that abused elders did not have significantly fewer individuals *overall* providing support and services than nonabused elders, for certain categories of supporters and helpers, there were significant differences.[10] Abused elders had significantly fewer individuals who called on the phone, fewer people with whom they could correspond, and fewer people available to call on in times of trouble than did nonabused elders. The abused elders perceived significantly less support from the individuals available in the social network than did nonabused elders. In addition, in the Phillips study a greater percentage of individuals in the abuse group had no individuals in every category of social supporters than did those in the nonabuse group. During Phillips's tests of a causal model constructed to explain elder abuse, the only category of social support that had a direct relationship to abuse was the number of family members in the household other than the caregiver available to help. The relationship was positive; the more people other than the caregiver available to help, the more abuse.

The results of investigations of mental and physical incapacities and resulting elder dependency in relation to elder abuse have been more conflicting. Data from studies by Block and Sinnott, Lau and Kosberg, and Rathbone-McCuan, for example, all seem to indicate a relationship between elder abuse and the presence of mental or physical impairments in the victim.[11] A study by Hickey and Douglass suggested a relationship between dependency of the elder and elder abuse.[12] Using case control methods, however, the results have been somewhat different. Phillips found no significant difference between abused and nonabused elders' abilities to perform activities of daily living; nor was the ability to perform such activities related to abuse in causal model testing.[13] Pillemer's data indicated that abused elders may actually be the less dependent, rather than the more dependent, partners in the elder-caregiver relationship.[14]

Similarly, Giordano and Giordano found that a victim's physical illness was a significant predictor of physical abuse among two comparative samples of elders, but that the relationship was negative, meaning that the more physical illness, the less physical abuse.[15] However, in this study, the victim's physical illness was found to be a significant predictor of neglect. The victim's physical illness was not a significant predictor of any other type of elder abuse, including psychological abuse, financial exploitation, and multiple abuse. In fact, physical illness was a variable that differentiated victims of physical abuse and neglect from those who experienced psychological abuse and financial exploitation.

The results of examining stress as a cause of elder abuse have also been conflicting. Several previously cited studies (O'Malley et al., Block and Sinnott, and Douglass et al.) found external stress, such as unemployment, medical problems, and life stress, to be an important variable for abused individuals. On the other hand, Phillips, using the Rahe Life Change Units Scale, found no significant difference between abused and nonabused elders' reports of their family's life change units.[16] In addition, in the Phillips study, life change units were not related to abuse in the causal model testing.

There are a number of reasons for the inconsistent fit between the situational model and the available empirical data. Probably the primary reason for the lack of fit relates to the many methodological problems that have plagued the studies that have focused on elder abuse in general,[17] and the studies that have investigated the explanatory power of the situational model in particular. The definitions of abuse have varied from study to study. Whereas some studies have focused only on physical abuse, others have made no differentiation among physical abuse, emotional abuse, neglect, and other forms of elder abuse. The kinds of individuals sampled in the investigations have varied among studies, with some researchers sampling the perceptions of health professionals, some sampling agency records, and some sampling the perceptions of elderly individuals. Few studies have employed comparison groups, and—with few exceptions—most have employed small, nonrepresentative samples. In addition, few systematic attempts have been made to actually test the situational model using appropriate statistical procedures. Instead, the majority of studies have simply sought to describe a sample of abused elders and to later generate a theoretical base to explain the observed data. As a result of these methodological problems, it is difficult to determine at this time whether or not the situational model provides a satisfactory explanatory base for elder abuse.

Another reason for the lack of fit between the situational model and the available data may be simply that portions of the model are not applicable to elder abuse in all its various forms. This model has been used in elder abuse under the assumption that since elder abuse, child abuse, and other forms of intrafamily violence share some obvious similarities, they can all be explained by the same theories. This assumption, however, has not been tested. Finkelhor and Pillemer argue that the parallels between elder abuse and other forms of domestic violence can be overdrawn and that, although sharing some similarities, elder abuse is different from other forms of family violence in some very important ways, among them the structural relationship between the victim and the abuser. It is, therefore, quite possible that even a powerful explanatory base for other forms of domestic violence may not be a satisfactory explanation for elder abuse. In addition, it is quite possible, as Giordano and Giordano suggest, that different theoretical explanations are appropriate for different forms of elder abuse—for example, the causes of physical abuse are quite possibly distinct from the causes of financial exploitation and/or neglect. If this is the case, then employing the situational model as a monocausal explanation of elder abuse may be theoretically and empirically inappropriate.

Social Exchange Theory

Another conceptual model that has been used to explain elder abuse has been derived from social exchange theory.[18] Social exchange theory is based on the idea that social interaction involves the exchange of rewards and punishments between at least two people and that all individuals seek to maximize rewards and minimize punishments in their interaction with others. Rewards are derived from the exchange of positive sentiments, instrumental services, and personal resources. Punishments include the exchange of negative sentiments, the withholding of resources and services, and the exchange of punishing behaviors. When all things are equal between two individuals, Homans[19] asserts that social interaction occurs according to the law of distributive justice, "which refers to a person's expectations of the rewards due to him and costs which he may incur—the proportion of his rewards to his costs; that these should be seen to be distributed in a fair ratio to each other."[20] Should this law be violated, the result is anger, resentment, and punishment. Between two people, over time, the just distribution of rewards becomes a value that is exchanged. When justice is exchanged as a value, the interaction conforms to the norm of reciprocity, which implies that each person in the relationship has rights and duties toward the other person, and patterns of exchanging goods and services between the two people are mutually satisfying.

In some relationships, all things are not equal. People have differential access to resources, including status, money, esteem, and prestige, as well as differing capabilities to provide instrumental services. As a result, there can be imbalances in social exchange that are termed power. As Dowd states, "From this perspective, power is synonymous with the dependence of Actor A and Actor B. It is based on the inability of one of the partners in the social exchange to reciprocate a rewarding behavior."[21] The person, then, who is less dependent and is perceived as contributing most to the relationship has the power advantage. When the dependent person has no choice about continuing the relationship, as in situations such as prisons and the armed services, the other has what is called "fate control." Fate control is converted to "behavior control" whenever the controlling person uses his or her power advantage to manipulate the behavior of the dependent person. When the dependent person has no choice about interacting with the other, the person with the power advantage develops a monopoly on rewards and has little to lose by being unjust.[22]

During the past decade, social exchange theory has been popular with theoreticians and researchers for explaining the situation of elderly individuals in families in general, and intrafamily violence and elder abuse, in particular. Although he did not specifically treat elder abuse, Dowd described the general aging condition (the context within which elder abuse occurs) in terms of the exchange paradigm. According to Dowd, as people age, they have less access to power resources and progressively less ability to perform instrumental services. In fact, with increasing physical infirmities, the individual begins to require more and more in the form of instrumental services. Therefore, when one is old and infirm, violating the law of distributive justice is relatively easy. In addition, because of the losses associated with aging, the individual's potential to supplement social ties and to extend a personal power base is reduced. As a result, the individual becomes less able to reciprocate rewarding behaviors and less likely to have a choice about continuing unrewarding or punishing social exchanges with those who perform an instrumental service. Figuratively speaking, the elderly individual must begin to live on the credit accumulated over the years because there are few ways to replenish the bank. One outcome of the aging condition that Dowd predicts is that as the imbalance in power increases, the older person is likely to display more passivity and compliance and more withdrawing behaviors in an effort not to alienate the remaining few people who can provide rewards and services.

Gelles and Straus have used social exchange theory as an explanation for child abuse and conjugal violence.[23] In both situations, the aggressor and the victim are viewed as having few alternatives to continuing the exchange, and the aggressor is seen as having a monopoly on rewards and thus little to lose from being unjust. When the aggressor determines that the personal rewards arising from the situation are not proportional to the personal costs being incurred, there is a violation of the law of distributive justice, which may result in violence within some relationships. Further, under such circumstances, the aggressor may gain rewards from an ability to inflict costs on the victim in response to the perceived injustice.

Conceptually, the exchange paradigm can be easily used to explain elder abuse under the assumption that abused elderly people are more powerless, dependent, and vulnerable than their caregivers and have fewer alternatives to continued interaction. Deriving empirical support for this stance, however, has been far less simple, although some research seems to support the exchange view. For example, in support of Dowd's argument that the more powerless the individual, the more passivity displayed, Phillips showed that abused elders demonstrated significantly more depression/dejection than nonabused elders.[24] In addition, between the two samples, abused and nonabused elders demonstrated similar amounts of anger and hostility. Similarly, Pillemer explained in his findings that social isolation is a contributing factor to elder abuse in terms of social exchange by asserting that "the costs of abusive behavior are far less when outsiders are not present to negatively sanction the behavior."

Phillips's inductive work, which was based on data obtained from abusive and nonabusive caregivers, demonstrated the importance of the principle of distributive justice for the caregiver's treatment of an elderly person.[25] A core category generated from those data was the caregiver's perceptions of the relative credits and debits of both the elder and the caregiver over years of interaction. These perceptions appeared to influence both the decisions of the caregiver about whether or not to provide care, and the evaluations by the elder regarding whether or not the care provided was appropriate. Among the data obtained from abusive caregivers were many examples of caregivers obtaining personal rewards as a result of punishing either current or past perceived injustices, as well as many references to the degree to which the caregiver's past and present credits far exceeded the caregiver's debts and elder's credits. Many of the abusive caregivers chose to participate in the study because they were seeking an outsider's opinion of whether or not they delivered more punishment than was warranted based on evaluations of the past and present credits of the elder. In the data from nonabusive caregivers, more common examples were those of caregivers perceiving their roles to be appropriate payment of past contributions of the elder, caregivers receiving payment for their role in the form of personal satisfaction, and the elder's past and present credits outweighing their past and present debts.

On the other hand, the failure of researchers to obtain unequivocal evidence that abused elders are more dependent than non-abused elders would seem to contradict the exchange paradigm by violating the essential assumption that abused individuals are more powerless and, as a result, caregivers have little to lose by their actions. Pillemer suggests an alternative view of how elder abuse fits the exchange paradigm that helps resolve this dilemma. Pillemer reports from a case-control study that in a small proportion of elder abuse cases the elder was excessively dependent, but that in the majority of cases, the reverse was actually true: The *abuser* was more dependent on the elder. Abuse, he argues, tends to arise when the abuser feels powerless and impotent and seeks to compensate for the lack of control or power loss with the resources available. When personal resources are limited, violence is a likely outcome. In support of this position, Pillemer provides empirical data indicating that (1) overall, the abused elders in the sample were no more physically impaired than a matched group of nonabused elders (in fact in some areas the abused elders were significantly more independent); (2) the nonabused elders were more financially dependent than their abused counterparts, although no significant differences were found between the groups for dependency related to housing, cooking or cleaning, household repair, companionship, and social activities; and (3) the abused elders were more likely than nonabused elders to report that their relative would be hurt financially if they left and to describe mutual dependence in other areas with their relative.[26]

A supplemental source of support for Pillemer's findings can be found among the interviews in Phillips's inductive studies. A number of the individuals who categorized themselves in the abuse group described their intense embarrassment, impotence, and subsequent frustration and anger arising from situations in which they were unable to control the elder's behavior. It was not uncommon for these incidents to be cited as the reasons for some of the punishments or abuses they used with the elder. Often the situations that involved the greatest sense of impotence were of two types. The first type involved everyday activities of daily living such as eating, toileting, or walking, where the elder was able to cope with the task independently but not in the way the caregiver considered appropriate or where the elder actually had ultimate control. The second type involved social situations in which caregivers felt a sense of responsibility for the elder's behavior and perceived that onlookers were negatively evaluating their performance as "good" caregivers. One incident illustrating the first type of situation was described by a caregiver who told of the elderly person insisting on washing her own underwear in the bathtub rather then letting the caregiver use the washing machine. In another incident, the caregiver described regularly taking the elderly person to the toilet only to have her become incontinent as soon as she stood up. Examples of the second type of situation included caregivers describing their embarrassment at taking the elderly person out to a restaurant and having the elder eat with his hands, drop and spill food on the floor, or make loud, inappropriate sounds or comments.

The empirical support that has been generated so far for the exchange paradigm as an explanation for elder abuse is not at all conclusive. In addition, by itself, social exchange theory does not afford a complete explanation for elder abuse. It does not, for example, provide the power needed to predict, given a similar set of circumstances, which individuals will use violence and which will not. On the other hand, more studies are beginning to use the exchange paradigm as a partial or complete theoretical base and empirical support, suggesting that its viability is beginning to accumulate. It would appear from these preliminary studies that further development and testing of exchange theory in this area of elder abuse is likely to be productive.

Symbolic Interactionism

Symbolic interactionism is a third theoretical explanation that has been advanced for elder abuse. Using the view developed by McCall and Simmons, symbolic interactionism is predicated on the assumption that social interaction is a process between at least two individuals that (1) occurs over time; (2) consists of identifiable phases that are recurring, interrelated, and loosely sequenced; and (3) requires constant negotiation and renegotiation to establish a "working consensus" (actually in the form of lack of disagreement rather than agreement) about the symbolic meaning of the encounter.[27] Extrapolating from the work of McCall and Simmons, the phases of social interaction include the cognitive process, the expressive process, and the evaluative process.

The cognitive process consists of the mental operations individuals use to organize their perceptions into a meaningful whole. The definition of the situation is a distinct part of the cognitive process in that it involves each individual assigning meaning to the encounter based on cultural beliefs, past experiences, and currently salient roles. The individual's definition of the situation determines his or her expectancy set and provides the background against which actions are planned based on perceived images of the self and the other, rather than any "true" reality. During this process, characteristics, motives, and goals are imputed to the other person based on perceptual images, and actions are formulated based on the imputed features of the other person. Initially, during an encounter, the individual unilaterally defines the situation. As interaction continues, however, and feedback is received, the individuals continually redefine the situation as a result of their perception of the degree to which each participant's role enactments mesh with expectancy sets.

During the cognitive process, individuals improvise roles for themselves, and impute role identities to others based on separate and negotiated definitions of the situation. Each individual can assume any number of roles, and the essence of the roles is stored within a behavioral repertoire. During the cognitive process of social interaction, each interactor calls forth from this "store" role identities that are deemed to be congruent with the perceived demands of the situation. The role each assigns to the other is based on what the individual would expect of himself under the same circumstances as well as his idealized view of the other. The concept of an idealized view of the other is an important one in relationship to the interactions between family members whose interactional and perceptual histories are long-standing. Goffman notes that under such circumstances each individual develops a constantly evolving "dossier" about the other person.[28] This dossier contains, among other things, a history of events, impressions, normative role expectations, and evaluations that uniquely identify the one person to the other. The dossier, or image of personal identity, is then used by the individuals as their "ready-made" definition of the situation. Whereas strangers and acquaintances must spend a considerable amount of time establishing the symbolic meaning of encounters, family members are able to abbreviate the process of role improvisation and role imputation to the other because they have preestablished expectancy sets based on perceptions of past history.

The expressive process is the phase during which actors display behaviors that are consistent with roles as improvised and with roles as imputed. During the expressive process, each interactor has a moral and social obligation to support the roles being portrayed by the other, as long as the other has misrepresented neither himself nor his role. This role support tends to assure the continuation of interaction as long as it is provided. Roles are synchronized within the interaction whenever the behavioral sets of the two people are mutually supportive, reciprocal, and compatible,[29] or at least not grossly conflicting. Role synchrony occurs when each person has a similar definition of the situation and has improvised and imputed role identities that are meshed. Role synchrony itself tends to assure the continuation of interaction, even when the roles are synchronized on invalid perceptions. For example, in a situation where an adult child has improvised the role of parent and imputed the role of child to the actual parent, interaction will continue without conflict so long as the elderly person improvises the role of child for herself and supports the adult child's portrayal of the parent role. Role asynchrony, on the other hand, occurs when there is a mismatching of either the definition of the situation or of the role identities that are assigned by each participant. The source of role asynchrony can arise from either participant in the interaction. If the people in an interaction have a choice about continuation of the relationship, role asynchrony will usually result in termination of the interaction and, eventually, the relationship. However, when there is no alternative but to continue the relationship, as is often the case with the elderly and their families, role asynchrony has negative results.

The evaluation process forms the basis for consensus negotiation as the actors alter their own behaviors and their expectations of the other in response to their independent assessments of the situation. During the evaluation process, each interactor judges the role enactments of self and the other person for adequacy and legitimacy. As a result of the evaluation process, the image of personal identity that each interactor holds for the other is reformulated and catalogued for retrieval during future encounters.

Viewed from within the framework of symbolic interactionism, elder abuse can be conceptualized as an inadequate or inappropriate role enactment arising from cognitive processes that alter role improvisation and role imputation for both the elder and the perpetrator (unless, of course, the elder is either cognitively or physically unable to participate in the process—for example, the elderly person is unconscious—in which case only the cognitive processes of the perpetrator are involved). The causal chain begins with (1) the symbolic meaning the family has created and perpetuated regarding negative behavioral expressions that influence role improvisation and role imputation,[30] and (2) the image of personal identity that each holds for the other and that influences the motives, characteristics, and goals that each ascribes to the other.

Phillips's inductive work using data derived from in-depth interviews with abusive and nonabusive caregivers has suggested the significance of the caregiver's image of an elder's identity to elder abuse.[31] According to these data, for elders and their family members, an important part of formulating personal images of the other person concerns reconciling the image of who this person was conceived to be in the past with the image of who this person is now conceived to be. In this process, the actual events involved in memories and observations are unimportant. Rather, the data suggest that the perceptions the individual has of the experiences and, as a consequence, the personal meanings that are attached to the experiences are important.

According to Phillips's data, past and present images can be deified, normalized, or stigmatized, depending on how well the individual's role performance is evaluated by the other.[32] The type of image formulated from both the past and present, and the amount of discrepancy between the past and present image, significantly influence the symbolic meaning of present encounters by affecting motives, characteristics, and goals that are ascribed to the other individual. Consequently, the families in which elder abuse was present were those in which the elders were stigmatized or those in which there was a large negative descrepancy between the past and present image of the elder. In these families, negative characteristics and ulterior motives were ascribed to the elder's behavior, and elders were viewed as willfully difficult or uncooperative. The conflict experienced regarding reconciling the past with the present image was particularly acute among adult children and elders who had not had a continuous live-in relationship throughout the years and among spouses where one spouse had sustained a personality-altering illness.

In the Phillips sample, evidence of caregivers having stigmatized images of the elder or images of the elder that were devalued over time was abundant. The abusive caregivers displayed more rigid, dogmatic expectations of themselves and elders than non-abusive caregivers. Another important relationship identified from these data is the degree to which the caregiver's perception of the elder's identity influenced the caregiver's own personal image and subsequent role improvisation. The abusive caregivers in the sample tended to ascribe negative motives and characteristics to the elders for whom they cared and sought roles from within their behavioral repertoire that were compatible with their negative images of the elder. For example, one caregiver indicated that she perceived the elder to be constantly testing the bounds of social acceptability. As a consequence, she perceived herself to be a "security guard" and enacted a punitive, controlling role that often involved abusive acts.

For the caregivers, formulating a personal image of self was particularly influenced by their currently salient roles. As family members aged, the constellation of roles stored within their behavioral repertoires naturally changed. New roles were adopted, some roles were modified, some roles were abandoned altogether, and some—the ones that were required in response to specific situations such as being a family caregiver—remained outside of the repertoire until the need arose. In formulating a personal image of self, caregivers were only able to call on those roles that had been learned and incorporated into the repertoire. Imaging and calling forth a role that was appropriate and consistent with a particular situation was next to impossible when the essence of that role was unavailable. For example, if the family member was required to perform the nurturing tasks associated with the role of caregiver but the individual did not have an image of self as nurturing, the role improvised was likely to be inappropriate. In addition, even if appropriate roles were available and the individual's perception of the other person's image could activate an image of self that was perceived by the person to be congruent with the situation, the subsequent role response could be inappropriate or inadequate. For example, if the family member perceived that the elderly person was willfully provocative, the image elicited could be that of aggressor or punitive parent, even though the elderly person's behavior was actually the result of a disease such as Alzheimer's.

The caregivers also indicated that elders could project inappropriate personal images. For example, an elder could maintain a personal image as parent or controller and could call forth that role long after the role was appropriate within the context of the situation. Negative consequences were the outcomes of such projections of personal image. Although the results of this qualitative investigation do not provide a test of symbolic interactionism as an explanatory base for elder abuse, they do suggest the potential importance of operationalizing a number of these concepts and testing the model by using appropriate statistical techniques.

Actual tests of the symbolic interactionist explanation of elder abuse are scarce. Phillips, however, used this framework in testing a causal model of elder abuse and found that the evaluation of roles devised for self by the elder (which was operationalized through a semantic differential instrument on which the elder evaluated roles such as parent, advice giver, and help giver) was related to anger/hostility ($B = -.27$) and depression/dejection ($B = -.22$), but neither anger/hostility nor depression/dejection were significantly related to abuse. The elders' perceptions of the caregiver's behavior ($B = -.62$), and other family members in the house who were also available to help ($B = .41$), were the only variables tested in that causal model that explained variance in abuse ($R^2 = .54$).

The use of symbolic interactionism as an explanatory base for elder abuse has certain advantages, as well as some inherent drawbacks. On the one hand, because of the nature of symbolic interactionism, many of the variables implied by the model are relatively inaccessible to empirical testing. Because the model deals primarily with cognitive processes and symbolic meanings, capturing more than the rudiments of the concepts in precise measurement systems is difficult. In addition, by itself, symbolic interactionism may not be able to provide the predictive power necessary to identify which families are likely to abuse and which are not.

On the other hand, symbolic interactionism clearly accounts for the interactional nature of abuse better than any other model. The situation model, for example, is static and takes the perspective of either the abuser or the abused but not the perspective of both simultaneously. There is every reason to believe that elder abuse is an extremely complex phenomenon that is rooted in the individuals' impressions of past experiences and caused by the interaction of multiple variables. For this reason, the symbolic interactionist perspective appears promising for capturing this complexity and for accounting for the dynamic nature of the situation.

Unresolved Issues Underlying Theory Development and Testing

Although Pedrick-Cornell and Gelles have suggested that theory development and testing is currently one of the most pressing needs of elder abuse research, devising theories to explain elder abuse has been and continues to be hampered by a number of unresolved issues. The major unresolved issues fall into four interrelated categories: (1) derivation of the theories; (2) operationalization of the dependent variable; (3) scope of the theories; and (4) method of testing theories.

Currently, controversy exists about the theoretical paradigm to which elder abuse belongs and consequently that from which testable hypotheses will be derived. Some researchers have chosen to identify elder abuse with other forms of family violence; they have applied to elder abuse the same theories used to explain other forms of family violence. Others have chosen to identify elder abuse with the family caregiving paradigm; they claim that elder abuse is simply an extreme example of the family caregiving relationship gone awry. There are, of course, strong arguments for each side of the controversy.

As we have seen, the similarities between elder abuse and other forms of family violence are striking, and there is reason to believe that a certain proportion of elder abuse is actually spouse abuse grown old. On the other hand, not all forms of elder abuse involve violence. In fact, some forms of elder abuse are intimately related to the manner in which the caregiver fulfills the caregiving role and not to precipitous violent episodes. In addition, some facets of elder abuse appear to be intimately related to questions raised in other caregiving research, such as: Who should provide care to aging individuals? What kinds of care and how much care should be provided? How do families mobilize to meet the needs of dependent elders? What is the role of society in supporting, augmenting, and supplementing the care that is provided by family members? Last, the elderly are much more vulnerable to abuse, such as financial exploitation, than are persons in other age groups; therefore, the situations of some elderly victims are fairly distinct from other kinds of victims.

A second, and closely related, controversy involves the appropriate operationalization of the dependent variable, abuse. In previous research, definitions of what constitutes abuse have varied widely, with some researchers considering only physical abuse (violence), some including all or a portion of a wide range of types of elder abuse, such as those identified by Block and Sinnott (physical abuse, medical abuse, and environmental abuse), and some having a broader view that includes abnormal expressions of the caregiving role as elder abuse. Some researchers have attempted to operationalize abuse based on the distinctions of intentional versus unintentional acts and acts of commission versus acts of omission. The use of instruments to quantify the presence and absence of certain acts has been another way researchers have attempted to increase precision.

In spite of all these efforts, however, facets of elder abuse have still eluded operationalization for a number of reasons. First, there are still no normative data that provide an indication of how frequent and severe negative acts must be before the situation is termed abusive. For example, does a caregiver slapping the hands of an elderly person constitute abuse? Or is hand slapping acceptable but face slapping not? Second, do characteristics of the elderly change the situation? For example, what if the elderly person has Alzheimer's disease, smears feces, and shrieks obscenities? Third, there are no guidelines for determining the degree to which family norms influence whether or not abuse is present. For example, is it abuse if the caregiver swears at the elder? Is it still abuse if the caregiver and elder have sworn at each other for the past forty years? Fourth, since elder abuse involves independent adults, there are no guidelines for determining the degree to which the elder's choices alter definitions of abuse. For example, is it abuse if the elder is required to live in a filthy room with no in-door plumbing? Is it still abuse if the elder *chooses* to continue in that place after alternatives have been presented? Finally, the issue of whether acts are abusive regardless of the knowledge or intentions of the perpetrator has not been addressed. For example, is it abuse if the caregiver pulls the elder's catheter out but doesn't know better? Or is it abuse if the caregiver force feeds the elder but does so because of an overwhelming desire for the elder to get better? These are only a few of the unanswered questions that arise when researchers attempt to operationalize abuse. Until some of these questions are answered, theory development in the area of elder abuse will be severely hampered.

A third issue in elder abuse theory development and testing is related to the scope of theories that are needed to satisfactorily explain elder abuse. The discussion in this chapter has presented three theories that have been used to explain elder abuse and has treated them as competing explanations. However, Gelles and Straus's work indicates that, in general, no one theoretical base will provide a comprehensive, all-inclusive explanation of elder abuse. In addition, there is reason to believe that different forms of elder abuse are explained by different theories. As a result, probably the best resolution to this controversy will be in efforts to integrate theoretical perspectives using those variables with the most explanatory power from any or all theories available. However, arriving at this resolution will require simultaneous testing of multiple theories in single studies in order to identify those variables from the various theories that are intercorrelated and those that do not have explanatory power for the phenomenon of elder abuse.

The last controversy to be considered relates to identifying appropriate methodologies for elder abuse theory development and testing. To date, three methodologies have been the most popular in elder abuse research: (1) survey/descriptive, (2) qualitative, and (3) causal model testing. The types of subjects measured have varied widely across categories (for example, those elders able to answer the telephone versus those elders who are confined to bed and incompetent or unconscious). In many ways, perpetuating this particular controversy is counterproductive. All of the methodologies that have been used (so long as the studies are well designed) are appropriate for different types of research questions and contribute to the expanding body of knowledge in different ways. The difficulty with all of these methodologies is not with the methods but with the interpretation of the data both by researchers and research consumers. The pressing need in elder abuse research is for theory generation and testing; a variety of methodologies can be used to meet this need.

Summary

This chapter has sought to explore three theoretical explanations for elder abuse and to raise some of the issues involved in the generation and testing of theory to explain elder abuse. The three explanations discussed are by no means mutually exclusive; nor do they include all of the explanations that have been advanced in the literature for elder abuse. The knowledge we currently have in the area of elder abuse is miniscule compared with that which is needed to ameliorate and prevent the problem. Only with empirically tested theories that clearly explain the phenomenon, identify the interrelationships of the variables involved, and predict which families are likely to abuse and which are not will it be possible to provide the information needed by elders and their family members, social planners, policy makers, and health professionals.

Endnotes

1. R. L. Douglass, T. Hickey, and C. Noel, "A Study of Maltreatment of the Elderly and Other Vulnerable Adults" (Ann Arbor: Institute of Gerontology, University of Michigan, 1980); M. R. Block and J. D. Sinnott, "The Battered Elder Syndrome: An Exploratory Study" (College Park: University of Maryland, Center on Aging, 1979); E. Lau and J. Kosberg, "Abuse of the Elderly by Informal Care Providers," *Aging* 299 (1979), pp. 10–15; H. O'Malley et al., "Elder Abuse in Massachusetts: A Survey of Professionals and Paraprofessionals" (Boston: Legal Research and Services for the Elderly, 1979); E. Rathbone-McCuan, "Elderly Victims of Family Violence and Neglect," *Social Casework* 61 (1980), pp. 296–304; S. K. Steinmetz, "Battered Parents," *Society* 15 (1978), pp. 372–75.
2. O'Malley et al., "Elder Abuse in Massachusetts"; Douglass et al., "A Study of Maltreatment of the Elderly"; Block and Sinnott, "The Battered Elder Syndrome"; L. R. Phillips, "Abuse and Neglect of the Frail Elderly at Home: An Exploration of Theoretical Relationships," *Journal of Advanced Nursing* 8 (1983), pp. 379–92; K. Pillemer, "Social Isolation and Elder Abuse" (Durham: University of New Hampshire, Family Research Laboratory and Department of Sociology, 1984).
3. O'Malley et al., "Elder Abuse in Massachusetts"; Douglass et al., "A Study of Maltreatment of the Elderly"; Block and Sinnott, "Battered Elder Syndrome"; Rathbone-McCuan, "Elderly Victims of Family Violence and Neglect"; Steinmetz, "Battered Parents."
4. T. Tiede, "Battered Oldsters," *The Arizona Daily Star*, May 21, 1977.
5. P. G. Archbold, "Impact of Parent Caring on Middle-Aged Offspring," *Journal of Gerontological Nursing* 6 (1980), pp. 78–85; P. G. Archbold, "Impact of Parent-Caring on Women," *Family Relations* 32 (1983), pp. 39–45; M. H. Cantor, "Strain Among Caregivers: A Study of Experience in the United States," *The Gerontologist* 23 (1983), pp. 597–604; V. G. Cicirelli, "A Comparison of Helping Behavior to Elderly Parents of Adult Children with Intact and Disrupted Marriages," *The Gerontologist* 23 (1983), pp. 691–725; C. L. Johnson and D. J. Catalano, "A Longitudinal Study of Family Supports to Impaired Elderly," *The Gerontologist* 23 (1983), pp. 612–18; S. W. Poulshock and G. T. Deimling, "Families Caring for Elders in Residence: Issues in the Measurement of Burden," *Journal of Gerontology* 39 (1984), pp. 230–39; S. H. Zaritt, K. E. Reever, and J. Bach-Peterson, "Relatives of the Impaired Elderly: Correlates of Feelings of Burden," *The Gerontologist* 20 (1982), pp. 649–55.
6. R. J. Gelles, *Family Violence* (Beverly Hills, Calif.: Sage Publications, 1979);

R. J. Gelles, *The Violent Home* (Beverly Hills, Calif.: Sage Publications, 1972).

7. R. J. Gelles and M. A. Straus, "Determinants of Violence in the Family: Toward a Theoretical Integration," in *Contemporary Theories About the Family*, ed. W. R. Burr et al. (New York: Free Press, 1979).

8. D. Finkelhor and K. Pillemer, "Elder Abuse: Its Relationship to Other Forms of Domestic Violence" (Paper presented at the Second National Conference on Family Violence Research, Durham, N.H., 1984).

9. N. R. Hooyman, "Elderly Abuse and Neglect: Community Intervention" (Paper presented at the Annual Meeting of the Western Gerontological Society, Seattle, 1981).

10. L. R. Phillips, "Abuse and Neglect of the Frail Elderly at Home."

11. Block and Sinnott, "The Battered Elder Syndrome"; Lau and Kosberg, "Abuse of the Elderly by Informal Care Providers"; Rathbone-McCuan, "Elderly Victims of Family Violence and Neglect."

12. T. Hickey and R. L. Douglass, "Neglect and Abuse of Older Family Members: Professionals' Perspectives and Case Experiences," *The Gerontologist* 21 (1981), pp. 171–76.

13. Phillips, "Abuse and Neglect of the Frail Elderly at Home."

14. K. Pillemer, "Dangers of Dependency: New Findings on Domestic Violence Against the Elderly" (Paper presented at the American Sociological Association, Washington, D.C., August 1985).

15. N. H. Giordano and J. A. Giordano, "Individual and Family Correlates of Elder Abuse" (Paper presented at the Annual Scientific Meeting of the Gerontological Society of America, San Francisco, 1983).

16. R. H. Rahe, "Life Change Measurement as a Predictor of Illness," *Proceedings of the Royal Society of Medicine* 61 (1968), pp. 1124–26.

17. C. Pedrick-Cornell and R. J. Gelles, "Elder Abuse: The Status of Current Knowledge," *Family Relations* 31 (1982), pp. 457–65.

18. L. R. Phillips, "Family Relations Between Two Samples of Family Elderly Individuals" (Ph.D. diss., University of Arizona, 1980).

19. G. C. Homans, *Social Behavior: Its Elementary Forms* (New York: Harcourt, Brace & World, 1961).

20. J. K. Chadwick-Jones, *Social Exchange Theory: Its Structure and Influence on Social Psychology* (London: Academic Press, 1976), p. 171.

21. J. J. Dowd, "Aging as Social Exchange: A Preface to Theory," *Journal of Gerontology* 31 (1975), pp. 584–95.

22. Chadwick-Jones, *Social Exchange Theory*; Homans, *Social Behavior*.

23. Gelles and Straus, "Determinants of Violence in the Family."

24. Phillips, "Abuse and Neglect of the Frail Elderly at Home."

25. L. R. Phillips, "Caring for the Frail Elderly at Home: Toward a Theoretical Explanation of the Dynamics of Family Caregiving" (Tucson: University of Arizona, College of Nursing, 1985).

26. Pillemer, "The Dangers of Dependency: New Findings on Domestic Violence Against the Elderly."

27. G. J. McCall and J. L. Simmons, *Identities and Interactions* (New York: Free Press, 1966).

28. E. Goffman, *Stigma* (Englewood Cliffs, N.J.: Prentice-Hall, 1962).

29. J. W. Thibaut and H. H. Kelley, *The Social Psychology of Groups* (New York: John Wiley & Sons, 1959).
30. E. J. Thomas, "Problems of Disability from the Perspective of Role Theory," in *Families in Crisis*, eds. P. H. Glasser and L. N. Glasser (New York: Harper & Row, 1970), pp. 252–72.
31. Phillips, "Abuse and Neglect of the Frail Elderly at Home."
32. Phillips, "Caring for the Frail Elderly at Home."

Chapter 9

MAJOR FINDINGS FROM THREE MODEL PROJECTS ON ELDERLY ABUSE

by Rosalie S. Wolf

In the summer of 1980, the federal government's most prominent agency in the field of social gerontology, the Administration on Aging (AOA), issued a request for proposals that would establish Model Projects on Elderly Abuse. Over two years had passed since a congressional subcommittee had been startled by a report on battered parents. The evidence from early studies and an investigation in 1980 by the House Select Committee on Aging that followed the testimony indicated that elder abuse was occurring nationwide and that the incidence of reports was increasing. Although these initial research efforts provided documentation about the characteristics and situations of the victims and the perpetrators, the studies suffered from small sample size, inconsistent definitions of abuse and neglect, and unverified suppositions about prevention and treatment.

Because of the sense of urgency with which members of the public and Congress regarded the problem, the AOA decided to allocate a portion of its 1980 discretionary funds to support several Model Projects, with the explanation that "the paucity of data should not be used as a reason to delay implementation of experi-

Note: Complete report can be found in Rosalie S. Wolf, Michael A. Godkin, and Karl A. Pillemer, *Elder Abuse and Neglect: Findings from Three Model Projects* (Worcester: University of Massachusetts Medical Center, University Center on Aging, 1984).

mental model programs to treat and prevent abuse."[1] The proposals submitted by the Massachusetts Department of Elder Affairs, the Metropolitan Commission on Aging of Onondaga County, New York, and the Rhode Island Department of Elderly Affairs were named recipients of the three-year AOA grants.

Model Projects were established in Massachusetts by one of the state's affiliated home care corporations, Elder Home Care Services of the Worcester Area, Inc., and by the Boston Commission on the Affairs of the Elderly (which terminated after the first year); in Onondaga County, New York, by Alliance Division of Catholic Charities of Syracuse; and in Rhode Island, by the state agency itself. The primary purpose of these Model Projects was to provide case work services to abused and neglected elderly and members of their families, including intervention in cases of maltreatment, introduction of services when appropriate, counseling for victims and relatives, and help conflict resolution between abusers and abused. In addition, the Model Projects were to function as coordinators among the service providers and as a focal point for action by local agencies on behalf of abused clients. Finally, all three projects had the responsibility of educating the community about elder abuse and neglect.

A grant for evaluating the three projects was given to the University Center on Aging at the University of Massachusetts Medical Center. Two questions were addressed in the evaluation: What is the nature of the phenomenon of elder abuse, its victims, perpetrators, and causes? and What was the impact of the Model Projects with regard to case resolution, community responses, and organizational replicability? This chapter reports on the results of the evaluation and then discusses some of the implications for future research, practice, and policy.

The Nature of Elder Abuse and Neglect

Five theories about the causes of elder abuse and neglect shaped the framework for this portion of the evaluation. These theories, which were culled from a review of earlier work on the subject, the sociological and psychological literature on family violence, and gerontological research on family relations, included (1) the psychological state of the perpetrator, (2) dependency and exchange relations between the abused and the abuser, (3) external stress, (4) social isolation, and (5) intergenerational transmission of violence ("cycle of violence"). Although by no means the only theories proposed by the investigators in these fields, these five were the most convincing and became the bases for the four analyses summarized below. (See Chapter 10 in this volume for further discussion of these theories.)

For purposes of this study, cases of elder abuse were limited to those in which the victims were 60 years or older and living in domestic settings, and those in which family members, neighbors, or other caretakers were the perpetrators. Institutional, professional, and paraprofessional abuse and self-abuse or self-neglect were excluded. After a review of previous research and legislative reports, a five-category definition of abuse/neglect was adopted that encompassed physical, psychological, and material abuse and active and passive neglect (see Figure 9–1).

Community Agency Case Reports

The first phase of the evaluation consisted of a survey of community health, mental health, social service, legal, law enforcement, and aging agencies in the Worcester area (city of Worcester and 15 surrounding towns), city of Boston, Onondaga County, and Rhode Island. In addition to answering questions on awareness, number

Figure 9–1 Definitions of Abuse and Neglect

Abuse

Physical Abuse: the infliction of physical pain or injury, physical coercion (confinement against one's will) e.g., slapped, bruised, sexually molested, cut, burned, physically restrained, etc.

Psychological Abuse: the infliction of mental anguish, e.g., called names, treated as a child, frightened, humiliated, intimidated, threatened, isolated, etc.

Material Abuse: the illegal or improper exploitation and/or use of funds or other resources

Neglect

Active Neglect: refusal or failure to fulfill a caretaking obligation, *including* a conscious and intentional attempt to inflict physical or emotional stress on the elder; e.g., deliberate abandonment or deliberate denial of food or health-related services

Passive Neglect: refusal or failure to fulfill a caretaking obligation, *excluding* a conscious and intentional attempt to inflict physical or emotional distress on the elder; e.g., abandonment, non-provision of food, or health-related services because of inadequate knowledge, laziness, infirmity or disrupting the value of prescribed services

of cases, service and training needs, the community agencies in the Massachusetts sites were requested to complete individual reports on all cases of abuse and neglect that they had seen in the previous six months. Data were obtained for 62 cases from the Worcester area and 65 from Boston.

Psychological abuse, present in over half the cases, was the most prevalent form of maltreatment reported by the two groups of Massachusetts agencies; physical abuse was next, in slightly less than half of the cases, followed by material abuse and passive neglect in about one-third. Finally, active neglect was reported in just under one-fifth of the cases. The profile of the abused in these samples was of a female, 70 years or older, with physical and mental impairments, and dependent on the abuser-caretaker for help with the activities of daily living and companionship. The person responsible for the abuse or neglect was usually a relative— frequently a son—who often had a history of mental illness, alcohol abuse, or medical problems and who had become financially dependent on the elderly individual. In many instances, both the victim and the perpetrator were caught in a web of interdependency and disability, which made it difficult for them to seek or accept outside help or to consider separation.

This portrait of the victim and the perpetrator, based on data collected retrospectively from community agency records, mirrored the findings of earlier studies. Although limitations in the methodology made it impossible to associate the various theories with causality, the results did suggest that psychopathology, dependency, and stress might be important factors. Unfortunately, not enough information was available about the past history of the perpetrators to test the "cycle of violence" theory, and the results about "social isolation" were not clear. Further investigation into the nature of this alarming phenomenon would be necessary.

Case Assessments

Another set of research data was obtained from the three Model Projects. Using a comprehensive questionnaire, which included detailed questions on the type of manifestations of abuse and the relationship of the perpetrator and victim, social workers from the Model Projects completed assessments on 328 cases (59 in Worcester; 135 in Onondaga County; and 134 in Rhode Island) for the period July 1, 1981 through June 30, 1983. In all sites these victims were usually female, "old-old" (mean age was 76), and living in a household with family members. The perpetrator was generally male and younger in age than the victim. Of the five types of maltreatment, the most common was psychological abuse, which occurred in three-quarters of the cases. Physical abuse was associated with about half the cases, and material abuse, with one-third. Both active and passive neglect were present, but in varying proportions in the three case loads. The Onondaga County project reported the most of both types; about one-quarter of their victims suffered from active neglect and one-half from passive neglect.

An analysis of the characteristics of abuse showed that physical maltreatment was most often evidenced by bruises and welts; psychological abuse, by verbal assault and intimidation; and neglect, by lack of support and companionship. Multiple manifestations were common in all case loads. For a large proportion of victims, ranging from one-third in Onondaga County to three-quarters in Rhode Island, these acts were very threatening or life-threatening, and had been ongoing for several years, and in some cases, decades. Usually, the victims had difficulties with the instrumental activities of daily living and were in poor emotional health. Many had little contact with other people besides the perpetrator or formal caregivers. Although the victims were dependent in large measure on the perpetrators for their daily needs, financial management, transportation, and companionship, they were relatively independent in terms of financial resources. In contrast, the perpetrators were apt to be dependent on the victims for financial support. The perpetrators' lives were stressful from the unrealistic demands of the abused/neglected person, changes in their own health status, or from financial problems. Evidence of mental problems was noted in at least one-third of the perpetrators, and a history of mental illness and alcohol abuse was noted in a somewhat larger percentage.

In general, the results of the Model Project case assessments brought into somewhat sharper focus the picture of elder abuse that appeared in the community agency reports and earlier studies. More complete information on the manifestations of abuse and the victims and perpetrators substantiated the seriousness of the cases and the complexity of the family relationships. Psychopathology of the perpetrator was present in a considerable proportion of cases; the dependency of the victim on the perpetrator and the perpetrator on the victim was graphically illustrated in some cases; and stress in the lives of the abusers was found to play a role. Social isolation, at least in some instances, also seemed to be a factor. The lack of data from a large enough sample of perpetrators in the three sites made it impossible to determine if family violence had been present in their earlier lives. To find out what factors might differentiate the victims and perpetrators of abuse or neglect from elders and their caretakers in nonabuse situations, a comparison study was undertaken as the third analysis in the series.

A Comparison of Abused and Nonabused Cases

For this research effort, the 59 Worcester project cases were compared with 49 cases randomly selected from the nonabuse case load of the same agency over the two-year period. The victims and the nonabused clients were similar in age, sex, and health status, and the two groups of caretakers were alike in age and health status. More perpetrators were male compared to the caretakers of nonabused clients. A majority of the victimized elders resided in households with family members, whereas a greater proportion of the nonabused/nonneglected older persons lived alone. Both the victims and the perpetrators in the sample were found to have more problems with psychological and emotional health than their counterparts in the nonabused case load. In spite of significantly greater functional and cognitive impairments, the abused elders did not appear to be more dependent than the nonabused group for most of their needs. Provocative behavior by victims, coupled with unrealistic expectations and financial and medical problems of the perpetrators, seemed to create a more stressful environment for the abused families than that found in the nonabused sample— a situation that was further exacerbated in some instances by fewer and less frequent social contacts. Although these findings supported the theoretical arguments proposed at the initiation of this evaluation, they did not shed much light on the dynamics of the problem. For greater understanding of the circumstances surrounding the phenomenon, a more discriminating procedure was necessary.

A Comparison Study of Cases by Type of Abuse and Neglect

To probe deeper into the nature of elder abuse, the cases were analyzed by type of abuse. Comparisons were made between cases in which, for example, physical abuse was present and those in which it was absent, for an array of sociodemographic and situational variables, for all types of abuse and neglect, and for all sites. Because a majority of the elderly clients suffered from more than one type of victimization, the categories were not mutually exclusive. Nevertheless, the methodology did allow for some tentative generalizations concerning the applicability of the theoretical framework that shaped the study.

Of the five types of maltreatment, neglect had the strongest relationship to the dependency needs of the victims. The neglected elderly had significant problems with cognitive and physical functioning, which made them dependent on their caretakers for many of the activities of daily living. They were likely to be more burdensome and stressful than victims of other forms of maltreatment because of a greater degree of impairment, advanced years, and a recent decline in mental health. In addition, perpetrators of passive neglect in the Onondaga County sample had experienced stress in their own lives with the significant likelihood of having gone through a recent divorce or separation. A tendency toward social isolation, associated with loss, was also a factor in the Worcester cases of passive neglect, which revealed a significant number of perpetrators without a person whom they could contact in an emergency.

The victims of psychologial abuse were quite different. In marked contrast to cases of neglect, they were relatively unimpaired, cognitively and functionally, and more independent in meeting their daily needs, but more likely to be emotionally ill. Psychological abuse appeared to be associated with the mental health of the participants and the pathological interpersonal relationship that existed between them. The data from both the Worcester and Rhode Island cases indicated that the victims of psychological abuse were likely to have poor mental health. Also, transactions between victims and perpetrators were apt to involve pathological behavior by the latter. A tendency at one site for perpetrators to have unrealistic expectations suggests that some psychological dependency on the elderly victim may exist. Indirectly, this finding was supported at a second site where a significant number of perpetrators of psychological abuse were provocative in their behavior toward their victims.

Material abuse seemed to be almost exclusively related to the financial needs of perpetrators, although the determination of a statistically significant relationship in the Worcester cases was not possible because of the small number. The relative social isolation of victims may have been a contributing factor in the other two sites, since the data showed that Onondaga County victims were likely to have suffered recent losses in their social network, and the Rhode Island victims tended to be unmarried. The perpetrators of material abuse were generally distant relatives or nonrelatives who were not emotionally involved with their victims but appeared to be motivated by greed for money.

The common denominators in cases of physical abuse in all three sites were the relatively poor emotional status of the perpetrators and the shared living arrangements and often pathological relationship of victim and perpetrator. In addition, the Onondaga County victims of physical abuse were likely to be seen as a source of stress, and the Worcester victims were apt to display provocative behavior toward the perpetrators, a significant proportion of whom showed a recent increase in dependency on the victim.

As a research effort, these four analyses had some inherent validity and reliability problems. Since the project staff were responsible for completing the assessment forms, the information that they provided reflected their perception and program orientation. Although attempts were made to ensure intra-site reliability by limiting data collection for each project to the two staff persons who were familiar with the cases, the nature of the assessment process made it impossible to carry out reliability tests. However, all the project staff took part in meetings, which included discussion of the definitions and instruments. Of still more uncertain quality were the data for the nonabuse/nonneglect cases that were collected by the home care case managers who did not have the intensive involvement with the project, although their data were checked for accuracy and interpretation by the Worcester program director. In spite of the attention given to the design of the case assessment instrument, the questions of function, health, and social contacts (which had been based on an existing form used by the Massachusetts Department of Elder Affairs) were worded in terms of "needs" rather than status, so that some necessary information never was obtained.

The Impact of the Model Projects

In addition to the investigations into the characteristics of the elder abuse phenomenon, the evaluation also focused on the effectiveness of the Model Projects. Three criteria were selected to measure the success of their efforts: case resolution, community response, and project replicability. Three sources of data were utilized. The case assessment and reassessment forms completed by the project staff at intake and at the close of the case furnished the information for measuring the success of the projects in preventing further maltreatment. Two community surveys—one conducted at the beginning of the grant period and the other two years later—provided statistics for assessing the response of the community to the projects, and interviews with the project and community agency personnel in the final year of the grant yielded information on the organizational models.

Case Resolution

Before analyzing the effectiveness of the Model Projects in preventing elder abuse, the case loads from the three sites were
compared for similarities and differences regarding sociodemographic characteristics of the victims and perpetrators, the "causes"
of maltreatment (psychopathology of the perpetrator, dependency,
stress, and social isolation), and types of maltreatment. On the
whole, the cases handled by the Model Projects were remarkably
similar. There were no differences among the victims at the three
sites in age, sex, marital status, living arrangements, and health
status; nor were there differences among the perpetrators in sex,
living arrangements, history of mental illness, and alcohol abuse.
Only the age of the perpetrators varied, with Rhode Island cases
having a significant larger percentage of abusers less than 50 years
of age.

An obvious difference among the sites was the variation in the
proportion of reports of physical abuse and passive neglect cases.
About one-half of the Rhode Island cases listed physical abuse as
the cause of the report to the Model Project in contrast to about
one-third of the Worcester cases and a little more than one-fourth
of the Onondaga County case load. On the other hand, almost one
out of five of the Worcester and Onondaga County cases listed
"passive neglect" as the precipitant of the report compared to one
in fifteen for Rhode Island. These differences may be due to the
fact that reporting of cases was mandatory during the grant period
in Rhode Island but not in New York or Massachusetts. It is
reasonable to assume that physical abuse, because it can be
verified more easily than other forms of mistreatment, may be
reported more readily than, for instance, passive neglect, which is
more elusive.

All the Model Projects recorded at the time the cases were
closed a large decrease in the number of manifestations of abuse
and neglect, their severity, and the level of threat they posed for
the victims. Each of the projects also made some headway in
reducing the dependency of the victims on the abusers and/or
family for companionship and daily needs and the dependency of
the perpetrator on the victim for financial resources. Two of the
projects (Onondaga County and Rhode Island) also noted improvement in the victims' independence in areas of financial management and transportation, in their emotional state and self-esteem,
and in the level of stress that they posed for the perpetrator.

The elimination of maltreatment in just under half the cases in
all the projects resulted from separation of the victim and the

perpetrator through nursing home placement, death, hospitalization or relocation into new community residences, or departure of the perpetrator. One out of four of the Onondaga County victims and one out of eight of the Worcester and Rhode Island groups were transferred to long-term care institutions. For some victims, remaining in the family setting, no matter how violent, was preferable to going into a nursing home. Other victims were reluctant to separate from the abusers to whom they felt obligated.

The most effective strategy for the three projects was the "changes in social/living situations"; the least was "changes in circumstances of the abuser which precipitated the abuse." Although the Worcester staff tended to regard all interventions[2] as more successful than the other two projects, they rated two-thirds of the cases as "resolved" or resolved "a lot" compared to the Onondaga County and Rhode Island staff, who placed three-quarters of their cases in these categories.

In order to determine what variables differentiated the cases that were resolved "completely" and "a lot" from those that were "not resolved" or resolved only "a little," the data from the three projects were pooled (to provide a large enough sample for the analysis). Of the long list of victim, perpetrator, and situation characteristics and intervention strategies, very few were significant. Resolution was apt to be identified with persons who were more dependent and neglected than those who were less dependent and physically maltreated. Apparently, more favorable results are possible in cases of neglect where the introduction of services, respite care, or relocation to a nursing home can have a salutary effect. Leaving the elderly victim in a situation where there is a symbiotic relationship or a mutual dependency may be more difficult to resolve, especially if the perpetrator is a spouse.

Community Response

In addition to treating cases of abused or neglected elders, the Model Projects served as a focal point for action in behalf of abused elders, as coordinators among the service providers in their area, and as organizers of education and training programs. Two community surveys furnished the information for evaluating the success of the Model Projects in carrying out these responsibilities.

During the first year of the grant period, a questionnaire was distributed to health, mental health, social service, elder service, legal, and law enforcement agencies in the geographic area of each of the Model Projects (survey I). It included questions on awareness of elder abuse or neglect, reluctance or willingness to report, number and type of cases referred to the particular agency in the previous six-month period, referral sources, service, and training needs. From the 212 survey forms that were returned in the three sites (86 in the Worcester area, 55 in Onondaga County, and 71 in Rhode Island), it was evident that almost all agencies were aware of elder abuse and not reluctant to report it. An attempt to obtain statistics on the number of cases of abuse and neglect, either in total or by type, was unsuccessful because of the difficulty in identification of cases, confusion between neglect by others and self-neglect, and perhaps the lack of experience on the part of the respondents with the classification system. Although there were variations among the three Model Projects in the relative importance given to the type of organizations involved in the communities' referral patterns, the agencies most often called upon for handling abuse and neglect in all sites included programs for the elderly, social agencies, home health organizations, and the police. Among the most needed service in all sites was emergency shelter; the most often mentioned training need was information about local resources.

Two years later the community survey was repeated (survey II), with a few changes in the wording for clarification purposes and the addition of a question on the degree of satisfaction of the community agency with service coordination. Completed survey II forms came from 213 agencies (101 in the Worcester area, 52 in Onondaga County, and 60 in Rhode Island). Slightly more than half of the agencies had known at least one case of elder abuse and neglect, and somewhat less than one-third were aware of the problem but had not encountered a case. A small percentage in all localities were not aware of such situations. These proportions are similar to those of survey I, which had been conducted at the beginning of the grant period. Because of the change in wording in the two questionnaires and the different group of respondents, no comparisons could be made about the impact of the Model Projects in increasing community awareness. Fewer than one out of two of the community groups had specific procedures to deal with cases of abuse, and of these, less than half were in writing—again, proportions that matched those found in survey I.

Over the two-year period, a change did occur in the community response system, with a larger proportion of agencies naming the Model Projects as the resource they would turn to or had turned to with cases of abuse/neglect than had been indicated in survey I. The social service and health agencies were apt to refer directly to the Model Projects, while the police, legal, and mental health groups and some state agencies usually investigated the situation first and then referred to the Model Projects if the case warranted referral. In both the Worcester area and the state of Rhode Island, the Model Projects were the major referral units for elder abuse and neglect; in Onondaga County the Model Project and the Adult Protective Services unit of the County Department of Social Services shared responsibility. The quality of the services provided by all Model Projects was rated as either excellent or good by the vast majority of community agencies that answered survey II. Many took the time to commend the Model Projects on the promptness with which they responded to the referrals.

Although the question of whether the Model Projects had an effect on case findings and reporting was not asked directly of community agencies, the survey forms did request information on the number and type of cases known to community agencies at the beginning of the grant period and two years later. Because of confusion about "cases" and definitions, data from the first survey could not be used. When the requests for information were repeated in survey II with more explicit definitions, the numbers given by the community agencies were much higher in comparison to those reported by the Model Projects for the same time period and geographical area. Whether this increase was due to several agencies reporting the same case or the fact that agencies did not refer all their cases to the Model Projects could not be determined. By law, the Rhode Island Model Project was to receive all reports of suspected abuse/neglect. The discrepancies in numbers suggest that community agencies were still having difficulty in differentiating, identifying, and referring domestic elder abuse/neglect cases.

Although all three Model Projects were responsible for helping to establish services in their localities (e.g., Worcester organized a 24-hour hot line), the extent of this type of activity could not be documented from the survey data. Respondents to survey I produced a long and varied list of service needs, but, except for emergency shelter and respite care, each need was mentioned only a few times. On survey II, the question was answered by only one-quarter of the responding agencies, and again no resource was cited more than three or four times. From the perspective of the community agencies, there appeared to be no real service gaps, although in the case assessments, the project staff in Worcester noted that they were hampered by scarcity of some services, particularly respite care; in Onondaga County nonreimbursement of certain services was cited, and in Rhode Island a lack of protective services was mentioned. Although the survey findings could not verify that the Model Projects had made a difference in the level of awareness of community agencies or had influenced case reporting or findings, they did confirm the fact that by the end of the grant period the Model Projects were the major referral agencies for cases of elder abuse and neglect in each of the sites.

Model Replicability

The final consideration of this phase of the evaluation concerned the replicability of the models. It is important to realize that although the Model Projects were similar in goals, target population, staffing, and operational definitions, each represented various approaches to elder abuse and neglect intervention. The Worcester project was located in an agency where the case workers had the authority to order a wide range of social services and thus had been designated as a "service brokerage" model. The Onondaga County project, on the other hand, functioned primarily as a coordinator of services supplied by other agencies and was termed a "coordination model," although it did also have direct control over a group of aides who worked with the most difficult cases. The Rhode Island project, identified as a "mandatory report model," had access to some direct services sponsored by the Department of Elder Affairs; it was also dependent on community agencies to assume responsibility for the cases once the situations had been investigated and the abuse alleviated. Consequently, a great deal of the Rhode Island staff effort was spent in working with community agencies and coordinating care plans. Also, because of the mandatory reporting, the Rhode Island agency, unlike Worcester and Onondaga County, was under pressure to respond to all calls within a certain time allotment.

Because of the variations in function and structure, the Model Projects faced different problems in developing and implementing their programs. For example, the Worcester project resolved an intra-agency problem by devising a plan of "co-management," so that the case managers in the agency could remain in charge of their abuse cases but also call on the Model Project staff for advice and direction. Similarly, the Rhode Island project handled an intra-agency problem with its information and referral workers by training all of them to accept elder abuse and neglect reports rather than having all such calls referred to a separate worker. All three projects established formal and informal procedures for promoting interagency coordination. To facilitate the process, the Onondaga County project organized a "team" to represent the relevant service providers for each case; the team met at intake and then as necessary to follow the progress of the case. Rhode Island made use of key councils, which were groups of elder service providers in the local communities who met regularly to discuss common cases. Both the Onondaga County and Rhode Island projects avoided conflict with their local adult protective services units, which were also charged with responding to cases of abuse and neglect, by showing their willingness to take on the most difficult cases.

A time study of the project staff indicated that the Worcester social worker spent about four times as long in direct service to clients in such areas as interviews and home visits than did the social workers in the Onondaga County and Rhode Island projects. This finding highlights the difference between the case management approach of the Worcester project and the "assessment, coordination, and referral" process utilized by the other two programs. The Worcester approach apparently did not result in a more favorable client outcome. As pointed out earlier, of the three groups, the Worcester project staff had a significantly smaller proportion of cases "resolved" or resolved "a lot" than did the Onondaga County or Rhode Island groups. Also, the Worcester staff appeared to have been less successful in changing the abuse situation than their counterparts, since they noted "no change" in the level of stress, emotional state, or problems for the perpetrators—aspects of cases that the Onondaga County and Rhode Island staffs noted as improvements, along with reduced hindrance from a variety of other barriers.

Although it would be difficult to compare the cases with regard to complexity, the data analysis does show that the victims and perpetrators in the three projects were not significantly different on the sociodemographic and health factors. They did differ in the type of maltreatment that precipitated the report, with Rhode Island having more cases of physical abuse and fewer of neglect, while the opposite was true for Worcester and Onondaga County. No differences were found in the proportion of psychological and material abuse or active neglect cases among all three sites. Since the passive neglect cases appeared to be resolved more easily compared with the physical abuse ones, the Rhode Island project would be expected to have the largest proportion of "unresolved" cases; in actuality, however, the reverse was true. It does not appear, at least from the data collected in this study, that the types of cases seen by the Worcester project were significantly different than those seen by the other two projects. If anything, since there was a smaller percentage of physical abuse cases in Worcester than in Rhode Island, the former cases as a group should have shown a higher percentage of cases resolved.

The Worcester group did, seemingly, experience more barriers to delivery of services. Of the three projects, the Worcester staff noted that delivery of care was hindered by lack of available services in about one out of five cases compared to approximately one out of twenty in the Onondaga County and Rhode Island sites. Also, the Onondaga County and Rhode Island staff noted significant improvements in many barriers by the time the cases were closed, but Worcester did not.

When the community agencies were asked to rate the performance of their Model Project, more than three-quarters of the respondents in the Worcester area checked "excellent" for the Worcester Project compared with only about one-half for Onondaga County and one-third for Rhode Island. Similarly, more than two-thirds of the agencies in the Worcester area stated that they were very satisfied with the degree of coordination and cooperation of services, but less than one-half for Onondaga County and one-third for Rhode Island believed that the services were well coordinated. The Worcester staff saw a much smaller number of clients whom they monitored over a longer period, often after the abuse and neglect situation had appeared to be resolved. Their style of practice involved more intensive and extensive work with families, whereas Rhode Island used a short-term intervention and referral strategy, and Onondaga County took a more middle-of-the-road approach, with greater emphasis on relocating clients into a new living arrangement. Rather than leading to a greater degree of case resolution, the Worcester method seemed to make the staff more aware of the underlying issues involved in the case. Because of their deeper involvement in these family situations, the Worcester staff appeared to be less willing to label the cases as "resolved," even though the immediate manifestations of abuse or neglect were gone. This interpretation may also explain why they found "receptivity of the abused and abuser" to be more of a barrier than either of the other two project staffs. A more extended follow-up of cases would be necessary to find out whether, in fact, the Worcester staff's view of the cases was a more accurate one than that of the Onondaga or Rhode Island staff.

Of concern was whether the projects could be replicated: Were they appropriate only in their own service environments or could their basic features be adopted by other agencies in other localities interested in providing protective services to abused and neglected clients? The circumstances of both the Worcester and Rhode Island projects were unique. Massachusetts, unlike almost any other state, has an extensive network of home care corporations that provide case management and social services to all frail elderly who meet the eligibility requirements (in fiscal year 1984, 43,400 elders were served at a cost of $84 million in state funds). Prior to the demonstration, the Worcester agency had established a Crisis Intervention Program to handle the protective service cases. It was the opinion of the agency administration that these cases required more highly skilled case workers, smaller case loads, and better trained homemakers than the usual clientele. This was not, however, the only model in use by home care corporations in Massachusetts.

One of the other tasks of this evaluative study was to compare two other programs—one in which the protective services component was contracted out to family service agencies, and one in which the abuse and neglect cases were assigned to the regular case management staff as part of their case load. After an analysis based on referral patterns, case coordination, service utilization, and management, the Worcester Model was judged the most efficient for the home care system and has since the end of the grant period been put into operation throughout the state.

Rhode Island also represents a special model. As part of a state agency that is both a state unit on aging and an Area Agency on Aging, it did have considerable leverage in working with other state agencies and the local communities. According to the response from community agencies, it was less effective than either of the other two projects in coordination and performance. The high client-staff ratio and the mandate to respond to all reports, as well as the normal tension that exists between the state and local groups, may explain these results.

Of the three projects, the Onondaga County model stands out as the easiest to replicate. Its record regarding case load and resolution was similar to that of the Rhode Island project, but its efforts at coordination of services were viewed more positively by community agencies. Using the team conference as a coordination strategy, the Onondaga County project was able to involve local service providers and the local Adult Protective Service unit (mandated by the state to respond to reports of elder abuse and neglect) in the case management process in a way that avoided issues of territoriality and conflict. Although it did not have control over a range of services as did the Worcester project, it did employ a group of aides who assisted in coordination and communication among the staff, clients, and service providers. Because no special sponsorship is needed, any human service organization can adopt the program. This flexibility, as well as the success in case resolution, the high case-staff ratio, and the effectiveness in coordination, makes the Onondaga County project a particularly attractive model for replication.

Conclusions and Implications

Even though the samples that explored the nature of elder abuse were obtained from many community agencies and three Model Projects, a certain consistency in results was evident. Psychopathology was present in cases of psychological abuse and to a lesser degree, physical abuse. Contrary to the minor role that the psychological state of the perpetrator is given in the family violence literature, it appears to be a major explanatory variable for elder abuse. Whether the cases seen by agencies are more likely to be psychopathological in nature than those that exist in the general community awaits the results of an incidence study of the general population, one of which is now underway under the auspices of the University of New Hampshire's Family Research Laboratory.

The findings of the evaluative research also suggest that the relationship of dependency to elder abuse/neglect found in the gerontological literature should be reexamined. The portrait of the victim as a very old, increasingly functionally disabled woman, totally dependent on an overburdened, neglectful, or abusive adult child is characteristic of neglect in this study, but not abuse. In cases of physical, psychological, and material abuse, dependency takes on another form. Not only is the victim dependent on the perpetrator, but the perpetrator is dependent on the victim.

Given the above findings, exchange theory may be an appropriate conceptual framework in which to study forms of abuse. It states that as dependencies increase, the cost of the relationship to the caregiver becomes greater, the rewards diminish, and the exchange is perceived as unfair. This interpretation has been employed to explain the abuse and neglect that results from the dependency of the victim on the caretaker. However, there is another view of exchange theory that has been used to explain acts of abuse when the perpetrator is dependent on the elderly victim. Finkelhor, writing on child and spouse abuse, believes that "acts of abuse can occur as a response to a lack or loss of power."[3] Pillemer suggests that the feeling of powerlessness experienced by an adult child who is still dependent on the elderly parent may be especially acute because it goes against society's expectation that adults function independently of their parents.[4] In these abuse situations, the individual may resort to violence and act out from weakness rather than strength.

Of lesser influence, according to these findings, are the sociological factors of external stress and isolation. Although present in the situations of the various types of abuse/neglect, these factors seem to exacerbate the situations rather than cause them directly. The role of the "cycle of violence" theory, which states that violence is transmitted from one generation to another, is still uncertain but should be pursued because of its prominence in explaining other forms of family violence.

Some of the limitations of the study have been presented earlier. As a product of evaluative research, the findings can only be considered as preliminary. They suggest the need for further investigation, using more rigorous research designs, into the circumstances leading to mistreatment of old people and the relationship of the participants and their early histories. Work has already begun on the development of assessment instruments and screening tools which, when tested, refined, and standardized, will answer some of the questions about causes and remedies. Similarly, a survey is already underway to measure the extent of the problem in the general population.

Yet, even the preliminary nature of the findings in this evaluation can be helpful in pointing to solutions to the problem. Each of the theoretical explanations found to have relevance to elder abuse also suggests an avenue to intervention. In view of the fact that many perpetrators have psychological problems and that victims suffer from emotional distress, mental health services would appear to be an absolute necessity in treating cases of abuse and neglect. Realistically, it is often not possible to provide this type of care, either because the participants are reluctant to accept help or because the situation is so critical that immediate action is required. Under these conditions, separation of the victim and perpetrator may be the only successful way to end the mistreatment.

Redressing the imbalance between dependence and independence within the family unit opens up several options for case resolution. Many services, such as homemakers, home health aides, chore helpers, and meals-on-wheels, can be brought into the home to assist caretakers who are overwhelmed with the burden of caring for an impaired elderly relative. Often, it may be desirable to arrange to have the older person attend a day-care program. Respite care on a weekly basis or for an extended two-week period may also be available for the caretaker. The objectives are to provide for the needs of the elderly victim and, at the same time, to make the elder less dependent on a caretaker-relative who is unwilling or unable to carry out daily tasks. Again, there are some cases, particularly those in which husbands are the perpetrators, that cannot be helped because health and social service personnel are not allowed into the home.

Abuse perpetrated by sons, daughters, or grandchildren who are dependent on the victim is not easily stopped. Alcoholism, mental illness, or developmental disabilities may be present. Often, finances are an issue. The strategy in these instances may be to provide the perpetrators with temporary housing, job counseling, and other supports to assist them in becoming self-sufficient and less dependent, while at the same time counseling the victims so that they will more readily accept the new relationship.

Although this research has not been able to define clearly the role of stress and isolation as causal factors leading to abuse and neglect, it is evident that many families associated with mistreatment of their elderly relatives are troubled by illness, unemployment, poverty, poor housing, and lack of contacts with the community. Linking these families to community agencies that can respond to their needs may be a solution to preventing further abuse. Through friendly visitor, senior companion, and local church programs, the social isolation of some of the households and potential for violence may be reduced.

Two other points about the nature of elder abuse and neglect drawn from the evaluation are important in designing intervention strategies. First, spouse abuse exists in fairly large proportions among the elderly victims. One-quarter of the cases from the Model Projects involved husbands and wives. Intervention in these instances may be more successful if some of the procedures used in spouse abuse cases involving younger victims, such as emergency shelter, assertive training, and victim support groups, are tried. Second, material abuse situations in which the perpetrator is likely to be a nonrelative and not a member of the same household, as well as cases of physical violence, may be more successfully resolved if viewed as a criminal act rather than a social problem. Recent work in spouse abuse has indicated that there was less recidivism when the perpetrators were put into jail for repeated offenses than when both parties were given counseling or when the perpetrator was sent away from the home for several hours.[5]

In addition to suggesting treatment modalities and areas for future research, the study also emphasized the importance of disseminating valid and reliable information about elder abuse and neglect to people in the aging field as well as others who may in some way be involved in the problem. So much of what has appeared in print in the past has been based on early studies that represented relatively few cases and, more seriously, that were methodologically flawed. Almost every national, regional, and state meeting dealing with problems of the aged has included at least one session about elder abuse, but the audiences have been relatively small; the result has been limited dissemination of materials. Even the concerted efforts made by the Model Projects reached only a portion of the community and human service providers.

Many states have established a network of agencies to respond to reports of abuse and neglect at the local level. The likelihood is that before long most if not all the states will have laws governing the reporting and investigating of elder abuse programs, service requirements, immunity, and competency. Social and legal services, health and mental health facilities, the police, courts, and churches are, or will be, involved. For all of these groups, education about the issues involved in elder abuse and neglect will be vital.

The findings of the study also have implications regarding the organization of a community response system. They reveal that to work with elder abuse and neglect cases, an organization must be (1) able to coordinate services and agencies, (2) flexible in its approach, and (3) creative in overcoming barriers to the delivery of services. The staff must be well trained, patient, and persistent, as well as knowledgeable about legal interventions and the community resources. A community environment with a well-organized human service system is important so that an elder abuse project can develop the linkages among the multiple organizations that are necessary for working with these difficult and complex cases.

Of the many groups that treat abuse cases (e.g., hospital teams, legal services, home health agencies, mental health centers, etc.), the social service agency appears to be the most suitable for handling the case management functions and brokering the many services that are often required. A "family systems" approach may be the most successful strategy, since abuse and neglect situations involve various family members within a household: spouses, children or grandchildren, siblings, or other relatives. Most of the states with elder abuse protection laws have elected to place their protective services units within departments of social services rather than in the state units on aging. With this arrangement there is the possibility that the older adults will not receive adequate attention. On the other hand, placing an elder abuse program within the aging network may require that the organization invest time and resources in working with nonelderly family members. These issues raise the question of the appropriateness of an age-segregated versus an age-integrated service delivery system, and ultimately where and how the problem of abuse and neglect should be addressed.

Endnotes

1. U.S. Department of Health and Human Services, Office of Human Services, Administration on Aging, *Guidelines for Preparation of a Grant Application Model Projects Title IV-C Fiscal Year 1980* (Washington, D.C.: DHHS, 1980).
2. Social workers were asked to note to what degree the various actions contributed to the resolution of the case, from very negative to very positive: removal of barriers, specific interventions, changes in the unhealthy interdependencies between abused and abuser, reduction in stress caused by abuse, reduction in life problems of the abuser, and changes in the circumstances of the abused which precipitated the abuse.
3. David Finkelhor, "Common Features of Family Abuse," in *The Dark Side of Families*, eds. David Finkelhor, Richard J. Gelles, Gerald T. Hotaling, and Murray A. Straus (Beverly Hills, Calif.: Sage Publications, 1983), p. 19.
4. Karl A. Pillemer, "Domestic Violence Against the Elderly: A Discussion Paper" (Paper presented at the Surgeon General's Workshop on Violence and Public Health, Leesburg, Virginia, October 27–29, 1985).
5. Lawrence W. Sherman and Richard A. Berk, "The Minneapolis Domestic Violence Experiment," *Police Foundation Reports* (April 1984).

Chapter 10

RISK FACTORS IN ELDER ABUSE: RESULTS FROM A CASE-CONTROL STUDY

by Karl A. Pillemer

Attitudes toward the elderly vary tremendously from culture to culture. In ancient China, filial piety was the norm; striking an aged parent was a crime punishable by death. The familiar Eskimo case demonstrates the opposite extreme: Elderly persons were sometimes abandoned to die of exposure when they became impaired or feeble. In contemporary America, proper behavior toward the elderly is by no means as clearly defined; we are often confused and ambivalent in our relationships with aged family members.

In the past few decades, researchers in sociology, social gerontology, and other disciplines have extensively explored the family lives of older people. One major area of interest for researchers has been determining what factors contribute to good relationships between elderly parents and adult children. For example, Johnson and Bursk found that health, living environment, finances, and attitudes toward aging were related to the quality of such relationships. Cicirelli emphasized the role of prior feelings of attachment in children's willingness to help elderly parents.[1]

In contrast, other researchers have approached the problem of the aging family from a different angle and have examined the *negative* aspects of family relationships in later life. Thus, Streib has suggested that older families' problems with health and finan-

Note: I am grateful to J. Jill Suitor for helpful comments on this chapter.

cial resources lead to poor relationships with kin. Kent and Matson highlight health problems in particular as causes of role disruptions, tension, and stress in family relationships. Another researcher has examined families who decided to institutionalize an elderly relative and has used these cases as examples of a breakdown in family caregiving.[2] In recent years, a number of investigators have turned their attention to a more direct manifestation of problematic kin relationships in later life: the abuse of the elderly by family members.

A considerable amount of research has been carried out in the area of domestic violence. Studies have focused in particular on the abuse of children by their parents and on the battering of women by men. Concurrent with this research effort has been the development of social programs to prevent these types of abuse and to treat victims of maltreatment when it occurs. It is only in the past few years, however, that researchers and policy makers have turned their attention to the abuse of the elderly. Thus, while elder abuse may not be a new phenomenon (see Chapters 1 and 2 of this book), it has come to the public's attention as a "social problem" only recently.

As many observers have noted, the research evidence on elder abuse is scanty.[3] In spite of this lack of knowledge, however, many states and localities are developing intervention programs for elder abuse and neglect, including mandatory reporting laws and protective services for the elderly. Among the most basic information needed to assist such programs is an answer to the question, Who is at greatest risk of elder abuse? To accurately assess and screen potential cases, it is critical to identify potential risk factors for maltreatment. The search for risk factors, currently a high priority for students of other forms of family violence,[4] must be extended to domestic violence against the elderly. This chapter presents the findings from a case-control study that attempted to identify risk factors for physical elder abuse.

Risk Factors: A Theoretical Review

Previous research efforts have tended to extend concepts relating to other forms of family violence to elder abuse and neglect. While consulting the family violence literature may be useful, it should be done only with the knowledge that the elderly occupy a special status in our society. Any attempt to understand the dynamics of abuse situations must take into account theory and research relating specifically to the aged. We must ask, What is it that makes the elderly vulnerable to abuse? How does being old specifically pattern family violence?

This chapter first reviews the sociological and psychological literature on spouse and child abuse and integrates it with available data on elder abuse. This is done in the context of identifying possible risk factors for elder abuse. Because the literature on these topics is broad, such a review must be quite selective; thus, only the most important issues have been outlined in a general way. The areas that emerged from the review as likely to be associated with elder abuse are as follows:

1. Intra-individual dynamics (psychopathology of the abuser).
2. Intergenerational transmission of violent behavior ("cycle of violence").
3. Dependency and exchange relations between abuser and abused.
4. External stress.
5. Social isolation.

Intra-Individual Dynamics

In the family violence literature, there has been controversy over intra-individual theories, which blame abuse on some pathological characteristic of the abuser. As Gelles has noted, many studies of child abuse have relied on the idea "that the parent who abuses his or her child suffers from some psychological disease which must be cured in order to prevent future abuse."[5] Studies of this kind have been primarily carried out by psychiatrists, social workers, and other clinicians. Some of these writers attribute abuse to sadistic personality traits. Young, for example, writes that "the outline of abuse" is "the perverse fascination with punishment as an entity in itself."[6] Others trace it to a flaw in the socialization process and tend to downplay social structural factors as important determinants of child abuse. A number of investigators have also traced wife battering to psychopathological traits in the perpetrator.[7]

Gelles severely criticizes such intra-individual explanations and argues that little agreement exists among various writers as to which pathological traits characterize abusers. Further, he suggests that these studies do not rigorously test hypotheses but instead offer after-the-fact explanations for deviant behavior that has already occurred. A final weakness, he claims, is reliance on clinical samples, without the use of non-abuse comparison groups. Gelles goes on to argue for a sociological approach to child abuse— one that examines independent variable such as socioeconomic class, economic stress, and unemployment.[8] In recent years, strictly intra-individual theories have been increasingly avoided by researchers.

One intra-individual characteristic, however, has gained some acceptance, at least as a partial explanation of why abuse occurs. This is the relationship between alcohol abuse and family violence. Numerous studies have in fact found support for such a relationship.[9] Alcohol consumption may act to diminish inhibitions against violence or simply provide a convenient excuse for violent behavior. In this study, alcohol abuse was considered to have a possible causal role in domestic violence against the elderly.

Although researchers in child and spouse abuse are now less prone to attribute family violence to the psychological state of the abuser, it is possible that persons who abuse elders may in fact have such problems. Douglass et al. include the "flawed development" of the abuser as one cause of abuse, which results from problems in the childhood of the abuser. Lau and Kosberg also refer to the problem of the "non-normal" child (e.g., mentally ill or retarded, or alcoholic) who has been cared for by parents all his or her life. If the parents become impaired, they may be placed in the hands of a person unable to manage his or her own life, let alone those of dependent elderly relatives. Further, research by Wolf et al. found a considerable degree of mental illness among abusers: 31 percent were reported to have a history of psychiatric illness, and 43 percent to have substance abuse problems.[10]

Intergenerational Transmission of Violent Behavior

Social learning theory holds that a child learns to be violent in the family setting, where a violent parent has been taken as a role model. When frustrated or angry as an adult, the individual relies on this learned behavior and lashes out violently. This theory has led to the concept of a "cycle of violence," which suggests, for example, that abused children grow up to become child abusers. Findings from a national survey conducted by Straus et al. support this notion.[11] This study revealed that a greater degree of physical punishment at the hands of either parent was positively associated with a higher rate of abusive violence toward that person's own children. Children who observed their fathers striking their mothers also had a higher rate of violence toward their children. This fits in well with Owens and Straus's findings, which showed that exposure to violence as a child is correlated with a general approval of violence as an adult.[12]

At present, we do not know whether elder abusers are more likely to have experienced violent upbringings, as no research has been conducted on this topic. Such a connection would indeed seem likely, based on the strength of this finding in other forms of abuse. It is important to note, however, that a difference exists between elder abuse and child and spouse abuse as regards the transmission of violent behavior. Obviously, children who abuse elderly parents were not *themselves* abused as elderly parents; the cycle of violence must therefore take a different form. Rather than becoming an abuser because one was abused by someone else, the cycle becomes more direct: the formerly abused child strikes out at his or her own abuser. This involves a different psychological process—one with elements of retaliation as well as imitation.

Dependency

Another commonly cited factor in elder abuse is the resentment generated by increased dependency of an older person on a caretaker. In fact, the belief that the dependency of elderly individuals is a major cause of abuse is probably the most widely held in the literature. Thus, Davidson ties abuse directly to the "crises" created by the needs of an elderly parent for care. Steinmetz has been perhaps the major proponent of this view, arguing that families undergo "generational inversion," in which the elderly person becomes dependent upon his or her children for financial, emotional, physical, and/or emotional support.[13] This leads to severe stress on the part of the caregiver. As the costs of the relationship to the caregiver increase and the rewards diminish, the exchange becomes perceived as unfair. If the caretaker feels unable to escape the situation, he or she may then become abusive.

However, many elderly are quite dependent on their relatives. The question therefore arises: Why are some of these dependent elderly abused and others not? In light of the fact that abuse occurs in only a small proportion of families, no direct correlation between the dependency of an older person and abuse can be assumed. Although it may seem contradictory, some research indicates that a more important cause of abuse may be the continued dependency of *abuser* on *abused*. Thus, Phillips failed to find any difference in level of impairment between a group of abused elderly and a control group. Wolf et al. found that in two-thirds of their cases, the perpetrator was reported to be financially dependent on his or her *victim*. Hwalek et al., in a case-control study, also found that the financial dependency of the abuser was an important risk factor in elder abuse.[14]

It is possible to speculate as to why the continued dependency of an adult child or spouse upon an elderly person might cause physical abuse. A theoretical explanation for this phenomenon can be based on a concept from social exchange theory: power. Finkelhor, in his attempt to identify common features of family abuse, notes that abuse can occur as a response to perceived powerlessness. Acts of abuse, he notes, "seem to be acts carried out by abusers to compensate for their perceived lack or loss of power."[15] Thus, spouse abuse has been found to be related to a sense of powerlessness, and the physical abuse of children "tends to start with a feeling of parental impotence." It may be that the feeling of powerlessness experienced by an adult child who is still dependent on an elderly parent is especially acute, because it goes so strongly against society's expectations for normal adult behavior. This perceived power *deficit* appears to have more explanatory power than the notion that the abuser holds much power in the relationship.

In summary, dependency seems to play a critical role in elder abuse, but it is not yet clear who is depending on whom in these abusive relationships. Does an elderly person come to make excessive demands on caregivers? Or are the abusers persons who have remained dependent on the abused into later life and have unrealistic expectations of what the latter can provide? A major goal of the present research was to shed light on these questions.

External Stress

A number of investigators have found a positive relationship between external stress (as differentiated from the stress that results from interpersonal relationships in the family) and child and wife abuse.[16] A stress perspective on abuse can be seen as an alternative to the theories previously discussed. In Gelles and Straus's terms, it is a "socio-cultural" theory rather than a social-psychological or intra-individual one, in that it emphasizes social-structural, macrolevel variables like unemployment or economic conditions.[17] However, the social stress model alone cannot explain elder abuse, as it does not account for why some families respond to stress with abuse and others do not. To date, no systematic exploration has been conducted of the relationship between stress and elder abuse. Based on the strength of findings relating stress to other forms of family violence, this area also appears to be an important one for investigators.

Social Isolation

Social isolation has been found to be characteristic of families in which child abuse and spouse abuse occur.[18] Violence that is considered to be illegitimate tends to be hidden. Detection of such violence can result in informal sanctions from friends, kin, and neighbors, and formal sanctions from police and the courts. Thus, all forms of family violence are likely to be less frequent in families who have friends or relatives who live nearby and interact with them frequently.[19] The presence of an active social support network may therefore have a deterring effect on elder abuse, for that is a highly illegitimate behavior. Phillips, in a case-control study, found abused elderly persons to have less social support.

Further, social support acts as a moderator of life stress and facilitates coping with crises,[20] and it is likely that active support from kin can reduce feelings of burden on the part of caregivers to the elderly.[21] It is possible that a lack of social support resources could negatively affect the ability of families to cope with stress that might precipitate elder abuse.

Summary

As this review indicates, no single theoretical paradigm has been developed to explain elder abuse. Instead, we are presented with an array of potential explanations for the problem. Further, the risk factors just discussed are not the only ones that could be included, although they are certainly among the most theoretically persuasive. For the purposes of an exploratory study such as that discussed here, the existing research appears to support focusing on the five areas outlined above. After describing the methodology of this study, the degree to which each of these factors was found to be related to the presence of physical abuse will be reported.

Methodology

A special study of a sample of physically abused elders was conducted as part of an ongoing research project: the evaluation of three Model Projects on Elderly Abuse, funded by the Administration on Aging. These sites, based in Massachusetts, New York, and Rhode Island, offered casework services to elderly (aged 60 and over) victims of maltreatment. In the three-year course of the demonstration, the Model Projects intervened in over 300 cases of physical and psychological abuse, financial exploitation, and neglect.

In order to improve on previous research efforts in this area, the present study had several important features. First, it focused only on one type of maltreatment: physical abuse. As others have noted, conceptual problems result from lumping together cases of abuse and neglect;[22] acts of *commission* differ substantially from those of omission. The sample therefore contained only elders who had experienced one or more acts of physical abuse, defined as the infliction of physical pain, injury, or physical coercion. This act could range from throwing an object at the other person to assaulting the person with a knife or a gun.

Second, the study did not rely, as most others have, on professional accounts of maltreatment, but instead involved direct interviews with clients. Third, and most important, the study included a matched control group of nonabused elderly. Without such a control group, it is impossible to isolate factors that are associated with elder abuse. It is necessary to contrast the characteristics of the abuse group with persons who are not maltreated, in order to establish characteristics unique to abusive families.

An attempt was made to interview all of the physical abuse cases at the three Model Project sites. In some cases, this was impossible due to the unwillingness or incapacity of the clients; roughly two-thirds of the active cases were actually interviewed at each site. A control group individually matched on sex and living arrangements was selected from the nonabuse case load of the Massachusetts project, a large, multiservice agency that served the elderly.

Case managers at this agency selected their most recent client who met the specifications provided them by the researcher; they were thus prevented from selecting particularly desirable or "interesting" cases. The case managers were asked to exclude any case in which they knew physical abuse had occurred. In spite of this restriction, three interviewees reported at least one violent incident and were therefore excluded from the control group and replaced.

One additional aspect of the design needs mention here. In the interview with the abuse victims, many of the questions dealt with the relationship with the abuser. In the control interviews, these questions were asked about a member of the household who occupied the same relationship to the control elder. Thus, if the abuser in one case was an oldest child, the control elder's oldest child became the subject of questions.

The final sample consisted of 42 physically abused elders and 42 controls. In both groups, 39 respondents were women and three were men. Both groups were predominantly white: 97.6 percent in the abuse group, and 95.2 percent in the control group. Incomes tended to be low, with 77 percent of the abuse group and 89 percent of the controls receiving less than $6,000 a year. Both groups were predominantly Catholic (71 percent of the abuse group and 69 percent of the controls). The abused elders tended to be younger (mean age 70) than the controls (mean age 75). This is due to the inclusion of three persons aged 56, 57, and 59 in the abuse group. These three individuals were severely disabled, and for this reason the Model Project staff suspended the age guideline. Of the abusers and comparison relatives, 14 (33 percent) were husbands, 14 (33 percent) sons, 10 (24 percent) daughters, 2 (5 percent) daughters-in-law, and 2 (5 percent) brothers.

All interviews were conducted in person by the same interviewer and lasted approximately 60 to 90 minutes. Quantitative measures were employed to explore a variety of areas: physical health, functional dependency, social support, and external stress, among others. Answers to open-ended questions were written down, and six tape-recorded interviews (three with abuse victims and three with abusers) were conducted to obtain more detailed accounts of the maltreatment. All these qualitative data were transcribed and analyzed. Here, I focus primarily on the quantitative findings, although qualitative material is occasionally used for illustrative purposes. The qualitative findings have been presented in more detail elsewhere.[23]

Findings

A number of items were employed to operationalize each particular risk factor. Here, it is not possible to discuss every measure that was employed; therefore, the presentation has been limited to the most important measures. The findings on the whole are relatively straightforward: A surprisingly clear and consistent picture of the abuse situation emerges.

Intra-Individual Dynamics

The first hypothesis to be examined is that which attributes abusive behavior to the psychological or emotional problems of the abuser. It was expected that the abusive relatives would exhibit such problems to a greater degree than the comparison relatives. The elderly respondents were asked two questions related to the possible psychological impairment of their relatives. First, each respondent was asked "Does [relative] have any mental or emotional problems?" The abused elders were much more likely to report psychological or emotional problems on the part of the abuser than were nonabused elders. In fact, 79 percent of the victims reported that the relative had mental or emotional problems to some degree, compared with only 24 percent of the controls ($p = .000$).[24] A more objective indicator of psycho-emotional illness is psychiatric hospitalization. The relatives of the abused elderly were considerably more likely to have been placed in a psychiatric hospital than the controls (35.7 percent to 7.1 percent; $p = .000$).

The study also examined the presence of alcohol abuse. It was determined at the outset of the project that questions relating to this issue would not be asked directly of the respondents, due to the sensitivity of this topic and the probability that the elders would underreport such behavior. Instead, the caseworkers involved with the victims and the controls were asked about the relatives' abuse of alcohol. This seemed a reasonable approach, as the caseworkers were very familiar with the respondents and their families. These workers were asked: "To the best of your knowledge, is [relative] an alcoholic?" The abusers were significantly more likely to be identified as alcoholics (45.2 percent to 7.1 percent: $p = .002$).

The qualitative component of the interviews also indicates that the victims frequently attributed the abuse they had suffered to pathological traits in the abuser. Many of the interviewees directly linked the maltreatment to psychosis, alcoholism, or other psychological problems. For example, in five cases, elderly women were assaulted by husbands who suffered from some form of dementia, whom they described as "out of control." Similarly, some parents reported that the abuser had suffered a "breakdown" of some kind and began at that time to become violent.

In fact, in over half of the cases, the victims cited character traits of the abuser as the primary cause of abuse. Some respondents blamed the maltreatment on substance abuse. As one mother put it, "I miss my son. But when he's on drugs, he's impossible." Sometimes they blamed themselves for the abuser's character flaws: "I raised him wrong," another mother reported. In other cases, the responsibility was placed on an "act of God." One woman reported that her son became abusive after a serious fall that caused brain damage, while others cited a stroke or Alzheimer's disease. In general, when asked "Why does he or she act this way toward you?" respondents were most likely to blame some flaw in the abuser's personality.

The question arises: Where do these findings point in our attempt to identify risk factors for elder abuse? Although the results presented here require further support and elaboration, the data argue for a consideration of individual psychopathology as a primary risk factor in elder abuse. The striking differences between the two groups on the measures described above, coupled with the victims' own perceptions, suggest that elder abusers may be especially troubled individuals.

One possible explanation as to why elder abusers would differ from perpetrators of other forms of family violence who have not consistently been found to be more mentally or emotionally impaired than the general population lies in the degree of normative prohibition against various types of family violence. Straus et al. found a great deal of popular approval for punishing children, and even a surprisingly high approval rate for spousal violence. However, it can be convincingly argued that it is a much more deviant act to strike an elderly person, and in particular a father or mother. There is no "normal" pattern for being violent toward one's elderly relatives; it is therefore a stronger normative violation than either child or spouse abuse. One might thus expect a greater degree of psychopathology on the part of elder abusers, as they engage in more deviant behavior than others.

Such an assertion will, of course, need to be borne out by further research. The findings reported here, however tentative, clearly argue for additional exploration of the role of the abuser's mental and emotional problems in maltreatment of the elderly. This focus need not have the overtone of labeling the perpetrators as "villains." It may simply mean, for example, that caregiving responsibility has fallen into the wrong hands. It is hoped that future studies will further illuminate this area.

Intergenerational Transmission of Violent Behavior

Somewhat surprisingly, the data do not show an association between physical punishment as a child and becoming an elder abuser in later life. In those cases in which the abuser was the child of the victim, respondents were first asked an open-ended question: "How did you usually tend to punish [child] when he or she was a child and teenager?" Responses to this question were coded as either "physical punishment mentioned" or "physical punishment not mentioned." Only one interviewee in each group spontaneously mentioned using physical punishment. Instead, the typical responses were: "I didn't have to punish," and "I never hit him."

Following this question, respondents were asked how frequently they had used physical punishment in the year in which they used it the most. The response categories ranged from "never" to "more than 20 times." No significant differences were found on this variable between the abuse and nonabuse groups. The same item was asked in reference to the use of physical punishment by the respondent's spouse; again, no significant differences were found. Most of the respondents reported that they had never used physical punishment, or that they had used it only once in that year.

While the data reported here are limited, they do not generally support the hypothesis that children who abuse elderly parents were themselves victims of abuse. The abuse victims reported that they rarely used physical punishment, and no difference was found between cases and controls on this issue. It is possible that this hypothesis is not a particularly promising one, and that stronger risk factors for elder abuse can be identified. Alternatively, it may be that the survey format employed in the present study is not the ideal one to obtain information regarding punishment and abuse of children. In fact, many of the respondents appeared to be uncomfortable with these questions. A future study could focus on this issue and conduct in-depth interviews with victims regarding their relationships with the abuser in childhood. Interviews could also be conducted with *abusers* regarding their child and teenage years. These methods may be more effective in exploring the role of a cycle of violence in elder abuse.

Dependency

Perhaps the most important findings in the study are those on the relationship between dependency and physical abuse of the elderly. As noted above, two contrasting views exist regarding the role of dependency in elder abuse. Many writers on the problem have postulated that the increasing impairment and frailty of the elderly person causes stress for the abuser, who responds with violence. An alternative hypothesis was advanced earlier in this chapter, in which abuse was attributed to a lack of power on the part of the *abuser*. In that case, we would expect to find perpetrators of elder abuse to be more dependent on the victim rather than the reverse.

The most important findings are presented here; a more detailed discussion is provided elsewhere.[25] The analysis will focus on three questions. First, Are abused elders, as some have asserted, more likely to be ill and to have diminished functional capabilities? Second, Beyond general impairment, are abused elders specifically more dependent on the abusers than are the controls on the comparison relatives? Third, Can the reverse of this configuration be considered—that is, are the abusers more dependent on their victims than are the control relatives?

The abused elderly do not, in fact, appear to be more physically impaired and in poorer health. One measure employed to test the first hypothesis is the inventory of illnesses from the Older Americans Resources and Services (OARS) instrument.[26] The abused and nonabused groups were compared on 24 conditions, ranging from arthritis and eye problems to heart disease and cancer. The respondents were asked whether they had the condition and, if so, the degree to which it interfered with their daily activities: not at all, a little, or a great deal. No significant differences ($p < .05$) were found on any of the illnesses with the exception of glaucoma; even on that condition, the difference was slight. Further, the groups did not differ significantly in whether the person was hospitalized in the past year, or in whether the respondent had experienced a decline in health status over the past five years or the past year.

Much research has shown, however, that diagnostic condition is not as reliable an indicator of the vulnerability of the elderly as is functional impairment. That is, to what extent is the individual unable to carry out basic functions essential to daily living? Some researchers have categorized these functions as personal activities of daily living ("ADLs": bathing, dressing, ambulation, etc.), and instrumental activities of daily living ("IADLs": food shopping, cooking, cleaning, etc.). Many instruments exist to assess functional status. For this study, the Index of Functional Vulnerability (IFV) was selected, which contains eleven items on mobility, orientation, and ability to perform activities of daily living.[27]

The hypothesis that the dependency of the victim leads to abuse would suggest that the abused elders should be more impaired on each item of the IFV. Tests for differences between the groups, however, found that this was not the case; in fact, the *reverse* appears to hold in some instances. No significant differences were found in the following variables: (1) needing help or having great difficulty with meal preparation; (2) being healthy enough to walk up and down stairs without help; (3) using a walker or wheelchair at least some of the time to get around; (4) being able to identify the correct year; (5) the number of days on which the person went outside of his or her dwelling in the past week; (6) being able to feed oneself; (7) or being unable to pursue desired activities because of poor health.

These data indicate that abused elderly persons were not more functionally impaired than the controls in many critical ADLs. In addition, the abuse group was found to be significantly *less* impaired than the control group in certain areas. The abused individuals were less likely to need help or have great difficulty with taking out garbage (45 percent in the abuse group to 71 percent of the controls; $p < .05$), and were more likely to report that they were healthy enough to do ordinary housework (62 percent to 38 percent; $p < .05$). The overall picture, then, is quite consistent: the abuse group is not more likely to be impaired in activities of daily living. Further, in some cases, they tend to be more *independent* than the controls.

Despite these findings, it would still be argued that while those in the abuse group are not more impaired in general, they may be more dependent specifically on the abusers. We must ask: Do abused elders depend more on the abuser (rather than on other potential helpers) than do the controls on their comparison relative? In one measure, respondents were asked whether there was someone who would care for them if they became seriously ill or disabled. Those who answered affirmatively were asked to identify the most likely helper. These responses were then coded as "Helper is abuser/comparison" or "Helper is other." The elders in the abuse group were much *less* likely to name the abuser as the person they would most likely depend on for help (26 percent to 63 percent; $p < .01$).

In another measure of the dependency of the elder on the abuser/comparison, the respondent was directly asked: "People depend on each other for many things. How much do you depend on [abuser/comparison] in each of the following areas?" Respondents were asked to answer "entirely dependent," "somewhat dependent," or "independent," in each of these areas: housing, cooking or cleaning, household repair, companionship and social activities, financial support, and transportation. No significant differences were found in five of the six areas. A difference was found in financial dependency, but the abuse group was more likely to be *independent* than the control group (69 percent to 48 percent; $p < .05$).

When the above measures are taken into consideration, the hypothesis that the impairment and dependency of an elderly person lead to physical abuse must be called seriously into question. None of the above data tends even slightly in that direction: Either no significant differences were found, or the abuse group was *less* dependent than the controls. Based on the exchange perspective outlined earlier, the alternative hypothesis must be explored—that the dependency of the abuser on his or her victim is a critical predictor of abuse.

Two measures were employed to assess the extent to which the abusers or comparison relatives were dependent on the elderly respondents. The first involved a dependency index identical to that just discussed, with the questions reversed. That is, the respondent was asked: "How much does [abuser/comparison] de-

Table 10–1   Dependency of Abuser/Comparison on Elder

	Independent No. (%)	Somewhat Dependent No. (%)	Entirely Dependent No. (%)
Housing			
Abuse group	19 (45.2)	5 (11.9)	18 (42.9)
Non-abuse group	29 (69.0)	6 (14.3)	7 (16.7)
Chi square: $p < .05$			
Household Repair			
Abuse group	33 (78.5)	2 (4.8)	7 (16.7)
Non-abuse group	40 (95.2)	0 (0)	2 (4.8)
Chi square: $p < .05$			
Financial Assistance			
Abuse group	15 (35.7)	21 (51.0)	6 (14.3)
Non-abuse group	26 (61.9)	14 (33.3)	2 (4.8)
Chi square: $p < .02$			
Transportation			
Abuse group	29 (69.1)	10 (23.8)	3 (7.1)
Non-abuse group	37 (88.1)	3 (7.1)	2 (4.8)
Chi square: $p < .05$			

Note: Due to small cell sizes, chi square was calculated by combining the "somewhat dependent" and "entirely dependent" categories. All three categories are presented here to provide readers with additional detail.

pend on *you* in these areas?" The abusers were found to be significantly more dependent on the elder in four areas: housing, household repair, financial assistance, and transportation (Table 10–1).

A second set of items was also included to further examine the imbalanced exchange between abuser and victim. The respondents were asked to imagine that they and their relative had decided to separate and establish separate residences and that contact between them was totally broken off. They were then told: "I'm going to read you things that could be affected by a break-up like this, and for each one, I'd like you to tell me who you think would be hurt more by it: you, the abuser [or comparison relative], neither of you, or both about the same."

While the abused elders less frequently identified themselves as likely to be hurt the most in the areas of performing household chores, being lonely, and being able to get around, the differences were not statistically significant. However, a significant difference was found in the question of who would be hurt more financially. The abused elders viewed their relative as much more likely to be hurt financially as the result of a separation than did the control group (53 percent to 7 percent; $p < .001$). This finding is of great importance, especially in conjunction with the data in Table 10–1, which show fewer than 36 percent of the abusers to be financially independent of their victims. Financial dependency on the part of the abuser may be an especially important predictor of violence.

Interestingly, the qualitative data collected in the study are highly consistent with the quantitative findings. If anything, the general portrait of abusers as persons with strong dependencies on their victims is even clearer than in the above discussion. To be sure, the issue of dependency is a complex one, and is likely to be mutual rather than entirely one-sided. While the predominance of cases (over two-thirds) involved abuser dependency on the abused, some relationships were at variance with that model. The following are some examples of relationships in which the abuser is heavily dependent:

- The daughter of one victim moved in with her and has never contributed in any way to her mother's support. "I support *her*. She has epilepsy and is on disability. She's supposed to give me $50 a month but she never does. She even stole a $25 gift certificate I won. We haven't gotten along ever. It's only nice when she's not here."
- An elderly couple had both been victims of their son's violent behavior. He was 30 years old and had lived on his own until he suffered a serious head injury with resulting brain damage. After the accident, he returned to their home. His behavior was erratic, and he shouted at his parents. He taunted his father and forced his mother off the telephone. His disability pension had been cut off, and he contributed little or no money to the household. His mother was injured trying to intervene in physical conflicts between father and son.
- The daughter of an elderly woman moved in with her following the daughter's divorce. The daughter had severe emotional problems and could not work. She struck her mother and threw a pan of scalding water on her. Her mother provided for her in almost every way. "My daughter never washes the dishes or the floor. I'd like her to go out and get a job. Her being unemployed makes it harder on our relationship, especially because she needs money. I support her entirely, financially. I'm pushed to the wall and I have to do this."

An interesting variant in this category was five cases in which wives were abused by severely disabled husbands they were caring for. For example:

- A frail woman, living in an elderly housing project, had had a stable relationship with her husband. He developed Alzheimer's disease and needed constant supervision. "He would beat me pretty bad, choke me. He grabbed me and said, 'I'll kill you.' "

These case descriptions, like the quantitative findings presented earlier, call into question the image of the elder abuser as a usually stable, well-intentioned individual who is brought to violent behavior by the excessive demands of an old person. In these examples, the abusers appear as persons with few resources who are frequently unable to meet their own basic needs. Instead, they are heavily dependent individuals: sometimes children who have been unable to separate from their parents; sometimes disabled or demented spouses. Rather than being powerful in the relationship, they are relatively powerless.

The findings reported in this section have major implications for the study of elder abuse. First, based on the data presented in this section, the hypothesis that the dependency of victim on abuser causes maltreatment should be seriously called into question. Instead, the hypothesis that the dependency of the relative leads to abuse was generally supported. Second, the typical abused elder tends to be an older woman who is supporting a dependent child, or, to a lesser degree, a disabled or cognitively impaired spouse. They tend to perceive the exchange relationships in which they are involved as highly imbalanced in the abuser's favor. They feel that they are giving much and receiving little.

Further research is needed to specify precisely why being dependent on an older relative would lead one to abuse that individual. From the examples given above, it is clear that financial exploitation is a factor: The abuser uses force to obtain money or goods from the victim. Certainly, the mental and emotional problems many abusers experience may make them less able to resolve differences in a nonviolent way. Finally, the theory that a sense of powerlessness in other areas can lead to the use of violence would appear to apply here. While the precise dynamics of this type of relationship remain to be determined, abuser dependency should be seen as a major possible risk factor in elder abuse.

External Stress

In this analysis, it was hypothesized that families in which elder abuse occurs would have experienced more stress from sources external to the family than the controls. It must be noted that many issues in the study of stressful life events remain to be resolved. These include how long the referent period for the reporting of events should be (e.g., six months versus one year) and whether "positive" stressors, such as taking a vacation, should be included in a life events scale. If the research project under discussion were one in which the study of stress was the primary issue, it would be important to address such technical problems. In the present case, however, the goal was simply to explore the role of external stress in elder abuse in a preliminary way.

For this reason, a relatively uncomplicated measure of stress was developed, based closely on that employed by Straus et al. in their national study of family violence. It uses the household, rather than the individual, as the unit of analysis, and it consists of events that are more likely to occur at the end of the family life cycle. Thus, respondents were asked whether any of a set of events had occurred within the past year, including a death in the household, the death of a close relative of someone in the household, and divorce or marriage of a household member. Respondents were also asked whether a household member had been ill or injured in the past year, whether someone had left or joined the household, whether someone had lost a job or retired, and whether the household had changed residence.

The results of this stress scale are inconclusive. When the abuse and control groups were compared, significant differences were found on only three items: someone was arrested, someone left the household, and someone joined the household. In each case, the abuse group was more likely to have experienced the stressful event than the control group. Unfortunately, however, the responses to these questions are confounded by the abuse situation itself. That is, in these three significant variables, the *abuser* was the person who was responsible for the event. In most of the incidents involving arrest, the abuser was arrested because of violence against the elderly victim. Similarly, a number of abusers entered and left the old persons' households in the same year, because the shared living situation became so tense and violent. If these three questions were dropped, none of the stress items would be significant.

A question was also asked about chronic financial stress, which can cause high levels of tension in households. Respondents were queried: "Sometimes financial problems can create stress. Is having enough money ever a problem for you?" No significant difference was found between the two groups. Thus, the data appear to indicate that the two groups did not differ in life stress that was *unrelated* to the abuser. The death or illness of household members did not strike the abusive families more frequently; nor did divorce, unemployment, or financial strain. The qualitative data do not shed much additional light on this issue. Stress was virtually never spontaneously mentioned by the victims as an explanation for the abuser's behavior. When asked an open-ended question— "What do you find stressful in your life right now?"—half of the respondents cited problems in their relationship with the abuser as the major stressor, rather than other aspects of their lives.

Two possible conclusions can follow from this evidence. The first is that stress has not been optimally measured here and that alternative indicators would achieve better results. This explanation is somewhat persuasive: Future studies should employ a more detailed measure of stress and carefully differentiate between stressful events that are related to the abusive situation itself and those that result from that relationship. It may be possible, alternatively, that the hypothesis that external stress increases the risk of elder abuse is not correct and that no relationship in fact exists. This second conclusion is supported to an extent by the material that has been presented in previous sections. The perpetrators have been found to have emotional problems, to be alcohol-dependent, and to be involved in long-term dependent relationships with the victims. The abuse may thus be more closely related to this configuration of factors than to the effect of stressful life events.

Social Isolation

As noted above, social support has been found to be an important moderator of life stress and may prevent family tensions from rising to unmanageable levels in a tense environment. Further, the presence of interested outsiders can make it more difficult to abuse an elderly relative. These individuals can intervene themselves or report the abuse to law enforcement or social service agencies. Thus, it is hypothesized that physically abused elders will be more socially isolated than the nonabused control group.

An in-depth look at social support was obtained by using the Social Resources Rating Scale (SRRS), which is part of the Older Americans and Services (OARS) instrument.[28] This scale measures the quality and quantity of relationships with family members and friends, as well as the availability of assistance, should older persons require it. The SRRS can be scaled into a number of indices of social support. Significant differences were found on two of these indices. The first index indicates the amount of contacts the old person has, coded as "few," "adequate," or "extensive." The abused elders were more likely to have "few" contacts with family members and friends than were the controls (36 percent to 17 percent; $p = .024$). The second index measures satisfaction with

these contacts. The data show that the abused elders were significantly more likely to find their social relationships to be unsatisfactory (39 percent to 20 pecent; $p = .019$). Another index measures
the availability of help from members of the informal support
network. No significant differences were found between the victims and controls. In most cases, elders in both groups did have
someone who would help them if necessary.

The abused elders, then, do appear to be more isolated than
non-abused elders. They tend to have fewer overall contacts and to
feel more negatively about their social situations. They are not,
however, less likely to have someone to help them if they require
it. It may be that the critical variable is the amount of involvement
of outsiders in the home; the greater this level of involvement, the
less easily a relative can be abusive without incurring the cost of
negative sanctions from others. Such a finding, as noted earlier, is
consistent with research on other forms of family violence.

These results, of course, do not prove that elder abuse is caused
by social isolation. In fact, the causal path may work in the opposite
direction. That is, the abusive relative may prevent or inhibit
contact with outsiders through threatening behavior or by creating
conflict in order to make visitors uncomfortable. The abused elders
frequently reported that the abuser had a negative impact on their
contacts with others. In some cases, the abuser directly prevented
interaction with friends and relatives. For example, one abusive
husband forbade his wife from calling her friends. Similarly, four
female respondents reported that their adult children's behavior
became worse when they (the mothers) were on the telephone.
One victim reported: "He makes it hard for me to talk on the
telephone. He mimics me while I'm talking. Sometimes I just
throw the phone down." This problem is a serious one, for the
telephone is frequently the most important source of contact with
others for elderly people.

Social contact was limited not only because the abuser expressly
forbade it, but because others found the erratic and antisocial
behavior threatening. One abused mother stated: "It's hard to
invite people over. I'm embarrassed. He talks out of line sometimes." Another woman quit her "Friendly Club" because her
daughter-in-law would "start screaming" whenever the club met in
her home. In another case, the husband's bizarre behavior frightened his young grandson so badly that the child was never brought
back to the house. Thus, the abuser can be an important factor in
reducing the victim's contact with the outside world. A vicious
circle appears to exist, in which persons who might be able to
intervene in the situation are driven away, allowing the abuser's
behavior to worsen; this, in turn, leads to further isolation.

Summary and Conclusions

In this study, 42 physically abused elderly persons were matched with a non-abuse control group to identify factors associated with this type of maltreatment. Five potential causes of abuse were examined: (1) intra-individual dynamics, (2) intergenerational transmission of violence, (3) dependency, (4) external stress, and (5) social isolation. It will be useful here to recapitulate the major findings.

1. *Intra-individual dynamics*. The abusers were much more likely than the comparisons to be identified as having mental and emotional problems and as abusing alcohol. They were also more likely to have been hospitalized for psychiatric reasons.
2. *Intergenerational transmission*. Findings in this area were not significant. Abused elders did not report more physical punishment of children; nor did they indicate that the perpetrator had been a victim of child abuse.
3. *Dependency*. Abused elders were not found to be more ill or functionally disabled than the control group; in fact, they were *less* impaired in a number of areas. The abuse group elders were not more dependent on their kin than the comparisons for assistance with activities of daily living. However, the abusers were more likely to be dependent on their elderly victims than were the control relatives.
4. *External stress*. These findings were somewhat ambiguous. While abusive families were more likely to experience three stressors (someone moving in, someone leaving the household, and someone getting arrested), these were usually actions of the perpetrator directly related to the abuse situation. The other, truly external events did not significantly differ between the two groups.
5. *Social isolation*. The abuse group scored more poorly on two social resources scales. They had fewer overall contacts and were less satisfied with those they did have.

Clearly, these findings need to be supported by future research. Based on the results presented here, however, it is possible to speculate on a configuration of factors that could place older persons at risk of abuse. Such a hypothetical "path diagram" appears in Figure 10–1. In this simple model, the abuser's mental and emotional difficulties, including alcohol abuse, lead in some cases directly to violence. They also cause the abuser to be dependent on the victim, which, following the exchange paradigm, can also lead to physical abuse. Social isolation is in a sort of

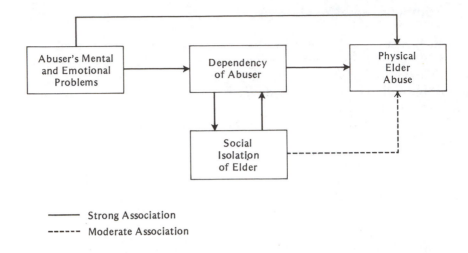

——— Strong Association

------ Moderate Association

Figure 10-1   Hypothetical Path Model for Physical Elder Abuse.

"negative feedback loop" with dependency: The isolation of the elder keeps others from intervening to change the abuse situation, but it is also a *consequence* of the abuser's behavior. A more complicated causal model could be constructed, which would involve multivariate statistical analysis of a larger sample to determine whether such a "path" to abuse exists. The conceptualization presented in Figure 10–1, however, seems plausible, based on the data collected for this study, and is supported by the qualitative findings reported here.

Implications for the Study of Elder Abuse

Two major themes have emerged from this study. The first is a general one: The theories of elder abuse that relate it to problems of the abuser, and to relationship between abuser and victim, were generally supported. Significantly less support was found for more "social-structural" causes of violence. To a sociologist, the dearth of findings that support a social-structural approach to the causation of elder abuse may be disturbing. The evidence is consistent, however. Thus, the "cycle of violence" theory was not supported here; that is, there did not appear to be a connection in this sample between physical abuse experienced and committing acts of elder abuse. It was noted above that the existence of such a cycle would lend credence to social learning theory, which holds that the family is the "cradle of violence." From the evidence presented here, the early family lives of the abusers do not appear to have been unusually violent. This sociocultural theory, then, does not seem to offer the explanatory power it had been found to have with other forms of family violence. It was also found that chronic economic stress and stressful life events played only a small role in the abuse situations.

The second theme relates to the dependency issues outlined above. Most important, the notion that physical elder abuse results from the strain of caring for a dependent old person found little support in this study. Instead, we are left with the image of an impaired, dependent perpetrator who uses physical violence to obtain money or goods or to compensate for a lack of power in his or her relationship with the victim. The findings of this study support a focus on the abuser and his or her troubles.

These results may make it necessary to question the conventional view of elder abuse. It has become fashionable to characterize the families of the elderly as willing, responsible caretakers. This view is largely due to research on caregiving, but also in part because families have come to be seen as a key component in reducing the public costs of long-term care. The resulting perspective taken by many persons interested in elder abuse was one that tended to blame the victim. The elderly, it has been held, are hard to care for. They create stress for their relatives, who in turn get angry, lose control, and strike the old person.

Based on the evidence provided here, we must be willing to shed, or at least suspend, accepted notions about the responsible behavior of some relatives of the elderly. In particular, elder abuse researchers must begin to view the phenomenon as domestic violence, rather than as only "caregiver" violence. We certainly do not wish to return to theories of a "criminal type" to explain deviant behavior such as elder abuse. We must, however, be open to the possibility that characteristics of the abuser, rather than those of the old person, may be strongly associated with violence against the elderly.

Endnotes

1. "Adult Children's Attachment and Helping Behavior of Elderly Parents: A Path Model," *Journal of Marriage and the Family* 45, no. 4 (1983), pp. 815–25; Victor G. Cicerelli, *Helping Elderly Parents* (Dover, Mass.: Auburn House, 1981); Elizabeth S. Johnson and B. S. Bursk, "Relationships Between the Elderly and Their Adult Children," *Gerontologist* 17 (1977), pp. 90–96.
2. Donald P. Kent and Margaret B. Matson, "The Impact of Health on the Aged Family," *The Family Coordinator* (January 1972), pp. 29–36; Marjorie Fiske

Lowenthal, *Lives in Distress* (New York: Basic Books, 1964); Gordon Streib, "Older Families and Their Troubles: Familial and Social Responses," *The Family Coordinator* (January 1972), pp. 5–19.

3. James J. Callahan, "Elder Abuse Programming: Will It Help the Elderly?" *Urban Social Change Review* 15, no. 3 (1982), pp. 15–19; Claire Pedrick-Cornell and Richard J. Gelles, "Elderly Abuse: The Status of Current Knowledge," *Family Relations* 32, no. 3 (1982), pp. 457–65.

4. Gerald Hotaling and David Sugarman, "An Identification of Risk Factors," in *Domestic Violence Surveillance System Feasibility Study, Phase I Report*, ed. G. Bowen (Atlanta, Georgia: Centers for Disease Control, 1984).

5. Richard Gelles, "Child Abuse as Psychopathology: A Sociological Critique and Reformulation," in *Violence in the Family*, eds. S. Steinmetz and M. A. Straus (New York: Dodd, Mead, 1974), p. 190.

6. L. Young, "Parents Who Hate," in *Violence in the Family*, eds. S. Steinmetz and M. A. Straus (New York: Dodd, Mead, 1974), p. 189.

7. M. Faulk, "Men Who Assault Their Wives," *Medicine, Science, and the Law* 14 (1974), pp. 180–83; John R. Lion, "Clinical Aspects of Wifebattering," in *Battered Women*, ed. M. Roy (New York: Van Nostrand Reinhold, 1977), pp. 126–36.

8. Gelles, "Child Abuse as Psychopathology."

9. Diane Coleman and Murray A. Straus, "Alcohol Abuse and Family Violence" (Durham: University of New Hampshire, Family Violence Research Program, 1981).

10. Richard L. Douglass, Tom Hickey, and Catherine Noel, "A Study of Maltreatment of the Elderly and Other Vulnerable Adults" (Ann Arbor, University of Michigan, Institute of Gerontology, 1980); Elizabeth Lau and Jordan Kosberg, "Abuse of the Elderly by Informal Care Providers, *Aging* (September-October, 1979), pp. 10–15; Rosalie S. Wolf, Michael Godkin, and Karl Pillemer, "Elder Abuse and Neglect: Report from Three Model Projects" (Worcester: University of Massachusetts Medical Center, University Center on Aging, 1984).

11. Murray A. Straus, Richard J. Gelles, and Suzanne Steinmetz, *Behind Closed Doors: Violence in the American Family* (New York: Dodd, Mead, 1980).

12. D. S. Owens and Murray A. Straus, "The Social Structure of Violence and Approval of Violence as an Adult," *Aggressive Behavior* 1 (1975), pp. 193–211.

13. Janice L. Davidson, "Elder Abuse," in *The Battered Elder Syndrome: An Exploratory Study*, eds. M. R. Block and J. D. Sinnott (College Park: University of Maryland, Center on Aging, 1979), pp. 49–55; Suzanne Steinmetz, "Dependency, Stress, and Violence Between Middle-Aged Caregivers and Their Elderly Parents," in *Abuse and Maltreatment of the Elderly*, ed. J. I. Kosberg (Littleton, Mass.: John Wright PGS, 1983), pp. 134–149.

14. Melanie A. Hwalek, Mary C. Sengstock, and R. Lawrence, "Assessing the Probability of Abuse of the Elderly (Paper presented at the Annual Meeting of the Gerontological Society of America, November, 1984); Linda Phillips, "Abuse and Neglect of the Frail Elderly at Home: An Exploration of Theoretical Relationships," *Journal of Advanced Nursing* 8 (1983), pp. 379–92; Rosalie S. Wolf, Cecile Strugnell, and Michael Godkin, "Preliminary

Findings from Three Model Projects on Elderly Abuse (Worcester: University of Massachusetts, University Center on Aging, 1982).

15. David Finkelhor, "Common Features of Family Abuse," in *The Dark Side of Families: Current Family Violence Research,* eds. D. Finkelhor et al. (Beverly Hills, Calif.: Sage Publications, 1983), p. 19.

16. David Gil, *Violence Against Children: Physical Child Abuse in the United States* (Cambridge, Mass.: Harvard University Press, 1971); Blair Justice and Rita Justice, *The Abusing Family* (New York: Human Sciences Press, 1976); Straus, Gelles, and Steinmetz, *Behind Closed Doors*.

17. Richard J. Gelles and Murray A. Straus, "Determinants of Violence in the Family: Toward a Theoretical Integration," *Contemporary Theories about the Family,* eds. W. R. Burr et al. (New York: Free Press, 1979).

18. Richard J. Gelles, *The Violent Home* (Beverly Hills, Calif.: Sage Publications, 1972); Gil, *Violence Against Children; Justice and Justice, The Abusing Family*.

19. Ivan F. Nye, "Choice, Exchange, and the Family," in *Contemporary Theories about the Family,* vol. 2, eds. W. R. Burr et al. (New York: Free Press, 1979), pp. 1–41.

20. Stanley Cobb, "Social Support as a Moderator of Life Stress," *Psychosomatic Medicine* 38 (1976), pp. 300–12; Thomas T. H. Wan, *Stressful Life Events, Social Support Networks, and Gerontological Health* (Lexington, Mass.: Lexington Books, 1982).

21. Steven H. Zarit, Karen E. Reever, and Julie Bach-Peterson, "Relatives of the Impaired Elderly: Correlates of Feelings of Burden," *Gerontologist* 20, no. 6 (1980), pp. 649–55.

22. Pedrick-Cornell and Gelles, "Elderly Abuse."

23. Karl Pillemer, "Merging Quantitative and Qualitative Methods in the Study of Elder Abuse," in *Qualitative Gerontology,* eds. S. Reinharz and G. Rowles (New York: Springer, 1986).

24. Unless otherwise noted, the test of statistical significance employed in this chapter is the McNemar test, which is a chi square test for related samples involving nominal scale dichotomous variables. See Quinn McNemar, *Psychological Statistics* (New York: John Wiley, 1969).

25. Karl Pillemer, "The Dangers of Dependency: New Findings on Domestic Violence Against the Elderly" (Paper presented at the Annual Meeting of the American Sociological Association, August 1985).

26. Linda K. George, R. Landesman, and Gerda G. Fillenbaum, "Developing Measures of Functional Status and Service Utilization: Refining and Extending the OARS Methodology" (Final report to NRTA/AARP Andrus Foundation, 1982).

27. John N. Morris, Sylvia Sherwood, and Vincent Mor, "An Assessment Tool for Use in Identifying Functionally Vulnerable Persons in the Community," *Gerontologist* 24, no. 4 (1984), pp. 373–79.

28. George et al., "Developing Measures of Functional Status and Service Utilization."

Part Three

TREATMENT AND PREVENTION OF FAMILY CONFLICT AND ELDER ABUSE

Chapter 11

DEVELOPING AND INTEGRATING FAMILY-ORIENTED APPROACHES IN CARE OF THE ELDERLY

by Mark A. Edinberg

We are at an interesting juncture in the care of the elderly. The increase in life expectancy and related crises in health care have meant that some older persons, particularly those in the oldest age groups, have become increasingly dependent on family members for assistance. Much of the response to these "new" demands on relatives (often referred to as "caregivers") has focused on development of services designed to ease the burdens of care, such as respite care beds in nursing homes or support groups for "children of aging relatives." There are, however, few attempts in the literature to tie this changing focus of care to theories and principles related to family systems, or to examine how such concepts can be translated into the realities of care of the elderly.

This chapter first outlines several aspects of what can be termed a "family-oriented approach" to the care of the elderly. It then examines some of the life-cycle crises faced by the elderly and their implications for family functioning. Finally, some recommendations are given for integrating family-oriented approaches into service delivery systems for the elderly, and for new directions in research, practice, and training.

A Family-Oriented Approach

Advocacy for a family-oriented approach to care of the elderly is as much a philosophical stance as a recommendation for specific modes of care. Most care of the elderly in our culture currently centers on the individual, with the family playing an important but secondary role. In emphasizing the need to think about diseases and conditions that affect the individual, the strong influence of the family system on the care, condition, and outcomes of interventions with the elderly is frequently ignored. The approach outlined here is presented to further our understanding of the functioning of the older person and her or his family.

The concept of "family orientation" is based on a system approach to families.[1] The following four axioms capture the main points of such an approach:

1. The total family system is more than the sum of its parts.
2. To understand the individual, one must also understand the total system and its relationships.
3. Relationships and behavior are interactive—that is, all events are part of a sequence. Each response in turn is a stimulus for other responses from family members. Relationships form an important context in which behavior takes place and can be understood.
4. To change individual behavior, the patterns, relationships, and communication styles of the family system must be changed, as systems work to maintain their current functioning (homeostasis).

These axioms lead to several considerations in conceptualizing the care of the elderly. One immediate consideration is that in this view, virtually *every* issue in the care of the older person is thought of as having implications for and responses from every family member. This in turn means that all members need to be considered before decisions are made as to how to inform older persons of their diagnosis, where and when relocation of an older person takes place, and similar issues.

Second, a family orientation presupposes that family dynamics, or systematic patterns of interaction, beliefs, and behavior among family members, are an important part of assessment, planning, and intervention in the care of the older person. Thus, the family becomes the unit of analysis, as opposed to the more customary approach of focusing on the individual client.

Third, a family orientation emphasizes interaction and relationships among family members as a focus of intervention. Such a perspective argues for the inclusion of all relevant family members—especially the older persons themselves—in decisions and discussions about living arrangements, medical regimen, and so forth.

Finally, a family-oriented approach allows us to use a nonpathological model in clinical practice. That is, family systems theories emphasize making the entire family functional rather than identifying any one member as pathological and "the problem." Since many of the stressors and conflicts faced by families with older members are not the result of "psychopathology" per se (see below), a family orientation may well promote greater understanding and better intervention models than more traditional individual perspectives.

Goals in Family-Oriented Approaches

Different schools of thought about family functioning have varying goals for work with families. However, they contain several consistent goals that in turn can serve as a starting point for work with older persons and their families. In addition to forming the basis for long-term counseling or therapy with families, these goals are also suitable for use in conjunction with other forms of intervention, including medical, nursing, social work, and outreach activities.

The first goal is to understand how the family's functioning affects the condition of the older person, the patterns of family caregiving, and the well-being of the family. This goal highlights the need to assess the family. This aspect of a family-oriented approach also leads to assessing the appropriateness of current programs such as respite care or support groups, as to their potential benefit for a given family system.

A second goal is to help the family improve its problem-solving ability in order to adapt to current crises.[2] A third goal is to help family members discuss uncomfortable feelings with each other in ways that are nondefensive.[3] Talking about a pending death, the possibility of institutionalization, or setting limits with an older relative as to the amount of time that will be spent in his or her behalf, is difficult and painful. However, such discussions can lead to better understanding, harmony, and an improved sense of self-worth in many situations. A related fourth goal is to help families give appropriate emotional support and encouragement to each other. Too often, both the power of reinforcement and the difficulties many families have with giving and taking affection and support from each other in times of crisis are underestimated.

A final goal is to work toward strengthening the family's functioning as opposed to working toward strengthening only the older person's position. That is, in one sense, a reiteration of the initial concepts of a family-oriented approach posed earlier, but it also carries with it the ideas that the self-esteem, growth, and relationships among all family members are equally important and can be viewed as relevant goals of intervention, even if they seem far afield from the present problem of the older person.

Sources of Stress and Change in Older Persons' Lives

Several age-related events may cause stress for older persons as they and their families age. These stressors include chronic illness and disability (including senile dementia of the Alzheimer type); divorce; death; moving in with family; institutionalization; and role reversal. While each potential stressor may have dramatic consequences for the older individual, there are likely to be equally important outcomes or changes in family functioning that in turn may be critical in planning and implementing interventions.

Illness and Disability

Chronic illness is highly correlated with age. Eighty-six percent of the elderly have at least one chronic condition, and 46 percent of the aged experience some limitation of activity due to these conditions.[4]

One common outcome of disability is that older men become afflicted with conditions that require wives to be caregivers for extended periods of time. Our social norms are quite strong about the "duties" of the wife in this situation, which may mean that she is uncomfortable discussing the extreme difficulties she experiences when she has to handle both her own physical condition while caring for her husband. The rest of the family may inadvertently reinforce her role as "martyr," or can alternatively be a source of strength to her as well as supplying needed relief from the duties of care. The values, beliefs, and hidden norms of the family may have to be assessed and addressed if the needed care and solutions to related problems are to be forthcoming.

The onset and diagnosis of dementia have such a tremendous impact on the family system that this problem deserves special mention. The older dementia patient is likely to need significant time and financial resources for care, which may conflict with other pressing priorities of the caregiving families, including child-rearing. Women, who have traditionally cared for aged relatives, are increasingly employed outside the home and are thus less available to fill the caregiving role. In addition, the needs for care, especially in more advanced cases of dementia, are quite demanding and can include assistance in feeding, bathing, and changing diapers and clothes if incontinence occurs. The impact of dementia can exacerbate existing conflicts in families, including those between spouses, between parents and children, and between home and work. Some family members may react with denial ("There's nothing wrong, really"), withdrawal, or resentment when faced with the need to care for a failing older relative. Other family members may take on the role of martyr, becoming overzealous and at some level, gaining satisfaction from being the "suffering hero(ine)." One rather impressive statistic in this area is that 55 percent of primary caregivers of Alzheimer patients in one study had "significant depressive symptoms."[5]

Beyond the external pressures on the family, family members may be torn between showing loyalty to the previously functional older adult and needing to take active steps (such as obtaining control over finances) to respond to the person's new situation. Another consideration is that in the course of dementia, the identified patient may become a dysfunctional family member. The past roles this person played in the family (e.g., father, mother, grandmother, grandfather, peacemaker, and so forth) become vacant. As the family adjusts, there are bound to be reactions to others taking the "place" of a family member who is not yet deceased.

Family dynamics and concerns may be exhibited in the decision to tell the client about his or her diagnosis and to discuss freely the client's condition. Frequently, the client is not told of his or her condition and its expected trajectory. The reasons given for such nondisclosure are that the client will forget anyway, not understand, or become too upset. In fact, in some cases, persons with organic brain syndromes *are* aware that something is seriously wrong. Not unlike the issues raised about telling terminally ill persons they are dying, it may well be that the difficulty family members have in handling their own feelings about the diagnosis is interfering with what is both a right and a need for the client to know what is happening. Even if the client forgets, misunderstands the information, or becomes upset, a frank and open discussion can establish trust and a sense that troublesome matters can be talked about.

This is not to argue that all persons should be told everything right away. In general, however, family members, including the client, have the right to know, unless extraordinary circumstances dictate otherwise. Rather than acceding to family wishes not to discuss a diagnosis, a family-oriented approach suggests assessing underlying motives for the request and then determining whether to accept the request, address the motives, or take other action.

Divorce

The number of divorces and divorced persons over the age of 60 is growing.[6] In many cases, an older husband leaves his wife; she is then left with no access to the husband's pension and/or social security benefits. In addition, the ex-wife may have a sense of stigma at having been "abandoned" in this way. In such a situation, family members may feel torn between loyalty to each parent— loyalty to the parent they "prefer," or loyalty to the parent who seems to be "right." The older woman who was "left for another woman" may well be viewed as a victim. There appears to be a narrow line between support that reinforces healthy behavior and a self-perpetuating blame of the departed spouse (and self) that leads to no movement or improved sense of self-esteem.

Death

The death of a family member creates a void in the family system that needs to be filled. Whatever roles were played by the now-deceased older person will eventually be occupied by other family members. This is of particular importance in the death of a spouse. How the family responds to the death will depend on the family's traditions, loyalties, rules, and adaptability. At times, such hidden loyalties and rules may lead to an uncomfortable resolution, such as when the family becomes the sole source of support, entertainment, and socialization for a widow because its members "feel obligated" to do so. A family-oriented approach to post-death care should include (1) attending to initial adaptation to the loss, (2) adapting to immediate and new demands for self-care of the widow(er), and (3) working with the family to allow the widow(er) to adapt to the social realities of singleness. Intervention may help relatives to weigh family and cultural traditions (for example, wearing black for the rest of one's life or keeping the memory of the spouse "alive" by never feeling attracted to another person of the opposite sex) with how the survivor is going to choose to live the remainder of his or her life.

Moving In

Increasingly, families are faced with questions about whether the older parent should move in with the children. Having an older relative living under the same roof as a younger family member raises important issues for family functioning. On a basic level, questions such as how the workload in the house is divided can surface. Certain subsystems (e.g., "adults" and "chore doers") may increase in numbers, with a new member having certain rights and potential responsibilities that have to be negotiated.

More important, unresolved or old family conflicts are likely to be rekindled by having the parents and their adult children in contact "24 hours a day." This situation is likely to occur when moving in occurs after some kind of loss—whether it be a loss of health, of financial resources, or of the older person's spouse. While moving in may be painful, it also provides an opportunity for family members to make peace as adults with the older relative, to develop appropriate interpersonal boundaries,[7] and to resolve unhealthy aspects of their relationships.[8]

Institutionalization

One of the greatest sources of family concern, guilt, resentment, and unresolved feelings is the issue of institutionalizing an older relative. Although less than 5 percent of all older persons are in institutions at any one point in time, 20 percent of the elderly population will spend some time in a long-term care facility.[9] Thus, many families are likely to be involved with the institutionalization of an older parent or in-law, even if only for a recuperative stay.

It is worth considering what institutionalization means to an older person. A formerly independent, fully functioning member of society has a decision made, *usually by others*, for him or her to leave the community in which he or she lives and go to a place that has a stigma associated with it. Further, the older person is mandated to live a more structured existence with less privacy, status, or choice over activity.[10] The change from being a community dweller to being an institutional resident often carries with it the sense that whoever makes the decision is taking some very important pieces of identity and life away from the older person.

The prospects of institutionalization raise a range of conflicts for families as well, many of which are characterized by feelings of guilt. Questions may focus on the appropriateness of institutionalization ("Are we doing the right thing?"), cost ("Should we pay to have Mom be a private patient?"), and finding a setting that is one in which residents are well cared for ("How good is this place?"). These questions reflect a number of concerns, including the fact that institutionalization can be perceived by the family as a failure to care for the older relative. Also, because many persons consider the institution as a "last stop" before death, some feelings and behaviors take place that are often associated with terminal patients (avoidance, not discussing things in front of the elder, or talking as if he or she were not present).

There are many reasons for the concerns and behaviors families exhibit when confronted by institutionalization, not the least of which concern the nature of institutions and the types of indignities that have taken place in the name of custodial care. However, it is also true that institutionalization is necessary in some cases and that, when ties are strong to begin with, families can experience an improvement in relationships after institutionalization.[11] A family-oriented approach to institutionalization can lead to interventions that will decrease family stress and improve the process of institutionalization. One example is mandatory family meetings that include the older person to discuss what is needed, what the options are, and ways of coming to grips with the strong feelings that are likely to emerge. In addition, programs such as the one described by Dye and Richards,[12] in which families and new residents were put in groups to discuss the first few weeks in the facility, may also be useful to help family members bridge the transition to institutional care.

Role Reversal

Unlike the potential stressors for the aging family previously discussed, role reversal is more descriptive of an interpersonal process than of a concrete event. Role reversal refers to the dynamic in which a child becomes a major source of emotional and material support for an older parent. Providing support in a new role to one's parents can be rewarding or painful, depending in part on the current relationship, level of communication, shared values, and each person's views of the new roles.

From a family orientation, several questions must be addressed: Can each person handle the change in historical roles without bringing in prior grievances or unresolved differences? Are other family members brought into the relationship in harmful ways?[13] Are roles and functions within the family strengthened or disturbed by this new relationship?[14] Are there conflicting values or beliefs that lead to discomfort with the new relationship, such as a sense of the parent's needs competing with the need to treat the older person as independent? When roles are reversed, there may be a lessening of the perception of reciprocity or exchange between the older person and the child now acting as parent. Along with working on the issues presented above, families may need to consider how they can gain some benefit, or at least have a sense of "appropriate" burden, from role reversal.

Implementing Family-Oriented Approaches: Barriers and Recommendations for Research and Practice

Although a family orientation offers the practitioner a useful framework for planning and implementing care of the elderly, it is rarely utilized in practice. In this section, some barriers to the use of family interventions with the elderly, even when such interventions are warranted, are identified.

Individual Orientation in Psychotherapy

Most health and mental health practitioners are trained in an individual orientation to diagnosis, planning, and treatment of "illness." A client is seen, diagnosed, and treated for a particular condition, with social and family factors relegated to secondary importance. Further, persons who choose to work with the elderly have, in a sense, identified themselves with one generation of a given family and may focus on the older person's needs, wishes, and behavior rather than giving equal weight to the family as a unit of care. There is also a tendency to view many problems of the aged as an individual failing rather than a "family problem." Dementia, delirium, or reactions to changes such as retirement or illness are not likely to be seen by either older persons or their families as a family problem. Although family members may admit that these events have an impact on the family, they generally perceive them as related to growing old and not having much to do with the total family system.

The primary model of care of the elderly in the United States is a medical one, which focuses on individual illnesses or pathology that can be remedied or managed by medicines or specific regimens focusing on the individual older client. Virtually all subsidized, third-party payments for care of the elderly reflect the medical model of care. Even when mental health services are needed, they are based on individual diagnosis and are poorly reimbursed under current funding and legislation. Payments for services are made on the basis of contact with the older client—not with families.

The issue of payment raises particular problems for family-oriented treatment or counseling, which may entail more than 40- or 50-minute sessions to get "air time" for all family members. Thus, family interventions may be viewed as less "time efficient" than working with the individual client. However, one counter-argument to the seemingly greater cost of family interventions is that problems in one generation may be prevented from being passed on to following generations. In addition, offering family-oriented counseling services may be cost-effective in that, by helping the family deal with increased responsibility for the older person, premature institutionalization may be prevented.

Role of the Older Client in the Family System

Family therapy and counseling were developed for use with psychiatric patients, many of whom were children. Most older persons facing the stressors discussed above are not labeled as "mental patients" but have family roles of mother, father, uncle, or aunt, and thus a position of implied leadership and prior child rearing. The older person, by virtue of these roles, is in a stronger position to refuse to have the family "drawn in." In addition, the older family member may not want family interventions as they can carry an implicit suggestion that the family has problems.

Institutional Reinforcement of Barriers to Family-Oriented Interventions

In nursing homes, mental institutions, adult day-care settings, and other service agencies, there is often an individual orientation to treatment, a medical basis for client selection, a reimbursement schedule based on individual pathology, and an emphasis on client (vs. family) problems. Several other aspects of these settings make family-oriented interventions difficult. One is the lack of suitable space for meetings with large families. In addition, there is often a sense that the family caregiving responsibilities have been some-how delegated to these service systems. While decreasing certain aspects of burden (e.g., "babysitting" or being worried about the safety of a parent living alone with Alzheimer's disease), many programs have limited resources to help the family "work through" or adapt in a healthy way to the changed status of the older client. Finally, in most of these systems, after the client leaves (be it for reasons of moving to a different level of care or death), there is no way in which the caregiving system continues contact with families for bereavement services, one exception being hospice programs.

Logistics

Bringing the family unit of an older person together is often hampered by geographic mobility, increased numbers of two-career families, and work schedules. The times when families *can* get together (vacation, holidays, or evenings) are when most practitioners prefer not to work.

Bias Against Older Clients' and Families' Capacity to Change

There is a belief that older people and their families have such a long history of maladaptive behavior or coping responses that any attempt to alter these dynamics is doomed to fail. From a practical viewpoint, it may well be that the goals of intervention with older families are more limited than with younger ones. Under these circumstances, the focus might be on adaptation, rather than "cure."[15] At the same time, there is no evidence that family-oriented interventions are less successful with older persons and their families than with "younger" families.

Lack of Integrated Models of Care That Include Family-Oriented Assessment and Approaches

The difficulty in combining family-oriented models with individually oriented models of care, as well as the relative separation of family interventions (usually thought of as family therapy) from more traditional medical and mental health care, has inhibited the development of models of care that include a family orientation. One consequence of these barriers is that the persons most likely to have contact with the elderly are not family therapists; nor are they family-oriented in their approach to care. Programs that are philosophically oriented toward the family, such as hospice, adult day care, and home care, despite their best intentions, have to overcome the previously mentioned obstacles as they make attempts to include the family in treatment.

Thus, while there is good reason to develop family-oriented approaches, there are also formidable barriers to using them. It is important to ask, Where do we go from here? The remainder of this chapter focuses on these three questions: (1) What do we need to know about families, care of the elderly, and assessment of family dynamics to be able to pinpoint when family-oriented interventions are needed? (2) How can we begin to integrate family-oriented interventions into existing systems that provide care to the elderly? and (3) What implications are there for the training of persons who work with the elderly?

What Should We Know?

From the clinical perspective, we need to address at least five issues in designing and implementing family-oriented interventions for the aged and their families:

1. We must work to identify the salient dimensions on which to assess and intervene with families. For example, should we begin to evaluate such theoretically developed dimensions as cohesion, adaptability, and communication to find out how they relate to the family constellation and predict its behavior.[16] Or, are we better off focusing on dimensions that on the surface seem to have a direct impact on care, such as flexibility, nature of family rules, use of power, communication patterns,[17] or should we focus more on functional and dysfunctional relationships in the family system?
2. Can clinically useful check lists, rating scales, or other measures be developed that can be used efficiently by persons other than highly trained family therapists? In reality, such methods must be easily administered and able to be completed in about 10 minutes to stand a chance of being added to assessment procedures used in many agencies, particularly those focusing on health care.
3. Assuming we can assess relevant dimensions of a family's functioning, definable family constellations should be identified that predict the need and potential effectiveness of different treatment modalities such as family counseling, respite care, family meetings, support groups or other forms of family interventions.
4. Related to this last concern, we must evaluate the way in which family-oriented interventions are distributed among the range of possible services. Given the barriers to a family orientation in care of the elderly, it is not surprising that at present there is financial support for important services as respite care and education but a relative lack of support for equally important services such as family counseling. A

radical approach that addresses this issue would be to mandate that requests for governmental funding for long-term care services include a budgeted proportion for direct family-oriented assessment and/or counseling.

5. Family intervention methods should be carefully evaluated. What types of outcomes can be expected both for the older adult and for the family (e.g., appropriateness of institutionalization, better allocation of family resources, decrease of pathology in families, decrease in tension among family members, improved decision making)? In order to justify their cost-effectiveness, family-oriented interventions should have a preventive function as well as show direct benefits for family members. Thus, there should be some substantiated impact on family functioning as well as demonstrated benefits for the older adult.

Applications for Practice Settings

Few persons currently working with the elderly and their families are trained in family-oriented interventions. This situation is unlikely to change overnight, even with the advent of certification and licensure in marriage and family therapy. We should expect therefore that in the foreseeable future, nonfamily therapists will frequently be assisting families in times of stress. Such encounters may take place in hospice settings, hospitals, home care, and long-term care settings. Other types of settings, including geriatric clinics, community mental health centers, ombudsman and elder protective service programs, and adult day care are more likely to have staff with appropriate expertise in family counseling, but those staff members may not have the time to work extensively with every family the agency serves.

Given this reality, we should consider transferring the "core technology"[18] to another group who are at present not considered to have appropriate "professional credentials" to treat families. Put in a slightly different light, it may be possible to "streamline" family assessment and intervention procedures for use in clinical settings by public health nurses, outreach workers, hospital discharge planners, case managers for frail elderly, or senior center and adult day-care center staff.

The question of adaptation of assessment and intervention skills for nonfamily therapists is testable and should be a focus of future research. Possible roles for family therapists and counselors in this process are those of trainer, supervisor, and consultant called in to work with particularly difficult families. Such limited use of "expensive" professional staff time has the potential to be cost-effective.

A second important practice application is to include family members in the planning and treatment of the older person's problems. They should be invited to participate in assessment, or even required to attend family meetings. At a very practical level, there needs to be space in clinical settings for families to participate in the interaction between professional and client. By inviting the relative(s) in for the examination, with, of course, the patient's consent, the professional can observe and interact with at least one part of the family system during the caregiving process.

Implications for Training and Education

In order to integrate family-oriented approaches into the existing service delivery system for the aged, it will be necessary to train or educate persons in family-oriented assessment and intervention. Adding this subject to existing curricula in the helping professions may be difficult, as many educators connected with such programs believe that there is already too little time to cover current content. The potential of this type of training to improve patient care, however, argues for its inclusion in nursing, medical, and social work training programs, among others.

A second possibility that may be easier to implement is continuing education and workshops for professionals. Since many professional groups require continuing education for licensure or accreditation, there are potential markets for training in family-oriented assessment and intervention skills through this structure. Families may also benefit from educational programs that can be developed by collaboration between national support networks such as the Alzheimer's Disease and Related Disorders Association and persons with expertise in family-oriented interventions.

A third educational initiative that could be considered is somewhat less conventional. Short-term sessions could be offered at professional meetings for researchers, clinicians, gerontologists, and policy makers, to talk about how they communicate, care for, suffer with, and otherwise cope with aging members *in their own families*. Professionals, like others, would benefit from a better understanding and appreciation of how their own patterns of family function influence their biases and interests. Most of us are affected by our own family issues as they relate to the elderly, and few of us have opportunities to improve our understanding of these issues. It may be time for professionals to confront aging in their own families, as well as the families with whom they work.

Endnotes

1. There is an extensive literature about family systems theory. A good overview for the interested reader is provided by Susan L. Jones, *Family Therapy: A Comparison of Approaches* (Bowie, Md.: Robert J. Brady Co., 1980).
2. John J. Herr and John H. Weakland, *Counseling Elders and Their Families: Practical Techniques for Applied Gerontology* (New York: Springer Publishing Company, 1979).
3. Virginia Satir and Michelle Baldwin, *Satir Step by Step* (Palo Alto: Science and Behavior Books, 1984).
4. Charles S. Wilder, "Chronic Conditions and Limitations of Activity and Mobility: United States, July 1965–June 1967," *Vital and Health Statistics,* Series 10, no. 61 (1971).
5. Donna Cohen and Carl Eisdorfer, "Depression and Attributional Style in Family Members Caring for a Relative with Alzheimer's Disease" (Paper presented at the Annual Meeting of the Gerontological Society of America, November 1984).
6. Peter Uhlenberg and Mary Ann P. Meyers, "Divorce and the Elderly," *The Gerontologist* 21 (1981), pp. 276–82.
7. Salvadore Minuchin, *Families and Family Therapy* (Cambridge, Mass.: Harvard University Press, 1974).
8. Murray Brown, "The Use of Family Therapy in Clinical Practice," in *Changing Families: A Family Therapy Reader,* ed. J. Haley (New York: Grune & Stratton, 1971), pp. 159–92.
9. Robert J. Kastenbaum and Sandra E. Candy, "The 4% Fallacy: A Methodological and Empirical Critique of Extended Care Facility Population Statistics," *International Journal of Aging and Human Development* 4 (1973), pp. 15–21.
10. Sheldon S. Tobin and Morton A. Lieberman, *Last Home for the Aged* (San Francisco: Jossey-Bass, 1976).
11. Kristen F. Smith and Vern L. Bengtson, "Positive Consequences of Institutionalization: Solidarity Between Elderly Parents and Their Middle-aged Children," *The Gerontologist* 19 (1979), pp. 438–47.
12. Carol J. Dye and Cherry L. Richards, "Facilitating the Transition to Nursing Home," in *Nontraditional Therapy and Counseling with the Aging,* ed. S. S. Sargent (New York: Springer Publishing Company, 1980).
13. Murray Bowen, "The Use of Family Therapy in Clinical Practice," in *Changing Families: A Family Therapy Reader,* ed. J. Haley (New York: Grune & Stratton, 1971), pp. 159–92.
14. Minuchin, *Families and Family Therapy.*
15. Herr and Weakland, *Counseling Elders and Their Families.*
16. David H. Olson, Hamilton I. McCubbin, Howard I. Barnes, Andrea S.

Larsen, Marla J. Muxen, and Marc A. Wilson, *Families: What Makes Them Work* (Beverly Hills, Calif.: Sage Publications, 1983).

17. Richard Bandler, John Grinder, and Virginia Satir, *Changing with Families* (Palo Alto, Calif.: Science and Behavior Books, 1976); Virginia Satir, *People Making* (Palo Alto, Calif.: Science and Behavior Books, 1972); Herr and Weakland, *Counseling Elders and Their Families*.

18. James D. Thompson, *Organizations in Action: Social Science Bases of Administrative Theory* (New York: McGraw Hill, 1967).

Chapter 12

RELIEVING INFORMAL CAREGIVER BURDEN THROUGH ORGANIZED SERVICES

by Francis G. Caro

Among the most challenging issues facing our aging society is the role of family members in providing long-term care for their aged relatives. An important minority of the elderly have a significant need for help in their activities of daily living. Although nursing homes and other institutions are frequent settings for the care of the elderly, the vast majority of the older population who need long-term care live outside of institutions. In recent years, organized home care programs for the elderly have expanded substantially in the United States. Nevertheless, informal caregivers—usually relatives—remain the most important providers of long-term care to the elderly living outside of institutions.

Debate over the degree of responsibility of family members as long-term care providers has emerged as a significant obstacle to proposals for expanded publicly funded home care. Proponents of home care have argued that subsidized services are needed because the informal system is often insufficient, and those in need lack adequate funds to pay for their own care. Further, as other

Note: Based on research supported by the Health Care Financing Administration, Grant No. 18-P-97462/2/01A1 and reported in *Home Care in New York City: The System, the Providers, the Beneficiaries* by Francis G. Caro and Arthur Blank, New York: Community Service Society of New York, 1985.

chapters in this volume indicate, family tensions and conflict may make relatives inappropriate caregivers. The critics maintain that subsidized services tend to substitute for care more appropriately provided by family members. Until ways are found to resolve the issues about the appropriate division of labor between the formal and informal system in the provision of home care, proposals for a federally funded, national, home care financing program for the elderly are likely to remain stalled.

This chapter has three major purposes: (1) to discuss the family responsibility issue as it affects publicly funded home care; (2) to present recent empirical data on the experiences of informal caregivers in the service-rich New York City environment; and (3) to discuss the policy implications of the findings.

The Issue of Family Responsibility

The need for long-term care among the noninstitutionalized elderly is substantial. In recent national studies, long-term care needs have been measured on the basis of activities of daily living (e.g., bathing, eating, and dressing) and instrumental activity of daily living deficits (e.g., meal preparation, shopping, and money management). In 1979 National Health Interview found that among those over 85, 43.6 percent needed help with at least one activity of daily living or instrumental activity of daily living task. A 1982 study of the noninstitutionalized Medicare population found that approximately one in five elders reported a deficit in at least one area.[1] Functional disability among the elderly is also age-related. In the Medicare study, 14 percent of persons between 65 and 74 reported a functional disability, whereas of those over 85, 51 percent indicated a need for help.

The extensive role of informal helpers in caring for the elderly at home is well documented. Brody, Poulshock, and Masiocchi estimate that 80 percent of all home care is provided by family members.[2] The responsibilities assumed by relatives have been described in a number of studies.[3] Although friends and neighbors often contribute significantly to the care of older people at home, relatives overall are by far the most important source of informal support. Gender is another important factor in caregiving. Specifically, wives and adult daughters are more active as informal caregivers than husbands and adult sons, who are generally less extensively involved. The pattern may be explained by the fact that elderly men in need of long-term care are more likely than women to have a spouse available to provide care and that, traditionally, the nurturing role has been ascribed to women. The help provided by family, friends, and neighbors takes a variety of forms: emotional support, direct services (e.g., personal care, housekeeping, and financial management), mediation with organizations regarding formal services (case management), and financial assistance.[4]

Although formal home care services for the elderly have existed on a small scale for many decades, the efforts to obtain substantial public funding for home care did not begin until the beginning of the 1970s. At that time, home care was proposed as an alternative to the high cost and questionable quality of publicly financed nursing home care. Proponents were particularly concerned about the plight of elderly people with inadequate informal support networks—those without close family ties and those whose relatives had significant disabilities themselves or other obligations that limited their ability to provide care.

The proposals for significant public funding for home care for the elderly have received a cautious response from policy makers. Undoubtedly, concern about high cost accounts for much of the reluctance to authorize a major national program to finance home care. Significant opposition, however, has also come from those who are concerned that publicly funded services might undermine the family's role in long-term care. Their argument is that care of the elderly is a traditional family role and that public programs should not interfere with it. The opponents of publicly funded home care are concerned that organized services will substitute for care otherwise provided by family members. Their question is, Why should the public be asked to pay for care that family members can provide without reimbursement?[5]

In acknowledging the role of family members in providing home care, the proponents of publicly financed home care are faced with some difficult policy problems. Should publicly funded home care be made available only to those lacking family resources? Should family caregiving capacity be excluded from consideration in establishing eligibility for a public program? Considering family caregiving resources in eligibility for a public program would meet the objections of those concerned about substitution. On the other hand, setting standards for family participation, determining the caregiving capacity of relatives of home care applicants, and enforcing caregiving by reluctant family members would pose problems for program administrators. Basing home care eligibility on family resources might also have the undesirable effect of weakening family ties. Adult children, in particular, might artificially distance themselves from a troubled parent to ensure the parent's eligibility for publicly funded home care. The exclusion of family caregiving capacity from consideration in setting eligibility for publicly funded home care would thus simplify administration of home care benefits, although it might add substantially to the public cost of a program.

One option would be to establish two home care systems—one for people with and another for those without informal assistance. A system designed explicitly to support older people who have informal help would presumably be more modestly funded than a system for functionally disabled elderly individuals who lack informal caregivers. For example, older people with informal supports could be offered any of a number of programs that have emerged with the express purpose of providing relief to caregivers. These "respite" services may take a variety of forms, including placement of the care recipient at an out-of-home facility during the day-time hours, a move to an institutional setting for a period as short as a weekend, or arrangements that bring a caregiver into the home. An early example of such an effort was the Natural Supports project of the Community Service Society of New York, which was designed to give relief to relatives extensively involved in care of a functionally disabled older person.[6]

In order to resolve this policy problem, attention must be paid to some underlying value questions, and in particular to the type of circumstances that would enable family members to get help from publicly funded services. Should there be some limit to the caregiving effort that can be expected of family members? Caregiving can have positive effects for relatives who provide care; informal caregivers, for example, can derive satisfaction from the experience of assisting a loved one. However, caregiving may also have negative consequences, such as emotional stress, excessive physical fatigue, and disruption of normal life patterns.

Conceptually, it is useful to distinguish between "caregiving effort," which simply refers to the tasks carried out by informal providers, and "caregiving burden," which refers to the negative consequences that can result from the dependency of an elderly relative. This distinction between effort and burden makes it possible to address questions about the often diverse and complex circumstances under which informal caregivers participate in long-term care.

The current analysis is based on a set of measurable and attainable objectives for publicly funded home care.[7] For example, prevention of institutionalization will not be considered as a policy objective for home care because there is no assurance that it is attainable. Similarly, improvement in the morale of service recipients is also not considered as a policy objective because of the difficulty in measuring morale. Proposed here is that for the functionally disabled, the major objective of nonmedical aspects of home care is simply to assure adequate solutions to problems of daily living—termed elsewhere as "quality of circumstances."[8]

A second major objective of publicly funded home care is to relieve relatives of the unreasonable burden associated with caregiving. The premise is that there should be limits to the caregiving burden expected of responsible relatives. Beyond some burden threshold, publicly funded home care should be available to provide relief to family members. If burden limitation is to be a factor in service authorization for publicly funded home care programs, it is desirable that caregiving effort and burden be measurable and that standards be established for what constitutes reasonable burden. The use of specific measures and explicit standards would help programs meet contemporary accountability requirements. In an era in which public expenditures for human services are sharply questioned, substantial public funding is more likely to be forthcoming if eligibility is based on objective criteria rather than on unverifiable claims of service applicants or judgments of professionals who serve as gatekeepers.

Empirical questions regarding the circumstances in which those with informal supports seek organized home care are also pertinent here: What happens to family participation when home care workers are present? To what extent do organized services complement the efforts of informal caregivers? To what extent do family members or friends actually curtail their caregiving when organized services are introduced? These questions are addressed in the remainder of this chapter.

Measuring Caregiving Effort and Burden

Research Objectives and Methods

This chapter reports findings from a research effort to measure caregiving effort and burden in the provision of home care to the elderly. The overall study was concerned with the implications of large-scale, publicly funded home care programs in New York City for the low-income, at-risk elderly and their caregiving relatives. New York City has extraordinarily well developed, publicly funded home care programs. In addition to conventional, Medicare-funded certified home health agency programs, the city, through its Human Resources Administration, operates programs that provide nonmedical home care for people meeting income eligibility standards. In 1982, these programs served an average case load of over 35,000 people at an annual public cost of close to $300 million. The largest of the programs, the Home Attendant Program, provided an average of over 50 hours per week of care to each client. Most of the funding was covered by Medicaid through a program option that allows states to finance personal care in home settings.

The policies and practices of the Human Resources Administration regarding family responsibility reflect the broader societal ambivalence toward family obligations in the provision of home care. The expressed policy of the Human Resources Administration is that when home care applicants reside with relatives, home care should not be authorized if a family member can be in the household to provide care. Home care, for example, may be authorized during the hours when the responsible relative is employed outside the household but not authorized during non-working hours when the relative might be at home. However, in actual practice, when family members refuse to participate in long-term care, the Human Resources Administration does not enforce this policy. Instead, it authorizes care according to the needs of the applicant. In the final analysis, home care is conceived by the Human Resources Administration as an individual entitlement; the ultimate public responsibility of the city is to assure adequate care for individual applicants.

A sample of 1,068 was recruited from among elderly patients at six large general hospitals in New York City. The sample was limited to patients over 60 years of age who would be leaving the hospital with a serious functional disability expected to be of long duration, and who were at a low or moderate income level. The fact that the study was restricted to patients capable of providing informed consent also had the effect of excluding those with severe mental impairments. The patients were studied for a twelve-month period beginning with the end of their acute care stay.

All patients were interviewed before discharge, and those who returned home were interviewed again at four and at twelve months after discharge. Patients were asked to identify a principal informal caregiver, if there was one. These family members or friends were interviewed four months after the patients had been discharged. At the four-month stage, 633 functionally disabled elderly and 422 of their helpers were interviewed. For two-thirds of the primary subjects, therefore, an informal caregiver was interviewed. Nearly 60 percent of the relatives lived in the same unit as the care recipients; 29 percent were spouses, and another

29 percent were daughters. Overall, 87 percent of the informal helpers interviewed were relatives.

In the measurement of caregiving effort and help received by the elderly, emphasis was placed on concrete aspects of care that could readily be understood by policy makers. Less tangible dimensions of care such as emotional support and companionship were deliberately excluded. The data on help received were obtained through a series of questions that began with an assessment of the ability of the subject to perform various self-care tasks. When a need for help was indicated, subjects were asked whether and how often help was provided for that task by a relative, friend, neighbor, or service worker. Interviews with caregivers were conducted in a similar fashion. Informal helpers were asked to indicate the older person's ability to perform various tasks independently. When a need for help was identified, the family members, friends, or neighbors were asked to indicate how often they provided help. Intensity-of-help (from the perspective of the care recipient) scores and caregiving-effort (from the perspective of the principal informal helper) scores were obtained by treating the data as if they were additive. All tasks were assumed to be of equal importance; the four frequency-of-care categories employed were scored on a zero-to-four basis. Standardized scores were calculated for each item and added together to form summary measures.

Patterns of Help

The elderly subjects indicated that both formal and informal services contributed importantly in the provision of needed care (Table 12–1). Over 80 percent of the subjects received some help. Forty percent relied entirely on informal providers; 18 percent received all needed care from organized services. Informal help was involved in 64 percent of the cases. Even in the service-rich

Table 12–1   Source of Help (Percent Distribution)

Source	Percentages
No help	18.5
Informal support only	40.3
Organized service only	18.0
Both informal support and organized service	23.2
Total percent	100.0
Total number	633

New York City environment, therefore, family members are extensively involved in providing care. When organized services are involved, the informal system characteristically also plays a role in providing care.

Functional disability was linked to source of help (Table 12–2). The elderly subjects were divided into three categories, according to the degree of their functional disability. Those in the low and moderate disability categories were more likely to rely entirely on informal caregivers for any help they received. In the case of the most severely disabled, however, there was a tendency to rely on a combination of formal and informal help.

An examination of shifting patterns of help over time sheds some light on the substitution question. Because the study lacked an experimental control group, it is not possible to speak precisely about the effects of help from organized services on the extent of help from informal providers. Changes in patterns of help over time were also expected to be influenced by other factors such as fluctuations in need for help. A multiple regression analysis was performed to explain differences in the overall intensity of informal caregiving between the four-month and twelve-month interviews (Table 12–3). The analysis shows, as expected, that changes in intensity of help from the informal system were affected by functional disability on both measures used (activities of daily living and instrumental activities of daily living). Of particular importance to the current discussion is the fact that the change in formal assistance had a significant, independent effect on the level of informal support. When formal care increased, there was a decline in the intensity of informal services. The extent of the apparent substitution is noteworthy. A four-unit increase in level of formal support was associated with approximately a one-unit decrease in intensity of help from informal sources. The rate of substitution, therefore, appears to be modest. What must be emphasized is that the data do not inform us about what triggered the change in

Table 12–2   Functional Disability and Helping Source (Percentages)

	Helping Source					
Level of Disability	None	Informal Support Only	Organized Service Only	Both	Total Percent	N
Low	60.6	30.0	7.5	1.9	100.0	160
Moderate	4.4	52.3	20.6	22.7	100.0	321
High	4.0	25.7	23.6	46.7	100.0	152

$X^2 = 310.82; P = .0001.$

Table 12–3 Regression of Change in Intensity of Help from Informal Caregivers (*T*12-*T*4) on Selected Variables

Variable	b	Standard Error	Signifi-cance
Intensity of help from informal caregivers (*T*4)	−0.41	0.07	.0001
ADL change (*T*12-*T*4)	2.61	1.13	.0226
IADL change (*T*12-*T*4)	6.09	1.84	.0012
Change in intensity of formal service (*T*12-*T*4)	−0.28	0.07	.0002
Constant	4.33	0.76	.0001

Adj. $R^2 = 0.36$; $N = 141$.

source of support. In some cases, the reduced availability of an informal helper may have led to the introduction of organized services. In other cases, the addition of formal services probably allowed an informal caregiver to reduce his or her caregiving effort.

Caregiver Burden

As indicated above, the research was concerned with broad questions about the circumstances in which caregiving effort is associated with burden. As other chapters in this volume have indicated, excessive caregiver burden appears to be associated with family conflict and even, in some cases, elder abuse. In this study it was expected that more extensive effort would lead to greater burden. Two aspects of caregiving burden were measured: that related to employment and to restrictions on personal domestic life. In the first area, informal helpers were asked whether the demands of caregiving prevented them from working. Those who worked were asked about potential restrictions such as the ability to leave work in case of emergency, the necessity to work close to home, and the availability to handle problems over the telephone. In the area of domestic life, family, friends, and neighbors who shared a residence with the primary research subject were asked whether their roles in long-term care affected their privacy, their free time, and their activities outside the household.

In examining the relationship between effort and burden, it was necessary to consider the caregivers who shared living arrangements with the elderly person separately from those who lived elsewhere. Among informal caretakers who shared a residence with the elderly disabled person, there was a positive relationship between frequency of help and caregiving burden (r = 20;

$p = .003$). When helpers lived elsewhere, however, there was no correlation between intensity of help and burden ($r = .01$). In the co-resident group, there was evidence that the relationship between frequency of assistance and burden was affected by the caregiver's relationship to the primary research subject (Table 12–4). In the case of spouses and daughters, there was a strong positive association between frequency of effort and burden ($r = .36$ and $r = .46$, respectively). When the informal support was a friend, however, the relationship was *negative* ($r = -.57$; $p = .05$). Although statistically significant, this finding should be interpreted with some caution, since it is based on only twelve cases. When frequency of help was examined for its relationship to the burden subscales, the same general relationship persisted. In the case of daughters, there was a statistically significant relationship between frequency of help and life-style restrictions ($r = 31$; $p = .02$).

For informal caregivers living outside the household, the implications of the relationship to the disabled person for burden were also examined (Table 12–5). Although differences were not statistically significant, the pattern was of interest. In the case of daughters, there was a suggestion of a slight positive association between effort and burden; in the case of friends, the direction was again negative.

Overall, the data suggested that the link between effort and caregiving burden is mediated by the nature of the relationship. When the informal helper is a close relative who shares a residence with the care recipient, frequency of effort is *positively* associated with burden. When the informal helper is a friend, effort, if

Table 12–4 Intercorrelations Between Caregivers' Frequency of Assistance and Caregiving Burden for Caregivers Who Live with the Care Recipient

Relationship to Care Recipient	Correlation Between Burden and Assistance	N
Spouse	.36*	91
Sibling	− .14	13
Son	.41	14
Daughter	.46*	58
Daughter-in-law	.35	5
Other relative	− .17	15
Friend	− .57†	12

* $P = .001$
† $P = .05$

Table 12–5   Interrelations Between Caregivers' Frequency of Assistance and Burden for Caregivers Living Apart from Care Recipient

Relationship to Care Recipient	Correlation Between Burden and Assistance	N
Spouse	—	—
Sibling	.34	5
Son	−.19	14
Daughter	.05	45
Daughter-in-law	−.05	4
Other relative	−.08	19
Friend	−.34	21

anything, is *negatively* associated with burden. The inconsistent pattern may be explained by the degree to which the help is voluntary or obligatory. Spouses and adult daughters who live with the care recipient may feel obliged to help. Because they feel they have little choice, the intensity of their effort may be linked to burden. In the case of friends, participation in care is more likely to be voluntary. Because friends choose to help, they experience less burden. They are in a better position than relatives to curtail their caregiving if it becomes burdensome for them.

Implications for Public Policy

The high prevalence of functional disability among the growing number of very old people and the strong preference of the elderly to remain in their own homes will lead to continuing pressure for publicly funded home care programs and to a greater commitment on the part of funding agencies to such services. In addressing questions about the interplay between organized services and informal care, we can learn from the New York City experience, which shows that a single home care system can serve both those with and without informal assistance. When formal caregivers are available, publicly funded home care can be designed to complement their efforts. The expectation that informal helpers will continue to participate in care can be taken into consideration when disbursing publicly funded services. As a result, those with informal support will need less publicly funded services, since the tasks which they perform can be taken into account in the design of the care plan.

The study findings provide some reassurance to advocates of

subsidized home care on the substitution issue. Further, the study results invite some question about the role of informal caregiver burden in the rationing of subsidized home care. Even in a situation in which extensive publicly funded home care is available, most help was provided by the informal system. Although the study design does not permit precise statements about the effects of publicly funded services on the participation of informal caregivers, the results are strongly suggestive. The use of organized services was particularly concentrated in cases in which functional disabilities were generally most severe. When help was provided by organized services, more often than not, informal caregivers were also active. The data suggest that the introduction of organized services leads only to a modest reduction in effort on the part of the informal caregivers. Organized services, therefore, are best seen as a *complement to* rather than *substitute for* informal caregiving.

How should the availability of family, friends, and neighbors as potential caregivers affect the allocation of publicly funded services in an era of austerity in the public sector? The research was based on the premise that when caregiving was burdensome to informal helpers, they might be relieved from some of their caregiving obligations. The research was based on the premise that informal helpers might be considered to have a right to live in a normal life pattern, that there might be limits in the extent to which caregiving should interfere with their opportunity to work or restrict their use of free time. The research findings show that under some circumstances, caregiving effort is linked to burden. The combination of a shared residence and a close relationship (spouse and adult daughter) produces a caregiving effort that may be burdensome and which can lead to family conflict.

Should informal helpers be expected to demonstrate that caregiving is burdensome for them if they wish to obtain some relief through the introduction of an organized service? In reality, such an eligibility test probably is not practical. Even though burden is operationalized here in relatively tangible terms (e.g., restrictions on freedom to work or availability of free time), claims of burden by family members or friends do not lend themselves to the verification needed in a tightly administered entitlement program. A more practical solution would be the specification of the *effort* expected of relatives or friends in providing care. Standards for the caregiving effort expected of informal helpers should be based on research evidence regarding negative effects of caregiving and societal norms regarding the degree to which the life patterns of caregivers should approximate those of noncaregivers. Research evidence on the degree to which the life patterns of caregivers differ from those of noncaregivers of similar age and social circumstances might be useful in setting standards. The standards should be explicitly sociocultural. They should reflect a balance between society's desire to enable caregivers to enjoy relatively normal lives and other important claims on public resources. Extensive citizen participation in the formulation of standards might be useful as a way of both assuring that the standards reflect societal norms and of gaining widespread support for them.

Although standards for informal caregiving should be officially promulgated, compliance should be voluntary. Enforcement of informal caregiving obligations among unwilling relatives would not be practical. When relatives refuse to do their share, publicly funded services should be provided at a level that assures adequate care for the functionally disabled person. The proposed approach differs in two ways from that of the New York City Human Resources home care programs: (1) a combination of social research and citizen participation would be used in setting standards for relative participation in home care, and (2) the voluntary nature of the standards for participation of relatives would be clearly stated to home care applicants.

The uneven relationship between effort of informal caregivers and burden has reassuring implications for those concerned about the aggregate costs of publicly funded home care. The fact that many family members or friends participate in providing home care without experiencing burden means that many would continue their effort in spite of the availability of publicly funded home care. Even knowing that they could obtain relief, many informal helpers would prefer to provide all or most needed care themselves. This finding is also interesting from the standpoint of understanding elder abuse and neglect. While intense caregiving effort may lead to feelings of burden and to family conflict, this is not necessarily the case.

Differential patterns of use of home care for caregiver respite could create equity problems, however. Some of the family members who chose to provide extensive care might be resentful of others who limited their caregiving by making extensive use of publicly funded services. The equity issue, however, could probably be kept under control if publicly funded services were accessible, if standards for informal caregiving were publicized, and if public appreciation were shown for the voluntary effort of informal caregivers.

Most crucial to the argument developed here is the point that organized home care for the elderly often has dual objectives. The welfare of both elderly care recipients and informal caregivers is at stake. Publicly funded services should encourage the continuing participation of the informal system. At the same time, the expected level of informal caregiving should be kept within reasonable limits. Informal caregivers should themselves be able to live normal lives. Striking a balance between family responsibility and formal support is of critical importance in developing a home care system that can reduce burden and family conflict, without incurring unreasonable costs.

Endnotes

1. R. Hanley, "Results from the 1982 Long-Term Care Survey: Age, Ethnicity, and Gender Differences in Daily Activity Limitations Among Elderly in the Community" (Paper presented at the Gerontological Society Meeting, 1984).
2. S. Brody, W. Poulshock, and C. Masioccia, "The Family Caring Unit: A Major Consideration in the Long-Term Support System" *The Gerontologist* 18, no. 6 (1978), pp. 556–61.
3. D. L. Frankfather, M. J. Smith, and F. G. Caro, *Family Care of the Elderly* (Lexington, Mass.: D. C. Heath, 1981); A. Horowitz and R. Dobrof, *The Role of Families in Providing Long-Term Care to the Frail and Chronically Ill Elderly Living in the Community* (New York: Hunter Brookdale Center on Aging, 1982); W. Poulshock, *The Effects on Families of Caring for Impaired Elderly in Residences* (Cleveland: Benjamin Rose Institute, 1982).
4. A. Horowitz, "Family Caregiving to the Frail Elderly," in *Annual Review of Geriatrics and Gerontology*, eds. M. P. Lawton and G. Maddox (New York: Springer, 1985).
5. V. L. Greene, "Substitution Between Formally and Informally Provided Care for the Impaired Elderly in the Community," *Medical Care* 6 (1983), pp. 609-19.
6. Frankfather et al., *Family Care of the Elderly*.
7. F. G. Caro, "Objectives, Standards, and Evaluation in Long-Term Care," *Home Health Services Quarterly* 2, no. 1 (1981), pp. 5-26.
8. F. G. Caro and A. Blank, *Home Care in New York City: The System, the Providers and the Beneficiaries* (New York: Community Service Society, 1985).

Chapter 13

MOBILIZING ADEQUATE HOME CARE RESOURCES: A MUTUAL AID RESPONSE TO STRESS WITHIN THE FAMILY

by Alan Sager

As the number of disabled, frail, and chronically ill older Americans steadily increases, the need for long-term care inevitably rises as well. However, the availability, ability, and willingness of families to help are eroding. Public programs cannot be expected to fill the gap; in the current political and economic climate, their resources per person in need can be expected to shrink. Consequently, greater stress will be placed on families. Some will be able to aid disabled parents and be glad for the chance. Others, who face competing demands, will aid parents only resentfully. Still others will not be in a position to help, and will experience varying levels of guilt. In the last two groups of families, neglect and even abuse of the older and disabled relative become possible.

We do not yet know the relative importance of psychological, social, and economic causes of elder abuse or neglect—the extent to which such maltreatment results from histories of unhappy personal relations (sometimes involving past abuse or neglect of the child); changes in social organization, family size, or family affiliations and responsibilities accompanying urbanization or industrialization; or a stark inadequacy of resources with which to serve a disabled person.

Regardless of the exact mix of causes of elder abuse, however, it is reasonable to expect that higher levels of external support to families will help prevent abuse or ameliorate its effects when it occurs. It also seems clear that we can expect long-term care needs to grow while traditional resources shrink. Can anything be done to prevent this? After eliminating what is impossible, whatever solutions remain—however unlikely—must be attempted. If public and family resources to provide long-term care become less adequate over the decades to come, substitutes must be found. One possibility will be to mobilize spare resources of time in American society.

A parallel can be drawn to the Great Depression of the 1930s. Then, observers sometimes noted the horrible juxtaposition of malnourished children and milk poured out in the street because its price did not warrant marketing. Massive economic dislocations prevented the joining of resource and need. Today, there are vast surplus resources in our society, but no method of mobilizing some of these on behalf of disabled older citizens and their families. One possible method of distribution is sketched in this chapter.

Although this proposal has enough merit to warrant testing, the argument of the chapter goes beyond one specific plan. Instead, it will be shown that traditional approaches to providing and financing long-term care services are leading our society down an unaffordable and inegalitarian dead end and that as these approaches become less able to satisfy needs for long-term care, we must generate and evaluate a variety of alternatives. Some of these alternatives will fail; a few will probably succeed. Therefore, we should stop wringing our hands or lamenting the current political climate. Instead, we should experiment, test, and put in place a satisfying, durable, and affordable long-term care system.

Needs and Services

Providing long-term care to family members is inherently stressful. This stress is magnified enormously by our society's public mechanisms for financing and delivering care. Certainly, there is ample reason to fear that evolving political, economic, and social circumstances will exacerbate tensions within families.

Stress

The process of providing long-term care can be difficult for all parties. The disabled person being aided may be fearful of death, ashamed of becoming a burden, resentful over needing to ask for help, anxious over growing dependence, worried by growing confusion, or afraid of being abandoned by the family and placed in an institution. Many nursing homes are well run, but some are not. Most older people say that they want nothing to do with them. Under these circumstances, some older people can become angry, withdrawn, passive, or even aggressive in demanding constant attention as proof that they will not be placed in "a home."

Families provide the great bulk of aid received by disabled older Americans.[1] But they are sometimes unable to give as much help as is needed or wanted by the parent, or as much as they or others believe they should give. The burden of aiding even a well-loved parent can become overwhelming, especially if the elder has become confused, incontinent, or bedfast, and therefore requires very frequent assistance.

Several factors cause stress in families who are caring for an older relative. First, the need for care is often unpredictable. A slowly developing case of arthritis or Alzheimer's allows time to plan; a stroke does not. Second, the need for care is pressing; usually, it cannot be deferred easily, especially when a person is very dependent. Caregiving cannot be juggled easily with other responsibilities, such as raising one's own children or working outside the home. Third, the burden of care usually falls principally on one person—typically a wife, daughter, or daughter-in-law. The job is rarely divided equally (except when the person is moved from one caregiver's home to another's). This inequality can make even conscientious family members resentful of their hard work. The resentment can grow under the often crushing burden of giving care around the clock, especially if the older person (for reasons just suggested) is not manifestly grateful. Fourth, families sometimes take on home care unwillingly. They may prefer nursing home care, while the elder expects aid from his or her children. Even if all parties agree that institutional care is preferable, an appropriate nursing home bed may not be available. In the home, combinations of resentment and guilt can intermingle with financial worries and psychological histories to help generate patterns of abuse or neglect. These can be difficult to detect, especially when there are few visitors.

American social and political institutions provide surprisingly little support to families who maintain disabled elderly persons at home. The result is that many of these families exist in a sort of "pressure cooker." Families blame themselves if they give care that is below their own or their relative's expectations. Instead of attributing a portion of their difficulties to the social circumstances that create or exacerbate the problems of caregiving, they feel guilt and self-blame. Few elders welcome the nursing home, and few families are satisfied if they are forced to institutionalize a parent. The lack of adequate publicly financed in-home services, however, can sometimes force such a decision.

Institutional Preference

While a very high proportion of older persons in need of long-term care declare that they prefer to receive it at home (80 percent in one study),[2] over 90 percent of public long-term care funds are spent on nursing homes.[3] In a democracy, so great a disparity merits explanation. As the proportion of old and very old citizens (many of whom survive with serious disabilities) has grown and as the need for long-term care has increased in this nation, we have tended to use public money to pay for institutional services. However, public resources will always be scarce. In a sense, publicly funded long-term care has been viewed as caulk: to fill some of the gap between human need and family capacity. It has generally been held necessary first to assure that the most disabled and needful citizens—those obliged to enter nursing homes—have first claim on those resources.

Thus, public policy in the United States in recent decades has worked to ensure that only very needful older people enter nursing homes with public financial support. Nursing homes have typically not been well reimbursed by Medicaid in most states. Individual states, which pay up to half the Medicaid bill, also control the nursing home reimbursement formula. They therefore have a clear incentive to hold down payment levels. One result is a lower perceived quality of care, which deters some people from seeking institutional residence at public expense. Because the nursing home provides a total package—room, board, and personal/nursing care—many impoverished and isolated older citizens might be tempted to give up some measure of independence and seek admission if the level of care seems decent enough. Limiting the acceptability of nursing home care is therefore important to cost control.

At the same time, the factors just noted have helped to make the institution itself the site of almost all public long-term care services. Paying to relieve impoverished or disabled citizens—or their caregiving families—outside the institution would boost the number of persons eligible for public aid to unaffordable levels. In effect, the combination of very weak public home care financing and generally unpleasant publicly funded institutional care keeps families on short tethers. They must continue assisting disabled elders at home, without much public support, or see them forced into what is generally perceived as a latter-day poor house.

Another explanation for the institutional preference has to do with the peculiar unfolding of public funding over the past twenty years. Medicare, and especially Medicaid, included nursing home coverage; this was done in large part in the hope that long-term care institutions would prove to be less expensive places in which to recuperate than hospitals. To some extent, then, these programs were aimed from the beginning to hold down acute care costs rather than to satisfy social needs. Further, once nursing homes were built, an industry heavily dependent on public funds evolved. Nursing home owners were able and willing to lobby for higher reimbursement rates. They were usually more persuasive than advocates for non-institutional long-term care programs.

Vladeck's sensible assertion that long-term care has never been on top of policy makers' agendas adds a final perspective.[4] If, as it appears, we have never thought through what we expect from publicly funded long-term care, we should not be surprised to find ourselves displeased. The harm to disabled older citizens and their families resulting from this thoughtlessness can be expected to increase in coming decades as need for care increases, public support shrinks, and family capacity declines.

Sources of Rising Stress on Families

Several years ago, a Health Care Financing Administration study projected nursing home bed need in the year 2030. This was done by applying 1977 rates of use of nursing homes, for various ages, to the projected 2030 population. The result was an expected increase from about 1.3 million beds to almost 3.0 million, a rise of 131 percent. This projection reflected in particular the expected increase in numbers of Americans aged 85 and above, about one-fifth of whom resided in nursing homes in 1977.[5] Assuming no change in the age-specific rates of nursing home use and no shift in the proportion of persons in nursing homes, it can be supposed that the need for all long-term care services would increase at similar rates. Unhappily, there is reason to fear a decline in both public and family care for disabled older citizens.

In the United States, interlocking ideological, political, and economic trends are resulting in reduced public spending per person in need of long-term care. Public programs are said to have failed; public efforts are held to be no substitute for family care. While this honors the family, it also hints at increased responsibility. Politically, huge federal deficits—manufactured but nonetheless now real—placed steady and (through Gramm-Rudman) institutionalized pressure on all federal programs. Opportunities for legislating costly new long-term home care programs are bleak, and the adequacy of future federal funding for nursing home services under Medicaid is uncertain. Congress tends to view Medicaid as an unpopular welfare program for poor people of working age, even though the great bulk of its funds support aged, blind, and permanently disabled individuals.[6] The federal government has recently urged the states to assume greater social welfare responsibilities. A renewed federal freeze on Medicaid contributions could force states to choose between raising taxes and constraining nursing home reimbursement. During the next recession, states will probably be obliged to do both.

Economically, the nation is facing hard times. The federal deficit and rising national debt are manifestations of these difficulties, as politicians struggle to maintain living standards in an economy that is less competitive internationally. This should not be shocking: Capital and technology are mobile, and many workers in politically stable nations are willing to work very hard for only a dollar or two per hour. It is unlikely that 240 million Americans will be able to sustain their present disproportionate enjoyment of the world's wealth.

The combination of these ideological, political, and economic forces will make any increases in public long-term care spending difficult to obtain; a drop in spending is more likely. In fact, powerful mechanisms exist for bringing about a reduction in resources. First, the rhetoric of competition masks budget-cutting: Free to compete, long-term care providers will be invited to do more with less, like the airlines and the hospitals. Second, state governments retain regulatory tools. Certificate of need and rate setting can restrain even badly needed nursing home construction. Third, some erstwhile long-term care beds in nursing homes are being occupied by convalescing short-term post-acute patients. Medicare's prospective payment system gives hospitals strong incentive to rapidly discharge such patients to nursing homes.

A Response

The combination of increased need for long-term care with reduced family and public capacity is ominous. Happily, there is one resource in our society that can be mobilized on behalf of dependent older citizens: *time*. The magnitude of this resource is difficult to estimate, but it is potentially a very rich one.

Time

Slack resources of time are more visible when they are clustered in large blocks. The perception of excessive "leisure" as a problem, drug-taking, and the boredom and lack of purpose suffered by some Americans all point to time that could be devoted to care for disabled individuals. Perhaps it is an error to regard time as either taut or slack. A conceptualization of one's own time as central or marginal/discretionary may be more helpful. There are 168 hours in a week. Some uses of time, such as sleeping and eating, are more central. Others, such as recreational reading or watching television, are more discretionary. At the margin, most Americans enjoy some time that is fairly free. Some individuals or groups have more than others, and the amount of free time varies from year to year. It is usually higher before starting a family, lower while raising children, somewhat higher as children grow, and very high after retirement.

Many of us are reluctant to use marginal time to aid others. One reason is that many of our social institutions may be so weak or brittle that we have come to fear that our aid to others will not be reciprocated. This discourages helping, as does the fear of appearing foolishly altruistic, of becoming known as a "sap," incapable of "looking out for number one." Individuals who do help others are motivated by varying combinations of altruism and self-interest. If the compassion and effectiveness of their care is adequate, we should be less concerned about motives than about results. Some mechanism that permits us to help others when we have time and that assures us that we will in turn be helped when needed would be effective in persuading more potential helpers to come forward.

One of the dilemmas of family provision of long-term care is that our parents may need our help while we are busy working or raising our own children. It would be valuable, therefore, to be able to *decouple* the time of our own helping from the time of our relatives' needs for help.

It is important to be aware that only a fraction of Americans ever need long-term care. This proportion may be as low as one-fifth, the proportion who reside in nursing homes at the time of their death,[7] and perhaps as high as one-third or even greater. Only a minority of these individuals come to need the around-the-clock care that poses the heaviest burden on families. Yet the need for care, when it comes, is often unpredictable and crushing. Can we devise a mechanism for sharing this burden?

Insurance

To finance privately one's in-home long-term care needs requires saving a huge sum of money. By pooling the risk, it would only be necessary to save the expected value of in-home care—that is, the average cost, across all individuals, and not the highest possible cost for any given individual. Societies devise insurance mechanisms to aid citizens under circumstances like these. A form of insurance could be appropriate to long-term care. It is probably preferable for the premiums to be paid in *time*, rather than in cash. First, cash represents a claim on the finite goods and services available in society. Given the pressures on the U.S. economy, it is not clear that we are willing to transfer large sums to finance long-term care. Certainly, we are not willing now to use public funds in this way. Second, individuals could use their own money to purchase long-term care insurance, but this proposal suffers from the defects of low demand, the possibility that long-term care may not *be* insurable, and the inequality of purchasing power.

Few individuals have been buying long-term care insurance at current prices, suggesting that they do not value this protection, are inclined to deny their need for it (owing to fear of contemplating dependence), or believe that Medicare will cover long-term care. Private long-term care insurance typically is tightly written with long waiting periods and high out-of-pocket costs, because insurers fear both adverse selection (those who are more likely to need the benefit sign up for it) and moral hazard (those who are insured seek to take advantage of the benefit for which they paid). Inequality of income and wealth means inequality of purchasing power generally and for long-term especially. Those likelier to need care, perhaps owing to enduring health or disability problems, will tend to have less money with which to buy insurance and may face higher experience-rated premiums.

A third reason for paying premiums in time is that a traditional, cash-financed insurance system will require hiring workers to deliver care. This will be costly. If the nation moves into an era of low unemployment rates, hourly wages will be high. And paid in-home care may be inherently inefficient, unless it is provided in volumes impossibly higher than can be imagined under private long-term care insurance. Inefficiency is caused in part by lengthy travel from workers' homes to those of recipients of care, and subsequently between recipients' homes. It is exacerbated by the costs of supervision (difficult to accomplish in long-term care) and of financial accounting, billing, and reimbursement.

Long-term care is more than lengthy in duration. It requires most of the time of a caregiver. Little long-term care is skilled; over 95 percent of all paid and unpaid help received by a sample of home care recipients in Massachusetts was unskilled.[8] In sum, time—not money—may be the more appropriate medium of exchange in long-term care.

Time Insurance: A Parallel Economy

The major problems with exchanging time are those plaguing any barter arrangement: the need for nearly simultaneous exchange and the question of comparative value. Bartering requires that two parties have goods or services that they wish to exchange at a given time. There may be some deferral, but not for long. Money permits the separation of transactions, for days or for centuries. Also, money obviates comparing the values of all combinations of items that could be bartered. Each item has its own value, and money settles differences. Using insurance in which time pays the premiums creates a parallel economy of long-term care services in which time is the medium of exchange. Such a system solves the problem of simultaneous exchanges. We can decouple the help we have time to give from the time our elderly relatives need our help. We can even transport regular help to relatives living far from us.

Several mechanisms for accomplishing this can be imagined. They range from restricted reciprocity within a closed community to local area exchanges to nationally interlocking networks. The basic idea remains the same.[9] Restricted reciprocity can be imagined within a congregate housing development for older citizens. On construction of the building, or subsequently, individuals needing help that cannot be provided by family or public resources could be identified. They might need aid with shopping, laundry, cooking, cleaning, supervision of medications, trips to physicians, and the like. Volunteers within the building could be recruited to assist with these tasks. Record-keeping could be either *loose* (all who participate as helpers are liable to be called on; all who need help are to be aided) or *strict* (hours given and taken are recorded). When those who had helped were no longer able to do so, they would become eligible for aid (if needed), especially from younger, newly admitted residents. Persons on the waiting list might also be included, as both helpers or recipients, as might residents of the neighborhood surrounding the congregate housing facility.

The key here is the involvement of an organization that persists over time—in this example, a congregate housing development. The organization is the guarantor that those who help will be helped. If record-keeping is loose, subsidies are possible. One individual may receive more help than he or she gave; another who gave much may need or seek none in return. There is an implicit insurance function.

What is lacking is any solid assurance that one who gave help would be helped, either commensurately or appropriately. Is such assurance necessary? If so, how could it be provided? Assurance is necessary if potential helpers demand it or if there is a fear that the age and disability composition of the population will become skewed toward those in need of aid. Assurance that residents will be aided could be given in three ways: (1) by admitting only able new residents who are willing to help, (2) by backing time with paid help, or (3) by broadening the base of helpers.

It would probably not be appropriate or legal to assess prospective residents' abilities or willingness to give help. Backing time with paid help would resemble the use of paper money supported by the promise to redeem with silver or gold. Individuals would be encouraged to help because they were confident that they would be helped in turn—either by a new and more able resident or, if necessary, by a paid worker. The promise to back time with paid help, if needed, may be a useful principle. But it probably should not be employed in restricted settings, such as single housing developments, in which demographics and the relatively unpredictable odds associated with small numbers of individuals make the need for paid helpers fairly likely.

Broadening the base of potential helpers, perhaps by including those on the waiting list for the congregate housing facility or the families of current residents, appears promising. But would it not then be desirable to assure these helpers that they, in turn, would be aided—even if they came to need help before they entered the facility?

This suggests the possibility of going beyond the housing development as an organizing unit. Other responsible organizations include the neighborhood, fraternal organization, labor union local, or religious congregation. These have several characteristics in common. They endure over time. Their members typically span at least two generations—and sometimes three or four. Their members know one another, for years or decades. These common qualities should make them appropriate backers for long-term care insurance. Health maintenance organizations, although looser in their members' sense of affiliation, might make suitable organizing vehicles because of their managerial competence.

Often, it is difficult to persuade individuals who are not managing well alone to accept long-term care. Individuals who have known one another for a long time may be more willing to aid one another when disability strikes. The fear of encountering and perceiving a person as *disabled* is reduced by the long-standing relationship. Helpers may be more willing to come forward to assist someone who is known. And those who are disabled may be more willing to accept help from those who are known—particularly if those who are helped had previously helped others.

Within each organization, record-keeping could again be loose or strict. Strictness would be more sensible initially, especially in organizations whose members did not know one another very well, until trust was built. Tokens or markers could be used to record the movement of help. Initially, each disabled person in need of help could be given (by the organization) a number of markers in some proportion to need for care that could not reasonably be met by relatives. The organization would continue to issue markers as long as individuals disabled before initiation of the time exchange, who could not have earned a sufficient number of markers, remained in need of help. This might be called "priming the pump" of the parallel economy of long-term care exchange.

Helpers would receive one marker for each hour of aid given. Helpers could bank their own accumulated markers until they needed assistance, or they could use them immediately to secure help for a relative or friend in need. Individuals could employ the markers they earned as they wished. They could, for example, use time earned to purchase marker insurance. Here, markers would be pooled, and individuals would lose control over them. A gatekeeper, some sort of case manager, would assess need for aid from the pool and release markers accordingly.

Marker premiums would be set in proportion to expected need for care. If, for example, it is assumed that (1) the average 60-year-old could be expected to have a one-in-four probability of needing long-term care; (2) that average need for this 25 percent would be 1,000 hours; and (3) that families would provide one-half of all aid, then the average premium should be set at 125 hour-markers (.25 times 1000 times .5). To guard against markers displacing family aid, the case manager might have the authority to negotiate to assure a reasonable level of continued family supports.

Both the responsible organization and the insurance pool should be required to maintain cash reserves and purchase reinsurance. The former would be used to purchase paid care for any individual holding a marker who was unable to find a volunteer willing to redeem it. (Public loans or grants might be required to help voluntary organizations meet their reserve requirements.) In this way, individuals would be encouraged to volunteer their time, because they would be assured that help given would be reciprocated when needed. The latter would provide a merging of risks to protect any one responsible organization, especially a small one, from an unpredictably great demand on its voluntary resources.

Some of these aspects seem complicated. But even relatively inexperienced local organizations could be encouraged to support time insurance if given technical support. Reserve and reinsurance requirements could be modeled on different assumptions; alternative management schemes could be tested and the results passed along to local organizations. Many of the issues that must be faced by local organizations resemble those tackled by the banking and insurance industries in past decades. Perhaps these organizations would be willing to share their expertise. For example, just as the local banks in the United States were obliged to give up their right to issue their own paper money during the nineteenth century, so local organizations backing time insurance might find it desirable in time to back a standard marker for long-term care. This would certainly make it easier for adult children to earn markers and mail them to a disabled parent living in another state.

Whether markers remain local or not, the question of their value must be addressed. There are three aspects. First, it would be simplest for the hour to remain the unit of currency. But some hours of help, such as cooking, may be easier to obtain than others, such as cleaning, personal care, or a ride to the doctor. It is likely that marker markets would arise in which demand and supply for discrete types of help would determine local prices. An hour of cleaning might command a price of three markers; an hour of reading, one-half marker. If a compelling idealistic commitment to the simplicity and the purity of the hour is absent, then even close policing would probably be inadequate to maintain it.

Beyond the micro-marker-market is the macro question of the overall marker price level: Is the market being inflated or deflated by macro-market conditions? For example, if too many markers were initially put into circulation, relative to the number of volunteers who came forward, the marker price of a given task would be inflated. Those who issue the markers would have to be sensitive to overall price levels. Otherwise, faith in their value would decline. If markers were to be effectively backed hour-for-hour by the time of a paid worker, this sets a floor under which their value would not fall. But if markers were to have this guaranteed value, what would prevent them from circulating in local areas as if they were really money? Those who did not earn them might buy them, perhaps at a discount, from those who had volunteered extensively. The ability to bank time raises the related question of the time-value of time—the right to earn interest.

Perhaps it would be best to keep local banking of time as simple as possible: One earns markers and must use them oneself. But this precludes insurance or movement of markers across space. A compromise position is possible. Marker exchanges might be made on the books (microcomputer) of the local organization. This could combat differential pricing of various tasks or the possibility that markers would circulate as currency. The hour-for-hour backing of the marker would prevent its value from falling very far. If its value started to rise, the local organization could simply put more markers into circulation. Marker exchanges from adult children to parents in another locality could be made by wired credit exchanges. Ultimately, if enough citizens were inspired to volunteer to aid others by this combination of altruism and self-interest, it might be possible to abandon record-keeping entirely, as individuals would be able to regard helping as casting bread on the waters.

Criticisms

A variety of objections, many of them well justified, could be raised against this approach. It could elicit accusations of undermining the proper spirit of aiding those in need of long-term care. The tainting of altruistic motives by coarse self-interest could lead to unsatisfactory care. This is certainly possible, but we should look at the motives of those who aid now. What is altruism, and when does it disappear into the depths of self-interest? Perhaps we should experiment with this approach and test whether compassion of care suffers a drop. Further, social cohesion might benefit from time insurance. The various organizations that endure over time and that chose to promote time insurance would be invigorated if the notion prospered. Citizens could help to rebuild a social institution intermediate between government and mass society.[10] De Tocqueville, pointing to the enthusiasm in this country for a wide variety of clubs, fraternal organizations, and mutual aid societies, noted the importance of voluntary institutions to American democracy.[11]

Time insurance could be labeled just another feeble way to

excuse government from its proper obligation to finance adequate non-institutional supports. Appeals to voluntarism have certainly been given a bad name by those who would use them as a smokescreen for mean-spirited government cuts. But adequate public non-institutional long-term care programs seem unlikely in any case. Government might even be encouraged by the mobilization of unpaid supports through time insurance: then, a public program would not be called on to do all that families could not or would not do; demands on a complementary public program might be manageable enough to finance. Time insurance can never substitute entirely for an adequate public noninstitutional care benefit. Many tasks are so intimate, physically demanding, or skilled that paid workers should typically do them. Millions of participants in a time insurance sector might evolve into the most effective lobby possible on behalf of adequate public funding for complementary in-home tasks.

A number of questions could be raised about those who help. Would enough volunteer? How should they be trained, supported, sustained, and encouraged? How do you match the right volunteers to the right tasks and recipients? These are all legitimate questions that need to be explored through pilot projects. Many of them are inherent in any noninstitutional long-term care program and do not particularly plague one employing time insurance.

Won't time insurance raise unemployment rates by substituting part-time volunteers for full-time homemakers and other paid in-home workers? And won't the volunteers, who are already busy, become taxed by yet another burden? Time insurance would not be likely to displace paid workers, because, unfortunately, so little publicly funded noninstitutional care is being provided in most states. A combination of honest political attention to our grave economic problems and current demographics should bring down unemployment rates steadily. Further, even if we could, do we really wish to employ large numbers of lower-income citizens in dead-end home care jobs at low wages, typically without fringe benefits? Isn't this the sort of work that a decent society should divide equitably? Individuals could volunteer at those phases of their lives when they had a bit of marginal time: perhaps when in school, when between jobs, and during and after paid employment.

How might we protect those who are being helped? What about the danger of theft, intimidation, and abuse? These are all possible, but a system that combines family aid with help from volunteers may be the best possible way of protecting a vulnerable older person from abuse or neglect by any caregiver. The presence of many helpers can be invaluable.[12]

Wouldn't time insurance discriminate against those who did not or could not volunteer? Wouldn't they be left to rely heavily on the nursing home if they became disabled? Existing social insurance and welfare programs in the United States do favor those who work. Social Security's disability insurance is far more generous than that under Supplementary Security Income. Time insurance would be less attractive to the non-altruist, the independent, and the private person.[13] And having decided not to volunteer, that person would not be eligible for time insurance benefits. But those unable to volunteer could be given markers with which to obtain aid. Deciding the difference between unwillingness and inability would not be easy, but equity requires some complexity.

Getting Started

A host of administrative, ethical, and financial questions would have to be answered to test time insurance as a method of mobilizing volunteer supports to older disabled citizens and their families. Happily, a number of intelligent efforts are already under way. Cahn has been working for some time to seek public financial backing for "service credits" earned by older workers. The District of Columbia government is considering such an approach.[14] Missouri has established a small pilot program in which credits are tracked by computer. And Florida has legislated a one-year demonstration.

In Los Angeles, Pynoos and colleagues[15] have been testing "intergenerational neighborhood networks" to aid frail older citizens. They report promising results. And in San Francisco, Hansen et al. have explored the use of a "voucher insurance plan" to summon forth informal supports. They have been investigating what tasks potential volunteers might prefer to do.[16] In the United Kingdom, Davies and his colleagues at the Kent Community Care Project have been exploring the uses of volunteer time.[17] The British "Link Opportunity" has organized voluntary exchanges by older citizens. Time stamps permit the banking of aid. We may be able to learn as well from experience in other areas. Babysitting cooperatives provide much practical information on organization, administrative rules, and human relations.[18]

In short, the possibilities of mobilizing surplus time on behalf of disabled older Americans have begun to attract the attention of several intelligent innovators. The results of their efforts demand careful evaluation and systematization. A host of enormous problems remains, including exposure of earned markers to federal income taxation. These issues will be explored in coming years. Early findings will probably be mixed; they usually are. Nonetheless, the enduring combination of increasing need for long-term care with declining traditional services should inspire us to continue to develop and test a variety of approaches to mobilizing volunteer aid. A gamble is always to be preferred to a certain loss.

Endnotes

1. James J. Callahan, Jr., Lawrence Diamond, Janet Z. Giele, and Robert Morris, "Responsibility of Families for Their Severely Disabled Members" (Waltham, Mass.: Brandeis University, University Health Policy Consortium, Heller School, 1979).
2. William G. Bell, "Community Care of the Elderly: An Alternative to Institutionalization" (Tallahassee: Florida State University, Program in Social Policy and the Aging, 1971).
3. Alan Sager, *Planning Home Care with the Elderly* (Cambridge, Mass.: Ballinger, 1983).
4. Bruce Vladeck, *Unloving Care* (New York: Basic, 1980).
5. Health Care Financing Administration, *Long-Term Care: Background and Future Directions* (Washington, D.C.: HCFA, 1980).
6. David E. Rogers, Robert J. Blendon, Thomas W. Moloney, "Who Needs Medicaid?" *New England Journal of Medicine* 307, no. 1 (1982), pp. 13–18.
7. Robert Kastenbaum and Sandra E. Candy, "The 4% Fallacy: A Methodological and Empirical Critique of Extended Care Facility Population Statistics," *International Journal of Aging and Human Development* 4, no. 1 (1973), pp. 15–21.
8. Alan Sager et al., "Living at Home: The Roles of Public and Informal Supports in Sustaining Disabled Older Americans " (Waltham, Mass.: Brandeis University, Levinson Policy Institute, Heller School, 1982).
9. Judah Drob et al., "Mutual Self Help Over Time: Can It Aid the Elderly" (Waltham, Mass.: Brandeis University, Levinson Policy Institute, Heller School, 1980); Alan Sager, "A Proposal for Promoting More Adequate Long-Term Care for the Elderly," *The Gerontologist* 23, no. 1 (1983), pp. 13–17.
10. Maurice R. Stein, *The Eclipse of Community* (Princeton, N.J.: Princeton University Press, 1960); George W. S. Trow, Jr., "Within the Context of No Context," *The New Yorker,* November 17, 1980, pp. 63–171.
11. Alexis DeTocqueville, *Democracy in America,* ed. Phillips Bradley (New York: Vintage, 1954).
12. Jane Lockwood Barney, "Community Presence as a Key to Quality of Life in Nursing Homes," *American Journal of Public Health* 64, no. 3 (1974), pp. 265–68; Jane Jacobs, *The Death and Life of Great American Cities* (New York: Viking, 1963).

13. Philip Slater, *The Pursuit of Loneliness* (Boston: Beacon, 1970).

14. Kathy Fackelmann, "Elderly Volunteers Will Get 'Credit' for Helping Sick Peers with Tasks," *Modern Healthcare*, August 2, 1985.

15. Jon Pynoos, Barbara Hade-Kaplan, and Dorothy Fleisher, "Intergenerational Neighborhood Networks: A Basis for Aiding the Frail Elderly," *The Gerontologist* 24, no. 3 (1984), pp. 233–37.

16. Berkeley Planning Associates, "A Voucher Insurance Plan to Mobilize Informal Support Among the Elderly" (Berkeley, Calif.: Berkeley Planning Associates, 1985).

17. Bleddyn Davies, "Proposal for the Study of the Reward System of Helpers in the Kent Community Care Project" (Canterbury, Kent: University of Kent, Personal Social Services Research Unit, 1977).

18. Marguerite Kelly and Elia Parsons, *The Mother's Almanac* (Garden City, New York: Doubleday, 1975).

Chapter 14

THE ENVIRONMENTAL PRESS MODEL: A THEORETICAL FRAMEWORK FOR INTERVENTION IN ELDER ABUSE

by Edward F. Ansello, Nancy R. King, and George Taler

The issue of elder abuse is still in its early stages of recognition and study. Since the signal works by Lau and Kosberg, and Block and Sinnott, research has centered on defining the nature and extent of this form of family violence.[1] However, as researchers are attempting to understand the problem, practitioners are being challenged to intervene in increasing numbers of abuse situations. Too often, intervention reduces to just one strategy: removing the elderly victims from the abusive environment, even when it is their own home, and placing them in an institution. In cases of imperiled safety, separation may be critical. However, this action may not be in the best interests of the victim or the abuser.

Clearly, there is a need for a theoretical model, based on our growing knowledge, that could provide a more comprehensive framework for intervention that might be successful in stopping elder abuse and responding to the needs of its victims. The environmental press model offers such a theoretical construct;[2] it is based on established social theory that serves to organize the several elements and stressors associated with elder abuse. We hope that this framework will provide a rational basis for effective intervention in elder abuse and a coherent model for future research.

What We Know About Elder Abuse

Research on elder abuse has been hampered by inconsistencies in terminology, reluctance in reporting, and, overall, a lack of well-controlled analysis of subject matter. Much of our research knowledge of elder abuse, with notable exceptions,[3] comes from a few studies involving small samples without controls; reports based on a few case studies have gained disproportionate attention. As yet, few population surveys and no national surveys have been conducted. As a result, basic information on the incidence and prevalence of the problem is lacking.

The forms of elder abuse vary. Although some researchers found significant levels of physical and psychological abuse within their samples,[4] others have found more passive forms of abuse, such as neglect, to be most prevalent.[5] Commonly, more than one type of abuse is present, and incidents frequently recur, sometimes over an extended period.

Victims are usually female and over the age of 75; most have some physical or mental impairment that limits their ability to function independently. Abusers tend to be related to victims and frequently live in the same household. Although researchers have identified several types of relationships between elder victims and perpetrators, often the relationship is characterized by dependence and isolation from others. The dependency relationship can manifest itself in two ways: in some cases the abuser is dependent on the victim,[6] and in others the victim is dependent on the abuser, who may be, in fact, the primary caregiver.

The model presented here is most relevant in situations in which the elder abuse is perpetrated by family caregivers on the elders in their care. We are operating under the assumption that caregivers who abuse their dependent elders have generally good intentions to provide quality care and would prefer to continue in their caregiving role if proper support were available. It should be stated that this paradigm is not necessarily applicable to the purely exploitive or pathologic relationship that characterizes some situations of elder abuse, such as those described by O'Malley and Pillemer.[7]

In many cases of abuse perpetrated by caregivers, the abuse begins after years of strenuous caregiving that equals the commitment to a full-time job. Surveys show that the majority of the caregivers who become abusive are themselves over age 50 and are frequently experiencing age-related problems of their own such as declining health and vigor, widowhood, and financial difficulties.[8] Alcohol and drug abuse and mental illness are sometimes factors in abuse. However, some abusers are basically unprepared caregivers who are overwhelmed by caregiving responsibilities.[9]

Establishing a Framework for Intervention

Intervention strategies are derived from the nature of the relationship between abuser and abused. O'Malley et al. were among the first to suggest that a "needs-oriented" definition of elder abuse might provide a better approach to intervention than would the typical categorizations of abuse (physical abuse, psychological abuse, sexual abuse, neglect, and financial exploitation).[10] A needs-oriented definition as applied to caregiver-perpetrated abuse focuses attention on the care needs of the elder victim. This definition suggests that three possible combinations of needs and caregiving services can result in inadequate care: (1) extensive care needs and extensive but inappropriate services, (2) extensive care needs and limited services, and (3) no care needs except those produced by the actions of the abuser. Intervention strategies would be aimed at redressing relevant inadequacies in care.

Our approach to intervention in elder abuse is to focus on the three aspects of the abuse situation: the victim, the abuser, and/or the victim/abuser relationship. Of course, an abuse situation may be multicausal—that is, rooted in more than one area. The victim may be a source of the problem when his or her dependence on assistance from the family caregiver is not accepted. This imbalance can result in anxiety, unreasonable demands, and severe psychological and behavioral disturbances by the dependent victim, such as belligerence, hostility, passive aggression, or regression, that may be focused on the caregiver.

The caregiver may be the major source of abuse in one or more of at least three ways. First, although he or she may genuinely wish to provide necessary care to the elderly relative, the caregiver may lack the information, skills, and/or resources to fill that role adequately. Second, the caregiver may be psychologically impaired to the extent that he or she is unable to provide adequate care. Third, the abuse may result from hostile and aggressive impulses.

The relationship between the elder and the caregiver may also be the source of the abuse. Although the victim has the capacity and resources to meet her own needs without excessive dependence on the abuser, and the abuser has the capacity and resources to provide the level of care needed by the victim, their unhealthy relationship may provide a foundation for abuse. In particular, this may characterize an abusive spousal relationship or another close familial relationship in which long-standing conflicts are unresolved.

The Environmental Press Model

Given the complex interaction of factors that comprise situations of elder abuse, designing an effective long-term intervention strategy is difficult. In dealing with the caregiver and the victim, researchers and planners have generally advocated two broad approaches to elder abuse: separation and support. The environmental press model assumes that, although temporary and, in some cases, permanent separation may be necessary, it is often possible to prevent or stop caregiver-perpetrated abuse by providing support. Support may take a variety of forms: psychological, medical, financial, social, or physical. It may include assistance ranging from education and skills training to extensive professional in-home support. Support can be provided for the abuser and/or the abused.

The environmental press model can thus be seen to relate to the overall situational complex in which elder abuse commonly occurs. This model is derived from research on an individual's "fit" with an environment. As such, it can be applied to the whole circumstance occurring in an instance of elder abuse and can facilitate an understanding of the likely causes of the abuse and potential remedial interventions (Figure 14–1). Moreover, the model is equally applicable for abuser and victim.

The environmental press model grew out of the pioneer research of Henry Murray, who examined the "demand factor" of the context in which a person behaves.[11] Since then, several researchers have noted that synchrony between an individual's level of "competence" and the environment's demand or "press" results in a minimal awareness of the demand, or what is called "adaptation."[12] Adaptation is the product, as it were, of a balanced relationship between competence and press. Under circumstances of adaptation to the environmental press, the individual can utilize fully his or her biological, sensorimotor, cognitive, and emotional competence. In other words, the individual is relatively unaware

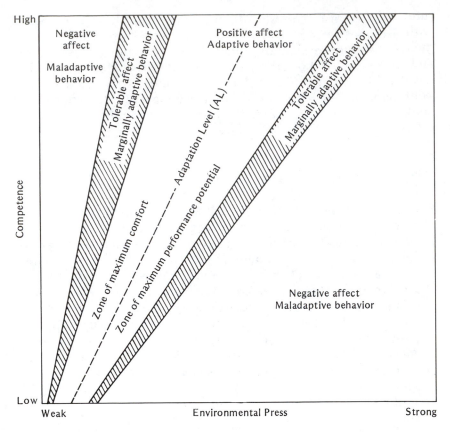

Figure 14-1 Environmental Press Model. *(From "Ecology and the Aging Process," by M.P. Lawton and L. Nahemow. In C. Eisdorfer and M.P. Lawton (Eds.),* Psychology of Adult Development and Aging. *Copyright 1973 by the American Psychological Association. Reprinted by permission.)*

of the demands of the environmental press—i.e., is adapted to the environment—and so can attend to other issues. Conversely, if competence and press are not in synchrony, "maladaptation" occurs. The strength or weakness of the environmental demand captures the individual's attention, essentially dictating responses. The outcome of either adaptation or maladaptation is expressed on two levels: behavior and affect.

Researchers who have examined the application of this theory of environmental press have most often worked within institutional settings, and their terminology reflects this experience. However, we are suggesting that the basic theoretical model has utility in understanding the circumstances of elder abuse in a family setting and in initiating interventions. In examining the terms that constitute this model, the relevance to the situations often associated with caregiver-perpetrated elder abuse is apparent; such situations include dependence, restricted environment, lack of preparation, and a sense of being overwhelmed by responsibilities.

Competence has been described in this research literature as being made up of four types: (1) biological or health—mobility, continence, ability to lift a certain weight, ability to bend over, etc.; (2) sensorimotor—how our senses take in information and our bodies react accordingly; (3) cognitive-intellectual skills or mental ability; and (4) emotional stability or ego strength. Each of us has different levels of competence.

Environmental press can be measured and quantified in different ways, according to research at the Philadelphia Geriatric Center and elsewhere.[13] These include:

1. *Stimulation.* The simplicity or complexity of the environmental demand reflects the quality of the sensory and social environment. A rich environment will include social, intellectual, sensorimotor, and emotional stimulation.
2. *Affect.* The environment can either encourage or discourage affectual (or emotional) expression.
3. *Impulse control.* To what extent does the environment offer immediate versus delayed gratification of needs?

All of these dimensions and several others identified can be reduced to three practical concerns: How much *stimulation, change*, and *responsibility* does the environment allow for a particular individual? In this case, the individual(s) is the abusive caregiver and/or the victim. The model maintains that the environmental press must be regularly renewing itself in order to maintain a given level of competence; if left alone, the press will drop from strong to weak.

Maladaptation occurs in these two scenarios:[14]

1. *Competence exceeds press.* Unfortunately, for most of us there is not a perfect fit between competence and environmental press. Sometimes we are more competent than the press. In this case "passive" maladaptation is typical. A competent person may be in an environment that is fairly unvaried, unstimulating, and predictable. Since the brain needs stimulation to survive, maladapted behaviors often result. For example, assembly line work can be boring and repetitious, with one's competence exceeding the environmental press. In this instance, the person may become passively maladapted to such work and engage in brain-

stimulating diversions such as withdrawal, daydreaming, escape, fantasy, sabotage—all predictable consequences of the situation. Under conditions of chronic, repetitious, unvarying press, the "cared-for" may become antagonistic in order to increase press, or may withdraw further into a self-created world of stimulation, while the caregiver may absent herself from the repetitious circumstances; absence may lead to neglect.

2. *Press exceeds competence*. When environmental press exceeds competence, there is likely to be a more "active" maladaptation. Acting-out behavior, aggression, anger, scapegoating, and, perhaps, abuse are likely to be the consequences. This does not necessarily mean that the persons involved are incompetent. They may be highly competent but functioning in an environment where press exceeds competence, especially in human services. "Burn out" is a typical result of press exceeding competence over a long term; burned-out caregivers—either professional workers or family members—are angry people. They see themselves as having given their all and feel that they have received little gratitude, recognition, and reward in return.

Neglect and abuse in institutions are beginning to be recognized as the consequences of an overloaded staff. That is, such behavior is more likely to occur when people who are too little recognized have just too much to do. When residents of institutions are systematically neglected, treated abruptly, or verbally or physically abused, this may be conscious or, more likely, the unconscious consequence of this active maladaptation. Similarly, this scenario may describe the situation of the family member facing years of chronic care of an elder whose physical or mental condition only worsens progressively. In the environmental press model, adaptation will not occur unless the caregiver's environmental press is appropriate for his or her level of competence.

Intervening on Behalf of Caregivers

Stress is intrinsic to prolonged caregiving. Full-time caregiving can be isolating and exhausting, and the rewards may be few. Efforts to provide comfort and care to frail elders cannot be expected to alter the natural progress of chronic disease that includes increasing functional limitation and dependence and eventual death. Caregivers may also be dealing with personal and marital adjustments, retirement, new grandchildren, and other stresses—positive and negative—of normal life. This set of changes, challenges, and responsibilities constitute a caregiver's environmental press.

Over the long term, caregiving may increasingly deplete a caregiver's physical and psychological resources and foster guilt, anger, hostility, depression, and other emotions that may be precursors to abuse. Steinmetz found in one study that the average length of care by the abuser prior to the first instance of abuse was over nine years.[15] In fact, the chronic presence of emotions such as anger and guilt is symptomatic of an excessive environmental press.

Caregivers may also lack the knowledge, skills, and personal resources to function effectively in an ever-demanding caregiving role. Although they may be highly competent in other areas of life, caregiving for a frail elder may involve new skills and information that are unpleasant and overwhelming. Feelings of inadequacy and frustration can overlay negative emotions produced by an excessive "press" and increase the chance of maladaptation expressed as abuse. Although causes of family violence are many and complex, in caregiver-perpetrated elder abuse situations, abuse can sometimes be seen as a reflection of maladaptation to the caregiving role.

Reducing Environmental Press for Caregivers

In providing support to the abusive caregiver, initial efforts should attempt to reduce the environmental press. This can be accomplished through separation of the abuser and the abused and/or by providing other types of support. The first step in a successful intervention effort is to identify the factors that are most demanding and fatiguing to the caregiver. The second step is to design and implement a strategy to eliminate these stressors or reduce their impact.

Separation of the victim and the abuser may offer several advantages, among them the following:

1. Immediate protection from further abuse for the victim.
2. An opportunity for detailed assessment and careful design of a strategy for meeting the victim's needs within the family system.
3. A "time-out," allowing an intensely emotional relationship to defuse.
4. At least temporary respite for the caregiver and an opportunity to rest and regroup.

5. A structured environment in which to bring the parties together for counseling in order to reevaluate the relationship and to either reaffirm or negate the caregiving contract.
6. Professional observation of the interaction between the abuser and abused, providing information that will be important in designing an intervention plan based on support.
7. An opportunity for medical and functional therapeutic intervention with elder and caregiver education in the disease process and skills instruction for the abuser.

It should not be assumed, however, that the abuse victim is the one to be removed from the abusive environment: In many abuse situations, it will be more appropriate to remove the abuser. Removal of a frail elder from his or her environment is likely to be traumatic and may contribute to accelerated physical and mental decline.

Respite care has been found to be one of the most effective interventions for overwhelmed caregivers. It gives caregivers a break from their responsibilities and an opportunity to participate in activities outside the home, reducing their isolation. Respite care, sometimes a lifeline for a caregiver, can be provided in the home or in a community or institutional setting. In-home respite care is available in many communities through public and private agencies. It includes homemaker services (e.g., help with meal preparation and housekeeping), personal care services (e.g., help with bathing and dressing), and skilled care (e.g., medical monitoring and physical therapy). In-home respite can also be provided by family members, neighbors, and volunteers (such as friendly visitors) who provide supervision and companionship for the impaired elder, freeing the caregiver to leave the house to shop, visit friends, and pursue enjoyable and fulfilling activities and interests. Weekend and other short-term in-home respite care allows a caregiver to get away for longer periods of time. Institutional respite care, available in some communities, can be provided for indefinite periods. Adult day care and recreational or therapeutic activities provided at senior centers or churches also provide respite for caregivers.

Skilled professional services can help reduce the environmental press on caregivers. For example, home health nurses can relieve caregivers of some of the more unpleasant and frightening obligations of care (e.g., disimpactions, catheterization, wound management, or nasogastric tube placement). Assistance in bathing a frail elder and performing other strenuous caregiving tasks is essential for the caregiver with limited physical strength. Support groups and professional counseling can be helpful in relieving the emotional stresses of caregiving and in resolving conflicts and feelings that contribute to a caregiver's emotional "press."

Another frequently overlooked source of stress for caregivers is the financial burden of care. Some caregivers leave paid jobs in order to provide care for family dependents. The loss of earnings may limit a family's ability to pay for educational expenses, weddings, vacations, or even essential needs and services. Nonreimbursable expenses of care for a frail elder—medications, insurance co-payments, supplies, and services—can be extremely costly. Families may feel trapped between the heavy financial cost of providing care at home versus the cost of placing the elder in an institution, which may deplete family funds even more quickly. Financial counseling and assistance can provide tremendous relief in reducing the environmental press of caregivers and their families.

Increasing Levels of Competence for Caregivers

In addition to decreasing the excessive environmental press of the caregiver, adaptation to caregiving can be facilitated by increasing the caregiver's competence. The environmental press model states that adaptation represents the point at which the environmental press is in synchrony with the caregiver's level of competence. When the environmental press is sufficiently strong that the caregiver is constantly aware of it, press can be functionally reduced by improving the level of the caregiver's competence. In other words, by increasing a caregiver's competence to do his or her job, environmental press and competence will more likely coincide. As noted, competence is an aggregate of physical health, sensorimotor functioning, cognitive skill, and ego or emotional strength. Although it may seem that the most appropriate interventions will be directed to improving cognitive and emotional competencies of the caregiver, in fact, long-term caregiving for a frail elder may well take its toll on all competencies.

Suggested cognitive-emotional competency interventions include self-help groups made up of other caregivers who are experiencing and struggling with similar challenges and frustrations. Self-help groups offer the added advantage of reducing the isolation of the caregiver and providing new information and ideas about how to approach a difficult problem. Contact with other caregivers can result in exchange arrangements in which one caregiver supervises two elders, providing a break for another caregiver in exchange for some time off. Individual and family counseling in which the abused elder is included can result in increased emotional strength for caregivers. Counseling that includes other members of the family can provide a forum for resolving long-term conflicts and finding practical solutions to day-to-day problems. Counseling could result in greater cooperation among family members and more sharing of responsibilities for the dependent elder, reducing the press of the primary caregiver.

Educational programs can enhance the cognitive and emotional competencies of caregivers. Short-term courses are available in many communities on financial management, behavior modification, community resources, public assistance, and processes of normal and pathological aging. Education by physicians and nurses about the diagnoses, prognoses, and potential medical interventions for chronic illnesses and other conditions can be invaluable in helping caregivers understand and more effectively handle the manifestations of the diseases they must deal with daily.

Caregivers will also benefit from information about drugs—both prescription and over-the-counter—being taken by the elder in their care or themselves, including possible interactions among drugs, side effects of drugs, and alternatives to drugs. Information on nutrition, special diets for special health problems, and drug-food interactions will also be important in increasing caregiver competence. Information about assistive devices such as prostheses and other durable medical supplies that may increase an impaired elder's mobility could lead to a reduction in an elder's dependence on the caregiver. Caregivers may not know that these labor-saving devices are available and sometimes paid for by Medicare or other insurance policies.

Skills training in meeting the physical or medical needs of the older person will be essential for some caregivers and helpful for all. Such training can teach caregivers how to monitor oxygen use for the emphysema patient; manage feeding tubes, catheters, and ostomies; use new products to deal with incontinence; and a host of other skills. Skills training can be provided at home by visiting nurses or through community education services at hospitals or senior centers.

Finally, interventions directed at improving the physical health and sensorimotor competencies of the caregiver may affect overall functional competence. For example, participation in an exercise program may enhance a caregiver's strength and endurance, increase her energy level, contribute to an overall sense of well-being, and offer both respite from caregiving and an opportunity for successful accomplishment of personal goals.

Intervening on Behalf of Victims

The primary goal of any intervention strategy for elder abuse victims must be to protect them from further abuse. Because of the age and frailty of most victims, all forms of abuse—whether it involves physical battering, verbal abuse, or neglect—should be considered serious. In some abuse situations, separation—at least temporary separation—is essential. But too often separation means institutionalization of the victim, and many elders choose to endure abuse rather than be placed in an institution. The environmental press model offers an approach that allows abused elders to avoid institutionalization and further maltreatment.

Goals implied by the environmental press model, when applied to the typical victim of elder abuse, are to *increase* competence and *increase* environmental press. Increasing competence will improve an impaired elder's ability to provide self-care, enabling him or her to exercise more control and become less dependent on the caregiver. Increasing environmental press will help to increase competence by focusing the frail elder's interest outside of self, improving physical and mental capacity, and enhancing overall sense of responsibility, control, and well-being.

Before any intervention approach for frail elders is designed, a complete physical, psychological, functional, and social assessment should be conducted. Information from the assessment will be critical in identifying appropriate approaches and services and in avoiding potentially harmful ones. Assessment should be conducted by professionals (optimally, a team that includes a physician, nurse, social worker, and appropriate specialists) and should involve a complete medical work-up that attempts to distinguish untreatable disease states from treatable conditions. It should also include a nutritional evaluation, an evaluation of prescription and nonprescription drugs (including alcohol), a psychological assessment, a functional assessment, and an assessment of the elder's living situation.

One objective of this assessment is to determine the potential for improvement in an elder's competence in all areas: biological, psychological, sensorimotor, and emotional. It is important not to underestimate an elder's capacity for improvement—a response that is a natural outgrowth of common misconceptions and stereotypes about the elderly. A second goal is to assess the limits of the elder in handling an increased environmental press—to ensure that intervention(s) will not "overpress" him or her and contribute to further distress and decline.

Increasing Competence

Interventions designed to improve a frail elder's competence might focus on any one or all of the following objectives:

1. Providing assistance in managing illness and disability through educational and skills-training efforts.
2. Improving physical and mental functioning through nutritional and medical interventions, exercise, and intellectual stimulation.
3. Improving capacity to provide self-care by teaching skills and changing the physical environment (such as installing grab bars in the bathroom and purchasing clothes that are easy to put on and take off).
4. Improving access to community resources and public assistance by providing information and arranging contact.
5. Providing assistance with financial management.

Medical and psychological interventions should be designed to reduce physical and emotional pain caused by disease states as well as anxiety, fear, grief, guilt, and depression. Psychological counseling can help elders to (1) understand and resolve conflicts with their caregiver and other family members, even past conflicts with those who are deceased; (2) accomplish the developmental tasks of old age that include coming to terms with significant loss and preparing for one's own death; and (3) find a constructive role and purpose in life.

Increasing Environmental Press

Unlike caregivers, abused frail elders are more likely to be living in a situation in which their environmental press is too weak. The elder's contact with other people is limited, responsibilities are few, and stimulation is minimal. To borrow from the language of the environmental press model, their environment *lacks* stimulation, responsibility, and change. Applying the confirmed adage, "use it or lose it," a weak environmental press will contribute to reduced competency.

As we have seen, a weak environmental press also leads to passive maladaptation, a situation that is commonly manifest in withdrawal, escape, and sabotage. It is not hard to see how the elements that characterize the lives of many dependent elders— lack of control over one's own body and environment, lack of involvement in events around them, lack of diversion from their own limited world, and dependence on others who may not function and respond in ways that they consider appropriate and necessary—can lead to frustration, depression, anxiety, anger, and a host of other emotional responses.

Successful efforts to expand an elder victim's environmental press will result in decreased isolation, boredom, excessive self-concern, depression, and anxiety. These outcomes will bring about a reduction in dependency on the caregiver and, as a result, a reduction in the caregiver's environmental press. A major goal of this intervention is to increase an abused elder's involvement with and visibility to others—professionals and peers. In addition to encouraging competence in all four areas, increased visibility to others, particularly professionals, will enhance the likelihood that a person outside the family will notice symptoms of abuse and ensure timely intervention. Indeed, professionals who work with elders should be trained to look for such symptoms.

Most of the activities and services designed to increase an elder victim's competence will also increase environmental press. Many communities provide a range of services that can facilitate progress toward these objectives. Adult day care provides recreation, rehabilitation, nutritious meals, and a rich social environment. Senior centers sponsor a range of educational, social, and therapeutic programs and services. They show movies, serve meals, and sponsor lectures and clinics (for example, to monitor blood pressure and diagnose glaucoma); they offer special exercise classes and sponsor card games, social events, trips, and other activities; some provide transportation.

In most communities in the United States, Area Agencies on Aging (AAAs) provide information and referral services to elders and their families. Although the availability and quality of these programs vary, information and referral services are mandated through the federal Older Americans Act and should be able to provide information about and contact with a variety of community services: medical and psychological treatment, home health care, legal counsel and advocacy, housing alternatives (permanent or temporary), transportation, financial management, rehabilitation, and recreation.

Case Management

Design, coordination, and overall monitoring of intervention strategies instituted on behalf of the caregiver or the care receiver should be the responsibility of one individual within an agency, rather than that of an entire agency or coalition of agencies. Since the presence of abuse may indicate a malfunctioning family system, in most cases the coordinator should be a nonfamily professional, paraprofessional, or trained volunteer. *An abused elder or an abusive caregiver cannot be expected to organize and manage a successful intervention system without assistance and support.*

Social workers are adept at providing case management as well as support services. They are knowledgeable about available community resources, assuring full advantage of all entitlements. They can provide an essential link between abusive caregivers, abused elders, and social and medical services; they can monitor intervention strategies and alert appropriate professionals and/or family members when additional intervention is needed. Social workers are also trained to provide individual and group counseling and can be an excellent source of information and support. The physician can serve in a pivotal role in the treatment plan but is also likely to be the least informed on nonmedical alternatives. However, information, skills training, and support offered by a physician are particularly valued, and, as a result, physician participation can improve compliance with intervention strategies.

Conclusion

The environmental press model offers a theoretical framework for providing support for caregivers and care recipients whether or not abuse is present. However, as should be clear, support will not be the appropriate approach in all elder abuse situations. If the abuse is malignant or severe, separation—perhaps permanent separation—is essential. Involvement by adult protective services and the criminal justice system may be necessary.

We have recommended consideration of the environmental press model in a variety of contexts. Excessive alcohol and/or drug abuse by the abuser or the victim and a history of violent or other criminal behavior suggest that intervention based on support will be inadequate to guarantee safety for the victim. It is possible, however, that successful alcohol treatment can precede other support strategies. If there is a known history of violence and/or other criminal behavior by the abuser, criminal justice involvement will be necessary. However, when elder abuse is present within a caregiving/cared-for relationship that becomes abusive over time, at least in part as a result of chronic stress produced by overwhelming caregiving responsibilities, the environmental press model can be valuable in understanding and intervening in abuse and in enhancing the quality of life for elders and their families.

Endnotes

1. M. Block and J. D. Sinnott, "The Battered Elder Syndrome: An Exploratory Study" (College Park: University of Maryland, 1979); E. Lau and J. J. Kosberg, "Abuse of the Elderly by Informal Care Providers," *Aging* (September-October 1979).
2. M. P. Lawton, *Environment and Aging* (Monterey, Calif.: Brooks/Cole, 1980); M. P. Lawton, "Competence, Environmental Press, and the Adaptation of Old People," in *Aging and the Environment: Theoretical Approaches,* eds. M. P. Lawton, P. G. Windley, and T. O. Byerts (New York: Garland STPM Press, 1980); M. P. Lawton and L. Nahemow, "Ecology and the Aging Process," in *Psychology of Adult Development and Aging,* eds. C. Eisdorfer and M. P. Lawton (Washington, D.C.: American Psychological Association, 1973).
3. K. Pillemer, "Domestic Violence Against the Elderly: A Case Control Study" (Ph.D. diss., Brandeis University, 1985).
4. Lau and Kosberg, "Abuse of the Elderly by Informal Care Providers"; H. O'Malley, H. Segars, R. Perez, V. Mitchell, and G. Kneupfel, "Elder Abuse in Massachusetts: A Survey of Professionals and Paraprofessionals" (Boston: Legal Research and Services for the Elderly, 1979).
5. Block and Sinnott, "The Battered Elder Syndrome"; T. Hickey and R. L. Douglass, "Neglect and Abuse of Older Family Members: Professionals' Perspectives and Case Experiences," *The Gerontologist* 21 (1981), pp. 171–76.
6. Pillemer, "Domestic Violence Against the Elderly"; R. Wolf, C. Strugnell, and M. Godkin, "Preliminary Findings from Three Model Projects on Elderly Abuse" (Worcester: University of Massachusetts, Center on Aging, December 1982).
7. T. O'Malley, H. O'Malley, D. Everitt, and D. Jarson, "Categories of Family-Mediated Abuse and Neglect of Elderly Persons," *Journal of the American Geriatrics Society* 32 (1984), pp. 362–69; Pillemer, "Domestic Violence Against the Elderly."
8. O'Malley et al., "Elder Abuse in Massachusetts"; S. Steinmetz, "Battered Parents," *Society* (July-August 1978), pp. 54–55.
9. G. Taler and E. F. Ansello, "Elder Abuse," *American Family Physician* (August 1985), pp. 107–14.
10. T. O'Malley, D. Everitt, H. O'Malley, and E. Campion, "Identifying and Preventing Family Mediated Abuse and Neglect of Elderly Persons," *Annals*

of Internal Medicine 98 (1983), pp. 998–1005; O'Malley et al., "Categories of Family-Mediated Abuse and Neglect of Elderly Persons."

11. H. A. Murray, *Explorations in Personality* (New York: Oxford University Press, 1938).

12. H. Helson, *Adaptation Level Theory* (New York: Harper & Row, 1964); E. Kahana, "A Congruence Model of Person-Environment Interaction," in *Aging and the Environment: Theoretical Approaches*, eds. M. P. Lawton, P. G. Windley, and T. O. Byerts (New York: Garland STMP Press, 1980); Lawton, *Environment and Aging;* Lawton and Nahemow, "Ecology and the Aging Process."

13. Lawton, "Competence, Environmental Press, and the Adaptation of Old People."

14. E. F. Ansello, "The Activity Coordinator as Environmental Press," *Activities, Adaptation, and Aging* 6, no. 3 (1985), pp. 87–97.

15. Steinmetz, "Battered Parents."

Chapter 15

SOCIAL POLICY AND ELDER ABUSE

by Stephen Crystal

Elder abuse has recently taken on a new visibility and has become a subject of public concern. It has received considerable attention from elected officials and the press, as well as from the social welfare community. This interest in the problem, and the concomitant pressure to "do something about it," has considerably outpaced research that would permit us to ascertain the extent of elder abuse, its relative severity, and the most appropriate means of addressing it.

As a particularly dramatic social problem, elder abuse captures the imagination in a way that other, more routine problems do not. Even though the available research is plagued with definitional and data problems, the public has been persuaded of the importance of the problem: 79 percent of the public believe elder abuse is a serious issue in the country, according to a Harris poll, and 72 percent believe it should be a "major responsibility" assumed by government.[1]

In seeking to respond to the public interest surrounding this "new" problem, categorical responses have frequently been proposed and often implemented. Such responses are aimed at establishing specific social service or law enforcement measures to address the problem of elder abuse. Elder abuse reporting laws, for example, are paradigmatic of such measures. These statutes have been widely enacted during the last several years, as attention has come to be focused on elder abuse. In 1980 they existed in 17 states;[2] by 1983, such statutes had become law in 33 states.[3]

Categorical Approaches

There are several problems with such categorical responses to the elder abuse problem. First, the nature and extent of the problem has not yet been clearly established, and there is no consensus or reliable knowledge base on the effectiveness of alternative approaches to resolving elder abuse when it occurs. Second, many of the responses that have been proposed or implemented in legislation are based on a false analogy to the child abuse problem. Third, categorical approaches by their nature tend to define the abuse element as the central problem to be addressed in what often turn out to be very complicated situations. Fourth, programs, policies, and legislation defined in terms of elder abuse establish a separate set of public responses, based on age, to problems that are shared with those of many nonelderly people.

These concerns, and others discussed below, center on the question of whether elder abuse is best responded to categorically, through legislative and programmatic solutions focused directly on the abuse issue, or whether it is best seen as a problem to be addressed mainly within more generic social service approaches and structures. The answers to these and related questions need to be based on as complete an understanding as we can muster of the incidence and nature of abuse.

A central question is whether abuse typically exists as a relatively self-contained problem that can be successfully addressed frontally and in its own terms, or whether it is typically a single dimension of a much more complex set of problems. Although the available research is limited, there appears to be good reason to believe that the latter of these situations is considerably more typical than the former.

Case Characteristics: The Scope of the Problem

An important issue that tends to confuse policy discussions on elder abuse is imprecision of definitions. The term "abuse" clearly connotes to the nonspecialist some type of direct physical harm or exploitation, and this is what is visualized in the public concern over the issue. Psychological abuse is a more elusive and subjective category than physical abuse but one that is at least a meaningful extension of the notion of a victim being actively abused. The inclusion of neglect as a type of elder abuse, however, although a frequent practice, considerably distorts commonsense semantics, particularly since care of a parent, as opposed to care of a minor child, is in general not a legal obligation. Even less helpful and confusing is the somewhat oxymoronic use of the term "self-neglect" as a form of abuse, which is often referred to in the literature and which has even appeared in statutory definitions of abuse.[4]

In statistics generated from studies or programs using such broad definitions, the more peripheral types of cases such as passive neglect are usually predominant. Such statistics generally reflect cases of a type very different from those envisioned by typical consumers of the statistics. Widely cited estimates, such as one million elder abuse cases per year (derived from Block and Sinnott[5] and used *inter alia* by the Senate Special Committee on Aging), are based on very broad definitions. The impression conveyed to the public and to policy makers—that a million elderly people are beaten up by their children or other caretakers each year—is palpably wrong. Carefully read, these studies typically reflect much lower rates of actual direct abuse; indeed, one of the problems in the research has been the difficulty in identifying sufficient numbers of truly abused victims to study.[6]

This is not to suggest that elder abuse is not a real problem, but that the responses to it need to be proportionate to its actual scope and its importance relative to other problems of the frail aged (e.g., lack of a caretaker as opposed to presence of an abusive caretaker). As discussed further below, public perceptions and the perceptions of social service workers serving frail elderly populations seem to diverge in the importance assigned to abuse in comparison with other typical problems of the frail elderly.[7] Since many of the types of intervention contemplated by legislative approaches to elder abuse, such as mandated central reporting and investigation, carry a risk of inappropriate intrusion and violation of elders' privacy and autonomy, it is all the more important that these risks be balanced accurately against the scope of the problem. In the discussion below, the term "abuse" is generally used to refer to some form of active harm.

Abuse is one of a number of forms of harm or endangerment that may call for protective intervention. While dramatic, it is not even necessarily the most severe or emergent, particularly when broadly defined. Experience with a broad range of programs organized to respond to harm and endangerment—adult protective services programs in particular—suggests that abuse is only one of a variety of problems encountered by impaired adults (those under 65 as well as the elderly); that it is not necessarily the most common or most severe form of harm or endangerment requiring protective intervention; and that where abuse does appear to be manifest, it is usually encountered as part of a complex set of problems, often revolving around an unmet or poorly met care need and/or an abuser who is himself or herself functionally compromised.

Between 1981 and 1986, the U.S. Department of Health and Human Services funded a national study on adult protective services, of which the author was the principal investigator. An initial one-year state-of-the-art assessment involved field work in California, New York, Minnesota, and Maryland, with national collection of information through correspondence and telephone contact. During three subsequent years, the project (Project Focus) worked with protective services programs around the country, providing training and technical assistance. In the large majority of programs encountered, both in the state-of-the-art assessment and in training sessions, elder abuse represented a relatively small proportion of cases encountered, many of which involved seriously endangered clients. Typical was the finding in Erie County, New York, for cases seen by the county Department of Senior Services. During a 15-month period in 1978 and 1979, approximately 5 percent of the cases seen (45 of 933 total adult protective services cases) had been victims of elder abuse. Protective services workers interviewed in Maryland, similarly, indicated that relatively few of the endangered clients they had contact with were victims of actual abuse. In New York City's adult protective services program, cases of actual physical abuse made up only about 6 percent of the case load; many more were severely endangered as a result of factors other than abuse.

The Child Abuse Analogy

Elder abuse statutes such as mandated reporting have frequently borrowed from the child abuse field. Despite the obvious lack of parallels between child abuse and elder abuse, many of the recently enacted statutes borrow directly from child abuse models, as does much of the literature on policy responses to elder abuse. Kerness, in proposing a model statute drawn mainly from child abuse statutes, is typical: "Experience under child protective reporting laws in the states as well as a growing body of professional literature argues in favor of a strong statutory reporting system as a powerful tool to protect vulnerable individuals against abuse and neglect."[8]

Yet the differences between the situations are fundamental. A minor child is assumed to require a guardian with custodial authority, while an adult is assumed to be competent to make basic life decisions on his or her own. Parents have both the responsibility to care for a child and the authority to make decisions for that child; in investigating the possibility of child abuse or neglect, the state acts in *parens patriae*, exercising its traditional responsibilities to look after the welfare of legal incompetents such as minors.

In overruling the professional confidentiality privilege of a physician or other professional, mandatory reporting statutes place the state in the position of substitute parent. The appropriateness of this in many cases of suspected elder abuse or neglect is dubious. The responsibility of an adult protective services worker or other worker dealing with possible elder abuse, unless and until the client's competency comes into serious question, should normally be to help the client make his or her own choices—not to make decisions on the client's behalf.

The parent of a minor child has the legal obligation to support and care for the child and the legal authority to have physical custody of the child. Where neglect or abuse is substantiated and counseling or casework assistance cannot ensure the child's safety, a central and crucial tool is temporary or longer-term foster care placement: substitution of the state's custodial authority for that of the parent and physical removal of the child. Child abuse investigation and enforcement revolves around custodial decisions; the difference between this situation and adult abuse is fundamental, both at a philosophical/legal level and at a practical service delivery level. At the former level, mandatory reporting and investigation of child abuse reflects society's *parens patriae* responsibility and authority toward individuals who by their age are *ipso facto* legally incompetent, and reflects the fact that the child can be assumed in virtually all cases to be both legally (as a ward) and factually incapable of dealing with the abuse. At the practical level, a large-scale system for reporting and investigation of child abuse makes sense in part because tools such as foster care placement exist as feasible remedies in many of the cases encountered. Neither assumption is necessarily valid for adults.

The child protective services system is backed up by an extensive array of services linked specifically to it; foster care placements made as a result of child abuse and neglect investigations represent billions of dollars annually in expenditures in the United States. There is no real analogy for foster care placement in the adult abuse situation; removal of an adult from his or her own home purely as a solution to abuse would seldom be appropriate, and, in fact, this possibility is of real concern as a possible outcome of elder abuse investigations.

Elder Abuse Legislation

The primary rationale for mandatory reporting is as a method of case finding. However, it is unclear whether these statutes actually serve this purpose. Cases are often already known to social agencies or other authorities.[9] In a Maryland study, 95 percent of cases were already known to authorities.[10] A Syracuse study reported that respondents in states with such statutes typically did not believe the mandatory reporting law in itself had actually resulted in an increase in the number of reports, but that publicity about the existence of the problem and the availability of resources to address was a much more important factor.[11]

This view is supported by the fact that in states where only certain categories of persons such as physicians are required to report many or even most reports often are found to come from nonmandated sources.[12] Cases are frequently reported by social agencies that might well be in as good a position to provide help as the agency to which the reports are made. Indeed, the possible negative effects on physician-patient confidentiality may be limited by noncompliance with a reporting law; at any rate, the number of reports from physicians tends to be very low. The Syracuse report cites one state in which, although physicians are the only source mandated to report, only 2 percent of reports received originated from that source. Such results are perhaps better understood in the light of a recent, as yet unpublished, study in Michigan and North Carolina (mandatory reporting states). In this study, it was reported that 71 percent of physicians surveyed did not know whether their state required the reporting of elder abuse, and an additional 12 percent believed it did *not* require reporting.[13]

If we assume that elder abuse, of whatever degree and however defined, is a problem of unique importance and priority, then perhaps it makes sense to concentrate efforts on case finding and investigation in this manner. If we look at the problem with the view that other, nonabusive situations—for example, nonavailability of care critically needed for safety or well-being—can be equally urgent, then it seems illogical to concentrate on case finding since in almost any given jurisdiction, large numbers of such cases are already known and do not receive adequate services.

The limited availability of services needed to adequately resolve many of these cases in the real world—a resolution that usually requires far more than simple enforcement—is in fact one of the principal problems with reporting laws. Intervention can break up what is often a complex social and economic equilibrium surrounding an at-risk individual; intervention can also lead to separation from another individual who, while possibly abusive, had functioned as a needed caretaker. In order to resolve the problems often presented by these cases without institutionalizing the elderly person, an array of services, ranging from financial management to home care to ongoing case management, may be necessary. Adequate levels of such services often do not exist in the community; in their absence, or in the absence of a healthy respect for the client's preferences, institutional care may in fact be the outcome. In Connecticut, it has been reported that 60 percent of those individuals receiving short-term medical care as a result of mandated reporting do not return home.[14] In a classic, early study of adult protective services in Cleveland, vulnerable elderly clients were randomly assigned to an intensive protective services case management program or left to existing community services. The most significant long-term outcome was a higher rate of mortality among those receiving the special intervention. The rate of nursing home placement in this group was much higher: Apparently, social service intervention resulted in many of the clients being judged to need institutional care for their own protection, and these placements resulted in mortality effects frequently associated with such placement.[15]

Inspection of the provisions of elder abuse statutes suggests that many are overly broad, particularly in terms of the definition of abuse. In fact, to the extent that these statutes contain penalties for abusive conduct (approximately 12 do so), many appear to be unconstitutionally vague. Mississippi's Adult Protective Services Act, for example, which includes penalties for abuse or neglect, defines neglect as "failure of a caretaker to provide the services which are necessary to maintain the mental and physical health of an adult." Oregon defines "abuse" as including "abandonment, including desertion or willful forsaking of an elderly person or the withdrawal or neglect of duties and obligation owed an elderly person by a caretaker or other person."[16]

One of the drawbacks of these statutes is their invasion of traditional privileged relationships with physicians, clergy, other professionals, and even spouses. As noted previously, this is not a real problem with child abuse reporting (particularly since the privilege may rest, *de jure* or *de facto*, with the parent who may be the abuser). But it can be a real problem to override an elderly individual's ability to control the use of information he or she has given to a professional, as well as that professional's own judgment that the problem might best be addressed without bringing in the authorities. Confidentiality provisions are overridden in part based simply on age, notwithstanding the absence of any finding of incompetency. This can be easily seen as infantilizing for the elderly. Spouse abuse, by contrast, is not dealt with in this way; battered spouses are entitled to discuss their problems with a professional in confidence and to decide whether or not they wish officialdom to become involved.

Investigations resulting from mandatory reporting laws can easily be intrusive and embarrassing to the elderly person, and they often lead to a "cure" that the elder perceives as worse than the disease—particularly where adequate patient follow-through does not take place and appropriate supportive services for nonrestrictive, nonpunitive solutions to the problems uncovered are not available. When so many of the basic services needed to support individuals with compromised functioning in the community are missing, including many services strongly desired by at-risk clients on a voluntary basis, the emphasis on case finding and an enforcement-oriented approach seems inappropriate.

Further, the rationale for remedies defined specifically by age is unclear. At least 13 states limit the statutory remedies, such as overriding the confidentiality of professional relationships, to those over 60.[17] Abuse among the elderly may involve a fully functioning, alert client; indeed, it may involve a spouse abuse situation indistinguishable from spouse abuse situations commonly encountered among the nonelderly. However, the statute seems to imply a presumption of less than full competency purely on the basis of age.

This author has argued elsewhere that much of our social policy on aging is flawed because of an inappropriate assumption that the elderly are typically feeble, poor, and sick, and that the differences in their situations and needs are less salient than their common disabilities.[18] Separate legislation for protecting the elderly in their interpersonal relationships smacks of similar stereotyping. A younger individual (such as one suffering from substance abuse, mental illness, or developmental disability) may well be less capable of self-protection and less "competent" than an elderly person. Use of "elder abuse" as a central concept in organizing legislation and programs creates an artificial split in the remedies and systems available to meet similar needs. Communities and states are usually hard-pressed to implement one adequate system for adult protective services, much less several.

In dealing with disability as a criterion for applicability of various provisions, statutes often do not distinguish clearly between conduct creating the presumption of judgmental impairment or risk and the status of being elderly. Thus, again, the implication is that age itself is a form of disability. Florida's statute defines an aged person as one "suffering from the infirmities of aging as manifested by organic brain damage, advanced age, or other physical, mental, or emotional dysfunctioning."[19]

Statutes providing for mandatory reporting or other intervention typically do not even include appropriations for the specific activities mandated, much less for improvements in ancillary services such as home care or financial management needed to support adequately the service plans that would result from appropriate assessment and planning in the cases investigated. The message is that the funds should be diverted from less visible, less dramatic social services activities, often those addressed to the same population.

Reporting and increased case finding and investigation alone will not improve matters (in fact, such measures may well not even succeed in identifying any significant numbers of previously hidden cases). Why, given the problems discussed above, are mandatory reporting statutes, in and of themselves, so popular? The political dynamic is familiar: Legislators and governors are anxious to find a way to "do something" about a highly visible problem without the need to spend substantial sums on new services. Hence, an approach that appears to address a problem with high visibility and a touch of the exotic through existing service programs has considerable appeal. The need to develop a comprehensive set of services to address a range of forms of endangerment, not merely elder abuse, lacks appeal by comparison. Topics such as the need for financial management, adequate adult protective services staffing, and guardianship services are complicated and lack popular appeal, while the problems of those who simply lack a caretaker (a much larger group than those abused by caretakers) are old hat and seem uncomfortable and costly to address, possibly creating an open-ended demand for services. Perhaps, then, in addition to the problems of effectiveness and appropriateness discussed above, the real problem with legislative approaches that center on mandated reporting is that they create an illusory sense of progress on these complex and difficult problems.

Endnotes

1. Louis Harris, "Americans Believe Government Should Take Major Responsibility in Coping with the Abuse Problem," News release, November 2, 1981, The Harris Survey.
2. Alliance/Elder Abuse Project, *An Analysis of States' Mandatory Reporting Laws on Elder Abuse* (Syracuse, N.Y.: Catholic Charities, 1983).
3. Jules Kerness, *Preventing Abuse and Neglect, Vol II: An Analysis of State*

Law and Proposed Model Legislation (Miami Shores, Fla.: Barry University School of Social Work, 1984).

4. Ibid.
5. M. Block and J. Sinnott, "The Battered Elder Syndrome: An Exploratory Study" (College Park: University of Maryland, Center on Aging, 1979).
6. Stephen Crystal, Edmund Dejowski, Sol Daiches, and Camilla Flemming, *Adult Protective Services: The State of the Art* (New York: Human Resources Administration, Project Focus, 1982), p. 209.
7. Ibid., pp. 201–15.
8. Kerness, *Preventing Abuse and Neglect*.
9. Lawrence Faulkner, "Mandating the Reporting of Suspected Cases of Elder Abuse: An Inappropriate, Ineffective and Ageist Response to the Abuse of Older Adults," *Family Law Quarterly* 16, no. 1 (1982), pp. 69–91.
10. Block and Sinnott, "The Battered Elder Syndrome."
11. Alliance/Elder Abuse Project.
12. Ibid.; Faulkner, "Mandating the Reporting of Suspected Cases of Elder Abuse."
13. James O'Brien, "The Role of the Physician in Identifying and Assisting Abused and Neglected Elderly" (Symposium discussion, Meetings of the Gerontological Society, New Orleans, November 23, 1985).
14. Faulkner, "Mandating the Reporting of Suspected Cases of Elder Abuse."
15. Margaret Blenkner et al., "A Research and Demonstration Project of Protective Services," *Social Casework* 52 (1971), pp. 483–99.
16. Kerness, *Preventing Abuse and Neglect*.
17. Ibid.
18. Stephen Crystal, *America's Old Age Crisis: Public Policy and the Two Worlds of Aging*, rev. ed. (New York: Basic Books, 1984).
19. Kerness, *Preventing Abuse and Neglect*.

INDEX